普通高等院校经济管理类"十三五"应用型规划教材
【国际经济与贸易系列】

国际商务函电双语教程

第2版

COMMUNICATING IN INTERNATIONAL BUSINESS

董金玲 郝景亚 郑凌霄 孙洁 编著

机械工业出版社
China Machine Press

图书在版编目（CIP）数据

国际商务函电双语教程 / 董金玲等编著. —2版. —北京：机械工业出版社，2016.11
（2025.11重印）

（普通高等院校经济管理类"十三五"应用型规划教材·国际经济与贸易系列）

ISBN 978-7-111-55302-1

I. 国… II. 董… III. 国际商务 – 英语 – 电报信函 – 写作 – 双语教学 – 高等学校 – 教材 IV. F740

中国版本图书馆CIP数据核字（2016）第256857号

　　本书体例安排新颖，语言简洁规范，通过大量的技能训练将基础英语技能和外贸英语知识有机结合起来，从而提高学生撰写国际商务英语书信的能力，实用性、针对性强。本书内容涉及国际贸易各个环节书面沟通的写作规范，以及经贸合同的写作技巧、其他主题的书信范例等。本次修订继续立足于国际贸易专业知识和英语语言技能于一体的教材编写思路，沿袭并更加突出"双语"这一课程特色，通过提炼两条知识主线，即外贸函电的文体特征和写作、国际贸易实务的具体流程和业务细节阐述，使专业教学和专业英语学习有效结合，最大程度降低学习的难度。

出版发行：机械工业出版社（北京市西城区百万庄大街22号　邮政编码：100037）
责任编辑：刘新艳　　　　　　　　　　　　　　责任校对：董纪丽
印　　刷：北京机工印刷厂有限公司
版　　次：2025年11月第2版第11次印刷
开　　本：185mm×260mm　1/16　　　　　　　印　　张：18
书　　号：ISBN 978-7-111-55302-1　　　　　　定　　价：59.00元

客服电话：(010) 88361066　68326294

版权所有·侵权必究
封底无防伪标均为盗版

Preface 前 言

作为国际经济与贸易专业的专业必修课,"国际商务函电"课程具有实践性强、对知识的综合运用程度高的特点,是在学生具备一定的外语水平,掌握了国际贸易理论与实务等相关知识的基础上开设的。尽管如此,在实际教学中,无论是教师还是学生都感到此课程难教、难学。究其原因,专业外语水平差异、对相关外贸交易程序及细节把握不系统是本课程难学的主要原因。总结长期的教学实践经验,我们深刻感受到,如果能将现有以外语为主的外贸函电教材改成双语模式,如果能将外贸业务的流程贯穿整个教材,而不仅仅是以英文函电格式、行文方法以及文体特点为主要内容,那么就会大大便利本课程的教学,降低学生学习和理解的难度,从而提高学生的综合应用能力。在借鉴国内、国际商务函电教材的成功经验,深入调查研究国际商务人才以及本、专科学生对国际商务函电教材需求现状的基础上,2011年7月,由董金玲、郝景亚、郑凌霄编写的《国际商务函电双语教程》由国家一级出版社机械工业出版社出版,被列入"普通高等院校经济管理类'十二五'应用型规划教材",成为国内为数不多的国际商务函电双语教材之一。因其新颖的体例,较强的实用性和可操作性,《国际商务函电双语教程》出版伊始即被众多院校选用为教材,受到了广大师生和经贸工作者的欢迎和好评,对此我们一直备受鼓舞,心存感激。近年来,随着国际经贸形势的发展和电子商务的普及,国际商务沟通的作用变得越来越重要,沟通的形式也发生了巨大变化,为适应这一变化,同时答谢读者朋友对本书的厚爱,我们对教材进行了修订。本次修订主要做了以下几方面的工作。

1. 更新和补充信例,以tips的方式增加国际贸易实践相关知识点的讲解和补充。对信例中出现的文体结构给予必要的解释,对涉及的语法现象、句型结构以及外贸专用术语进行细致讲解;新增适合国际经济与贸易专业学生认知水平的教学内容,附录中增加国际贸易实践中外贸单证的实例。

2. 增加课后练习的题量和形式。在现有练习的基础上,增加练习题的量和深度,同时在课程结束后增加五套综合练习题,以便测试学生综合运用知识的水平。

3. 对部分外贸术语以及英文表达过时陈旧的地方给予更新、替换,对上一版中的内容逐字逐句勘误,使其表达更为清晰和流畅。

4. 充实与该教材配套的电子教学资料,使内容进一步充实,语句更加精练,重点更加突出,案例更加接近贸易实践。

本书第1版出版时,我们对全网有关教材进行了搜索,发现以中英文对照的双语模式进行编写的教材为数不多。五年来的实践告诉我们,这种体例对于学生理解和掌握专业知识具有非常大的帮助，极大方便了老师的教学和学生的自学，增强了教材的可读性、应用性。本次修订继续立足于国际贸易专业知识和英语语言技能于一体的教材编写思路，沿袭并更加突出"双语"这一课程特色，通过提炼两条知识主线，即外贸函电的文体特征和写作、国际贸易实务的具体流程和业务细节阐述，使专业教学和专业英语学习有效结合，最大程度降低学习的难度。

  本次修订工作由编写组共同完成。董金玲负责全书修订工作的总体设计和协调工作，具体负责1、7、10、11、14章的补充和修订，提供了综合练习题等相关素材；郝景亚负责2～6章的补充和修订；郑凌霄负责8、9、12、13章的补充和修订；孙洁负责tips内容的补充。

  长久以来，机械工业出版社对本书的出版、发行都给予了鼎力支持，出版社的编辑对本书的出版、发行及修订工作提供了不遗余力的指导和帮助，正是他们及时反馈本书的使用情况及修订建议，才使我们的修订工作更具针对性和客观性，在此表示诚挚的谢意！本书在修订过程中参阅了大量文献资料，使用本书的相关高校教师提供了许多无私的建议，在此一并表示深深的谢意！

  "国际商务函电"是一门实务性很强的课程，需要较为深厚的理论知识及实践积淀。由于水平有限，书中不妥之处在所难免，恳请各位读者多提宝贵意见。

编 者

2016年8月

Suggestion 教学建议

"国际商务函电"是国际经济与贸易专业的专业必修课,是一门实践性很强的综合性应用型课程。它以进出口业务的各个环节为主线,对商务信函的特点、结构、写作方法及商务文化一一解析。通过学习本课程,学生能掌握外贸英语的专业词汇、专业术语以及基本句型,掌握进出口业务过程中各个环节往来信函的写法、常用单证的审阅和缮制,并能在实际中熟练使用。

本课程是在学生具备一定的外语水平、掌握大量英语词汇及国际贸易等相关知识的基础上开设的课程,因此,在学习本课程之前学生应先修基础英语、国际贸易理论与实务等课程。

本课程以课堂教学及情境式教学为主。教学中,应将商务英语与国际贸易实务紧密结合在一起,根据外贸交易业务过程中的各个环节,讲授涉及的专业术语及句型、信函的撰写要点及相应的单证;教师应充分发挥教学的主导作用和学生的主体性,以学生为中心组织课堂教学,建议每讲完一章,采取商务模拟的形式,由学生扮演商家进行外贸函电往来,并依据每一章的内容做相应练习,根据练习情况进行总结,使学生全面了解外贸业务,达到应用目的。

本课程总学时为42个学时,各章学时分配建议如下。

章	教学内容	总学时	理论讲授学时	课内实践学时
Chapter 1	Basic Knowledge of Business Letters and Foreign Trade Procedures	4	3	1
Chapter 2	Establishment of Business Relationships	3	2	1
Chapter 3	Inquiries and Replies	2	1	1
Chapter 4	Quotations, Offers and Counter-offers	3	2	1
Chapter 5	Orders, Acceptances and Rejections	2	1	1
Chapter 6	Terms of Payment	4	3	1
Chapter 7	Packings and Marks	3	2	1
Chapter 8	Insurance	3	2	1
Chapter 9	Commodity Inspection	3	2	1
Chapter 10	Shipment	3	2	1
Chapter 11	Complaint, Claim and Settlement	3	2	1
Chapter 12	Promotion	2	1	1
Chapter 13	Agency	3	2	1
Chapter 14	International Business Contracts	4	3	1
合计		42	28	14

课程考核以闭卷为主。考核时应适当加大作业、课堂表现、学生实践能力等的平时成绩所占的比例;要精心设计和合理安排考试类型,句型翻译、信函写作、单证缮制等题型应占较大比重。建议平时成绩所占比例为30%~40%,期末考试成绩所占比例为60%~70%。

目 录 Contents

前　言
教学建议

第1章　商务信函基础知识与外贸交易程序　1
Chapter 1　Basic Knowledge of Business Letters and Foreign Trade Procedures　1

1.1　商务信函概览及写作指导　/1
An Overview of Business Letters and Writing Guidelines　/1

1.2　商务信函的结构　/6
Structure of Business Letters　/6

1.3　商务信函的格式　/11
Format of Business Letters　/11

1.4　信封的写法　/14
Envelopes Addressing　/14

1.5　商务信函的其他形式（传真、电子邮件）　/15
Some Other Forms of Business Letters (Fax, E-mails)　/15

1.6　国际贸易的一般程序　/17
General Procedures of Foreign Trade　/17

1.7　商务谈判的一般程序　/21
General Procedure in Business Negotiation　/21

1.8　有用的短语和句子　/24
Useful Expressions　/24

练习　/26
Exercises　/26

第2章　建立贸易关系　28
Chapter 2　Establishment of Business Relationships　28

2.1　背景知识　/28
Background Information　/28

2.2 信例 /30
Sample Letters /30

2.3 有用的短语和句子 /39
Useful Expressions /39

练习 /41
Exercises /41

第3章 询盘与回复 43
Chapter 3　Inquiries and Replies　43

3.1 背景知识 /43
Background Information /43

3.2 信例 /46
Sample Letters /46

3.3 有用的短语和句子 /53
Useful Expressions /53

练习 /55
Exercises /55

附录3A 国际贸易价格术语 /57
Appendix 3A　Terms of Price in International Trade /57

第4章 报价、发盘及还盘 58
Chapter 4　Quotations, Offers and Counter-offers　58

4.1 背景知识 /58
Background Information /58

4.2 信例 /61
Sample Letters /61

4.3 有用的短语和句子 /68
Useful Expressions /68

练习 /69
Exercises /69

第5章 订购、接受和拒绝 71
Chapter 5　Orders, Acceptances and Rejections　71

5.1　背景知识　/71
Background Information　/71

5.2　信例　/74
Sample Letters　/74

5.3　有用的短语和句子　/78
Useful Expressions　/78

练习　/80
Exercises　/80

附录5A　订单　/82
Appendix 5A　Order　/82

附录5B　销售确认书　/82
Appendix 5B　Sales Confirmation　/82

附录5C　原产地证明书　/86
Appendix 5C　Certificate of Origin　/86

第6章 付款条件 87
Chapter 6　Terms of Payment　87

6.1　背景知识　/87
Background Information　/87

6.2　信例　/91
Sample Letters　/91

6.3　有用的短语和句子　/96
Useful Expressions　/96

练习　/100
Exercises　/100

附录6A　信用证　/102
Appendix 6A　Letter of Credit　/102

附录6B　开立不可撤销信用证申请书　/103
Appendix 6B　Irrevocable Letter of Credit Application Form　/103

附录6C　汇票　/107
Appendix 6C　Bill of Exchange　/107

第7章　包装与标志　108
Chapter 7　Packings and Marks　108

7.1　背景知识　/108
Background Information　/108

7.2　信例　/111
Sample Letters　/111

7.3　有用的短语和句子　/115
Useful Expressions　/115

练习　/119
Exercises　/119

附录7A　装箱单　/121
Appendix 7A　Packing List　/121

第8章　保险　122
Chapter 8　Insurance　122

8.1　背景知识　/122
Background Information　/122

8.2　信例　/128
Sample Letters　/128

8.3　有用的短语和句子　/132
Useful Expressions　/132

练习　/134
Exercises　/134

附录8A　保险单　/137
Appendix 8A　Insurance Policy　/137

第9章　商品检验　138
Chapter 9　Commodity Inspection　138

9.1　背景知识　/138
Background Information　/138

9.2 信例 /139
Sample Letters /139

9.3 有用的短语和句子 /143
Useful Expressions /143

练习 /146
Exercises /146

附录9A 检验证明书 /147
Appendix 9A Inspection Certificate /147

附录9B 出口货物报关单 /148
Appendix 9B Goods Declaration for Exportation /148

第10章 装运 150
Chapter 10 Shipment 150

10.1 背景知识 /150
Background Information /150

10.2 信例 /153
Sample Letters /153

10.3 有用的短语和句子 /157
Useful Expressions /157

练习 /159
Exercises /159

附录10A 提货单样本 /162
Appendix 10A Bill of Lading /162

附录10B 商业发票样本 /163
Appendix 10B Commercial Invoice /163

第11章 投诉、索赔和理赔 164
Chapter 11 Complaint, Claim and Settlement 164

11.1 背景知识 /164
Background Information /164

11.2 信例 /167
Sample Letters /167

11.3　有用的短语和句子　/172
Useful Expressions　/172

练习　/174
Exercises　/174

第 12 章　促销　176
Chapter 12　Promotion　176

12.1　背景知识　/176
Background Information　/176

12.2　信例　/177
Sample Letters　/177

12.3　有用的短语和句子　/181
Useful Expressions　/181

练习　/184
Exercises　/184

第 13 章　代理　186
Chapter 13　Agency　186

13.1　背景知识　/186
Background Information　/186

13.2　信例　/189
Sample Letters　/189

13.3　有用的短语和句子　/194
Useful Expressions　/194

练习　/196
Exercises　/196

附录 13A　代理协议　/198
Appendix 13A　Agency Agreement　/198

第 14 章　国际商务合同　200
Chapter 14　International Business Contracts　200

14.1　国际商务合同简介　/200
A Brief Introduction to International Business Contract　/200

14.2 国际商务合同的语言特色 /202
Language Features in International Business Contracts /202

14.3 合同样例 /206
Sample Contract /206

14.4 有用的短语和句子 /211
Useful Expressions /211

练习 /212
Exercises /212

附录14A 贸易单证实例1 /215
Appendix 14A Trade Documents 1 /215

附录14B 贸易单证实例2 /223
Appendix 14B Trade Documents 2 /223

综合练习题1　228
Comprehensive Exercises 1　228

综合练习题2　234
Comprehensive Exercises 2　234

综合练习题3　237
Comprehensive Exercises 3　237

综合练习题4　240
Comprehensive Exercises 4　240

综合练习题5　244
Comprehensive Exercises 5　244

练习答案　248
Key to Exercises　248

综合练习题答案　267
Key to Comprehensive Exercises　267

参考文献　275
Reference　275

Chapter 1
第 1 章

商务信函基础知识与外贸交易程序
Basic Knowledge of Business Letters and Foreign Trade Procedures

Learning Objectives

Enable students to master the principles of business letter writing; to become acquainted with the general layout of most business letters; to be able to write structural parts of business English letters with proper styles; to be familiar with the procedures of foreign trade, parties and documents involved.

使学生掌握商务信函的写作原则,熟悉商务信函的结构;能熟练运用适当的格式撰写商务英语信函;同时了解外贸交易的相关程序、涉及的各方当事人以及相关单证。

1.1 商务信函概览及写作指导
An Overview of Business Letters and Writing Guidelines

Business communication is a process through which the parties involved establish partnerships or relationships, negotiate terms, and complete transactions. Every company, big or small, communicates with many different firms and companies everyday. Although new information technologies are increasingly used, business letters are still the main channel and medium of business communication. Even though the way of transmission of the business letters is changing, the essential act of sending a message from one person to another remains the same. Therefore, it is necessary to be aware of the importance of business letter writing.

In business world, words are as important as figures. By words we make sales, create good will, win customers and hold old ones. Words can let us obtain credit, get bills paid, report on new ideas and products, and launch sales campaigns. So success in writing is a key to success in business.

商务交流是有关各方建立合作关系、商讨贸易条款、完成交易的过程。每家公司,不管是大还是小,每天都要与其他公司打交道。尽管现在大量使用信息技术,但是商务信函仍然是交流的主要渠道和媒介。即使商务信函的传播方式发生了变化,但人与人之间传递信息的基本行为仍然是相同的。因此,了解商务信函写作的重要性非常有必要。

在商业世界,文字与数字一样重要,我们用文字去销售,实现美好愿望,赢得新客户,维持老客户。文字也能获得信誉,得到货款,展示新的思想和产品,进行营销活动。因此,成功的信

Business letters can be roughly grouped into three categories in terms of their purpose: to get action; to build goodwill; to furnish information. If you want to write successful business letters, always keep in mind that you are going to have a talk with your reader. The most effective letters are messages from one real people to the other. They should be easy to read and understand, and they must be friendly and courteous.

There are some common requirements in the writing of a business letter, especially for the body of the letter, which are known as the "7Cs": correctness, conciseness, clarity, concreteness, completeness, courtesy, and consideration. These "7Cs" principles are virtually reflected at different levels of a business letter, which refers to the language, content, attitude and form of the letter.

函是交易成功的关键。

根据写信的目的，商务信函可大体分成三种类型：实施某种行为，建立美好愿望，提供某些信息。成功地写好一封商务信函，一定要牢记，你是在与读者交流。最有效的信函是信息从一个真实的人向另一个真实的人传递。这些信息应当易于阅读和理解，友好而礼貌。

商务信函的写作有一些基本要求，尤其是信的主体部分，要遵循"7C"原则：正确、简洁、清晰、具体、完整、礼貌和体谅，这"7C"原则反映了商务信函的不同层面，包括语言、内容、态度以及信函形式。

1.1.1　正确
Correctness

Correctness not only refers to the correct grammar rules, contents and forms, but also reflects in the style, language and typing. To choose the right words that can most closely convey the meaning of your thoughts is one of the ways to improve the readability of your business writing. At the same time, the right tone is also significant. Usually, mistakes with tone can be avoided by using the following techniques:

(1) Place more emphasis on the reader than yourself;

(2) Avoid extreme cases of humility, flattery, and modesty;

(3) Avoid condescension;

(4) Avoid lecturing.

正确不仅是指符合语法规则、内容和形式正确，而且还指风格、语言和文字的正确。选择最能确切表达你想法的词是增强商业信函阅读性的方法之一，同时，正确的语气也很重要。一般来讲，可以通过运用下列技巧避免使用错误的语气。

（1）把重点放在读者身上，而不是你身上；

（2）避免过度谦卑、奉承和谦虚；

（3）避免傲慢；

（4）避免说教。

1.1.2　简洁
Conciseness

Conciseness is often considered to be the most important writing principle and language feature. It enables to save both parties' time. Conciseness also means you should clearly express what you would do in a short and pithy style of writing as possible as you can. To achieve this, the following guidelines must be observed:

简洁常被视为商务信函写作的重要原则和语言特色。它可以节省双方的时间。简洁也意味着你应该以一种短小精悍的写作方式表达你的想法，要做到这一点，应遵循下列原则：

（1）Make a long story short and try to avoid wordiness;
（2）Avoid the out-of-date commercial jargons and try to use modern English;
（3）Avoid unnecessary repeat;
（4）Build effective sentences and paragraphs.

Compare the following sentences:

（1）长话短说，不要啰唆;
（2）不要使用过时的语言，要运用现代英语;
（3）避免不必要的重复;
（4）使用有效的句子和段落。

比较下列句子:

Wordy 冗长	Concise 简洁
We would like to know whether you would allow us to extend the time of shipment for twenty days and if you would be so kind as to allow us to do so, kindly give us your reply by fax without delay. 我们想知道你是否允许我方延长装运期20天，如果允许，请立刻传真告知我方。	Please reply by fax immediately if you will allow us to delay the shipment until April 21. 请传真告知你是否允许装运期推迟到4月21日。
They attend the Guangzhou Trade Fair for the purpose of finding a business partner. 他们参加广交会的目的是寻找商业伙伴。	They attend the Guangzhou Trade Fair to find a partner. 他们参加广交会寻找合作伙伴。

Out-of-date Commercial Jargons 过时的语言	Modern English 现代英语
due to the fact that 由于……的事实	as, because or since 因为
terminate 结束	end 结束
attached hereto 随函附	Enclosed is/are 随函附
acknowledge receipt of 确认收到	Thank you for... I received... 感谢……今收到……
Inst. 本月	this month 本月
up to this writing 在写这封信的时候	so far 到目前为止

1.1.3 清晰/清楚
Clarity/Clearness

A point that is ambiguous in a letter will cause trouble to both sides. In this way, clarity is often considered to be one of the main writing principles and language features. To achieve clearness and clarity, you should first have a clear idea of what you wish to convey in the letter, such as the purpose, the attitude, and the matter concerned. The following rules should be followed:

（1）Avoid to use the words which have different or unclear meaning;
（2）Pay attention to the position of modifiers;
（3）Pay attention to the rationality in logic.

Compare the following sentences:

信函表达含糊会给双方都带来麻烦，因而，表达清晰常常被看作是信函写作的主要原则和语言特色之一。要做到这点，在写作信函的时候，头脑中就要有一个清晰的想法，比如写作的目的、态度、所涉及的问题等。要遵循下列原则:

（1）避免使用有歧义的文字;
（2）注意修饰语的位置;
（3）注意语言的逻辑性。

比较下列句子:

Ambiguous 模棱两可	Clear 清晰
We sent you 5 samples yesterday of the goods which you requested in your letter of May 25 by air. 我方根据你方 5 月 25 日来函要求，昨日航邮 5 份样品给你。	We sent you, by air, 5 samples of the goods yesterday which you requested in your letter of May 25. 根据你方 5 月 25 日来函要求，我方于昨日航邮 5 份样品给你。

1.1.4 具体
Concreteness

Business writing should be vivid, specific and definite rather than vague, general and abstract, especially when the writer is requiring a response, solving problems, making an offer or acceptance, etc. We need to use specific facts, figures and time to stress concreteness. Try to heed the following tips:

(1) Complete with the 6W's: Who? What? Why? How? Where? When?

(2) Concreteness in action: using specific language to make our information more concrete and convincing;

(3) Using concrete words.

商务信函要生动、具体和明确，而不是含糊、一般和抽象，尤其是写作者需要得到某种回应、解决问题、做出发盘或接受报价时，更需使用具体的语言、数字和时间强调其具体性。记住下列要点：

(1) 写信时要考虑 6W 原则，即谁？什么？为什么？怎样？哪里？何时？

(2) 写信时要具体：使用确切的语言，使得信息更具体，细节更完整；

(3) 要使用具体词汇。

Vague 含糊	Concrete 具体
We have drawn on you as usual under your L/C. 与往常一样我方已开具了信用证项下的汇票。	We have drawn on you our sight draft No. 345 for the Invoice amount, US $ 560.00, under your L/C No. 234 of the China Bank. 我方已就中国银行开立的 234 号信用证，向贵方开具了 345 号汇票，金额为 560.00 美元。
We wish to confirm our fax dispatched yesterday. 希望确认昨天发给你的传真。	We wish to confirm our fax dispatched on September 12, 2010. 希望确认 2010 年 9 月 12 日的传真。

1.1.5 完整
Completeness

A business letter should include all necessary information. It is essential to check the message carefully before it is sent out. As you work hard for completeness, keep the following guidelines in mind: Why do you write the letter? What are the facts supporting the reasons? Have you answered the questions asked?

完整意味着一封商务信函应该包含所有必要的信息，因而有必要在信函发出之前检查一遍。要做到这一点，应记住下列原则：为什么写信？支持你写信的依据是什么？你是否已经回答了对方提出的问题？

1.1.6 礼貌
Courtesy

Courtesy plays a considerable role in business letter writing as in all business activities. It is not the mere politeness. By courtesy we mean trading people with respect and friendly human concern. In order to make a business letter courteous, try to avoid irritating, offensive, or belittling statements. To answer letters promptly is also a matter of courtesy. Following rules should be followed:

(1) Change the commanding tone into requesting tone;

(2) Use mitigation and avoid overemphasizing your own opinion or irritating your partner;

(3) Passive voice should be adopted accordingly;

(4) Try to avoid using the words with forcing tone or arousing unpleasantness;

(5) Use expressions about joy and willingness, thanks and regret, etc.

Compare the following sentences:

像所有的商业活动一样，礼貌在商务信函中起着非常重要的作用。礼貌不仅仅意味着彬彬有礼，还意味着与人交易时要尊敬和友好待人。要做到这点应避免使用进攻或轻视性的语言，另外及时回信也是礼貌的表现。应遵循下列原则：

(1) 变命令式的语气为征求式语气；

(2) 语气要缓和，避免过分强调你的想法或激怒对方；

(3) 相应地使用被动语态；

(4) 尽量避免使用带有强制性的语言，防止引起不愉快；

(5) 使用表达高兴、意愿、感谢和遗憾之类的文字。

比较下列句子：

Poorer 较差	Better 较好
Tell us more detailed information on your requirements. 告诉我们你们的具体要求。	Will you please tell us more detailed information on your requirements? 请告诉我们你们的具体要求好吗？
You can make shipment a little later, that is, by June 10. 你们可以装运晚一点，即6月10日。	You might make shipment a little later, that is, by June 10. 你们可以考虑装运晚一点，即6月10日。
We can't deliver the goods all at one time. 我们不可能同时交货。	I'm afraid we cannot deliver the goods all at one time. 恐怕我们无法同时交货。
You did not enclose the price list in your letter. 你们没有在信中附价格单。	The price list was not enclosed in your letter. 贵方信中没有附价格单。
We must refuse your offer. 我们拒绝贵方报价。	We regret that we are unable to accept your offer. 很遗憾我们不能接受贵方报价。

1.1.7 体谅
Consideration

Consideration means thoughtfulness. So you should always put yourself in your reader's place. That is, to emphasize You-attitude rather than We-attitude. When

体谅意味着要为他人着想，即要把自己摆在对方的位置，强调以对方为主，而不是以自己为

writing a letter, keep the reader's request, needs, desires, as well as his or her feelings in mind. Plan the best way to present the message for the reader to receive. In addition, we should try to discuss problems in a positive way rather than in a negative way.

主。写信时要谨记对方的要求、需要、愿望和感受，用最好的方法向对方传递可以接受的信息。此外，还应以肯定而不是否定的方式来讨论问题。

Make a comparison between the following:

比较下列各句：

We-attitude 以我为主	You-attitude 以对方为主
We would like to take the opportunity to demonstrate our full range of products and services which we can offer our customers. 我们想借此机会向您展示我们可以给客户提供的全套产品和服务。	Please join us at the fair and you will have the chance to see how our products and services can benefit you and you company. 请与我们一起参加展会，您将有机会看看我方产品和服务是否对贵公司有益。
We allow 2% discount for cash payment. 我方对现金付款有2%的折扣。	You earn 2% discount when you pay cash. 如果贵方付现金可以有2%的折扣。

Negative 否定	Positive 肯定
Your order will be delayed for 2 weeks. 贵方订单将延误2周。	Your order will be shipped in 2 weeks. 贵方订单将于2周后装运。
We regret our inability to serve you at this time. 很遗憾我方不能在这时向你提供服务。	Perhaps next time we can send you what you require. 或许下次我们可以发送你需要的货物。

1.2 商务信函的结构
Structure of Business Letters

A typical business letter consists of the following parts: letterhead, the date line, inside address, the attention line, salutation, subject line, body, complimentary close, signature, enclosure (Enc.) and postscripts (P.S.). Figure 1-1 is designed to illustrate the position of each possible part mentioned above.

典型的商务信函由下列几部分组成：信头、日期、封内地址、注意项、称呼语、事由、正文、结尾敬语、签名、附件、附言等。图1-1这封信列出了上述提到的各部分的具体位置。

1.2.1 信头
The Letterhead

The letterhead is the heading at the top of a letter. It usually consists of the name, address, telephone number and fax number of a company who delivers the letter. The letterhead can be typed out, but it is usually printed on the company's stationary (such stationary is also called letterhead) in the up-center or at the left margin of a letter. In addition, the printed letterhead may also include other items such as the company logo, website, e-mail address, etc.

信头位于信的最上端，通常由写信人的公司名称、地址、电话、传真等组成。信头可打印出来，但多数都事先印在了公司的信纸上方中间的位置或者在信的左边空白处。此外，印好的信头还可包括其他内容，如公司标识、网址、电子信箱等。

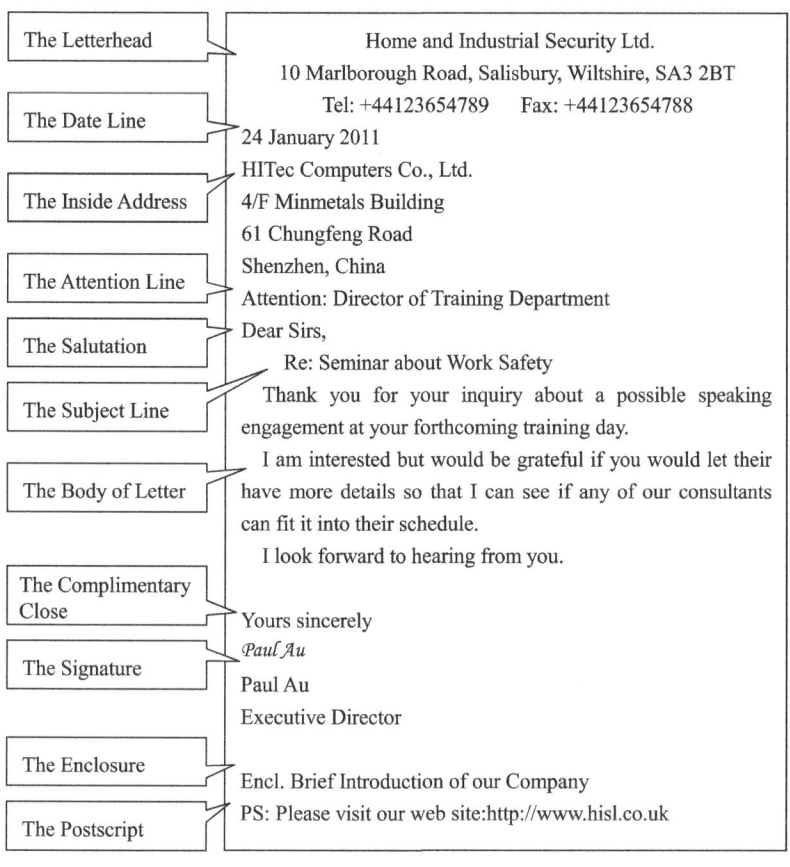

图 1-1

1.2.2 日期

The Date Line

The format of the date line differs from country to country. The common ones are M/D/Y (typical American), D/M/Y (typical British).

e. g. 02/12/2010

This form in Britain could be taken as December 2, 2010, but in American and some other countries it would mean February 12, 2010. So the month written in letters is preferred because figures may create confusion.

The date is typed a few lines below the last line of the letterhead. Different from the place in a Chinese letter, the date in an English letter should be put above the inside name and address.

日期的形式因国家的不同而不同，通常的方式是：月/日/年（美国），日/月/年（英国）。

比如：02/12/2010

这个形式如果在英国表示 2010 年 12 月 2 日，但是在美国等国家则表示 2010 年 2 月 12 日。因此，最好用字母来写月份，以免引起混淆。

日期一般要写在信头下面几行的位置，不同于汉语写信日期的位置，英文写信日期应放在封内地址的上面。

1.2.3　编号和封内地址
The Reference and Inside Address

The reference may include a file name, departmental code or the initials of the signer followed by that of the typist of the letter. Many letterheads provide space for references.

e. g. Your ref:

Our ref:

The inside address is the recipient's address, which should be identical to the delivery address on the envelope. The inside address serves as the delivery address. It is typed at the left-hand margin two lines below the date. The information should be given in a way like this:

(1) Receiver's name or his official title;
(2) Company's name;
(3) Number of the house and name of the street;
(4) District, name of the town or city;
(5) State or province, ZIP code;
(6) Name of country.

Courtesy titles such as Mr., Ms., etc. are commonly used to address one person. Use Ms if you do not know whether a lady is married or not. If there is any official position of that person, his or her official position should follow the name.

e. g. Mr. John Smith, President

Messrs is also a common courtesy title, only used for companies or firms, the name of which includes a personal element, like Messrs. J. Henry & Co. It is not used when the name already carries a courtesy title, like Sir James Fred & Co.

编号包括文档名称、部门号、签署人名字的首字母以及打字人名字，许多信函会留下空间用于输入编号。

如：贵方编号：
我方编号：

封内地址指的是收信人的地址，这个要与信封的地址一致。封内地址就是寄信地址，位于日期栏下方几行左首的位置，具体内容是：

(1) 收信人的名称和职务；
(2) 公司名称；
(3) 街道、门牌号；
(4) 地区、城市名；
(5) 州或省，邮编；
(6) 国家。

信寄给某个人时，要用表示礼貌的词如 Mr. 或 Ms.。如果不了解女性的婚姻状况，则用 Ms.。若有职务，则其姓名后面要加上其职务。

如：Mr. John Smith，董事长

Messrs 同样表示礼貌的称呼，但只用于称呼公司或者公司名是由人名命名的，如 Messrs J Henry & Co.。如果公司名已经有类似的礼貌用语如 Sir James Fred & Co.，则不需要再用 Messrs。

1.2.4　注意项
The Attention Line

If you want your letter attended by or directed to a specific person or department, add an attention line. This will speed up the sorting process within a company.

e. g. Attention: Sales Manager

如果信是寄给某个具体的人或部门，则需要加上"注意项"一栏，这样有助于提高信件处理的速度。

如：请交销售经理

1.2.5 称呼语
The Salutation

The salutation is the greeting to your recipient. It is usually two lines below the inside name and address without any indentation, including a personal or professional title and the name of the recipient. The salutation varies according to the writer-recipient relations and the formality level of the letter.

The following table shows some common salutation:

称呼语是对收信人的称呼,通常位于封内地址下两行的位置,不用缩行,主要包括收信人的姓名和职务。根据与收信人的关系和信的正规程度,称呼也有所不同。

下表列出了常用的称呼语:

Salutation 称呼语	People to Address 称呼对象
Dear Mr. ×××	Men 男性
Dear Mrs. ×××	Married women 已婚女性
Dear Miss. ×××	Unmarried women and girls 未婚女性
Dear Ms. ×××	Women, marital status unknown 女性,婚姻状况不明
Dear Dr. ×××	Physicians, PH. D. holders 医生、博士
Dear Prof. ×××	Professors and any holder of a professional rank 教授、拥有职称的人
Dear Sir (s)/Madam	No specific reference, formal 没有具体的对象、正式用语
Gentlemen	No specific reference, formal 没有具体的对象、正式用语
Ladies and Gentlemen	No specific reference, formal 没有具体的对象、正式用语
To whom it may concern	You don't know yet who is the recipient 不清楚给谁
(Dear) First name only	Close friend, informal 朋友,非正式

1.2.6 事由
The Subject Line

The subject line is placed one line below the salutation. It helps both the sender and the recipient identify the subject matter. It is used to call reader's attention, therefore, you may underline it or make it in boldface letters. Below are some samples of the subject line:
- Subject: Order No: 12345
- Subject: S/C No. 345
- <u>Re: Invoice 567</u>
- Re: Your L/C No. 678

事由位于称呼的下一行,其目的是帮助双方了解信的主要内容,引起对方的注意,因此可以在事由下面画线或加黑。下面是有关事由的几种常用格式:
- 主题:12345 号订单一事
- 主题:345 号售货合同一事
- <u>关于:567 号发票一事</u>
- 关于:贵方 678 号信用证一事

1.2.7 正文
The Body of The Letter

This is the most important part of any business letter. It is typed two lines below the salutation or subject line. No matter whether your letter is long or short, it usually

这是商务信函最重要的组成部分,通常位于称呼语和事由项下两行。不管信函长短,通常要

consists of three paragraphs: the opening paragraph which is to give a subject introduction of the letter; the middle paragraph to discuss the details of the transaction; and the closing paragraph to end the letter in a way of summation, further request or suggestion. And when writing the letter, you should attach great importance to the 7Cs' principles: Clearness, Conciseness, Consideration, Courtesy, Correctness, Concreteness and Completeness. It is advisable to keep the following tips in mind:

(1) Write simply, clearly, courteously, grammatically, and to the point;

(2) Paragraph correctly, confining each paragraph to one topic;

(3) See that your typing is accurate.

有三段：开头段，主要介绍信的主题；中间段，讨论交易的细节；结束段，进行总结，给出进一步的要求或建议。写信时，要遵循"7C"原则，即清晰、简洁、体谅、礼貌、正确、具体和完整。要注意下面几点：

（1）文字要简单、清楚、礼貌、符合语法、恰到好处；

（2）段落划分准确，每段讲述一个主题；

（3）确保文字正确。

1.2.8 结尾敬语
The Complimentary Close

This part is like bidding farewell to someone with a handshake, a wave of hand, or a kiss. Like the salutation, the complimentary close has various styles: formal, semi-formal and informal. The style shall match that of the salutation. For example:

(1) Dear Sirs matches Yours faithfully;

(2) Gentlemen matches Yours truly;

(3) Dear Mr. James matches Yours sincerely.

Some samples of the complimentary close are as below:

这部分就如同是向某人道别、挥手或吻别。像称呼一样，结束语风格多样，有正规、半正规和非正规等形式。但注意，敬语要与称呼语匹配，如：

（1）Dear Sirs 与 Yours faithfully 搭配；

（2）Gentlemen 与 Yours truly 搭配；

（3）Dear Mr. James 与 Yours sincerely 搭配。

下表给出了结尾敬语的几个样例：

Formal 正规	Semi-formal 半正规	Informal 非正规
Yours faithfully	Sincerely yours	Sincerely
Yours very truly	Cordially yours	Cordially
Faithfully yours	Very cordially yours	Best regards

1.2.9 签名
The Signature

The signature is generally placed two lines below the complimentary close. It consists of a handwritten signature

签名位于结尾敬语的下面两行处，由手签（手签往往难以辨

(by hand and in ink, usually illegible), the typed-out name and a title.

认）、打印名和职务三部分组成。

1.2.10 附件
The Enclosure

When something else is sent together with the letter, you add the enclosure to inform the reader what is enclosed. For example:
(1) Enclosure: Sales Contract
(2) Encl:
　　Packing List
　　Commodity Inspection certificate
　　Insurance Policy

当有其他文件随信寄送时，加上"附件"以告诉对方附件是什么。如：
（1）随函附：售货合同
（2）随函附：
　　装箱单
　　商品检验证书
　　保险单

1.2.11 附言
The Postscript

The postscript is used to add an afterthought, aiming at the drawing of the reader's attention to a point you wish to emphasize or something you forget to mention. The note of a P.S. should be avoided as far as possible, since it may suggest that you have failed to plan your letter well. It is strongly advised to rewrite the letter instead of using the afterthought when you forget to mention something important.

As a special device, the postscript is placed two lines below at the left margin.

附言主要用于事后想起的事情，目的是让对方注意到你强调的或者你忘记在信中提及的事情。但要尽量避免使用附言，因为这可能会使对方认为你没有组织好信函，所以写信的时候忘记谈及某个重要的事情时，建议重写而不要使用附言。

附言通常放在信的左下方空白处。

1.3 商务信函的格式
Format of Business Letters

Generally speaking, there are three basic forms of letter. They are block form, indented form and semi-block form with indented paragraphs.

通常，信函的格式有三种：缩进式、齐头式和半齐头式（或混合式）。

1.3.1 缩进式
Indented Form

The main feature of this style is that each line of the inside name and address should be indented 2~3 spaces, and the first line of each paragraph should be indented 3~5 spaces. This is a traditionally conservative format of layout.

这种格式的主要特点是：封内地址每行都应缩进2~3个空格，每段的第一行也要缩进3~5个空格，是较为传统的信函格式。

THE EASTERN SEABOARD CORPORATION

350 Park Avenue, New York, 10017, USA

Tel: 225-2788 Fax: 225-2780

E-mail: ESCO. @ CA. com

Our Ref: QW9807
Your Ref: UI-87

January 4, 2011

Kanto Mercantile Corporation
  2-1 Nihonbashi
    Tokyo 89
      Japan
Dear Sirs,

Price list

Here is the price list you asked about.

You will be happy to know that all of the items listed on pages 5~7 will be marked down 30% between February and March. If you would like to take advantage of this special opportunity, please fill out the enclosed order form and return to us by the end of January.

Thank you for writing.

Yours faithfully,

THE EASTERN SEABOARD CORPORATION

James Baton

Vice President

1.3.2 齐头式
Block Form

In the block form, all typing lines, including those for the date, the inside name and address, the salutation, the subject heading and the complimentary close, begin at the left-hand with no indention in the letter.	齐头式中各行，包括日期、封内名称和地址，称呼、事由以及结尾敬语等都是从左边边缘打起，整封信无行首缩进。

MARIWANG PTE. LTD.
402, ORCHARD ROAD # 08-09
DELFI ORCHARD, SINGAPORE 0928
TEL: 65-7548-9824 FAX: 65-7548-9825

January 4, 2011

Beijing Textile Imp. & Exp. Corp.
102 Fengqi Road
Beijing 100002

Dear Sirs,
We have been informed of your company and address through the Chamber of Commerce in Beijing. We are interested in your cotton blankets and bed-sheets for sales in Singapore market.
We would like you to send us details of your various ranges, including size, colors, prices and samples of the different qualities of material used. We trust that you will make an effort to quote us most favorable terms for large quantities.
Looking forward to establishing direct business relations with you.

Yours faithfully,
MARIWANG PTE. LTD.
Adam Smith
Adam Smith
Manager

1.3.3 半齐头式或混合式
Semi-block Form with Indented Paragraphs

In this form, the inside name and address is typed in block form, but the paragraphs forming the body of the letter are all indented 3 or more spaces.

半齐头式封内地址是齐头式，但段落要缩进3个或更多的空格。

```
                        Armstrong Cork Company
                          Lancester, PA, 17884
                                                    December 19, 2010
Mr. Thomas Carlin,
Alexander Hamilton Institute, Inc.
123 East 42nd Street
New York, N. Y. 10017

Dear Mr. Carlin,
    Thank you for your recent letter requesting copies of the types of written communication
which we employ. We very much appreciate your interest in Armstrong.
    I have enclosed samples of the types of communication which we have available. I hope that
the material is helpful and that you find it interesting and informative. If there is something more
that we may do for you, please don't hesitate to let me know.
    Thank you again for your interest in Armstrong Cork Company. On behalf of the Company,
may I wish Mr. Elfen every success with his new book.
                                                              Sincerely,
                                                            Thomas L. Burgum
                                                         Public Relation Department
```

1.4 信封的写法
Envelopes Addressing

Envelope addressing calls for accuracy, legibility and good appearance. Like the inside address, the address on the envelope can be written in two forms: the indented form and the block form. Usually no punctuation is used on the envelope. No matter in which way the address on the envelope is written, it should conform to the inside address in both style and content. Generally speaking, the address of the envelope should be written in the following order:	信封要求文字准确、清晰、整洁。如同封内地址一样,信封地址可以有两种形式,即缩进式和齐头式。通常不使用标点符号。不管信封用哪种方式写,都应与封内地址一致。一般按下列顺序:
(1) Name of the addressee;	(1) 收信人姓名;
(2) Number and street;	(2) 门牌号;
(3) City, state and zip code;	(3) 城市、州、邮编;
(4) Country.	(4) 国家。
Figure 1-2 is a sample of an envelope.	图 1-2 是样例。

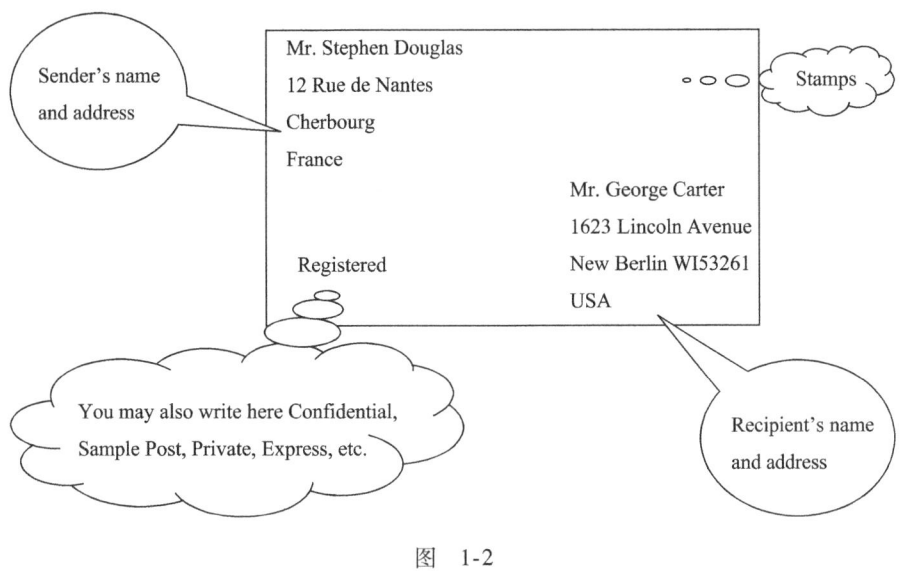

图 1-2

1.5 商务信函的其他形式（传真、电子邮件）
Some Other Forms of Business Letters (Fax, E-mails)

Although business correspondence has undergone significant changes in forms and style with the fast development of technological developments, the electronic correspondence remains the means and ways by which transactions in foreign trade are discussed.

In international trade, there are usually four types of electronic correspondence, namely telegraph, telex, fax and E-mail. Due to the fast development of internet, telegraph and telex are seldom used today. What follows is a discussion of two communication methods: fax and e-mail.

随着科学技术的快速发展，商务信函虽在形式和风格上经历了显著的变化，但电子信函仍是国际贸易使用的主要手段和方法。

国际贸易中，通常有四种电子信函，即电报、电传、传真和电子邮件。随着互联网的发展，电报和电传现在已很少使用。下面主要探讨传真和电子邮件两种通信方式。

1.5.1 传真
Fax

Fax machine provides an easy way to send documents over phone lines. It's faster than regular mail and more affordable than overnight delivery. While e-mail has begun to supplant the fax in many businesses, fax machine is still indispensable for immediately sharing contracts, proofs and other written documents. People can use fax to send all kinds of messages, such as letter, diagrams, graphs, tables or even signature etc. So knowing how to write a fax message in the correct form becomes a must for

传真机为通过电话线传送文件提供了方便，它要比一般的信函快，而且可以夜间传送，尽管电子邮件在许多商业领域开始取代传真机，但传真在发送合同、证据以及其他书面文件方面仍是不可或缺的。人们可以用传真机传送各种信息，如信件、数字、图表甚至签名。因此，学会如何

all who want to go into the business world.

Fax messages are divided into two parts. The top of it contains details of the sender and recipient, date, and the subject. Some companies have their printed fax coversheet with the fax heading displaying the company contact details. The second part is the body of the fax.

Here are some tips on writing a fax:
(1) Write a correct heading so that the receiver knows:

to whom it is designated—to
from whom it comes—from
on which date—date
for what purpose—ATTN:/Subject:
(2) Indicate the number of pages to follow;
(3) Use simple language and be concise.

以正确的形式写传真对于从事商业活动的人非常重要。

传真由两部分组成。第一部分，即最上端一般是发信人和收信人的详情、日期和事由。一些公司有其自己印制好的传真纸，上面有信头，写明公司的联络方式。第二部分是传真的正文。

下面是写传真的一些要点：
（1）正确书写信头，以便使收信人知道：
信是给谁的，
谁发来的，
日期是什么时候，
什么目的；
（2）写明传真的页码数；
（3）使用简单的语言，文字要简洁。

To: Hill Company
Attn: Mr. Conrad Smith
Fax: 1-403-234568　　　　　　Tel: 1-403-234569
From: George Bill
Date: 06/09/2010
Fax: 86-516-5879212　　　　　Tel: 86-516-5879213
Number of pages to follow: 1
Dear Mr. Smith,
　　It was a pleasure meeting you this week and learning of your interest in our promoting project.
　　Please find enclosed detailed information of our special promotion package for the March issue. As time is short final deadline has passed. Your prompt confirmation would be highly appreciated.
　　Thank you for your kind attention and I look forward to your prompt reply.
Best regards!

1.5.2　电子邮件
E-mail

Business e-mail consists of the heading, the body, and a signature block. Depending on the nature of its cor-

电子邮件由信头、正文和署名组成。根据信函性质的不同，

respondence, business e-mail may also include a salutation and a complimentary close. The pre-set format of e-mail makes them even easier to write than business letters. The sender's email address and the date are generated automatically by the computer, what you have to do is to type in the recipient's email address.

Here is a sample of an E-mail:

电子邮件还可以包括称呼语和结尾敬语。事先设置好格式的电子邮件写起来要比普通商务信函容易得多。计算机可以自动生成寄信人的地址和日期,你所要做的就是输入收信人的地址。

下面是一封电子邮件样例:

From	"John Song" <johnson@sina.com.cn>
Date	SUN, 23 JAN 2011 23:25 PM
Subject	Business in Canada
To	"Kevin lee" <kevin@gmail.com>

Dear Mr. Lee,
　　We thank you for your cooperation for our business for the past five years.
　　Now we are desirous of enlarging our trade in staple commodities, but have had no good connections in Canada. Therefore we shall be obliged if you could kindly introduce us to some of reliable importers in Canada who are interested in these lines of goods.
　　We await your immediate reply.

1.6　国际贸易的一般程序
General Procedures of Foreign Trade

　　The procedures of foreign trade are so complicated that it may take quite a long time to conclude a transaction. Varied and complicated procedures have to be a good through in the course of export or import transaction. From the very beginning to the end of the transaction, the whole operation generally undergoes four stages: preparing for exporting or importing, business negotiation, implementation of the contract, and settlement of disputes (if any). Each stage covers some specific steps. No matter what way the negotiations are held, in general, they consist of the following links: enquiry, offer, counter-offer, acceptance and conclusion of sales contract, among which offer and acceptance are two indispensible links for reaching an agreement and concluding a contract. Since the export and import trades are two sides of the same coin, and one country's export is another country's import, hence, we will take the procedures of export transaction in the following diagram to illustrate the general procedures of export and import transaction.

　　进出口贸易的程序非常复杂,往往要花很长一段时间才能完成一笔交易。在一笔进出口贸易中,要经历各种各样复杂的程序。从开始到结束,整个交易过程经历四个阶段:进出口准备、商务谈判、合同执行以及纠纷解决(如果有的话)。每个阶段包含一些具体的步骤。但不管磋商以什么样的方式开始,它通常包含下列几个环节:询盘、发盘、还盘、接受和签订销售合同。其中,发盘和接受是达成协议和签订合同不可缺少的环节。既然进出口贸易是同一件事情的两个方面,即一个国家的进口就是另一个国家的出口,在这里我们用出口贸易步骤的流程图来说明进出口贸易的一般程序。

1.6.1 出口的程序
Procedures of Export

The most difficult part of exporting is taking the first step. Different countries have different economic policies or systems. So before doing business with foreign countries, one has to understand the whole procedures of export.

There may be 3 steps for an exporter to conclude a transaction of export: to prepare for exporting; to have business negotiation; to carry out the contract.

The preparation for export involves market survey, pricing, preparing goods, advertising, contacting the clients, etc. To some extent, the preparation for export lays a good foundation for the next stage.

The negotiation of terms and conditions is to maximize the exporters' profit. Generally speaking, a business negotiation goes through such steps as inquiry, offer, counter-offer and acceptance before a contact is conducted.

To ensure the fulfillment of a contract for export business, an exporter should see to it that everything concerning the export business to be done without failure, in particular with such affairs as to prepare goods for exports, to secure documentary credit, to arrange for shipment, and to get ready for all shipment documents for settlement (See Figure 1-3).

对于出口来说，最困难的是迈出第一步。不同的国家有不同的经济政策和体制。因此，在与外商做生意之前，必须了解出口交易的整个程序。

一般出口商达成一笔出口交易需要三步：准备出口、交易磋商以及合同执行。

出口准备涉及市场调研、定价、准备货物、广告、与顾客联系等。从某种程度上，出口准备为下一步交易奠定了良好的基础。

交易条款的磋商是为了确保出口商利益的最大化。通常交易磋商在达成协议之前要经历询盘、发盘、还盘和接受四个阶段。

为确保出口合同的顺利执行，出口商应确保与出口有关的一切事务万无一失，尤其是出口货物的准备、单证的信用保证、装运安排、结算用装运单据的准备等（见图1-3）。

1.6.2 进口贸易的程序
Procedures of Import

Somewhat similar to those of export business, the basic procedures of import business may be divided into three major stages, but naturally the focus of each stage differs from that of export business.

The market survey still plays an important role in import business. The market survey helps collect necessary information for the importer's analytical study of the capacity, reputation, credit standing and business mode of both the producers and the suppliers and the comparison of prices, qualities, specifications and technology of similar products so as to select reliable clients and minimize the importing cost.

类似于出口交易，进口交易的基本程序也可以分成三个阶段，但每个阶段的重点不同于出口交易。

市场调研在进口交易中仍然起着十分重要的作用。市场调研有助于获得必要的信息以供进口商分析生产者和供货商的市场容量、声誉、信用状况、商业模式，比较同类产品的价格、质量、规格和技术以便选择可靠的客户，减少进口成本。

The process of the negotiation of terms and conditions aims at reducing the importer's cost and safeguarding the importer's profit. But after the negotiation, the importer needs to sign the purchase contract or conformation with the foreign exporter so as to clarify both parties' obligations and enable the fulfillment of the contract.

If the import business is concluded on the basis of FOB or FCA and requires payment by document credit, the importer has the obligation to open a L/C through a bank, book shipping space or charter a ship, advise loading date, arrange for insurance, take the delivery of the goods, make payment, make import entry at customs and import inspections, etc. With the completion of this stage, the whole import business ends (See Figure 1-4).

合同条款的磋商过程旨在降低进口商的成本，确保进口商的利润。但是磋商后，进口商需要与外国出口商签署购货合同或确认书，以便分清彼此的责任和义务，确保合同的执行。

如果进口交易是以 FOB 或 FCA 成交并以跟单信用证成交，进口商则有义务通过银行开立信用证、预定舱位或者租船、通知装运时间、安排保险、提交货物、付款、进口通关、进口检验等。伴随着这一系列手续的完成，整个进口交易结束（见图1-4）。

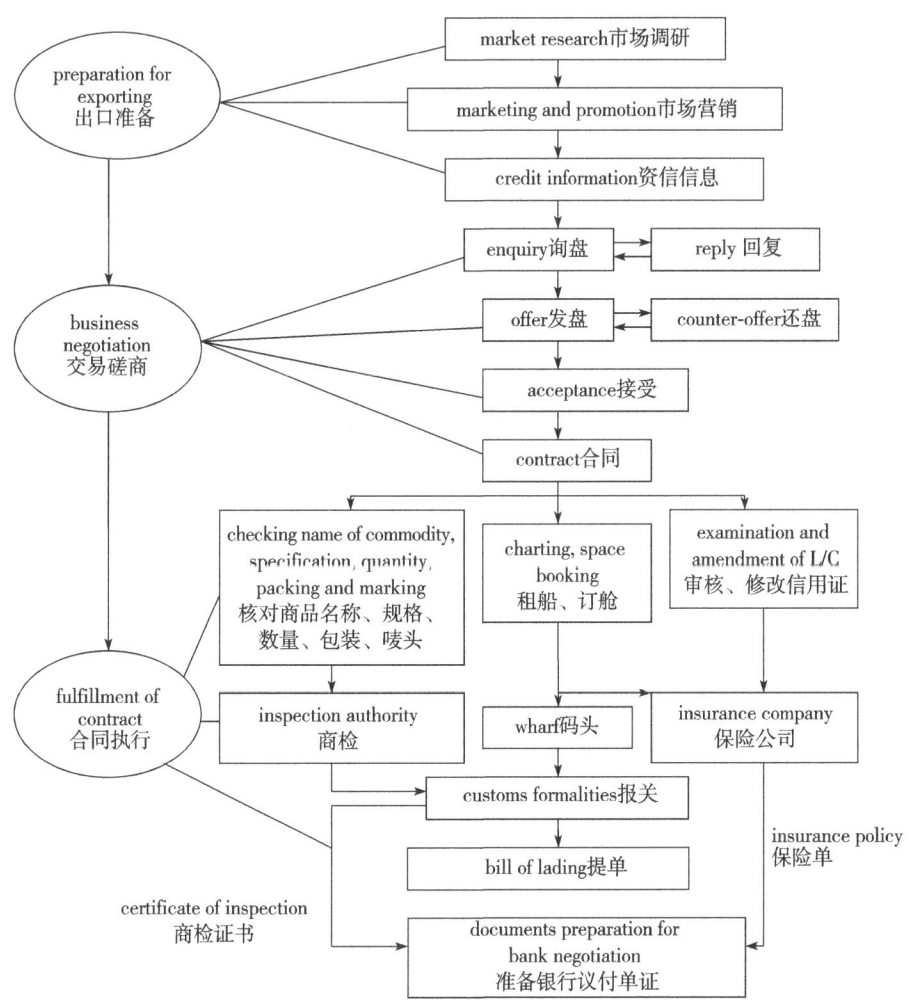

图 1-3　Procedures of Export Transaction 出口交易程序

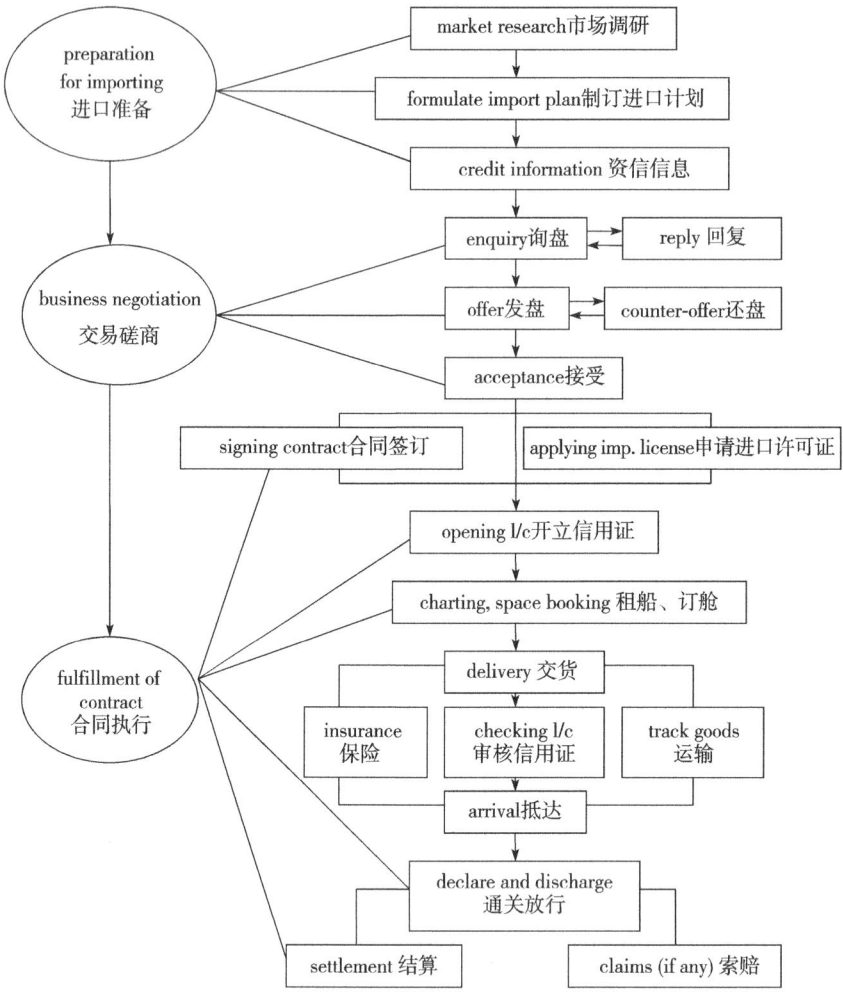

图1-4 Procedures of Import Transaction 进口交易程序

1.6.3 外贸交易的当事人
Parties Involved in Foreign Transaction

The basic parties are the buyer who purchases the goods and the seller who provides the goods. Main parties involved in an export and import transaction are as follows:

(1) The exporters;

(2) The shipping agents at the port or airport of loading;

(3) The railway in the exporter's country;

(4) The road hauler in the exporter's country;

(5) The port authority;

外贸交易的主要当事人是购买货物的进口商和出售货物的出口商。进出口业务中涉及的主要当事人是：

(1) 出口商；

(2) 装运港或机场的运输代理人；

(3) 出口商所在国的铁路部门；

(4) 出口商所在国的陆路承运人；

(5) 港口当局；

(6) The shipping company;
(7) The airline (for air freight);
(8) The insurance company or broker;
(9) The exporter's bank;
(10) The importer's bank;
(11) The railways in the importer's country;
(12) The road hauler in the importer's company;
(13) The shipping agent at the port or airport of discharge;
(14) The importers.

(6) 船务公司；
(7) 航空公司（对空运货物）；
(8) 保险公司或经纪人；
(9) 出口商银行；
(10) 进口商银行；
(11) 进口商所在国的铁路部门；
(12) 进口商所在国的陆路承运人；
(13) 装卸港或机场的运输代理；
(14) 进口公司。

1.6.4 进出口交易所需基本单证
Basic Documents Needed in Export and Import Transaction

Usually the number and type of documents needed depend on the specific requirements of the exporter and importer. The common used documents are as follows:
(1) Bill of lading;
(2) Commercial invoice;
(3) Proforma invoice;
(4) Consular invoice;
(5) Packing list;
(6) Weigh memo;
(7) Certificate of origin;
(8) Certificate of inspection;
(9) Insurance policy;
(10) Sales contract;
(11) Sales confirmation.

通常，单证的数量及类型取决于进出口商的具体需要。常用的单证如下：
(1) 提单；
(2) 商业发票；
(3) 形式发票；
(4) 领事发票；
(5) 装箱单；
(6) 重量单；
(7) 原产地证明书；
(8) 商品检验证书；
(9) 保险单；
(10) 售货合同；
(11) 售货确认书。

1.7 商务谈判的一般程序
General Procedure in Business Negotiation

The business negotiation usually goes through 5 steps, namely, enquiry, offer, counter-offer, acceptance and conclusion of a contract.
(1) enquiry.
Business negotiation in international trade usually begins with an enquiry by an overseas buyer to a seller, inquiring upon the terms of a sale. Enquiry is often made by

商务谈判通常要经历5个环节，即询盘、发盘、还盘、接受和合同成立。
(1) 询盘。
国际贸易中的商务谈判通常都是以海外买方向卖方发起询盘，询问销售条款而开始的。询盘通

the buyers without engagement to get information about the goods to be ordered, such as the commodity's name, quality, price, mode, the desired quantity and delivery date and other terms.

Sometimes a seller can also initiate the negotiation by making an enquiry to a foreign buyer, including his intention of selling certain goods to the latter, which is also called an invitation to offer or invitation to make a bid. It is worthy of note that whoever makes an enquiry is not liable for the buying or the selling, and, the opposite party, at the same time, can make no reply at all. However, in practice, the receiver of an enquiry will respond without delay in the usual form of a quotation, an offer or a bid. An enquiry can be made not only to one party but also to several clients. In this way, the enquirer can make a comparison between the terms of sales stated in the different replies and thus trade beneficially with the one who has quoted or offered the best terms.

(2) offer.

An offer is a proposal of terms and conditions presented in a potential contract by one party, called the offeror, to another party, called the offeree. For the sake of the agreement to be binding, the offeree must first accept the offer, otherwise, there is no legal contract.

Like an enquiry, an offer can be made either by a seller or by a buyer. The offer made by the seller is called "selling offer" in which such wording as " can supply " "supply" "offer" "offer firm" is mostly used. If the offer is made by the buyer, it is commonly called "buying offer". In it different wording is used, such as "book" "order" "bid". In general, it is the seller, the offeror, who offers the sale of certain commodities to the buyer, the offeree.

(3) counter-offer.

A counter-offer is an offer made by an offeree to an offeror, accepting some terms. It can be made verbally or in writing. Once the counter-offer is made, the orginal offer made by the offeror loses its effectiveness. Therefore, a

常是无约束力的,买方借以获悉预订商品的信息,如品名、质量、价格、型号、预购数量和交货期等。

有时,卖方也可通过询盘外国买方发起谈判,表达其想出售某种商品给后者的愿望,通常也叫作要约邀请或者邀请递盘。值得注意的是,不管是谁发起询盘,都不承担买卖责任,与此同时,另一方完全可以不予理会。但在实践中,询盘的接受者往往会以报价、发盘或递盘的方式对此立即做出回应。询盘不仅可以向一方发出,也可向几个客户发出,通过这种方式,询盘方可以对不同回复中所提出的销售条款加以比较,从而与报价或发盘最有利于自己的一方进行交易。

(2) 发盘。

发盘是由一方(发盘人和发价人)向另一方(受盘人或被发价人)提出的订立合同的条款。为了使此协议有一定的约束力,受盘人必须首先接受发盘,否则该合同不是合法契约。

如同询盘,发盘既可由卖方发出,也可由买方发出。由卖方发出的叫卖盘,常用"可供""供应""发盘""发实盘"等字眼。如果由买方发盘,则叫买盘,常用"预订""订购""递盘"等字眼。一般,卖方(发盘人)提出销售某种商品给买方(受盘人)。

(3) 还盘。

还盘是由受盘人在接受发盘人的一些条款的情况下向发盘人发盘,既可以是口头的,也可是书面的。一旦还盘,原来的发盘

counter-offer, in fact, is a rejection of the offer. Hence, it is a new offer and at the same time the original offer lapses. In a counter-offer a new price as well as other new terms is suggested. When used, it is often simply worded with only the new suggested terms stated in order to make certain that other terms embodied in the original offer remain unchanged and the date and/or reference number of orginal offer is usually so referred to in the counter-offer as to be no mistaking what it is aimed at.

(4) acceptance.

An acceptance is the assent to the terms of an offer, which is required before a contract can be valid. It must be absolute and unconditional (otherwise it is not an acceptance but a counter-offer), and it may be tendered only by the person to whom the offer is directed, and must conform to any conditions which are set forth in the offer.

An acceptance can only be made in the form of a statement or any other conduct by an offeree, the particular person or a group of persons, who are clearly stipulated in a firm offer. Either a verbal or a written statement is good for this purpose. The conduct that the seller delivers the goods or the buyer makes the payment also serves. Inactivity is by no means an acceptance. An acceptance must be unconditional. It should be an unreserved assert to all the terms designated in the offer. If any additions, modifications or limitations to the offer are made, they are a counter-offer, not an acceptance.

(5) contract.

A contract is an agreement that creates an obligation, which is a binding, legally enforceable agreement between two or more competent parties. A written contract is often signed to bind on both the seller and the buyer. A formal contract should be prepared in duplicate. Each copy should be signed by both parties, and each party should keep a signed copy of it.

Forms of contract are various. Contracts, confirmation, agreements and memorandums can all be adopted. In our foreign trade business, we mainly adopted the sales contract, sales confirmation, purchase contract and purchase confirmation.

即失去了效力。因此，还盘事实上是对发盘的拒绝，是一次新的发盘，同时也是原发盘的失效。还盘时会提出新的价格及其他条款，常用一些简单的字眼对相关条款提出建议，同时确保原发盘中的其他条款保持不变，原发盘的日期和编号通常作为还盘的依据，以便还盘时不会出错。

(4) 接受。

接受是对发盘条款的同意，是合同签署前所必需的，是绝对无条件的（否则就不是接受，只能是还盘）。接受是接受发盘的一方做出的，必须与发盘中设定的条款相一致。

接受既可以以声明的形式做出，也可由受盘人、实盘中指定的人或一群人发出，要么是口头的，要么是书面的。卖方交付货物以及买方支付的行为同样也要说明。不反应绝不意味着就是接受，接受必须是无条件的，它应是对发盘中所设定条件的无保留的主张。如果对发盘提出任何附加条款、修改或者限制，那只能是还盘，不是接受。

(5) 合同成立。

合同是缔结双方或有法定资格的多方之间的一项注明义务并具有法律约束力和法律效力的协议。书面合同要签名以约束买卖双方。正规合同应一式两份，每份都应由双方签署，双方各持一份。

合同的形式是多样的，合同、确认书、协议或者备忘录都可以。在我国的对外贸易中，主要采取售货合同、售货确认书、购货合同和购货确认书等。

> **Tips**
>
> **1. 简单直接的商务信函**
>
> 商务信函不是发挥创意的场所,只要按照习惯行事就可以了。因此写作商务信函不需要使用华丽优美的句子,所需要做的就是用简单朴实的语言,准确表达自己的意思,让对方可以非常清楚地了解你想说什么。
>
> **2. 商务邮件怎样分段合适**
>
> 商务邮件的写作除了要遵循 7C 原则之外,还应注意不宜过长,要有条理地把事情说清楚,简洁明了。除了称呼和落款,尽量控制在 3 段,6~8 句话,中间段落作为邮件的核心部分,文字应多于其他两段。
>
> **3. 英汉表达中句子的长短**
>
> 同样的一句话,用汉语表达可能需要由几个短句组成,它们之间靠意义联系起来,而用英语表达往往可以借助关系代词或者关系副词连成一个较长的句子。因而,在用英语撰写商务信函时,对于较短的、结构较松散的句子,应尽量用各种方法将几个部分组合在一起,成为一个由短语或者从句构成的、结构复杂的长句,只要表达得当,层次分明即可。如 "非常感谢贵方订单,需要说明的是,因无货源,我方只得取消贵方的订单",可以译为 "While thank you for your order, we have to explain that without supplies we have no alternative but to decline your order"。

1.8 有用的短语和句子

Useful Expressions

1. Common Used Phrases in Business Letter 商务信函常用词组

   sample 样品
   printed matter 印刷品
   private 亲启
   confidential 密函
   urgent or immediate 急件
   please readdress 请转寄
   introducing Mr... 兹介绍……先生
   carbon copy(C. C.) 抄送
   kindness of Mr... or per favor of Mr... 敬烦……先生转交
   with compliments 赠品
   photo only 内有照片,请勿折叠
   personal 私函
   registered 挂号
   forward(care of, c/o) 请转交
   poste restante 留存邮件
   commercial papers 商务文件
   care postmaster 留存邮局

2. If undelivered, please return to...
   若无法投递,请退回原处……

3. After 10 days, please return to...
   10 天后请寄回……

4. Return postage guaranteed.
   回信邮资已付。

5. We have received your letter of May 18, 2010, for which we thank you.
   收到贵方 2010 年 5 月 18 日函,谢谢。

6. In accordance with the instructions given in your favour of the 10th May.

遵照贵公司 5 月 10 日来函指示。
7. Thank you for your letter dated August 12, informing us of the opening date of the fair.
感谢贵方 8 月 12 日来函，告知交易会开幕日期。
8. Further to our letter yesterday, we now have the pleasure of informing you that...
续谈我方昨日函，现欣告知……
9. We must apologize for the delay in replying to your letter of...
迟复贵方……月……日函，甚歉。
10. In reply of your letter of... we are glad to...
兹复贵方……的来函，我方很高兴……
11. For your information we would like to add that...
我方要补充说明……仅供参考。
12. If you are interested in the article, please let us know as soon as possible.
如对该货感兴趣，请尽早告知。
13. We are pleased / glad to inform you that...
兹欣告贵方……
14. We would remind you that we have not had a reply yet from you to our question...
我们提醒贵方，我方尚未收到贵方对……问题的答复。
15. We are sending you herewith / under separate cover...
兹随函/另封寄上……
16. Please accept our thanks for the trouble you have taken.
有劳贵方，不胜感激。
17. We are obliged to thank you for your kind attention in this matter.
不胜感激贵方对此事的关照。
18. We tender you our sincere thanks for your generous treatment of us in this affair.
对贵方在此事中的慷慨之举，深表感谢。
19. Allow us to thank you for the kindness extended to us.
对贵方之盛情，不胜感谢。
20. We thank you for the special care you have given to the matter.
贵方对此悉心关照，不胜感激。
21. We should be grateful for your trial order.
如承试订货，不胜感激。
22. We should be grateful for your furnishing us details of your requirements.
如详述具体要求，不胜感激。
23. It will be greatly appreciated if you will kindly send us your samples.
如承惠寄样品，则不胜感激。
24. We shall appreciate it very much if you will give our bid your favorable consideration.
如承优惠考虑报价，不胜感激。
25. We are greatly obliged for your bulk order just received.
收到贵方大宗订货，不胜感激。
26. We assure you of our best services at all times.
我方保证向贵方随时提供最佳服务。

27. If there is anything we can do to help you, we shall be more than pleased to do so.
    贵公司若有所需求,我公司定尽力效劳。
28. It would give us a great pleasure to render you a similar service should an opportunity occur.
    我方如有机会同样效劳贵方,将不胜欣慰。
29. We spare no efforts in endeavoring to be of service to you.
    我方将不遗余力为贵方效劳。
30. We take this opportunity to re-emphasize that we shall, at all times, do everything possible to give you whatever information you desire.
    我们借此机会再次强调,定会尽力随时提供贵方所需的信息。

练习

Exercises

Ⅰ. Comprehension Questions
  1. What are the principles of good business letters' writing?
  2. How many principal parts does a business letter consist of?
  3. Discuss how to make a business letter effective and productive?
  4. What's the format of business letters? How about envelopes addressing?
  5. What are the procedures of foreign trade?
  6. Discuss the parties and documents involved in foreign transactions.

Ⅱ. Translate the Following Terms and Expressions
  1. inside address   2. Ref. No
  3. semi-block format   4. subject line
  5. complimentary close   6. enclosure
  7. 经办人   8. 左边空白处
  9. 缩进式   10. 混合式
  11. parcel post   12. commercial copy
  13. printed matter   14. 赠阅
  15. 样品邮件

Ⅲ. Arrange the Following Information in Proper Form as They Should Be Set Out in a Letter
  1. Sender's name: Manley Ventilations PLC
  2. Sender's address: 22 Warden Hill Street, Padiham, Burnley BRO 1 RQ, England
  3. Sender's telephone: 3021 4567
  4. Sender's fax: 0321 6789
  5. Sender's website: manley@ bigbiz. co. uk
  6. Date: September 21, 2009
  7. Receiver's name: Atomic Shielding International
  8. Receiver's address: 234 Park Avenue, Cranford, NJ07015 USA
  9. Receiver's telephone: 973-778-1234
  10. Receiver's fax: 973-778-4321
  11. Salutation: Dear Sirs

12. Subject: Household Porcelain Articles
13. The message:

  We have received your letter dated September 2, 2009. We are very much interested in your household porcelain articles produced by your company.

  We shall greatly appreciate it if you will kindly forward us some samples and relative pamphlets for our inspection.

  Thank you for your attention to this matter and looking forward to your early reply.

14. Complimentary close: Yours faithfully

Ⅳ. Address an Envelope for the Above Letter

Ⅴ. Please arrange a letter of indented form, block form and semi-block form with indented paragraphs according to the following information.

发信人：浙江义乌玻璃制品有限公司

地址：义乌市中山北路 19 号，邮编：322000

电话：86-0579-88957213

电子邮箱：ywglass@hotmail.com

发信时间：2016 年 5 月 10 日

收信人：Fox International Co.

  150 Fifth Avenue, New York, NY231, USA

事由：玻璃制品

信函内容：你方所购玻璃杯样品已于 5 月 8 日寄出，该玻璃制品在欧美市场一直很畅销，请收到后速回订购信息，谢谢。

Chapter 2
第 2 章

建立贸易关系
Establishment of Business Relationships

Learning Objectives

Enable the students to know about the importance of establishing business relationships; to be familiar with the channel of obtaining business information; to master steps and procedures of writing letters of establishing business relationships.

使学生了解建立贸易关系的重要性；熟悉获得贸易信息的渠道；掌握书写建立贸易关系相关信函的步骤及流程。

2.1 背景知识
Background Information

The main purpose of business communication is to establish business relations or maintaining the goodwill. When a company wants to conclude a business with a foreign company, it must firstly establish business relations. It is the first step for a company to establish good business relationships so as to open up its business, because all businesses happen after establishing business relationships. So, either for a newly established firm or an existing one that wants to enlarge its business scope and turnover, establishing good relationships with prospective clients is one of the main measures. Both importers and exporters may benefit from favorable business relations.

When a company needs to open up a new market to sell to or buy from other foreign companies, seeking a prospective partner is one of the main measures. Company can

商务交流的主要目的是建立贸易关系或维系良好的关系。当公司想与一个外国公司做成一笔生意时，它必须要与其先建立贸易关系。因此，对于一个公司而言，建立良好的贸易关系是开始和扩展生意的第一步，因为所有的贸易都发生在贸易关系建立后。无论对于新兴的公司还是想进一步扩大自己市场的老牌公司而言，同潜在客户建立良好的贸易关系是其中一个至关重要的手段。并且，无论是进口商还是出口商都会从一个良好的贸易关系中受益。

当一家公司开拓海外市场，向国外其他相关公司出售和购买货品时，寻找潜在贸易合作对象是重要

get informations of its needed prospective consumers through the following sources:

(1) Banks;
(2) Trade directories of importers and exporters;
(3) Chambers of commerce both at home and abroad;
(4) Commercial counsellor's office;
(5) Advertisements;
(6) Exhibitions and trade fairs;
(7) Market investigations;
(8) Enquires received from foreign merchants;
(9) Self-introduction or introduction from his business connections;
(10) A branch office or representative abroad;
(11) The internet;
(12) The introduction from your partners;
(13) Other sources.

Above sources, chambers of commerce both at home and abroad, commercial counsellor's office and the introduction from your partners are usually the most reliable. When you choose one foreign partner, you need to do some researches as follows so as to have a better understanding of this country or region:

(1) Business policies and customs;
(2) Political and economic stability;
(3) Diplomatic relationships;
(4) Culture and interests of potential consumers;
(5) Geographic conditions;
(6) Natural environment.

When we want to establish relations with foreign companies, we usually contact them by the following channels:

(1) Communication by mails (E-mails, faxes, letters, etc.);
(2) Attendance at the export commodities fairs;
(3) Contact at exhibitions held at home or abroad;
(4) Mutual visits by trade delegations.

Constantly, the first media is widely used in business activities. After obtaining the name and address of prospective company from above sources, the company can send letters to them. The first letter is crucial for opening and enlarging market, because the first impression is very

举措之一。公司可以利用以下资源获得它所需要的潜在客户的信息：

（1）银行；
（2）进出口商行业名录；
（3）国内外商会；
（4）商务参赞处；
（5）广告；
（6）展览与贸易交易会；
（7）市场调研；
（8）外商的询函；
（9）自我介绍或商务关系的介绍；
（10）国外分公司或代表；
（11）国际互联网；
（12）贸易伙伴的介绍；
（13）其他渠道。

以上资源中，通常以国内外商会、商务参赞处以及贸易伙伴的介绍最为可靠。此外，在选择一个国外合作伙伴时，为了对该国家或地区了解得更为全面，一般要做以下相关方面的一些调研：

（1）贸易政策和习俗；
（2）政治和经济稳定；
（3）与本国的外交关系；
（4）潜在消费者的消费文化及喜好；
（5）地理条件；
（6）自然环境。

当有意与国外的公司建立贸易关系时，通常通过以下渠道联系它们：

（1）信件交流（主要通过邮件、传真和信函等）；
（2）参加出口商品交易会；
（3）在国内外的展览会接触；
（4）贸易代表团互访。

在以上渠道中，长久以来，第一个渠道方式在商业活动中被广泛使用。利用上面提到的资源，公司获得欲洽谈业务公司的名称与地址后，就可以发信给该公司。

important.

Generally, the letter basically includes the following information:

(1) How and where to get the receiver's address and name;
(2) Purposes and desires of writing this letter;
(3) Business scope of your company;
(4) Financial status and business scopes of your company;

Simultaneously, we also need to remember the following writing principles:

(1) Short content, no more than one page;
(2) Polite language with courteous and sincere attitude;
(3) Show your intention in the first paragraph and express cooperating desire in the letter;
(4) Say something highly about your company, if allowed, list some of the famous companies you have cooperated.

However, establishing good business relationships needs not only good language communicating skills, but also practicing business techniques, especially when you try to establish business relationships with potential customers.

第一封信函对于打开和扩大市场至关重要,因为第一印象非常重要。

一般,该类信函基本要包括如下信息:

(1) 获得收信人名称和地址的渠道;
(2) 目的与意图;
(3) 本公司的业务范围;
(4) 本公司的资信及经营情况;

同时,要遵守以下几个写作原则:

(1) 内容简短,不超过一页纸;
(2) 措辞礼貌、谦虚、诚恳;
(3) 第一段就讲明意图,并在文中明确表达合作愿望;
(4) 对本公司做积极评价,如情况允许,列举一些已经合作过的知名公司。

建立良好的贸易关系既要有语言交流技巧,还要有实际的商务谈判技巧,特别是尝试与新的潜在客户建立贸易关系。

2.2 信例
Sample Letters

Letter 1 An Introduction of an Exporter

CHINA AGRICULTURAL PRODUCT EXPORT CORPORATION XUZHOU BRANCH

Xuzhou, China Tel: 86-0516-76767676

September 6, 2010
Farmer Food Corp.
5 Victoria Street
Brisbane, TT23134
Australia

Dear Sir,

　　We owe your name and address to the Commercial Counselor's office of Australian Embassy in Shanghai who have informed us that you are in the market for agricultural product.

> We are an individual-owned enterprise, handling export of agricultural product. We wish to establish trade relationship with you by the commencement of some practical transactions.
>
> In order to acquaint you with our agricultural products available now for export, we enclose a catalogue and a price list for your reference.
>
> Should any of the items be of interest to you, please let us know. We shall be glad to give you our lowest quotations upon receipt of your detailed requirements.
>
> We look forward to receiving your specific enquiries.
>
> Yours faithfully,
>
> CHINA AGRICULTURAL PRODUCT EXPORT CORPORATION XUZHOU BRANCH
> (Signature)
> Bruce Wang
> Director
>
> Encl.

Notes

1. We owe your name and address to... 承蒙……告知贵公司地址和名称。
   类似的表达方法有:
   Through the courtesy of ...
   We have obtained your name from ...
   We are indebted to ... for your name and address.
   Your name has been recommended/ given/ introduced to us by ... as...
2. Commercial Counsellor's office of Australian Embassy 澳大利亚商务参赞处
3. in the market for something 是书面语言,表示想买进某物;除此以外,也可以引申为"乐于接受某物"。
   in the market 想要买(或卖)
4. inform 通知,告诉,报告
   (1) inform sb. of sth.
       Please inform us of time of shipment. 请告我们装运时间。
   (2) inform sb. that/what/which
       We wish to inform you that business has been done at 1 200 yuan per metric ton. 我们已以每吨1 200元的价格成交,特此通知。
   (3) Please be informed that...
       Please be informed that we have already sent the clothes required. 兹通知贵方,我方已将所需衣服寄出。
   (4) keep sb. informed of/that...
       keep sb. advised of/that...
       keep sb. posted of/that... 随时告知

We hope you will keep us informed of the financial status at your end.
希望随时报告贵方的财务状况。

5. individual-owned enterprise 私营企业
   state-owned corporation 国有公司
   state-run enterprise 国有企业
   state-designated second grade enterprise 国家指定二级企业
   collective-owned enterprise 集体企业
   private-owned enterprise 私营企业
   merchandising enterprise 商业企业
   small and middle/medium enterprise (SME) 中小企业
   township/ rural enterprise 乡镇企业
   enterprise for joint venture, for cooperative and with sole foreign capital investment 三资企业

6. export（单数）出口；（复数）出口货物
   有关 export 的常见短语有：
   amount of exports 输出额   export control 出口管制
   export declaration 出口申报单，出口申请书   export drawback 出口退税
   export dumping 出口倾销   export document 出口单据
   export entry 出口报关   export license 出口许可证
   export-oriented economy 出口导向型经济   export quota 出口限额
   export volume 出口量   export subsidies 出口补贴

7. acquaint sb. with/of sth; acquaint sb. that
   使某人熟悉，使了解，使认识
   You will have to acquaint us with the details.
   你们必须让我们了解详情。
   be/get acquaint with...
   认识……/熟悉……
   We are well acquainted with the market condition in American.
   我们对美国市场行情很了解。

8. We enclose a catalogue and a price list for your reference.
   我们随函附寄产品目录和价格表各一份，供参考。
   Enclosed is our revised quotation, subject to our confirmation as usual.
   随函附上修改后的价目表，同往常一样以我方确认为准。

9. Should any of the items be of interest to you, please let us know.
   如贵方对我们的产品感兴趣，敬请告知。
   "should"在此是助动词，该句运用主谓倒装，省略"if"，来充当条件句，表示"万一""如果"。当 if 条件句中有助动词 should、had 或 were 时，则可以省去 if，而将 should、had 或 were 置于句首，从而构成倒装虚拟句，意义不变，如：
   Should you be unable to deliver the goods by the time stated, please get in touch with us immediately. 如果到了指定的时间贵方仍不能交货，请立即同我方联系。

10. upon/on receipt of... 一旦收到……即……
    Upon receipt of your instructions we will send the goods. 一收到贵方通知，我方即发货。

Letter 2 Positive Reply from an Importer

FARMER FOOD CORP.
5 Victoria Street, Brisbane, TT23134
Tel: 1234567789

October 27, 2010

Mr. Bruce Wang
China Agricultural Product Export Corporation Xuzhou Branch
15 Huaihai West Road, Quanshan District
Xuzhou 221000, China

Dear Mr. Bruce Wang,

  Thank you for your letter of September 6, 2010 from which we learn that you are doing the business of agricultural product. We shall be glad to establish business relations with you.

  We are interested in buying variable beans. We would like you to send us details of your beans, including colors and prices, and also samples of the different colors.

  We look forward to a productive trade and the opportunity to work together with you in the future. We await your early reply.

Yours faithfully,

(Signature)

Amy Harry

Notes

1. would like... 想要……
2. We look forward to a productive trade and the opportunity to work together with you in the future. 我们期望贸易富有成效，并能有机会在未来合作。

Letter 3 Negative Reply from an Importer

FARMER FOOD CORP.
5 Victoria Street, Brisbane, TT23134
Tel: 1234567789

October 27, 2010

Mr. Bruce Wang
China Agricultural Product Export Corporation Xuzhou Branch
15 Huaihai West Road, Quanshan District
Xuzhou 221000, China

Dear Mr. Bruce Wang,

  Thank you for your letter of September 6, 2010 showing your interest in doing business with us. We really appreciate your interest.

However, we very much regret that we are not in a position to establish business relations with you at present. We currently have another company as our agricultural products supplier in Suzhou. According to the contract conditions, we are banned from importing agricultural products from other companies.

As this is not an appropriate time to cooperate with your company, we would like to wait. But we will keep your letter on file and will get in touch with you when this contract expires.

We really hope that we have the chance to cooperate in the near future.

Yours faithfully,

(Signature)

Amy Harry

Notes

1. appreciate 感谢，感激（可接动名词，不可接不定式）；理解，体会
   We highly appreciate your kind cooperation. 我们十分感激贵方的合作。
   （1）习惯上不接不定式作宾语，其后可接名（代）词、动名词、名词性从句等作宾语，但不能接不定式：
     We shall appreciate hearing from you again. 能再次收到你的来信，我们将十分感激。
   （2）习惯上不用"人"作宾语，其后只能接"事"作宾语，而不能接"人"作宾语。
     正：I appreciate your kindness. 谢谢你的好意。
     误：I appreciate you for your kindness.

2. We very much regret that...
   regret 抱歉，惋惜，遗憾；其后可跟名词、动名词，也可跟从句。We regret 和 That we regret to say 用法不同。如果为自己一方的不足或过失而表示遗憾，两个句子都可以使用；如果对别人的不足或过失表示遗憾，则只能说 We regret to say。另外当 regret 被状语 very much 修饰时常放在 regret 的前面。

3. be in a position to do sth. （其处境）有权，有资格，有办法，能够（做某事）
   financial position 财务状况
   cash position 现金头寸
   easy position 头寸宽裕
   to cover position 轧平头寸
   long/ bull position 多头交易，买空交易
   short/ bear position 空头交易，卖空交易

4. We will keep your letter on file and will get in touch with you when this contract expires.
   我们将保留贵方信函，待合同到期后再与你联系。

5. We really hope that we have the chance to cooperate in the near future.
   我们真心希望未来能有机会合作。

Letter 4　Introduction of an Importer

FARMER FOOD CORP.
5 Victoria Street, Brisbane, TT23134
Tel: 1234567789

October 12, 2010

China Agricultural Product Export Corporation Xuzhou Branch
15 Huaihai West Road, Quanshan District
Xuzhou 221000, China

Dear Sir,

　　We have obtained your address in the China Daily and are now writing you for the establishment of business relations.

　　We are very well connected with all suppliers of agricultural products. Now, we are very interested in your beans and wheal and feel sure we can sell large quantities of them if we get your offers at competitive prices.

　　For our credit standing, please refer to the following bank:
　　　　　　　The Bank of Australia and New Zealand, Australia
　　Your immediate reply would be highly appreciated.

Yours faithfully,

(Signature)
Amy Harry

Notes

1. be connected with... 与……保持联系（络）
2. get your offers at competitive prices 得到具有竞争力的报价
3. Please refer to the Bank of China, Suzhou Branch for our credit standing. = For our credit standing, please refer to the Bank of China, Suzhou Branch. 请向中国银行苏州分行查询我方资信情况。
   refer to sb. for sth. 向某人打听（查询）某事
   credit standing 资信状况
   Please refer to the following bank. 请向下面银行咨询。
4. The Bank of Australia and New Zealand 澳新银行
5. Your immediate reply would be highly appreciated. 若蒙贵公司及时回复，将不胜感激。

Letter 5 Reply from an Exporter

CHINA AGRICULTURAL PRODUCT EXPORT CORPORATION XUZHOU BRANCH
Xuzhou, China   Tel: 86-0516-76767676

November 7, 2010

Farmer Food Corp.
5 Victoria Street
Brisbane, TT23134
Australia

Dear Sir,

Your letter of October 27, 2010 addressed to our Shanghai Branch Office has been passed on to us for attention and reply. We shall be pleased to enter into trading relations with you.

In compliance with your request, we are sending you, under separate cover, our latest catalogues and price list covering beans.

Payment should be made by an irrevocable and confirmed letter of credit.

If you feel that business is possible, please contact us for specific offers.

Your effort and reply is greatly appreciated. I look forward to a successful business relationships in the future.

Yours sincerely,

(Signature)
Bruce Wang

Notes

1. Your letter of October 27, 2010 addressed to our Shanghai Branch Office has been passed on to us for attention and reply. 贵方 2010 年 10 月 27 日寄到我方上海分公司的信已送达并回复。
2. enter into... 开始（某种关系、事业、谈判等）；缔结（契约等）
   We wish to enter into business relations with your company for the supply of electrical products. 我方愿与贵公司建立贸易关系，以便取得电气产品的供货。
3. in compliance with... 依从，按照，该短语多在句中引导状语
   In compliance with your request, we are sending you, under separate cover, our latest catalogues and pricelist covering beans. 按照贵方要求，现另封邮寄我方豆类的最新目录和价目表。
4. under separate cover 另封邮寄
5. covering 关于，有关的
6. an irrevocable and confirmed letter of credit 不可撤销的保兑信用证
7. specific offers 具体报价

Letter 6　Credit Inquiry

CHINA AGRICULTURAL PRODUCT EXPORT CORPORATION XUZHOU BRANCH
Xuzhou, China　Tel: 86-0516-76767676

The Bank of Australia and New Zealand
1423 Victoria Street
Brisbane, TT23134
Australia

Dear Sir,

　　Your name has been given to us as a credit reference by Farmer Food Corporation, 5 Victoria Street, Brisbane, who wants to enter into business with us. We should be highly obliged if you could let us have your opinion on their reputation and their financial standing.

　　Any information given to us will be surely treated in strict confidence. We thank you in advance for your courtesy.

Yours faithfully,

(Signature)
Bruce Wang

Notes

1. credit inquiry 资信调查
   客户资信调查的内容和范围：
   （1）国外企业的组织机构情况，包括企业的性质、创建历史、内部组织机构、主要负责人及担任的职务、分支机构等。调查中，应弄清厂商企业的中英文名称、详细地址，防止出现差错。
   （2）政治情况，主要指企业负责人的政治背景，与政界的关系以及对我国的政治态度等。
   （3）资信情况，它包括企业的资金和信用两个方面。资金是指企业的注册资本、财产以及资产负债情况等；信用是指企业的经营作风、履约信誉等。这是客户资信调查的主要内容，特别是对中间商更应重视。例如，有的客户愿和我们洽谈上亿美元的投资项目，但经调查其注册资本只有几十万美元。对这样的客户，我们就该打一个问号。
   （4）经营范围，主要是指企业生产或经营的商品、经营的性质，是代理商、生产商还是零售批发商等。
   （5）经营能力，每年的营业额、销售渠道、经营方式以及在当地和国际市场上的贸易关系等。此外，对客户资信进行调查后，应建立档案卡备查，分类建立客户档案。总之，要善于利用不同类型客户的长处，为我方服务。
   客户资信调查的途径有：
   （1）通过银行调查。这是一种常见的方法，按国际习惯，调查客户的情况属于银行的业务范围；在我国，一般委托中国银行办理。向银行查询客户资信，一般不收费或少量收费。

（2）通过国外的工商团体调查。如商会、同业公会、贸易协会等，一般都接受国外厂商委托调查所在地企业情况，但通过这种渠道得到的资信，要经过认真分析，不能轻信。

（3）通过我驻外机构和在实际业务活动中对客户进行考察所得的材料，一般比较具体可靠，对业务的开展有较大的参考价值。此外，外国出版的企业名录、厂商年鉴以及其他有关资料，对了解客户的经营范围和活动情况也有一定的参考价值。

2. Your name has been given to us as a credit reference by... ……告知我公司，贵行是其资信证明人。

3. We should be highly obliged if you could let us have your opinion on their reputation and their financial standing. 若贵行能提供对该公司信誉及资金状况的意见，将不胜感激。

4. Any information given to us will be surely treated in strict confidence. We thank you in advance for your courtesy. 我公司保证对贵行提供的任何资料严格保密。在此对贵行的帮助预致谢意。

Tips 1. 开发信的写作

所谓"开发信"就是告诉客人你是谁、你做什么以及你的优势。要尽量模仿外国人的行文方式，避免中国人的行文和思维方式，要按照欧美人的习惯去思考和写作。

实际业务操作中开发信有三个要素：①简洁。三段以内，每段两三句话即可。②简单。用简单的词，避免生僻、晦涩的词汇。③准确。内容到位，不说废话，切中要点，不要漫无边际。

在写开发信的时候常见的错误：①过长。一般情况下，国外客户每天都会收到大量的开发信，浏览每封信的时间只有几秒钟，因而不宜长篇大论。②没有明确的主题。注意写出吸引人的标题。③大篇幅地介绍自己的公司。只要一两句话突出自己的优势即可，也不要炫耀自己的英文水平，使简单的问题复杂化。④使用奇怪的字体和颜色。会使客户觉得不够严肃和专业。⑤主动语态使用过多。变 I... 或 We... 的句子为被动语态比较符合外国人的表达习惯，如 We'll send you the samples asap（as soon as possible），最好改为 Samples will be sent asap. ⑥提无意义的问话。如 How is your business recently 或 Would you like to corporate with us，以及 Do you want our products，诸如此类中国式思维习惯的客套话。

通常情况下，此类信函遵循以下步骤。

（1）指明自己如何获知对方的资料和信息（如从本国驻外国使馆商务参赞处、商会、商务办事处获悉，或经某一银行或其他公司和机构介绍，或者是在大众传媒、展览会上认识等），如 Having obtained/had your name and address from... (Commercial Counselor's office of our embassy in your country) 从……（我国驻贵国使馆商务参赞处）得知贵公司的名称及地址。On the recommended to us by... (Mr. Zhang, CEO of China's import and export Co., Ltd.) 由……（中国进出口贸易有限公司总经理，王先生）推荐给我们。We have learned from... (The internet, our local newspaper) 我方从……（互联网或报纸）得知……

（2）介绍致函的目的。一般出口商主动联系进口商，总是以扩大交易地区及对象、建立长期业务关系、拓展产品销路等为目的。

如 We are writing to you to see if we can establish/enter into long-term business relation with you. 今致函你方希望能与贵公司建立业务联系。

（3）概括介绍自己的公司。主要包括对公司性质、业务范围、宗旨等基本情况的介绍，以及公司某些相对优势的介绍，如贸易经验丰富、供货渠道稳定、销售渠道广泛等。

如 We are a leading company with many year's experience in machinery export business. 我公司在机械类产品出口领域处于领先地位，有多年的出口经验。

（4）简要介绍一些自己公司的产品。在较为明确对方需求时，可以选择特定产品进行具体的推荐性介绍；否则，通常只介绍公司产品的整体情况，如对质量标准、价格水平、销售情况等做笼统介绍，并附上目录、报价单或另寄参考样品等。

如 Article No. 76 is our newly launched one with superb quality, fashionable design, and competitive price. To give you a general idea of our products, we are enclosing our catalogue for your reference. 76 号商品是我公司新开发的产品，其质量优良、设计时尚，并且价格公道。为让贵公司能对我公司产品有一个大概的了解，我们随附了产品目录以供参考。

（5）激励性结尾。作为建立业务关系的商业促销信函，在结尾部分通常都会写上希望对方给予回应或劝服对方立即采取行动（如询价、递盘等）的语句。

如 We are looking forward to your earlier reply/receiving your reply. 我们期待你的早日回复。

2. 广交会（Canton Fair）

广交会即广州交易会，创办于 1957 年春季，是中国目前历史最长、层次最高、规模最大、商品种类最全、到会客商最多、成交效果最好的综合性国际贸易盛会。它的官方名称是"中国进出口商品交易会"（The China Import and Export Fair）。

3. Tendency Fair 和 Ambiente Fair

Tendency Fair 是德国法兰克福秋季消费品博览会，每年 8 月举行；Ambiente Fair 是法兰克福春季消费品博览会，是和秋季博览会对应的，每年 2 月举行。这两个博览会对于开发欧洲市场十分重要，特别适合消费品、礼品和杂货类产品，每年都汇聚了大批的欧洲进口商和零售商，以及世界各地的参展商和专业买手，在行业性展会里有着举足轻重的地位。

2.3 有用的短语和句子

Useful Expressions

1. Through the courtesy of... we learn that you are one of the leading importers of ... in your country and wish to enter into business relations with us.
   由于……的好意，我方获悉贵方是贵国……最大的进口商之一，欲与贵方建立贸易关系。
2. We owe your name and address to the Chamber of Commerce in your country, through whom we learned that you are in the market for silk products.
   承蒙贵国商会的介绍，我们得知贵公司想要购买丝绸制品。
3. We got the information from our sales manager that you have the desire to cooperate with our firm

in marketing our silk products.
从我方销售经理处得知,贵方愿与我公司合作,销售我们的丝绸制品。

4. We are willing to enter into business relations with you on the basis of equality, mutual benefit and exchanging needed goods.
我方愿与贵方在平等互利、互通有无的基础上建立业务关系。

5. We are glad to send you this letter, hoping that it will be the prelude to our friendly business cooperation in the coming years.
我们欣然寄发这封信,希望这会成为未来几年里我们友好商务合作的前奏。

6. We are one of the largest . . . importers in our country and have handled various kinds of the products for about. . . years.
我方是我们国内……最大的进口商之一,已经营各类产品达……年。

7. Our corporation is a group enterprise integrating scientific research, business, production and service. As a joint venture, our corporation has won a prominent position in the field of agricultural products in China.
我公司是一家集科学研究、商贸、生产和服务于一体的企业集团。作为一家合资企业,公司已经在中国农产品领域赢得显著地位。

8. We invite you to send us details and prices, possibly also samples, of such goods as you would be interested in selling, and we shall gladly study the sales possibilities in our market.
我们邀请贵方将贵方感兴趣销售的商品详细资料和价格发送给我们,如果可以,将样品也发送给我们,我们很乐于研究其在我方市场上销售的可能性。

9. We look forward to receiving your order and meanwhile enclose a copy of our catalogue as we feel you may be interested in some of our other products.
我们盼望收到贵方订单,同时随函附上一份目录,因为我们认为贵方会对我们的其他产品感兴趣。

10. In recent years the company has experienced a serious difficulty in finance and delayed in executing their normal payment. We would suggest you to pay more attention to the business with them. However, this is just our personal opinion and we wish you to make further information.
最近几年该公司在财务上经历严重危机而延误正常的付款,谨建议贵公司与其谨慎交易,此乃我们个人意见,希望贵公司做进一步调查。

11. We take the liberty of writing to you with a view to building up business relations with your firm.
我们冒昧通信,以期与贵公司建立业务关系。

12. We have the pleasure of introducing ourselves to you with the hope that we may have an opportunity of cooperating with you in your business extension.
我们有幸自荐,盼望能有机会与你们合作,扩大业务。

13. We are looking forward to your early reply.
期盼贵方早日回复。

14. Your early reply will be highly appreciated.
如能早日回复,我方将不胜感激。

15. Awaiting your favorable reply.
期盼佳音。

16. The above information is given confidentially and without responsibility on our part.

对以上情况请保守秘密，我方对此不负责任。
We take the liberty of writing to you with a view to building up business relations with your firm.
我们冒昧通信，以期与贵公司建立业务关系。
We have the pleasure of introducing ourselves to you with the hope that we may have an opportunity of cooperating with you in your business extension.
我们有幸自荐，盼望能有机会与你们合作，扩大业务。

17. The purpose of this letter is to explore the possibilities of developing trades with you.
    本信目的是探索与你们发展贸易的可能性。
18. We are glad to send you this introductory letter, hoping that it will be the prelude to mutually beneficial relations between us.
    我们欣然寄发这些自荐信，希望是互利关系的前奏。
19. In order to expand our products in South America, we are writing to you to seek cooperation possibilities.
    为扩大我方产品在南美的销售，现致信你方寻求合作的可能性。
20. We are one of the leading importers/exporters engaged in ...
    我们是……行业进口商/出口商的排头兵。
21. We are one of the representative importers/exporters in the line of ...
    我们是……行业的代表。
22. We are enjoying an excellent/high reputation in the circle of textile.
    我公司在纺织品行业圈内享有很高的信誉。
23. We have a good variety of colors and sizes to meet your different needs.
    我公司产品的颜色、规格齐全，一定能满足您的不同需求。
24. Our products have enjoyed a high reputation/popularity in Asian market.
    我们公司的产品在东亚市场享有很高的声誉/极受欢迎。
25. To give you a general idea of our products, we are enclosing our catalogue for your reference.
    为让贵公司能对我公司产品有一个大概的了解，我们随附了产品目录以供参考。

练 习
Exercises

Ⅰ. Comprehension Questions
  1. Why should we need to establish business relations with other companies at present?
  2. Through what kinds of channels can a company secure the necessary information about prospective trade partner?
  3. What knowledge of other respects you also need to research before establishing business relations?
  4. Tell basic information and principles of basic writing letters on establishing business relation.
  5. Do you, as a business person, enjoy receiving unsolicited letters?

Ⅱ. Translating the Following Terms and Expressions
  1. be in line with   2. get in touch with
  3. business partner   4. open an account
  5. inquire for   6. 商务参赞处

7. 财务状况 8. 想要购买
9. 在某人方便的时候 10. 售后服务

Ⅲ. Fill in the Blanks

We desire to _____ the business we _____ Middle East countries, and would be grateful if you could provide us _____ a list of reliable business _____ in your area who might be interested in _____ Chinese electronic products.

We are a well-established exporter of all kinds of Chinese goods, especially electronic and hi-fi products (see _____ catalogs). _____ seen in this line for more than 30 years, we are confident we can give our customers complete satisfaction.

_____ our credit and financial _____, we refer you _____ the Bank of China and the Chamber of Commerce in Guangzhou.

Ⅳ. Translating the Following Sentences

1. We want to know if order 2 000 dozens, what discount can be given.
2. Your letter of Feb. 23 has been received and passed on to Shanghai branch. They will reply directly as the commodities you enquired are handled by them.
3. We have done metal products many years, hoping we have a chance to cooperate with your company.
4. We are convinced that with joint efforts business between us will be developed to our mutual benefit.
5. As requested, we airmailing to you, under separate cover, a sample each of Art. No. 1025 and 1026 for your reference.
6. It will be greatly appreciated if you will give us your cooperation.
7. 所附小册子会向贵方提供我们真空吸尘器的详细情况。
8. 本地的中国银行海外部推荐了贵公司，说贵方有意与一家中国公司建立贸易关系，以推销贵方的轻工业产品。
9. 按贵方要求，今特寄去我们的新产品样品，但愿样品能及时到达贵处。
10. 请告知贵方能按什么价格、什么条款、多少数量供应下列商品。

Ⅴ. Translating the Following Letter into English

本公司是中国最大的电气设备出口公司之一。随函附上一份有关我公司目前可供货物所有详情的目录，希望贵方能对其中的一些产品感兴趣。

若承蒙收到贵公司对其中产品的询价，我公司将不胜感激，并报我公司最低价。

若贵公司不进口上述商品，恳请贵方将此信转交给经营此类商品的进口公司。

我公司希望收到贵方及时、有利的答复。

Ⅵ. Write an English Letter in a Proper Form Based on the Following Information

Write a letter to Foothill Enterprises Trade Development Co., Ltd. (P. O. Box 22789 Taiz Street, Sana'a, Republic of Yemen) telling them:

1. You are introduced by the Commercial Counselor's Office of their embassy in Beijing （驻北京的大使馆商务参赞处）;
2. You wish to set up business relations with them;
3. The main scope of your business is exporting chinaware;
4. Samples and catalogues will be sent to them upon receipt of their specific inquiries.

Chapter 3
第 3 章

询盘与回复
Inquiries and Replies

Learning Objectives

Enable the students to know the definition of inquires, the basic content and kinds of the inquiry; to be familiar with the differences of general and specific inquiry, the important principles of inquiry and reply; to master basic sentences and expressions in the letter of inquiry and reply.

使学生了解询盘的定义、询盘的基本内容和种类;熟悉一般询盘与具体询盘的区别、回复的基本内容,以及询盘和回复要注意的事项;掌握此类信件的基本句型及表达方式。

3.1 背景知识
Background Information

Generally, if an importer wants to do some importing transactions, he can send the exporter an inquiry to get information of needed imports. So, inquiry is the basis of transaction and a very important step connecting buyers and sellers in international business. Through comparing inquiries, the importer can choose the most favorable exporter.

The definition of inquiry is that one party in transaction asks the other conditions of this transaction, when he or she prepares to buy or sell products. Inquiries can be made through letter, fax, telephone, or face-to-face communication. However, inquiry is not a necessary procedure of every deal. If both parties acquaint with each other, they do not need to inquiries about conditions and possibilities of business. In this case, they can directly make an offer instead of an inquiry.

一般情况下,如有意做进口贸易,进口商可以给出口商发一个询盘,得到相关要进口商品的信息。因此,询盘是交易的基础,是在国际贸易中把购买者和销售者联系起来非常重要的一步。通过比较询盘,进口商选择最合适的出口商。

询盘也叫询价,是指交易的一方准备购买或出售某种商品,向对方询问买卖该商品的有关交易条件。询盘可以通过信件、传真、电话甚至是面对面交谈进行。但是,询盘不是每笔交易必经的程序,如交易双方彼此都了解情况,不需要向对方探询成交条件或交易的可能性,则不必使用询盘,可直接向对方发盘。

In a regular inquiry letter, importer usually writes all needed information concisely and correctly, including catalogue, pricelist, sample and so on. According to different contents, inquiries are always divided into two kinds: general inquiry and specific inquiry. The former usually inquiries general information of product such as pricelist, catalogue, sample and terms of payment, while the later generally expresses clearly his ideas about specific information of a specific product such as price, quantity, way of shipping, and packing. "The first inquiry" is sent to a supplier whom you never contact with. In this case, in the beginning of your inquiry letter, you need to tell where and how you get his name and your detailed introductions such as the major products needed, quantity, and way of trade. Tell any information as much as you can in order to let the supplier know what part he or she can help you. In order to let the reader get the main point of your letter, you can write the name of product in the subject line, when inquiring.

Nowadays, many companies use printed inquiry instead of letter. They just need to fill some needed information in the form. Also, some companies provide on-line inquiry system which makes the inquiry easier and faster.

Letter of inquiry generally includes three parts:
(1) In the first part, show the interests, purposes of writing, and brief introduction of yourself;
(2) In the second part, directly tell the detailed information of inquiry, and/or explain purposes and requests;
(3) Finally, thank for the receiver's future reply, and hope he or she can reply earlier.

Simultaneously, you also need to comply with the following principles:
(1) Before sending inquiries, you need to consider which countries or regions you will send inquiries, and how many inquiries you will send in the same regions. After that, you choose carefully several companies instead of

在常规的询盘信中，进口商一般清楚准确地告知他所需要的一般信息，包括目录、价目单和样品等。按照内容的不同，询盘一般分为两种类型：一般询盘和具体询盘。前者一般询问关于产品的大概信息，如价目表、目录、样品和支付方式。后者如果情况允许，一般表达出对具体产品的确切想法，如关于价格、数量、运输方式和包装的具体信息。第一次询盘是指将询盘信发给一个从来没有打过交道的供应商，因此开头要告知是如何获得它的名字的，介绍自己以及需要的商品、数量和贸易方式。告知任何可以告知的信息，从而使供应商知道它在哪方面可以帮助你。在询盘时，为了使读者能立即得知信件的主题，可以在主题行写上产品名字。

现在，很多公司都使用打印的询盘代替信件，它们只需要在表上填上要填的一些信息。还有一些公司提供在线询盘系统使得询盘更为方便快捷。

询盘信一般包括三大部分：
（1）第一部分说明询盘人的兴趣，写信目的，并简单介绍自己的情况；
（2）第二部分明确提出询盘的详细信息，和/或对目的、请求做出解释；
（3）最后对对方的回复表示感谢，盼其早日答复。

同时，询盘要遵守以下几个基本原则：
（1）要事先考虑向哪些国家或地区发出询盘，以及在同一地区要发出几份询盘。确定国家和地区后，要再次仔细选择其中几

all of them, which can avoid suppliers raising the price owning to the thought of you are eager to get products;

(2) Express detailed requests but not promise to buy;

(3) Emphasize the importance of the information you need, in order to get more information;

(4) Ask them reply definitely;

(5) Trade is made between two companies, not a private business. So, the letter needs to be sent to the company instead of a specific person;

(6) Language needs to be polite.

Inquiry means possible business, so reply need to be fast and polite and cover all needed information. If they request samples, you should send to them as soon as possible. Of course, you can ask them to share the post fee of sending samples. In some cases, sample fee is also a very heavy burden. If products needed are not available, or conditions cannot be satisfied, you should not refuse them so directly which would offend them and hinder future cooperations. At this moment, you also need to thank them for being interested in your products and provide information of other products. In reply letter, you must make sure you have answered all information. If questions are too many, you can use number to sort. If inquiry is the first inquiry, you may clearly tell them advantages of your products.

Letter of reply usually includes three parts:

(1) In the beginning, you should make your appreciation about their inquiries, and tell them which date you received the letter, and summarize the content of their letters;

(2) In the second part, answer all questions of inquiry in detail;

(3) Finally, hope your information be useful and get reply as soon as possible.

Simultaneously, the letter of reply generally bases on the following principles:

(1) If you can only satisfy with some requests, you

家发出询盘，而不是同时向所有的供应商都发出，这样避免使得供应商们认为你很急迫地需要产品，从而提高价格；

（2）阐述具体要求但不承诺购买；

（3）强调你所需要的信息的重要性，以获得更多信息；

（4）请对方明确回复；

（5）买卖是公司间的交易，而不是私人间交易，因此询盘应寄给公司，而不应该寄给个人；

（6）去信询问要客气礼貌。

询盘意味着可能的贸易往来，所以回复应该迅速、礼貌，以及答复信息要全面。如果对方索要样品，应尽可能以最快的速度发给对方。当然也可以要求对方共同承担样品的运费，因为有些时候，这也是个巨大的负担。如遇到询问目前不再供应的产品，或是不能满足对方的一些条件，不要直接拒绝，以免得罪对方，而阻碍日后的合作，要同样感谢对方对我们产品感兴趣，可以提供一些其他产品信息。回信时，要确定回答了所有信息，如问题较多，可以用序号。如果询盘是第一次，可以明确告诉对方产品的优势。

回复一般包括三个部分：

（1）第一部分要感谢对方的询盘，并告知自己收到询盘信的日期，并概括询盘信内容；

（2）第二部分详细回答询盘问题；

（3）最后，希望你的信息能对对方有用，并盼尽快回复。

同时，回复一般要遵守以下几个原则：

（1）如果只能满足对方部分

need to tell what parts you can satisfy with, then explain what you cannot do;

(2) If you cannot satisfy with all of requests completely, you should appreciate their inquiry, then give your apologies;

(3) Language must be sincere and polite.

要求，要告诉你能满足哪些部分，然后解释你不能做的原因；

（2）如完全不能满足，要首先表示感谢对方询价，然后致歉你无法做到；

（3）措辞要真诚、礼貌。

3.2 信例
Sample Letters

Letter 1 General Enquiry

<pre>
                    M&N COMPANY
                       1234 Lowe
                    Boston, U.S.A.
                  Tel: 001-123-2345566
</pre>

August 12, 2010

C. C. , Ltd.
1123 Cambridge
London, British

Dear Sirs,

We have seen your products at the British Summer Trade Fair in June this year and are particularly interested in your products. It would be appreciated if you send us the details of your various ranges, including sizes, colors, prices, and also samples of different qualities of material used.

We are a leading dealer in home products and believe there is a promising market in our area for moderately priced goods.

Please give us detailed information on CIF Boston prices, discounts, and terms of payment.

We hope this will be a good start for a long and profitable business relation.

We look forward to hearing from you soon.

Yours faithfully,

M&N Company
Manager

Notes

1. British Summer Trade Fair 英国夏季交易会

2. It would be appreciated if you send us your catalogue soon. 如贵方尽快寄来商品目录，我方将不胜感激。

   It would be appreciated... 对……不胜感激
3. various range 各类产品

   range 的含义有：

   （1）行，列，系列；种，类

   　　a full range of samples 一整套样品

   　　a full range of shipping documents 一整套装运单据

   （2）范围，区域；界限，差距

   　　There is only a narrow range of prices. 价格仅有很小的距离。

   （3）从……到……涉及

   　　Our scope of business ranges over an extensive line of electrical products. 我们的经营范围包括多种电器产品。
4. price 价格

actual price 实际价格	advantage price 上涨了的价格
base price 基价，底价	bid price 买方出价，标价
bottom price 底盘，最低价	closing price 收盘价格
competitive price 竞争价格	cost price 成本价格，生产价格
current price 市价，时价	external price 国外价格，对外价格
fair price 合理价格	favorable price 优惠价格
fixed price 固定价格	floor price 最低价格
forward price 期货价格	fresh price 最新价格

5. dealer 商人，商号（多用复数）

   a leading dealer 主要的经销商

   licensed dealer 有照商人

   securities dealer 证券商

   dealership 经销权，代理权
6. a promising market 销路良好的市场

   与 market 有关的短语有：

   at the market 照市价，照当前最好的行情

   bring to market, put on the market, come into the market 在市场上出售，投放市场

   lose one's market 失去做买卖的机会

   at the market price 按市价

   price out of the market （商品）定价过高而无人购买

auction market 拍卖市场	bond market 债券市场
corner the market 囤积居奇	exchange market 外汇市场
financial market 金融市场	futures market 期货市场
niche market 利基市场	service market 劳务市场

7. CIF 价格术语，"Cost, Insurance, and Freight"（成本、保险加运费）的缩写，通常称为"到岸价"。

8. discount
   （1）折扣；贴现；减价
       The rate of discount in New York is now 8%. 现在纽约的贴现率是8%。
   （2）贴现，打折扣，不完全置信
       If you can discount your price by 15%, we are ready to take 400 bales. 如果贵方价格能予以8.5折处理，我方乐于接受400包。
9. terms of payment 支付条件，也可以说 payment terms
10. profitable 有益的，有利的，可获利的
    profitable fields of investment 有力的投资场所；net profits 净利润，纯利润；total profits 总利润；profit ratio 利润率；gross profits 总利润；毛利

Letter 2　Reply to General Inquiry

C. C., Ltd.
1123 Cambridge
London, British
Tel：123-12344344

August 16, 2010

M&N Company
1234 Lowe
Boston, U.S.A.

Dear Sirs,
　　We are very pleased to receive your inquiry of August 12, 2010 and enclose our illustrated catalogue and price list giving the details you ask for. Also under separate cover, we are sending you some samples and feel confident that when you examined them you will agree the goods are both excellent in quality and craftsmanship. If you are in need of any other information not contained therein, please feel free to let us know, we shall satisfy you to the best of our ability.
　　We allow a proper discount according to the quantity ordered. Your payment term by Letter of Credit at sight is acceptable to us.
　　Thank you again for your interest in our products. We are looking forward to receiving your orders soon.

Yours faithfully,

C. C., Ltd.
Manager

Notes

1. We are very pleased to receive your inquiry of August 12, 2010 and enclose our illustrated catalogue and price list giving the details you ask for. 我们感谢贵公司 2010 年 8 月 12 日的询盘，现随函寄上我方附插图的产品目录和价目表。
2. under separate cover = by separate post = by separate mail 另封；另邮寄
   We are mailing you, under separate cover, photographs of the offered goods. 我们另寄你所订货的照片。
3. sample
   （1）样品
       The sample is for reference only. 样品仅供参考。
       full range of sample 全套样品
       free sample 免费样品
       outturn sample 到货样
       random sample 随意取样
   （2）取样以做检验
       We sampled some goods to test their quality. 我们取一些产品做检验以测试其质量。
4. examine 检验，审查
   辨析：examine 和 check
   examine 表示严密调查，以确定某一事实、某事的真正性质、特征、状况或测定某事的质量、效力、真实性或功能等。
   check 认真仔细检查以便看到一切都正确。
5. be excellent in... 在……方面优异
6. craftsmanship（工匠的）技术，技艺
7. If you are in need of any other information not contained therein, please feel free to let us know, we shall satisfy you to the best of our ability. 如果你需要的信息没有包含在内，请告知我们，我们会尽力满足贵方需求。
8. letter of credit 信用证
   在商业书信中常用大写，单数为（a）Letter of Credit，复数为 Letters of Credit，且常用大写缩写形式，即 L/C 和 Ls/C。当用 credit 表示信用证时，复数为 credits。信用证有即期和远期之分，即期信用证可以表示为：a letter of credit available by draft at sight = a letter of credit payable against draft sight = a letter of credit available by = a letter of credit at sight = sight letter of credit。远期（或迟期）信用证是 time L/C 或 term L/C，常见的有见票后 30（60、90）天议付的信用证，如 time L/C at 30 days after sight。
   其他一些词组：
   confirmed L/C 保兑信用证
   revolving L/C 循环信用证
   documentary L/C 跟单信用证
   reciprocal L/C 对开信用证
   irrevocable L/C 不可撤销信用证
   transferable and divisible L/C 可转让与可分割信用证

Letter 3　Specific Enquiry

M&N COMPANY
1234 Lowe
Boston, U.S.A.
Tel: 001-123-2345566

12th August, 2010

C.C., Ltd.
1123 Cambridge
London, British

Dear Sirs,

Re: "Australian Royal" wool blanket

　　We are now considering buying large quantities of your "Australian Royal" wool blanket. There is always a ready market here for "Australian Royal" wool blanket, provided it is of good quality and competitive price. We should be thankful if you would send us its full details concerning the price, discount, term of payment, delivery date, packing and so on. It would also be appreciated if you could forward your samples.

　　When quoting, please let us have your prices on both FOBC 3% Keelung and CIFC 3% HongKong. If your terms are favorable, we shall probably order about 10 000 dozens and open L/C in your favor in time.

　　We look forward to hearing from you by return.

Yours faithfully,
M&N Company
Manager

Notes

1. ... provided it is of good quality...
   provide 的过去分词形式 provided 和 V-ing 形式 providing 均可作连词，用来引导条件从句，意为"如果……的话；只要……"。可直接接从句，也可加上 that，二者可互换，但在正式文体中多用 provided。
   provide against... 为……做好准备；预防……
   provide for 提供生活费，养活
2. concerning 关系到
   concern oneself with/in/about sth. 忙于某事；关心某事；so/as far as... be concerned 就……来说/而论；be concerned with / in... 与……有关；Where... be concerned 在牵扯到

……的时候／情况下

3. We should be thankful if you would send us its full details concerning the price, discount, term of payment, delivery date, and packing and so on. 如果你寄给我们关于价格、折扣、支付方式、装运期和包装等详细信息，我方将不胜感激。

4. if you could forward your samples... 如果你能够寄送你的样品……

forward 常见词组：

amount brought forward 上期结转   amount carried forward 结转金额
balance forward 余额移后   balance brought forward 上期结转
balance carried forward 余额结转下期   carriage forward 运费交货时照付
charges forward 运费等由收货人在货到后自付   dating forward 预填日期
demand carried forward 结转需求   dollar forward 美元期货
duty forward 预付关税   freight forward 运费由提货人照付，运费到付
spot and forward 即期外汇与远期外汇   store and forward 储存和转送

5. FOBC3% Keelung 在基隆船上交货价包含3%佣金
CIFC3% HongKong 到香港货价、保险价、运费包含3%佣金

Letter 4 Reply to Specific Inquiry

C. C., Ltd.
1123 Cambridge
London, British
Tel：123-12344344

16th August, 2010

M&N Company
1234 Lowe
Boston, U.S.A.

Dear Sirs,
Re: "Australian Royal" wool blanket

    We warmly welcome your inquiry of 16th August and thank you for your interest in our "Australian Royal" wool blanket.

    We have pleasure in sending you a copy of the catalogue and samples of the full range of colors and the prices. They will reach you after 5 working days. You will see detail information about "Australian Royal" wool blanket on page 5 of the catalogue. Besides, "Australian Royal" wool blanket is packed in plastic bags, with 1 piece in each bag, 5 bags in a paper box, 10 boxes in a carton reinforced by hook iron. We give 12% discount on orders of $40 000 or more, and payment must be made by confirmed, irrevocable Letter of Credit payable by draft at sight. Our time of delivery is within 30 days after receipt of your L/C.

> All orders entrusted to us are given our careful and prompt attention. We sincerely desire to have the pleasure of receiving an order from you.
>
> > Yours faithfully,
> >
> > C. C. , Ltd.
> >
> > Manager

Notes

1. working day = workday = weekday 工作日
2. "Australian Royal" wool blanket is packed in plastic bags, with 1 piece in each bag, 5 bags in a paper box, 10 boxes in a carton reinforced by hook iron. 每一片"澳大利亚皇家"羊毛毯样片被独立装在一个塑料袋内，5个袋子装在一个纸盒里，10个盒子放在一个纸箱内，外用铁钩固定。
3. We give 12% discount on orders of $40 000 or more, and payment must be made by confirmed, irrevocable Letter of Credit payable by draft at sight. 对于4万美元或超过4万美元的订单，我们给予12%的优惠。至于付款条件，我方通常要求是保兑的、不可撤销的即期信用证。
4. All orders entrusted to us are given our careful and prompt attention. 我公司一向慎重并及时办理所接到的订单。
5. We sincerely desire to have the pleasure of receiving an order from you. 我们真诚地希望能得到你的订单。

Tips

1. 及时回复询盘

虽然询盘只是卖方或买方试探贸易可能性的一种做法，它对买卖双方都不具有法律约束力，收信方也没有一定要回复的义务，但是在实际业务中，收信方通常都应及时予以回复，可以以报价或者发盘的方式回复，如索要样品应酌情寄送。

2. 筛选后再回复

企业的邮箱里可能会出现大量的询问信函，那么是不是都要一一回复呢？当然不是，我们的时间、精力有限，回复一些不必要的信函会影响我们找到真正有价值的客户。所以，首先要做询问邮件的筛选：打开一封邮件，如果有称呼，同时明确提到某种具体产品，并简单介绍自己公司的背景，这样的发信人通常比较仔细用心，有明确的合作意向，并有心引起你的兴趣，是有回复价值的询盘；如果一封邮件既没有称谓，也没有提到某种产品，只是标准格式的询问信，那么发信人只是广泛乱发的，你只是他随机碰到的一个而已，不回复也罢。

3. 得体的否定对方

在商务信函往来中，在否定对方的观点、建议或者要求的时候，直接否定会让对方觉得不够礼貌，不利于双方友好合作关系的建立，需要有技巧地拒绝或者否定，如可以使用 unfortunately, scarcely, hardly, rather, almost, slightly 等副词使否定程度有所弱化，从而有利于建立平等、友好的沟通氛围。

发询盘时一般不直接用"询盘"的术语，通常用下列词语：

请告…… Please advise. . .
请电邮告知…… Please advise by e-mail. . .
对……有兴趣,请…… Interested in . . . please. . .
请报价…… Please quote. . .
请发盘…… Please offer. . .

3.3 有用的短语和句子
Useful Expressions

1. We read with interest your advertisement in China Daily and should be glad to receive particulars of your tender for port construction.
   我们对你方在《中国日报》上刊登的广告很感兴趣,现请你方寄送港口建设投标的详细情况。
2. We are interested in the mechanical toys demonstrated at the recent Guangzhou Trade Fair and should be glad to have details of your export terms.
   我们对你们最近在广州交易会上展列的机械玩具感兴趣,请详细告知出口条件。
3. We have seen your advertisement in the "Foreign Trade" and should be glad if you would send us by return patterns and prices of good quality cottons available from stock.
   我们已经看到了贵方在"对外贸易"上的广告,如果贵方能够给我们发送优等棉花的现货来样和价格,我们将很高兴。
4. We were pleased to know from your letter of 24th June of your interest in our products and enclose the catalogue and price list giving the details you asked for. Also enclosed you will find details of our conditions of sale and terms of payment.
   我们很高兴地从贵方6月24日的来信中获悉,贵方对我们的产品感兴趣,附函的目录和价格单给出了贵方要求的详细资料,同时附有我方的销售条件和支付条件。
5. We are making you the following offer, subject to your reply reaching here within five days.
   我们给出以下报价,以贵方5天内回复为准。
6. We shall be pleased if you will furnish us with your lowest quotation for the following goods.
   如果你们为我们提供下列产品的最低报价,我们将会很高兴。
7. If you think this offer is acceptable to you, please fax us immediately for our confirmation.
   如果贵方认为此报价可以接受,请立即向我们发出传真以便确认。
8. Under separate cover, we are sending you one sample pad for the synthetic fabric dress materials we are exporting at present. We hope some of the designs and colors will prove to your liking.
   另封寄上我方目前出口的合成纤维衣料,希望某些花样及颜色能使贵方喜欢。
9. We have been importers of. . . for many years. At present, we are interested in extending our range and would appreciate your catalogues and quotations.
   多年来,我公司经营……进口生意。现欲扩展业务范围,盼能惠寄商品目录和报价单。
10. We specialize in supplying small stores in rural areas. Over 3 000 of these stores virtually depend on us, and this assured sales outlet enables us to dispose of fairly large quantities.

我们专向乡镇小商店供货。3 000 家以上此种商店靠我们供货，这些有保证的销路足够我们大量推销。

11. Your samples should give us an idea of the colors and quality of the products.
    贵公司寄来的样品，使我们对贵公司产品的色彩与品质有一定了解。

12. We cannot take anything off the price.
    此价不能再减。

13. One of our clients has sent us a quotation for 2 000 units of refrigerator to be sold in the countries in South-east Asia. Please quote us your best terms CIF Manila and let us know what quantities you are able to deliver at regular intervals.
    我方一客户发来询盘，要求 2 000 台销往东南亚国家的电冰箱报价，请贵方报 CIF 马尼拉最优惠交易条件，并请告知贵方能定期提供的数量。

14. We have the pleasure of sending you a direction of how to operate our new dishwashing machine.
    现寄上关于如何使用我们新式洗碗机的说明书一份。

15. If the prices quoted are competitive/workable, and the quality up to standard, we will place orders on a regular basis.
    如果贵方报价有竞争力/可行性，产品质量达标，我方将长期订购。

16. We trust you will give this enquiry your immediate attention and let us have your reply at an early date.
    我方相信贵方会对此询盘予以重视并及早回复。

17. We have been informed by the Bank of Canada, Vancouver that you are one of the leading exporters of textiles in Shanghai.
    加拿大银行温哥华分行告知我们，贵公司是上海的主要纺织品出口商之一。

18. We are on the look-out for the following items and should be grateful if you would send samples of the same.
    我们欲求购下列产品，如贵公司能寄来其样品，我们将非常感激。

19. In reply to your enquiry dated November 25, we are sending you here with our quotation, along with various samples of leather gloves closely resembling to what you want.
    应贵公司 11 月 25 日来函询问，现寄上我方的报价和几副式样不同的与贵方要求相近的皮手套样品。

20. You will find that we have given you the most favored quotation for the same products.
    你将会发现，我们给贵公司的报价是相同产品中最低的。

21. We shall be glad to settle the deal with you if the price is lowered by another 5%.
    如果你方能将价格再降 5%，我们将很高兴与你方敲定这笔生意。

22. We look forward to receiving your firm offer at your early convenience.
    我方期望贵方早日报出实盘报价。

23. As soon as we receive your firm offer, we will inform you whether your price is acceptable to us.
    一旦接到贵方实盘报价，我们将通知贵方是否接受报价。

24. Meanwhile, please make sure that you include all requirements in your inquiry.
    同时，请确定贵方询盘中已包涵了所有要求。

25. Regarding your enquiry of September 1, please kindly advise us the quantity you require as soon as possible.

关于贵方 9 月 1 日的询盘，请尽快告知我方贵方所需数量。

26. We have to ask you to reduce your price to a competitive level as the price of the similar line has been lowered to the 80% of last year.

    由于同类产品价格已降至去年的 80%，我们不得不请贵公司将价格削减到有竞争力的水平。

27. In view of our long term friendly relationships, we make our favorable offer subject to your reply by March 31.

    鉴于双方的长期友好关系，特向贵方报出优惠报盘，3 月 31 日前答复有效。

28. Our annual order will be increased by 15% in next three years together with the increase of market shares.

    随着市场份额的增加，我们在未来三年中，每年的订货量会增加 15%。

练习
Exercises

Ⅰ. Comprehension Questions
  1. In international trade, what is an inquiry?
  2. What are the differences between general inquiry and specific inquiry?
  3. What are the principles of writing an inquiry and a reply?
  4. Suppose the goods inquired about are out of stock. What are the possible replies? Please list them out.
  5. In the first inquiry, what items do you need to consider?

Ⅱ. Translating the Following Terms and Expressions
  1. quantity discount   2. spoil one's credit
  3. enjoy credit   4. current price
  5. original price   6. 特殊折扣
  7. 单独邮寄   8. 质量一般的产品
  9. 出货书   10. 畅销市场

Ⅲ. Fill in the Blanks
  1. One of the customers is also interested _____ thermos bottle.
  2. Please quote us you lowest prices _____ the following items.
  3. If your prices are favorable, we are prepared to order the beans _____ large quantity.
  4. We have an inquiry _____ Groundnut Kernels and shall be pleased if you quote us your lowest price _____ C. I. F. basis, stating the quantity available.
  5. Please send us _____ parcel post samples representing your current stocks.
  6. Please let us know if you can supply us with 200 cases of Luncheon Meat for _____ shipment.
  7. We are interested in the _____ goods, and shall be obliged if you will send us quotations on C. I. F. Liverpool basis, including 2% commission for us.
  8. If the following items are available in your _____ stock, please quote your lowest price with full details of specifications and origin.

9. We hope to _____ the business to our mutual benefit.
10. We _____ you of our readiness to serve you in this end all future business.
11. As one of the largest extractors and processors of food oil in China, our _____ (年需求量) for soy bean is 100 000 MT.
12. We sincerely wish to establish a _____ (双赢) business relationship with you, who are an important provider of soy bean in Brazil.
13. We _____ (诚恳地) wish to establish a win-win business relationship with you, who are an important provider of soy bean in Brazil.
14. We will _____ (感谢) it if you can offer us a competitive price.
15. However, we have to ask you to quote us a more favorable price _____ (由于) the stronger competition this year.
16. For the _____ (同类的) pens, the price is only 60% of that in last year.
17. We are a _____ (主要的) importer of medical equipments in Tianjin, China.
18. We are now looking for the opportunity to order ten _____ (套) of Electron Microscope with a magnification of 80 000 times.
19. As we maintain a long term relationship with our clients, we keep a very thin _____ (利润).
20. They are able to fulfill the _____ (要求) for regular blood and cell examination.

Ⅳ. Translating the Following Sentences

1. Fragile goods should be handled carefully.
2. We learned from ABC Co. that you are in a position to supply fruit and dried fruit.
3. As soon as we receive your specific inquiries we will make you best offer on CIF Lagos basis.
4. As for terms of payment, we need irrevocable L/C payable by draft at sight.
5. We enclose quotation sheet against your Inquiry No. 16 and look forward to your confirmation.
6. 由于自去年以来对我们茶叶的需求量不断增加，所以我们无法按贵方的要求报价。
7. 该报价为最惠价，恕不还价。
8. 我们同意贵方的建议。
9. 我们的一位商业合伙人建议我们向贵公司求助。
10. 正如你们所知，我们是经营此类商品已有多年的国有公司。
11. 强烈的市场竞争使得该产品价格下降了20%。
12. 请向我公司发出七英寸①灰色泰迪熊的离岸价，包装为纸板箱，每打一箱。
13. 我们在此想提请贵方对市场潜力给予关注。
14. 如能收到贵方有竞争力的报盘，我方将立即向贵方发出 500 打电动玩具车的订单。
15. 我公司在硅谷的合作伙伴将贵公司推荐给我们，请回复我们关于数据库系统软件的询盘。

Ⅴ. Translating the Following Paragraphs into English

我们想大量购买各种型号的铁钉，请报每吨尼日利亚拉哥斯到岸价。同时，如能收到贵方寄来的样品和（或）小册子则不胜感激。我们过去常从他处购买此货，但是，现在我们宁愿向贵公司购买，因为我们得悉贵公司能以更吸引人的价格大批量供货。另外，我们十分相信中国产品的质量。

---

① 1 英寸 = 0.025 4 米。

附录3A 国际贸易价格术语
Appendix 3A Terms of Price in International Trade

根据《2000年国际贸易术语解释通则》，所有的术语基本分为四种不同的类型。第一组"E组"（EXWORKS），指卖方仅在自己的地点为买主备妥货物；第二组"F组"（FCA、FAS和FOB），指卖方将货物交至买方指定的承运人；第三组"C组"（CFR、CIF、CPI和CIP），指卖方须订立运输合同，但对货物灭失或损坏的风险以及装船和启运后发生意外所发生的额外费用，卖方不承担责任；第四组"D组"（DAF、DES、DEQ、DDU和DDP），指卖方须承担把货物交至目的地国所需的全部费用和风险，见表3-1。

表 3-1

类别	名称	交货地点	运输	保险	风险转移	出口结关	进口结关	运输方式	各组特点
E组发货	EXW 工厂交货	卖方工厂				买方		各种运输	内陆交货
F组主要运费未付	FCA 货交承运人	交承运人（买方指定）	买方	买方	交货时				装运合同运费未付
	FAS 船边交货	指定装运港船边						海河内河	
	FOB 船上交货	指定装运港船上							
C组主要运费已付	CFR 成本加运费	装运港船上		买方	装运港船舷		买方	海河内河	装运合同运费已付
	CIF 成本、保险费加运费	装运港船上		卖方					
	CPT 运费付至	交第一承运人		买方		卖方		各种运输	
	CIP 运费、保险费付至	交第一承运人							
D组到达	DAF 边境交货	边境指定地点（不卸货）	卖方	卖方	交货时			陆上运输	到货合同
	DES 目的港船上交货	目的港船上（不卸货）						海河内河	
	DEQ 目的港码头交货	目的港码头（卸到码头）							
	DDU 未完税交货	指定目的地（不卸货）						各种运输	
	DDP 完税后交货	指定目的地（不卸货）					卖方		

Chapter 4
第 4 章

报价、发盘及还盘
Quotations, Offers and Counter-offers

Learning Objectives

Enable the students to know the definition of quotation, offers and counter-offers; to be acquainted with the differences between firm offer and non-firm offer, the main components of letters of quotation, offers and counter-offers; to master basic expressions and write principles of letters of quotation, offers, and counter-offers.

使学生了解报价，发盘和还盘的定义；熟悉实盘和虚盘的区别，报价、发盘和还盘信函主要组成部分，还有发盘和还盘信函的写作宗旨；掌握这类书信的基本用语和句型。

4.1 背景知识
Background Information

In international business practice, companies always go through the process of "quotation-offer-counter-offer-acceptance". This process can be oral, face-to-face or telephone communication. However, written forms such as letter and e-mail are often used. By quotation sheet which includes all necessary information requested, the seller replies the buyer's inquiry of supply. Quotation is a promise based on conditions agreed, always considered as a non-firm offer. After quoting, potential buyer has no obligation to buy. Besides, if the seller would not like to sell, he has also no obligation to sell the quoted commodities. Quotation has no legal enforcement, although it also uses accurate language like firm offer. If commodities are too many, quotation can be made in form of sheet. When we send quotation, we always use letter to tell the buyer that there is a quotation attached in the letter, show thanks for

在国际贸易实务中，公司一般经过"报价—发盘—还盘—接受"这个流程达成一桩买卖。这个过程可以是口头的，也可采取面对面或电话交流，但是普遍采取书信形式，如信件和邮件。一般卖方通过报价单回复买方的询盘，报价单包括询盘中所要求的所有必要信息。报价是一种按约定条件供货的承诺，被认为是一种虚盘。请求报价后，未来买主没有义务非买不可；如果卖方后来决定不卖，也没有义务一定出售以前报过价的商品。报价不具法律约束力，尽管它也像实盘那样使用了某些严谨的说法。当商品繁多的时候，报价单可以采取

their inquiries, or introduce quoted commodities and hope to get the reply of them. Letter of quotation generally includes the following parts:

(1) Thanks for the former inquiry;
(2) The name, quality, quantity and specifications of commodities;
(3) The details of price, discount and term of payment;
(4) Clearly introduce price involved, such as packing, freight, premium, etc. ;
(5) Packing and delivering;
(6) Express the hope of accepting quotation.

Offer is the reply of the seller to the inquiry of buyer. In order to sell their commodities, the seller may directly make an offer rather than waiting for the inquiry. The offer must have specific receiver, and clear content. Because quotation does not mean promising sell, it is not an offer but inviting buyer to inquire or send an order. If quotation promises to sell, includes key conditions such as price, quantity and so on, and claims that these terms need to be clarified in the contract, the quotation can be considered as an operative offer. The offer can be divided into firm offer and non-firm offer. If the receiver does not agree, the sender promises not to withdraw and change the content of offer in the time limit without the permission of the receiver, that is firm offer. If the receiver accepts in the time limitation, the transaction is concluded, and the content of offer is the part of contract. A complete firm offer shall include specific terms of transaction such as the name of commodities, specification, quantity, price, and term of payment, time of shipment as well as validity of the offer. Besides, it is necessary to clarify that it is a firm offer. Non-firm offer is that the sender agrees to make a deal based on some specific conditions. Non-firm offer is not limited by its content, or make any promises, some phrases such as "be valid after the final confirmation", or "offer has no obligation" are often used.

表列式。在寄送报价单时，通常都用一封专函，告知对方信内附寄报价单，并对询盘表示感谢，或介绍所报商品，希望获得对方的订单。写报价信一般包括以下几部分：

（1）感谢之前的询盘；
（2）商品的名称、质量、数量和规格；
（3）有关价格、折扣和付款条件的细则；
（4）详细表明价款所包括的方面，如包装、运费、保险费等；
（5）包装、交货日期；
（6）表示希望接受所给报价。

发盘是卖方对买方询价的回复。为了销售自己的商品，卖方可以不等对方询盘即主动发盘。发盘必须有明确的受盘人，其所有内容必须十分确定。因为报价没有承诺出售，所以不是发盘，而是邀请买方询盘或发出订单。如果报价承诺销售，包含价格、数量等关键条件，并说明这些条件需在双方协议中加以明确，那么这个报价就可被视为可操作的发盘。发盘分为实盘和虚盘两种。实盘是发盘人承诺在一定期限内，受发盘内容约束，非经接盘人同意，不得撤回和变更。如接盘人在有效期限内表示接受，则交易达成，实盘内容即成为买卖合同的组成部分。一个完整的实盘应包括明确肯定的交易条件，如商品名称、规格、数量、价格、支付方式、装运期等，还应有实盘的有效期限并应明确发盘为实盘。虚盘是发盘人有保留地表示愿意按一定条件达成交易，不受发盘内容约束，不作任何承诺，通常使用"须经我最后确认方有效""报盘不具责任"等语。

Letters about offer generally bases on the following steps:

(1) Firstly, express thanks for the inquiry, show what date or which inquiry you are answering;

(2) Make clear the nature of the offer. If it is a firm offer, state the period of validity. If not, state that the offer without engagement;

(3) State clearly the name of the commodity, quality, specification, quantity, details of prices, time of shipment, and terms of payment;

(4) Provide information as much as possible;

(5) In the final part, hope the buyer will be satisfied with the offer and accept it.

Writing the letter of offer generally bases on following points:

(1) Reply in time;

(2) Clearly and correctly reply;

(3) Include all terms of trade;

(4) Clarify it is firm offer or non-firm offer;

(5) Introduce the advantages of commodities.

Counter-offer is one of trade forms, in which the receiver accepts the offer but suggests amending some of the content. The nature of counter-offer is some kinds of refusing to the former offer and giving the new offer as the position of sender. So, after counter-offer, the former offer expires, and new offer becomes the basis of negotiation. If the other party continues to disagree with the content of counter-offer, he or she also can do the counter-counter-offer. Counter-offer can repeat between two parties. The content of counter-offer usually only involves in terms to be changed or added. In the international trade, counter-offer and counter-counter-offer may repeat many times, and then final agreements can be achieved.

Writing the letter of counter-offer always bases on the following steps:

(1) Firstly, express thanks for the offer;

(2) In the second part, clearly apologize and show your reasons for disagreement to certain term (s);

写发盘信函一般按照以下几个步骤：

(1) 感谢对方的询盘，表明是对方哪一天或哪一次的询盘；

(2) 明确发盘的类型，如果是实盘，明确有效期，如果不是，表明发盘不具效力；

(3) 明确商品的名称、质量、规格、数量、价目明细、装运时间和付款方式；

(4) 提供尽可能多的信息；

(5) 表示希望买方对发盘感到满意并接受。

发盘信函一般遵守以下几点：

(1) 及时回复；

(2) 明确、准确地答复；

(3) 包含所有的贸易条件；

(4) 明确实盘还是虚盘；

(5) 渲染商品优点。

还盘是交易方式之一，即接盘人对所接发盘表示接受，但对其内容提出更改。还盘实质上构成对原发盘某种程度的拒绝，也是接盘人以发盘人地位所提出的新发盘。因此，一经还盘，原发盘即失效，新发盘取代它成为交易谈判的基础。如果另一方对还盘内容不同意，还可以进行反还盘（或称再还盘）。还盘可以在双方之间反复进行，还盘的内容通常仅陈述变更或增添的条件，对双方同意的交易条件无须重复。在国际贸易中，往往经过多次的还盘、反还盘，才最终达成协议。

还盘信函一般按照以下几个步骤：

(1) 对发盘表示感谢；

(2) 明确地表达对发盘中部分条款的不赞同，并说明原因；

(3) Put forward concrete suggestions or amendments to the former offer;

(4) In the end, express hopes of reply earlier and make a deal.

Writing the letter of counter-offer always based on the following principles:

(1) Be polite but directly tell the subject;

(2) List what you disagree;

(3) Clearly make your suggestions.

(3) 对发盘提出明确的修改建议；

(4) 表达希望早日回复并做成交易。

还盘信函一般遵守以下几点：

(1) 措辞礼貌但要直奔主题；

(2) 明确列举哪些部分你不能接受；

(3) 清楚地写出你的建议。

4.2 信例
Sample Letters

Letter 1 Quotations

May 23, 2010

Dear Sirs,

"Australian Royal" wool blanket

We thank you very much for your Inquiry List No. 234 and enclose our Quotation No. 452 for the captioned goods.

Being requested, we enclose our latest price list and catalogue of this month by air. A very full range of the blankets have been sent to you by sample post today, and we are confident that, after examining that, you will see the quality and the prices of the goods we offer you compare favorably with any others, for the same class of goods. We are continually issuing new designs and we are delighted to submit further samples to you if there are orders from you in succession from now on.

On order for 600 pieces or more we allow a special discount of 6% and look forward to receiving your order.

Yours faithfully,

M&N COMPANY

(SIGNATURE)

Bruce Lee

President

Notes

1. the captioned goods 标题项下的货物

   类似的表达法还有：

the subject article (goods)
the good (article) mentioned in the subject line
2. by air 空邮
3. A very full range of the blankets have been sent to you by sample post today, and we are confident that, after examining that, you will see the quality and the prices of the goods we offer you compare favorably with any others, for the same class of goods. We are continually issuing new designs and we are delighted submit further samples to you if there are orders from you in succession from now on. 今天将所有不同种类毯子的样品一并寄送贵处。我们相信，经过检验，贵公司将会发现我方提供的这些商品的质量、价格和其他同类商品相比毫不逊色。如果贵公司今后陆续给我们订单，我们会不断地给你们发布最新产品设计，并向贵方提交其样品。
4. Issue 发行、发布。常用短语有：
   bonus issue 红利股（即作为红利发行的股票）　　capital issue 股票发行
   conversion issue 证券转换发行，调换发行　　currency issue 货币发行
   current issue 现期刊物，即期　　custom union issue 关税同盟争论
   debenture issue 债券发行　　economic issue 经济问题
   excess issue 超额发行，限外发行　　expiry issue 迄期期次，最末供应的一期
   extra-limit issue 限外发行
   fiduciary issue 信用发行，保证准备发行（即以政府证券做准备的发行）
   fractional free issue 小额免费发行证券　　free issue 自由发行
   government issue 公债券发行，国家证券发行　　guaranteed issue 保证发行
   hot issue 上市后不久价格猛涨的股票　　initial issue （债券等的）首次发行
   intra-limit issue 限内部发行　　live issue 尚在争论中的问题
   long standing issue 长期存在的问题　　low price issues 冷门股票
   marketable issue 适销证券　　maximum issue 发行极度
   missing issue 期刊缺期　　monetary issue 货币发行
   new issues （纸币、证券等的）新发行，新的争论点　　new bond issues 新债发行
   new capital issues 新发行的资本股票　　new foreign bond issues 新的外国债券
   non-supplied issues 未供应卷期　　note issue 纸币发行，通货发行
   over issues 过量发行的印刷品　　par issue 平价发行

Letter 2　Firm Offer 1

Dear Sirs,
　　Thank you for your inquiry dated July 17 and, as requested, we are airmailing you, under separate cover, one catalogue and three sample books for our Australian Royal wool blankets. We hope they will reach you in due course and will help you in making your selection.
　　We are pleasure of making the following offer, subject to your reply reaching us by 5 p.m. our time, Tuesday, August 16, as follows:

Article: Australian Royal wool blanket

Art. No.: 123445

Quantity: 6 000 pieces

Packing: standard export wooden case

Price: US $ 79 per piece CIFC 3% Singapore

Shipment: 7 days after receipt of order

Payment: By confirmed, irrevocable L/C payable by draft at sight to be opened 30 days before the time of shipment.

We look forward to receiving your trial order and assure that it will receive our prompt attention.

Yours faithfully,

M&N COMPANY

(SIGNATURE)

Bruce Lee

President

Firm Offer 2

TO: NEO GENERAL TRADING CO.

FROM: DESUN TRADING CO., LTD.

DATE: OCT. 16, 2005

Dear Andy Burns,

We have received your letter of Oct. 14, asking us to offer the chinaware and highly appreciate that you are interested in our product.

Comply with your kindly request, we are please to offer our best price as follows.

1.

Commodity	Article Number	FOB Shanghai per set	CFR Toronto per set	CIF Toronto per set
20-Piece Dinnerware Set	DR 2010	USD 17.69	USD 20.12	USD 20.34
47-Piece Dinnerware Set	DR 2202	USD 19.81	USD 24.63	USD 25.01
95-Piece Dinnerware Set	DR 2211	USD 23.09	USD 30.85	USD 31.26
15-Piece Tea Set	DR 2300	USD 12.30	USD 15.61	USD 15.83
35-Piece Dinnerware and Tea Set	DR 2401	USD 21.35	USD 25.12	USD 25.58

2. The total price according 20' FCL

3. Quantity: (DR 2010: 400 boxes; DR 2202: 343 boxes; DR 2211: 254 boxes; DR 2300: 437 boxes; DR 2401: 542 boxes)

> 4. Package: DR 2010, DR 2300 set / carton, two sets / box; DR 2202, DR 2211, DR 2401 set / carton (DR 2010: 400 boxes; DR 2202: 343 boxes; DR 2211: 254 boxes; DR 2300: 437 boxes; DR 2401: 542 boxes).
>
> 5. Payment: L/C AT SIGHT
>
> 6. Shipment: Not later than Dec. 16, 2005
>
> 7. Insurance: 110% of invoice amount insured by WPA, broken and war risk insurance.
>
> 8. Air samples have been sent for.
>
> Noted: Our quotation remains effective until Oct. 23, 2005.
>
> PLS kindly pay attention to the fact that we have not much ready stock on hand. Therefore, it is very important to reply us before Oct. 23.
>
> Looking forward to hearing from you soonest.
>
> Best regards
> DESUN TRADING CO., LTD
> Minghua Zhao

Notes

1. as requested 根据贵方要求，应贵方要求

   As requested, we enclosed our catalogue and price list. 应贵方要求，我方随函附寄目录和价格单。

2. We hope they will reach you in due course and will help you in making your selection. 我们希望这些能准时送到贵方以供选择。

   in due course 在适当的时候

3. We are pleasure of making the following offer, subject to your reply reaching us by August 16, as follows. 现报盘如下，此报盘以我方时间8月16日收到贵方答复有效。

   (1) pleasure 愉快，快乐，高兴，满意

   　　to have/ take pleasure in doing (to do) sth. 乐于做某事

   　　to have/ take the pleasure of doing (to do) sth. 乐于做某事

   　　at one's pleasure = at will/ at discretion 听便

   　　with pleasure 愉快地接受、同意

   (2) offer 报盘（包括货品、数量、规格、价格、船期、有效期等，通常和介词 for、of 或 on 连用）

   　　Please make us an offer CIF London for (on) 20 metric tons groundnuts. 请给我们提供20吨花生伦敦到岸价格的报盘。

   　　We offer... subject to our final confirmation. 我方报盘……以我方最后确认有效。

   　　We make you an offer subject to the goods being unsold. 我方向你方报盘，以未售出为准。

   　　常用词组有：

   　　to accept offer 接受报盘　　　to confirm offer 确认报盘

   　　to decline offer 拒绝报盘　　　to entertain offer 考虑报盘

   　　to extent offer 延长报盘　　　to withdraw offer 撤回报盘

	to renew offer 恢复报盘	to reinstate offer 恢复报盘（恢复过期较久如十天前的报盘时）
	combined offer 搭配报盘	lump offer 综合报盘
	package offer 一揽子报盘	

4. article 商品
5. Art. No. 商品号码（指在目录和样品簿中某一商品的编号）
6. Packing：standard export wooden case 包装：标准出口木箱
7. Payment：By confirmed, irrevocable L/C payable by draft at sight to be opened 30 days before the time of shipment. 付款：装船前30天开出保兑的、不可撤销的信用证，见票即付。
8. We look forward to receiving your trial order and assure that it will receive our prompt attention. 我们期望能收到贵方试订单，并保证会及时关注。
9. We have received your letter of Oct. 14, asking us to offer the chinaware and highly appreciate that you are interested in our product. 我们已经收到了贵方10月14日来函要求我们报瓷器价格，非常感谢您对我们的产品感兴趣。
10. Comply with your kindly request, we are please to offer our best price as follows. 根据你方要求，现提供最优报价如下。
11. PLS kindly pay attention to the fact that we have not much ready stock on hand. Therefore, it is very important to reply us before Oct. 23. 另请注意，现有手头库存不多，请一定在10月23日前回复我们。

Letter 3　Non-firm Offer

Dear Sirs,
　　We have received your kind inquiry dated May 23, 2010. In compliance with your request, we included in this letter our quotation sheet for Australian Royal wool blankets Art No. 132.
　　The respective quantities are quoted on the basis of CFR Port New York. This offer is subject to our final confirmation. The price quotes include packing and delivery terms and are subject to 6% trade discount for purchase larger than 6 000 items. As usual, we require payment to be made by a confirmed and irrevocable Letter of Credit, payable at sight against presentation of documents. We can guarantee delivery within 15 days after we receive the L/C. If you need any further information about our products, please do not hesitate to let us know by return.
　　What you mentioned in your letter in connection with the question of agency has been taken into our account. We shall revert to the matter later on.
　　Awaiting your esteemed favors and orders.
Yours faithfully,

Notes

1. In compliance with your request, we included in this letter our quotation sheet for Australian Royal wool blankets Art No. 132. 按照贵方的请求，我们随信寄去132号澳大利亚皇家羊毛毯的报价单。

in compliance with 依从，按照

a compliance to... 对……的称赞，赞扬……

Please forward the following articles. Your compliance with our request will be highly appreciated. 请发送以下商品，如贵方照办，则不胜感激。

2. respective 各自的（一般接名词复数）
3. subject
   （1）be subject to 支配，从属于；是英语一个很重要的短语，特别是在商贸英语中出现的频率很高，不少人由于没有真正了解它的用法，而不能正确使用它，下面做简要介绍。

   subject to 中 subject 作形容词用，其基本含义是"受限于……""服从于……""易受……"。

   Also, these fuels, especially oil, are subject to uncertainties over price and future supply. 此外，这些燃料，特别是石油，易受到价格和将来的供应等不稳定因素的影响。

   （2）be subjected to 接受，经受，遭受，使经受，使遭受等
4. confirmation 确认，证实，保兑

   Your immediate confirmation of our offer is appreciated. 感谢贵方迅速确认我们的发盘。
5. payment 支付，付款

   当数量条款定有溢短装条款时，付款条件中也应有所反映：

   Payment: By confirmed, irrevocable L/C payable by draft at sight. The L/C should include a clause 5% more or less for both the quantity and the amount allowed. 支付：保兑的、不可撤销的信用证付款。信用证必须包括装货数量和总值都有 5% 溢短的条款。
6. hesitate 犹豫不决，迟疑

   If you need any further information about our products, please do not hesitate to let us know by return. 如需要更多关于我们产品的资料，请立即回信告诉我们。
7. taken into our account 考虑，顾及
8. revert to 回复到，重议

   What you mentioned in your letter in connection with the question of agency has been taken into our account. We shall revert to the matter later on. 我方已考虑贵方来信中所提及的关于设立代理处的问题，以后会和贵方重议此事。
9. Awaiting your esteemed favors and orders. 殷盼惠示并订购我们的商品。

Letter 4　Counter-offers

Dear Sirs,

　　We thank you for your Quotation No. 12344 for your Australian Royal wool blankets, and we have given it very careful consideration.

　　We regret to say that we find your price rather high and we believe we will have a hard time convincing our clients at your price. Besides, there is keen competition from supplier in Japan and China. You cannot ignore that. We find that we can obtain from another firm in China a price of 10% lower than that of yours.

> If you would reduce your price to that extent, we will be pleased to place with you an order that will carry us for the rest of this year.
>
> Hope to hear from you soon.
>
> Yours faithfully,

Notes

1. regret 遗憾
   regret to do sth. 很遗憾地/抱歉地做……（事情还没有做）
   regret doing sth. 很遗憾/后悔做了……（为已经做过的事而感到遗憾）
2. convince 使相信（信服），说服；使承认；使悔悟；使认错（罪）
   convince sb. of sth. 使某人相信某事
   convince sb. 说服某人
   convince sb. to do sth. 说服某人做某事
3. We regret to say that we find your price rather high and we believe we will have a hard time convincing our clients at your price. 很抱歉，我们觉得你的价格相当高，对此我们很难让客户接受这个价格。
4. competition 竞争，竞赛
   表示"激烈竞争或残酷的竞争"有许多可以替换的形容词，如 keen, strong, formidable, fierce, bitter, cut-throat, severe, intense, dog-eat-dog competition。
5. ignore 不顾，忽视
6. obtain from 得到
7. If you would reduce your price to that extent, we will be pleased to place with you an order that will carry us for the rest of this year. 如果你能在一定程度上降低价格，我们很乐意下这一年剩下几个月的订单。

Tips

1. 实盘、虚盘、递盘

实盘（offer with engagement/firm offer）：指发盘人（发价人）对接受人所提出的是一项内容完整、明确、肯定的交易条件，一旦送达受盘人（接受人或称受发价人），则对发盘人产生拘束力，发盘人在实盘规定的有效期内不得将其撤销或加以变更。

虚盘（offer without engagement/non-firm offer）：虚盘又称非确定报价，指不含明确意义的报价，也就是发盘人有保留地愿意按一定条件达成交易的一种表示。虚盘的主要作用是试探对方的交易诚意；吸引对方向我方递盘或订货；可以为我方保留对交易的最后决定权。

递盘（bid）：交易磋商过程中，卖方对当前的市场情况不清楚，或卖方还不了解买方是否有诚意购买，常常要求买方首先发来发盘，这种由买方发来的发盘为递盘。实际上，递盘就是一种发盘，所以它也有实盘和虚盘之分。前者内容明确、肯定，对买方有约束力；后者内容不明确、不肯定，对买方没有约束力。

2. 还盘的构成条件

还盘在法律性质上与要约相同，对发出还盘方也具有约束力，即一旦对方表示接受，则负有与对方成立合同的义务。区别在于：①它可以在内容上仅就受要约人的修改进行表述，而不需要重复要约中并无不同意见的其他内容；②一经还盘，原要约对要约人的约束力（义务）即被解除，并且承诺的权利从原受要约人转移到原要约人。

4.3 有用的短语和句子
Useful Expressions

1. We have pleasure in offering (quoting) you the following goods.
   我们很高兴就以下产品向贵方报价。
2. We have learned that there is a good demand for walnut in your market, and take this opportunity of enclosing your Quotation Sheet No. 1234 for your consideration.
   获悉贵地市场对核桃有较大需求，现寄上 1234 号报价单供参考。
3. Thank you for your letter of December 23 asking us to offer you 10 000 metric tons of the subject wheat for shipment to Singapore and appreciate very much your interest in.
   感谢贵方 12 月 23 日的来信，要求我方报盘运往新加坡的 10 000 吨标题小麦，十分感谢你对我们产品的兴趣。
4. These quotations are all subject to the fluctuations of the market.
   这些报价是随市场波动而变动的。
5. This offer is to be withdrawn if not accepted by May 10.
   如果贵方没有在 5 月 10 日前接受该报盘的话，它将无效。
6. This offer will remain effective (valid, firm, open, available, good) until…
   该盘有效期到……为止。
7. On condition that you take more than 2 000 sets, we are prepared to offer this special price of \$ 9.15 per set, 5% discount.
   如订购 2 000 台以上可给予特别报盘，每台 9.15 美元，5% 的折扣。
8. Thank you for your kind cooperation in meeting our demand. We hope you will furnish us with further mutually profitable offers in the future.
   感谢贵方合作，满足我们的要求。希望将来能以更优惠的报盘提供给本公司。
9. We have accepted your firm offer. I am afraid the offer is unacceptable.
   我们已经收到了你们报的实盘，恐怕贵方的报价不能接受。
10. Your offer is unacceptable unless the price is reduced by 5%.
    除非你们减价 5%，否则我们无法接受报盘。
11. You could benefit from higher sale with a little concession, say a 2% reduction.
    只要稍做让步，比方说降价 2%，就可得到一大笔交易。
12. Their fine quality, attractive designs and the reasonable prices at which we offer them will convince you that these materials are really of good value.
    它们的良好品质、诱人的花样以及我们所报的合理价格将会使贵方相信，这些料子是货真价实的。
13. We trust that you will be able to accept our offer, which shall be kept open against reply by fax.
我们确信，贵公司会接受我们的报价。此报盘至复传真为止有效。
14. We were very pleased to receive your enquiry of 2nd July and now confirm our fax offer of this morning, as follows.
谢谢 7 月 2 日来函。兹确认今天早晨的传真报价如下。
15. We must stress that this offer is firm for three days only because of the heavy demand for the limited supplies of this velvet in stock.
本公司必须强调，此报价仅有效 3 天，此乃因为天鹅绒的存货有限，需求量过大。
16. We thank you very much for your kind order of February 25, being accompanied by your check, value ＄2 000, which we received today.
今已收到贵方 2 月 25 日订单及随附价值 2 000 美元支票一张，非常感谢。
17. We are arranging for dispatch next month, we feel sure that you will be satisfied with the goods.
我们正在安排下个月的装运，并相信贵方会对我们的商品感到满意。
18. We assure you that this order and further orders shall have our immediate attention.
我们保证此次订单和以后的订单均会得到我们及时的重视。
19. We are glad to confirm your order which we have accepted on the terms.
我方很高兴确认贵方的订单并已接受贵方的条件。
20. Please note that goods supplied on approval must be returned, carriage paid, within 7days if not required.
请注意，试销货物，如不需要，必须在 7 天内退回，运费先付。

练习

Exercises

Ⅰ. Comprehension Quotation
  1. What are quotation, offer, and counter offer?
  2. What are the differences between firm offer and non-firm offer?
  3. What principles do we need to know before writing a letter of offer?
  4. Under what circumstance should we use non-firm offer?
  5. Is a counter-offer made to direct only against price?

Ⅱ. Translate the Following Terms and Expressions
  1. make a concession   2. effect shipment
  3. a firm offer   4. extend offer
  5. 与……一致   6. 提高 8%
  7. 接受还盘   8. 询价单

Ⅲ. Fill in the Blanks
  1. We shall be glad to receive an offer _____ you _____ bicycles.
  2. We offer firm CIF, Lagos shipment _____ 30 days, subject _____ your reply here _____ 10 a.m., our time.
  3. We offer firm the following _____ the same terms and conditions as the previous contract, subject to your reply here _____ one week _____ today.

4. The letter of credit has been opened _____ your favor.
5. Owing _____ unusual shortage _____ stock, this offer is made subject to the goods being unsold.
6. Black tea, first grade, is out _____ stock now.
7. I'd like to direct your attention _____ the quality _____ the goods which is superior _____ that of other makes.
8. We have _____ present only 50 tons Bitter Apricot Kernels _____ stock.
9. We can supply walnuts _____ stock.
10. On orders _____ 500 pieces or more we _____ a special discount _____ 4%.

Ⅳ. Translate the Following Sentences
1. Although we are not in a position to satisfy your special requirements, we still send you another copy of our price list.
2. We are sending you a firm offer, subject to your reply here by 5 p.m. our time, Tuesday, July 10.
3. You are cordially invited to take advantage of this attractive offer. We are anticipating a large order from the United States, and that will cause a sharp rise in price.
4. We believe that you will place a large order with us owing to the high quality and reasonable price of our products.
5. We are studying the offer and hope that it keeps open till the end of the month.
6. 本报盘 5 日内有效。
7. 我方报价如有变更不另行通知。
8. 如果贵方认为这一报盘可以接受,请即来电,以便我方确认。
9. 为了开展双方间具体的业务,我们很高兴向贵方报特盘,须以我方最后确认为准。
10. 如果贵方能将 9 月 3 日的报价单上的价格降低 3%,我公司将乐意接受你们的报价。

Ⅴ. Translate the Following Paragraphs into English
　　我们仔细研究了贵公司 9 月 18 日来函。贵公司与我公司业务往来多年,照理应该同意贵公司关于降低我产品价格,但困难不少。在过去四个月内原料成本上升很快,如按贵公司所提减价 20%,很难不影响产品的质量标准,而这不是我公司愿采取的做法。我们建议凡订单超 5 000 美元的,减价 15% 而不是 20%。这样做将不会因减价而影响货品质量。

Ⅵ. Try to write letters of quotation, offer and counter-offer according to the information given below.
1. 浙江盛辉公司(Shenghui Trading Co.)的 Frank Luo 收到美国 Sunshine Trading Co., Ltd. 的经理 Adam 初次询盘,并按其要求及时寄出商品目录和价目单,同时致谢对方的询盘,表达了希望与对方建立业务关系的愿望。
2. 美国客商在收到材料后,表示需求量较大,对其中三款角磨机(angle grinder)感兴趣,并寻问 Frank Luo 能否报 FOB 宁波价、最惠价、最低订货量等问题。三款角磨机型号分别为 AG105L, AG203S, AG880H,并希望寄送样品,费用自付。
3. 收到询盘后, Frank Luo 给美国客商寄送了样品,回复三款产品的报价为 Art No. AG105L: USD 25.30/PC FOB Ningbo; Art No. AG203S: USD 30.50/PC FOB Ningbo; Art No. AG880H: USD 13.00/PC FOB Ningbo。
4. 美国客商对样品很满意,但还是不能接受盛辉公司给出的优惠价,如果订购 5 000 套希望对方能再降 5%。
5. 在收到美国 Sunshine Trading Co., Ltd. 的还盘后,盛辉公司的 Frank Luo 表示商品单价不变,但为了合作,愿意给出 5% 折扣,同时提醒对方要抓住机会。
6. 美国客商感谢对方的退让,高兴地接受了修改后的报价。

Chapter 5
第 5 章

订购、接受和拒绝
Orders, Acceptances and Rejections

Learning Objectives

Enable the students to know the definitions of order, acceptance and contract; to be acquainted with the main components of the letters of order, acceptance and reject; to master typical sentences and expressions of this kind of letter and learn to write and fill different kinds of order form and contract.

使学生了解订购、接受和合约的定义；熟悉订购、接受、合约和拒绝信函的主要组成部分；掌握写作此类书信的典型句型和表达用语；学习撰写或填写不同类型的订购和接受订购的合约。

5.1 背景知识
Background Information

After inquiry, offer, repeat offer and counter-offer, under the agreement of both parties, the buyer will place an order, at this time, the transaction comes into a very important phase. Order is an instruction sent to supplier. It can be either the buyer's acceptance to offer, or directly order according to catalogue, price list and sample. In order to avoid mistakes, the content of ordering must be clear and correct. The buyer can use letter to order. However, many trade companies use printed formal order form in order to make sure no condition be omitted. If formal printed order form is used, a short complimenting letter often follows.

在经历了询盘、报价，以及反复多次的报盘、还盘后，在双方都同意的情况下，买方就会下订单，交易也到了非常重要的阶段。订购是向供货者发出的供货指示，既可以是买方对报盘的接受，也可以是买方根据目录、价格表和样品直接订购。为了确保所订购的产品无误，订购内容一定要准确清楚。买方可以用书信方式订购，但现在许多贸易公司都使用打印好的正规订单进行订购，以确保不会疏漏任何重要的条件。如订货时使用正规印刷订单，通常附寄一张简短问候信即可。

Letter about order always includes:

(1) Referring to the previous contact, acknowledge that you have accepted the offer;

(2) Give the description in great detail of your order:
- Name of goods, catalogue No. and sample No.;
- Price of goods, including unit price, total value;
- Quality requirement, grade, model name/ specification;
- Quantity of goods;
- Origin and material;
- Weight, dimensions, color and pattern;
- Packing and marking;
- Terms of payment;
- Delivery requirements, including place, date, mode of transport, whether the order will be carriage paid or carriage forward, etc.
- Documents such as bill of lading, commercial invoice, insurance policy, etc.
- Special points and others, for example, alternatives if goods required are not available.

(3) Expressing your good will in cooperation.

An acceptance or a confirmation is in fact an unreserved assent of the buyers or the sellers who, after mutual negotiation, are willing to enter into a contract or accordance with the terms and conditions agreed upon. There are many reasons for the sellers to reject the order. For example, price is too low, no stock, unacceptable delivery terms and so on. However, the seller should explain the reasons in his reply letter, expressing the regret and showing the hope for next cooperation. When receiving order, the seller should reply in time, and had better repeat terms of order, express good wills in the end and thanking for this order, and appreciate their orders.

Letters about acceptance usually include:

订购信函主要包括以下内容:

(1) 基于前次联系,告知你接受发盘;

(2) 详细描述你的订购:
- 商品名称、目录和样品编号;
- 产品价格包括单价和总价;
- 质量要求、品级、型号/规格;
- 商品数量;
- 原产地、使用材料;
- 重量、尺码、颜色和式样;
- 包装和标志;
- 付款条件;
- 送货须知,包括地点、日期、运输方式、运费到付还是运费付讫等;
- 货运单据,比如提货单、商业发票、保险单等;
- 特殊性能和其他注意事项,例如,如果所要的商品没有现货供应,是否同意以别的商品替代等。

(3) 表达你方希望合作的意愿。

接受或确认是受盘人在发盘的有效期内,无条件地同意发盘中提出的各项交易条件,愿意按这些条件和对方达成交易的表示。当然,一些情况下,卖方会因为一些原因拒绝订单。例如,价格太低,没有存货,不能接受的运货条款等。但是,在回执信里,卖方需要解释原因,表达歉意以及期待下一次的合作。收到订单要及时回复,最好在回复时重申订单条款,同时在结尾时表达良好的祝愿,称赞对方的订货是明智的;对这次惠顾表示感谢。

接受订单的信函内容包括以下几部分:

(1) Express pleasure at receiving the order;
(2) Add a favorable comment on the goods ordered;
(3) Ensure to attach importance to the order;
(4) Draw attention to other products;
(5) Hope for further orders.

Letter of rejecting including:

(1) Thanks for the orders;
(2) Reject the order and explain the reasons;
(3) Offer the substitute;
(4) Expectation to the reply.

A successful deal means it bases on the firm offer of the seller is accepted by the buyer, or a non-firm offer is confirmed by the seller under the buyer's acceptance. As a result, the contract is set up. But, in international business, as usual practice, after the agreement is made, it is necessary to sign the contract so as to clarify both parties' rights and obligations in written form. The business contract has two main functions: Firstly, it proves rights and obligations, especially for some deal made in oral. Secondly, it acts as regulations of transaction during the implement of transit. In China, the written contract mostly adopts two forms: one is official contract that has full-scale content and conditions such as import contract, purchase contract, export contract, and sales contract; the other one is simple contract, such as sales confirmation and purchase confirmation. Which one to use depends on the variety of the commodity, the relationship with your partner and your personal preference. If you make a small business with a familiar partner, the sales or purchase confirmation can replace the official contract. Although it is simple, sales or purchase confirmation has the same legal binding force.

（1）表达收到订单的喜悦；
（2）对订购的产品高度评价；
（3）保证重视订单；
（4）引起对其他商品的注意；
（5）期盼将来的订单。

拒绝订单的信函主要包括以下几部分：

（1）感谢订单；
（2）拒绝订单并说明原因；
（3）建议其他替代；
（4）期望回复。

交易成功建立在卖方的实盘被买方接受，或一个虚盘在买方确认接受后被卖方确认。在这种情况下，合同即告成立。但在国际贸易实务中，按照一般习惯做法，买卖双方达成协议后，通常还要制作书面合同将各自的权利和义务形式加以明确。合同在贸易中起到以下两个主要作用：第一，它是权利和义务的另一个证明，特别对于一些已经口头上达成协议的交易特别重要。第二，它在双方实施交易过程中起到条例作用。我国的贸易中，书面合同主要采用两种形式：一种是条款较完善、内容较全面的正式合同，如进口合同、购货合同、出口合同、销售合同；另一种是内容较简单的简式合同，如销售确认书、购货确认书。采用何种形式合同，要根据交易的商品种类、你与对方的关系和你个人的喜好。如果和一个熟悉的贸易商进行较小的贸易，可以使用购货或销售确认书来代替正式的合同。尽管较为简单，但购货或销售确认书具有相同的法律效力。

5.2 信例
Sample Letters

Letter 1　Placing an Order

P J ANGEL & CO. , LTD.

1989 Queen Street, Victoria, Brisbane, Australia

Tel: 12345578　Fax: 1233445

ORDER FORM

July 12, 2010

Order No. 123

To: America B H Clothing Corporation

Boston, America

Please supply:

Quantity	Item	Catalogue No.	Price	Subtotal
100	Skirt	12	$ 20.00 each	$ 2 000.00
100	Sweater	234	$ 100.00 each	$ 10 000.00
200	Trousers	456	$ 40.00 each	$ 8 000.00
			Sales tax	30%
			Shipping charge	$ 600.00
			Total	$ 26 600.00

Packing: Each set to be packed in a plastic bag, with a wooden case as an outer package.

Delivery: 15 days after receipt of L/C.

Insurance: W. P. A for 10% over the invoice amount.

Payment terms: By irrevocable letter of credit.

P J Angel & Co. Ltd
Jenny Brown
Manger

P J ANGEL & CO. , LTD.

1989 Queen Street, Victoria, Brisbane, Australia

America B H Clothing Corporation

Boston, America

Enclosed please find our order No. 123.

We would appreciate prompt shipment.

WITH COMPLIMENTS

Notes

1. place an order 下订单
   一般来说，在一封订购信里包括一个订购单，简洁地覆盖所需信息，订购单的内容不需要在信中重复。订货时使用正规印刷订单，通常情况下附寄一张简洁问候信即可。
   一般情况下，订单的基本内容根据需要可做相应修改，但是，现在仍有很多公司选择按自己的需要书写订单信函，因为有时有些事先印好的订单不是很合适或它们不能完全覆盖对方所需要的特殊信息。因此，了解一封订购信如何书写仍很重要。
2. Packing：Each set to be packed in a plastic bag, with a wooden case as an outer package. 包装：用塑料袋包装，外包装用木箱。
3. Delivery：15days after receipt of L/C. 交货：收到信用证15天内。
4. Insurance：W. P. A for 10% over the invoice amount. 保险：按超出发票金额10%投保水渍险。
5. Payment terms：By irrevocable letter of credit. 支付方式：不可撤销信用证。
6. Enclosed please find our order No. 123. 随函附上我方123号订单。

July 12, 2010

Re：Order No. 1234

Dear Qing Wang,

 Thank you so much for your letter of July 9 and the catalogues. Pursuant to our email since that date, we have decided to place an initial order as follows：

Item	Item No.	Color	Price ($)	Quantity	Subtotal ($)
Coat	123	Purple	120.00	100	12 000.00
		Brown	120.00	100	12 000.00
		Black	120.00	100	12 000.00
		Pink	125.00	100	12 500.00
Blouse	234	Blue print	16.00	200	3 200.00
Blouse	345	Red print	16.00	200	3 200.00
		Total		800	54 900.00

 We expect to find a good market for the above and hope to place further and large orders with you in the near future. Our usual terms of payment are D/P at 60 days and we hope they will be satisfactory to you. Meanwhile should you wish to make enquiries concerning our financial standing, you may refer to the following bank：ANZ bank 123 Queen street, Victoria, Brisbane, Australia.

 We look forward to a long and successful cooperation.

Yours faithfully,

Jenny Brown
Manager

Notes

1. pursuant to 根据
   We reaffirm the commitment of developed-country members to provide incentives to their enterprises and institutions to promote and encourage technology transfer to least-developed country members pursuant to Article 66.2. 根据第66.2条，我们重申发达国家成员向其本国企业和机构提供优惠措施来促进和鼓励向最不发达国家成员进行技术转让的承诺。
2. meanwhile = meantime 其间，其时

Letter 2　Acceptance

AMERICA BH CLOTHING CORPORATION
Boston, America

May 21, 2010

P J Angel & Co., Ltd.
　　1989 Queen Street, Victoria, Brisbane, Australia

Dear Madam,

　　We are pleased to receive your order No. 123 female clothes. We accepted the order and are enclosing you our Sales Confirmation No. 231 in duplicate of which please countersign and return on copy to us for our files. We trust you will open the relative L/C at early date.

　　As to skirt and sweater, we shall arrange delivery as soon as we receive your L/C, and for trousers we shall ship accordingly.

　　Hoping the goods will turn out to your entire satisfaction and we may have further orders from you.

Yours faithfully,

Notes

1. We accepted the order and are enclosing you our Sales Confirmation No. 231 in duplicate of which please countersign and return on copy to us for our files. 现随函附寄我方的231号销售合同一式两份，请会签并寄回一份给我方以便存档。
2. Hoping the goods will turn out to your entire satisfaction and we may have further orders from you. 希望货品能令贵方完全满意，同时也希望继续收到贵方订单。

Letter 3　Confirmation

Dear Sirs,

　　We hereby confirm having sold to you the under mentioned goods, subject to the terms stated below:

> Quantity: 2 000 dozens.
> Description: Wool Blanket our usual standard.
> Price: $ 200 per blanket CIF London.
> Shipment: Prompt shipment, sailing direct to port of destination, transhipment allowed.
> Payment: by an irrevocable letter of credit payable against presentation of shipping document.
> Insurance: insurance to be covered by us.
> No claim can be entertained unless made within 10 days of arrival of goods at the port of destination.
> Remark: Kindly sign and return one copy, each of the original and duplicate here is evidence of your acceptance.
>
> Yours faithfully,
>
> Encl: Enclosing a sales confirmation

Notes

1. We hereby confirm having sold to you the under mentioned goods, subject to the terms stated below. 我们确认向你们销售上述货物,并按下列条款签订合同。
2. No claim can be entertained unless made within 10 days of arrival of goods at the port of destination. 如果货物 10 天内抵达目的港,不接受索赔。
3. Kindly sign and return one copy, each of the original and duplicate here is evidence of your acceptance. 请会签并退回我方一份,每份原件和复印件均可证明你方已接受。

Letter 4　Sending the Contract

> Dear Sirs,
> 　　　　　　　　　　Re: Contract No. 1234
> 　　We are enclosing herewith the captioned contract in two originals, of which please return one copy to us duly countersigned for our records.
> 　　Thank you for your kind cooperation.
>
> Yours faithfully,

Notes

1. We are enclosing herewith the captioned contract in two originals, of which please return one copy to us duly countersigned for our records. 今寄上标题合同正本一式两份,会签后寄回一份,以便存档。
2. Thank you for your kind cooperation. 感谢贵方合作。

Letter 5 Failure to Supply

Dear Sirs,

Your Order No. 123

　　Referring to 2 000 dozens of dresses under your Order No. 123, we regret to tell you that we have no stock of the goods you required for the time being and do not expect further deliveries for at least another three months. Before then you may have been able to obtain the goods elsewhere, but if not we will revert to this matter as soon as our new supplies come up.

　　We are enclosing 2 copies of our catalogue covering all the articles available at present. If you need any of the items please inform us. We assure you that your requirement will receive our prompt attention at all times.

Yours sincerely,

Notes

1. We regret to tell you that we have no stock of the goods you required for the time being and do not expect further deliveries for at least another three months. 非常抱歉，贵方订购的货品我方时下无货，而且三个月之内不可能有新的进货。
2. But if not, we will revert to this matter as soon as our new supplies come up. 如果不能，我方愿意在有了新货之后重新考虑此订单。
3. We assure you that your requirement will receive our prompt attention at all times. 请相信，贵方的要求随时都会得到我方即时处理。

Tips 直接写作和间接写作

　　商务信函所传递的信息根据性质可以分为：正面或积极信息（positive message）、负面或拒绝信息（negative message）、说服性或者鼓动性信息（persuasive message）。

　　相应地在撰写信函时应该采用不同的策略和方法。传递正面信息时，可以开篇就切入主题，直接说明有关信息，或答复对方的要求，直截了当，给出积极回复后再做出相关的细节解释。传递负面信息或者说服性信息时要采用迂回策略，不要直接生硬地告知对方坏消息或否定部分的信息，而是在信函开始时提及与否定信息相关的客观因素，说明情况并解释原因，然后水到渠成地表达拒绝之意，以创造友好气氛，利于将来可能的合作。

5.3　有用的短语和句子
Useful Expressions

1. It is appreciated that you handed us your order No. 123 for 2 500 women's shirts. Enclosed is a copy of our Sales Note No. 45.

非常感谢贵方的 123 号订单向我们订购 2 500 件女式衬衫。随信附上我方的 45 号销售确认书一份。

2. Referring to your letter of January 15, we shall be obliged if you will forward to us the following at an early date.

已获悉贵方 1 月 15 日来信，如能及早发送以下货物将不胜感激。

3. We are delighted to receive your letter of August 20, and thank you for your esteemed order for...

非常高兴收到贵方 8 月 20 日来信，并感谢订购……

4. We have pleasure of placing the following order with you, and hope you kindly send by fast freight.

非常高兴向贵方订购以下商品，并希望贵方尽快发货。

5. Thank you very much for your order, but we are sorry that we are fully occupied with contract orders. As it is the case, we have no other alternative but to decline your order of this time. But we look forward to your future favors and attention.

非常感谢贵方的订单，但很抱歉，我们目前的合同订单已满。鉴于此，我们不得不婉拒贵方订单，并期盼贵方今后订单的惠顾。

6. Delivery will be made immediately on receipt of your letter of credit.

一旦收到贵方信用证明，立即发货。

7. With reference to your letter of December 4, we have pleasure in informing you that we have booked your order for 2 000 alarm clocks. We are sending you our S/C No. 100 in duplicate, one copy of which please sign and return for our file.

据贵方 12 月 4 日来信，我方很高兴通知贵方 2 000 台闹钟订单已确立，现送我方第 100 号售货合同一式两份，一份签字后寄回，以便我方保存。

8. We trust that this initial order will lead to further dealings between our two companies.

我们相信这第一笔订单会使我们两家公司之间的生意源源不断。

9. While thanking you for your order, we have to explain that without supplies we have to no alternative but to decline your order.

非常感谢贵方订单，需要说明的是，因无货源，我方只得取消贵方订单。

10. We thank you for your quotation and have noted the price and terms are acceptable, and we request you to put all items in hand as soon as possible.

感谢贵方报价，我们已经注意到价格及有关条款可接受，因此要求贵方尽快将所有货物发往我方。

11. Thank you for sending your catalogue and price list. We enclose the order form and would be grateful if you would send the goods as soon as possible.

感谢贵方寄来目录本和价目表。现随函寄去我们的订单，如贵方能尽早发来货物，我们将不胜感激。

12. If this first order is satisfactorily executed, we shall place further orders with you.

如果贵方首次订货圆满执行，贵方将有大量订货。

13. We enclose a trial order. If the quality is up to our expectation, we shall send further orders in the near future.

我方随附试订单，如贵方产品质量达到我方期望，不久将有大量订货。

14. I'm sure that our quotation is more favorable than any one you can receive from other sources.

    相信我方报价比贵方从他处能得到的任何报价都要优惠。

15. We cannot do more than a 2% reduction.

    我们至多降价2%。

16. If we had not thought of our long term business relationship, we wouldn't have made you a firm offer at this price.

    若不是我们有长期的业务关系，我们是不愿意以这个价格报实盘的。

17. We are sorry that we are unable to entertain any counter, offer, for this offer is firm, subject to the receipt of reply by us before December 21.

    很抱歉我方无法考虑任何还盘，因为这是一个实盘，并以12月21日以前收到我方回复为准。

18. For acceptance within 10 days.

    此报盘必须在10天之内接受有效。

19. We quote you our best prices for the following goods, and shall be pleased if you can favor us with your orders.

    在此就以下商品向贵公司报我方最低价，盼惠顾试购。

20. The quotation we offer you at exceptionally low prices are subject to reply by return of post.

    破例所提供的优惠报价，以贵方回信确认为准。

练习

Exercises

Ⅰ. Comprehension Questions

1. What should be included in an order letter?
2. What is the definition of order, acceptance and contract?
3. What should be included in an acceptance and contract?
4. Does an order have any restriction before the seller accepts it? If so, what are they?
5. What functions does contract have?

Ⅱ. Translating the Following Terms and Expressions

1. old hand   2. keep upright
3. bilateral trade   4. bilateral clearing
5. marine policy   6. 托收汇票
7. 收盘汇率   8. 出口信贷
9. 出口额   10. 书面证明

Ⅲ. Fill in the Blanks

We have _____ with thanks your _____ No. 369 of 8 July in confirmation of Indent A26 issued by your _____ house—Messrs Thomson Co., Ltd. .

We can _____ your order except for the first item Stainless Plates. Only yesterday we received from Messrs Thomson Co., Ltd. their amended Indent _____ which this item is excluded, _____ to the imposition of a new duty. You will soon hear _____ them on this subject.

Your _____ Order Sheet and the relative L/C at the earliest date will be _____ .

IV. Translating the Following Sentences

1. We are pleased to enclose herewith our contract No. 4567 in two originals for your counter-signature. Please send one copy back to us at your earliest convenience.
2. The conclusion of the dealing is certainly not the ending. It is only the beginning, and a good one, of the long and friendly business relations between us.
3. Please supply in assorted colors: preferably 6 dozens each of red, yellow, green, blue and brown.
4. Because we are already heavily burdened with the outstanding orders, it is impossible for us to accept new orders for delivery within this year.
5. We refer to our order No. 675 dated May 15. As we have, up till now, received no any information from you that goods have been sent, we have no alternative but to cancel this order.
6. 请按照贵方6月10日的报价和样品提供下列货物。
7. 由于最近各方对我们的传真机需求量很大，我们无法保证在11月30日前交付新订单。
8. 这批货物须在5月31日前及时运抵，以此为条件，我们订购此货，如延期交货，我们保留取消订单和拒绝提货的权利。
9. 由于货源难觅，我们别无选择，只得谢绝你们的订购。
10. 由于贵方没能在规定时间交货，我们只得取消订购。

V. Translate the Following Paragraphs into English

　　对这批订货，我方客户已同意分运，这样将促使你方可以从4~6月份分三个月装运。如贵方能按一定比例分月装运，而不是把100吨整批货物集中在同一个月内装运，将大大有利于我们的客户。有关的客户都是我市最大的食用油进口商，它们很可能在本月内将再次向你们订货。

VI. Translate the Following into Chinese

Dear Andy Burns

　　We have received your e-mail of Oct. 19, 2015. After the consideration, we have pleasure in confirming the following offer and accepting below:

　　Article No. DR2010 USD 19.00 CIF Toronto per set

　　Article No. DR2202 USD 23.80 CIF Toronto per set

　　Article No. DR2211 USD 30.00 CIF Toronto per set

　　Article No. DR2401 USD 23.50 CIF Toronto per set

　　We are pleased to accept your letter, price and other terms set out in. Number of orders for the NE0911 have been attached.

　　Look forward to more cooperation.

Best regards

附录 5A 订单
Appendix 5A Order

Number   124
Date: July 12, 2010
Salesperson: Andrew
Address: 123 Victoria Street, Queensland, Australia
Sold to: 1234 Five Avenue, New York, America   Shipped to: B H Corporation
Phone: 123456   Shipped by: Australia Clothing company

Quantity	Item/Description	Price/Item	Subtotal
123	Dresses	US $	US $

Sales Tax
Total
Shipping Charge
Amount Due

附录 5B 销售确认书
Appendix 5B Sales Confirmation

SALES CONFIRMATION

卖方 Seller:	××××× CO., LTD. Room 2901, HuaRong Mansion, GuanJiaQiao 85#, Shanghai 200005, P. R. China TEL: 021-4711363 FAX: 021-4691619	NO.: DATE: SIGNED IN:	DS2001SC205 Mar. 23, 2001 SHANGHAI, CHINA
买方 Buyer:	SAMAN AL-ABDUL KARIM AND PARTNERS CO. POB 13552, RIYADH 44166, KSA TEL: 4577301/4577312/4577313 FAX: 4577461		

经买卖双方同意成交下列商品，订立条款如下：
This contract is made by and agreed between the BUYER and SELLER, in accordance with the terms and conditions stipulated below:

唛头 Marks and Numbers	名称及规格 Description of goods	数量 Quantity	单价 Unit Price	金额 Amount
				CFR DAMMAM PORT, SAUDI ARABIA
N/M	CANNED APPLE JAM 24 TINS X 340 GMS	2 200CARTONS	USD 6.80	USD 14 960.00
	CANNED STRAWBERRY JAM 24 TINS X 340 GMS	2 200CARTONS	USD 6.80	USD 14 960.00
	Total:	4 400CARTONS		USD 29 920.00

总值 TOTAL U.S. DOLLAR TWENTY NINE THOUSAND NINE HUNDRED AND TWENTY ONLY.

Transhipment（转运）：
☑ Allowed（允许）　　□ not allowed（不允许）
Partial shipments（分批装运）：
☑ Allowed（允许）　　□ not allowed（不允许）
Shipment date（装运期）：
Jun. 05, 2001
Insurance（保险）：
　　由_____按发票金额110%投保_____险，另加保_____险至_____为止。
to be covered by the _____ FOR 110% of the invoice value covering _____ additional _____ from _____ to _____ .
Terms of payment（付款条件）：
□ 买方不迟于_____年_____月_____日前将100%的货款用即期汇票/电汇送抵卖方。
The buyers shall pay 100% of the sales proceeds through sight (demand) draft/by T/T remittance to the sellers not later than _____ .
□ 买方须于_____年_____月_____日前通过_____银行开出以卖方为受益人的不可撤销_____天即期信用证，并注明在上述装运日期后_____天内在中国议付有效，信用证须注明合同编号。
The buyers shall issue an irrevocable L/C at _____ sight through _____ in favor of the sellers prior to _____ indicating L/C shall be valid in China through negotiation within _____ day after the shipment effected, the L/C must mention the Contract Number.
□ 付款交单：买方应对卖方开具的以买方为付款人的见票后_____天付款跟单汇票，付款时交单。
Documents against payment (D/P): The buyers shall duly make the payment against documentary draft made out to the buyers at _____ sight by the sellers.
□ 承兑交单：买方应对卖方开具的以买方为付款人的见票后_____天承兑跟单汇票，承兑交单。
Documents against acceptance (D/A): The buyers shall duly accept the documentary draft made out to the buyers at _____ days by the sellers.

Documents required（单据）：

卖方应将下列单据提交银行议付/托收。

The sellers shall present the following documents required for negotiation/collection to the banks.

☐ 整套正本清洁提单。
   Full set of clean on Board Ocean Bills of Lading.

☐ 商业发票一式 _____ 份。
   Signed commercial invoice in _____ copies.

☐ 装箱单或重量单一式 _____ 份。
   Packing list/weight memo in _____ copies.

☐ 由 _____ 签发的质量与数量证明书一式 _____ 份。
   Certificate of quantity and quality in _____ copies issued by _____ .

☐ 保险单一式 _____ 份。
   Insurance policy in _____ copies.

☐ 由 _____ 签发的产地证一式 _____ 份。
   Certificate of Origin in _____ copies issued by _____ .

Shipping advice（装运通知）：

一旦装运完毕，卖方应即电告买方合同号、商品号、已装载数量、发票总金额、毛重、运输工具名称及启运日期等。

The sellers shall immediately, upon the completion of the loading of the goods, advise the buyers of the Contract No, names of commodity, loaded quantity, invoice values, gross weight, names of vessel and shipment date by TLX/FAX.

Inspection and Claims（检验与索赔）：

1. 卖方在发货前由 _____ 检验机构对货物的品质、规格和数量进行检验，并出具检验证明书。

The buyers shall have the qualities, specifications, quantities of the goods carefully inspected by the _____ Inspection Authority, which shall issue Inspection Certificate before shipment.

2. 货物到达目的口岸后，买方可委托当地的商品检验机构对货物进行复检。如果发现货物有损坏、残缺或规格、数量与合同规定不符，买方须于货到目的口岸的 _____ 天内凭 _____ 检验机构出具的检验证明书向卖方索赔。

The buyers have right to have the goods inspected by the local commodity inspection authority after the arrival of the goods at the port of destination if the goods are found damaged/short/their specifications and quantities not in compliance with that specified in the contract, the buyers shall lodge claims against the sellers based on the Inspection Certificate issued by the Commodity Inspection Authority within _____ days after the goods arrival at the destination.

3. 如买方提出索赔，凡属品质异议须于货到目的口岸之起 _____ 天内提出；凡属数量异议须于货到目的口岸之日起 _____ 天内提出。对货物所提任何异议应由保险公司、运输公司或邮递机构负责的，卖方不负任何责任。

The claims, if any regarding to the quality of the goods, shall be lodged within _____ days after arrival of the goods at the destination, if any regarding to the quantities of the goods, shall be lodged within _____ days after arrival of the goods at the destination. The sellers shall not take any responsibility if any claims concerning the shipping goods is up to the responsibility of Insurance Company/Transportation Company/Post Office.

Force majeure（人力不可抗力）：

如因人力不可抗力的原因造成本合同全部或部分不能履约，卖方概不负责，但卖方应将上述发生的情况及时通知买方。

The sellers shall not hold any responsibility for partial or total non-performance of this contract due to Force Majeure. But the sellers advise the buyers on time of such occurrence.

Disputes settlement（争议的解决方式）：

凡因执行本合约或有关本合约所发生的一切争执，双方应协商解决。如果协商不能得到解决，应提交仲裁。仲裁地点在被告方所在国内，或者在双方同意的第三国。仲裁裁决是终局的，对双方都有约束力，仲裁费用由败诉方承担。

All disputes in connection with this contract of the execution thereof shall be amicably settled through negotiation. In case no amicable settlement can be reached between the two parties, the case under dispute shall be submitted to arbitration, which shall be held in the country where the defendant resides, or in third country agreed by both parties. The decision of the arbitration shall be accepted as final and binding upon both parties. The Arbitration Fees shall be borne by the losing party.

Law application（法律适用）：

本合同的签订地，或发生争议时货物所在地在中华人民共和国境内或被诉人为中国法人的，适用中华人民共和国法律，除此规定外，适用《联合国国际货物销售公约》。

It will be governed by the law of the People's Republic of China under the circumstances that the contract is signed or the goods while the disputes arising are in the People's Republic of China or the defendant is Chinese legal person, otherwise it is governed by Untied Nations Convention on Contract for the International Sale of Goods.

本合同使用的价格术语系根据国际商会《国际贸易术语解释通则1990》。

The terms in the contract based on INCOTERMS 1990 of the International Chamber of Commerce.

Versions（文字）：

本合同中、英两种文字具有同等法律效力，在文字解释上，若有异议，以中文解释为准。

This contract is made out in both Chinese and English of which version is equally effective. Conflicts between these two languages arising therefrom, if any, shall be subject to Chinese version.

本合同共 _____ 份，自双方代表签字（盖章）之日起生效。

This contract is in copies, effective since being singed/sealed by both parties.

The Buyer	The Seller
SAMAN AL-ABDUL KARIM AND PARTNERS CO.	××××× CO., LTD.

附录 5C 原产地证明书
Appendix 5C Certificate of Origin

CERTIFICATE OF ORIGIN

Shipper/exporter (name and address including zip code): Baking Technologies, Inc. 45 South 7th Street Minneapolis, MN 55402	*Booking/shipment number*: FYF101	*B/L or AWB number*: MXVZ 9707503
	Export references: Baking Technologies, Inc. quote number BT 10102 Mendez Panaderias S. A. purchase number M 3652	
Consignee (name and address): Mendez Panaderias S. A. Col. Roma Mexico D. F., C. P. 06760	*Forwarding agent (name and address - references)*: Yellow Freight 12400 Dupont Avenue South Burnsville, MN 55337	
Intermediate consignee/notify party (name and address): Galfiro Montemayor Avenida de Colombia 1025 Veracruz, Mexico	*Point (state and country) of origin*: MN, U. S.	
	Domestic routing / export instructions: Yellow Freight Minneapolis, MN to Houston, TX	
Pre-carriage by: Yellow Freight	*Place of receipt*: Minneapolis, MN	
Exporting carrier: American President Line	*Port of loading/export*: Houston, Texas	*Transportation method*: Ocean Vessel
Foreign port of unloading (vessel and air only): Veracruz, Mexico	*Place of delivery by on-carrier*: Mexico, D. F., C. P. 06760	*Containerized (vessel only)*: ☒ YES ☐ NO

Container No. / Seal No. / Marks and Numbers:	Number of Packages:	Description of commodities, Model/Serial number, harmonized number	Gross weight (kg):	Measurement
Model BT002043 Addressed and Numbered 1 of 4...	4 Crates	Baking/Kneading Equipment Tariff Classification 8438. 10	2 722	1 680 Cubic Feet

The undersigned _____ (Owner or Agent), does hereby declare for the above named shipper, the goods as described on the above date and consigned as indicated and are products of the United States of America. Dated at _____ on the _____ day of _____, _____.

Sworn to before me this _____ day of _____, _____. _____ (Signature of Owner or Agent)

The _____, a recognized Chamber of Commerce under the laws of the State of _____, has examined the manufacturer's invoice or shipper's affidavit concerning the origin of the merchandise, and, according to the best of its knowledge, finds that the products named originated in the United States of America.

Secretary,
_____

Chapter 6 第 6 章

付 款 条 件
Terms of Payment

Learning Objectives

Enable the students to know the definition and function of international business payment, and the definition and kinds of bills of exchange, promissory notes and checks; to be familiar with the definition, parties and kinds of remittance, collection and letter of credit; to master the skills of writing the letters of urging to establish, amend, and extend letter of credit.

使学生了解国际贸易货款支付的定义和作用,汇票、本票与支票的含义和种类;熟悉汇付与托收的含义、当事人和种类,以及信用证含义、当事人及信用证支付货款种类;掌握催开、修改与展延信用证信函的写作与基本用语。

6.1 背景知识
Background Information

In international business, payment is very complicated. It means the settlement of debts or the transfer of currency. International payment usually involves in payment instrument, payment methods, and payment time and place, which have great influence on the currency safe transfer.

The main instrument of international payment is financial document that is a written debt voucher with fixed form. It includes fixed value and date, and can be used to get money from drawer or specific drawee. Financial documents used in international trade primarily include bill of exchange, promissory note and check, among which bill of exchange is popularly used. Bills of exchange is a bill signed by the drawer, requiring the entrusted payer to make unconditional payment of certain sum of money on

在国际贸易中,货款结算通常非常复杂,货款结算意味着债务清偿或转移资金。国际贸易货款结算一般涉及支付工具、支付方式和支付时间及地点,它们在很大程度上影响货币的安全周转。

国际结算的主要工具是票据,它是具有一定格式的书面债据,上面载明一定的金额与日期,持票人可根据此向发票人或指定付款人支取款项。票据有汇票、本票、支票,其中汇票最常被使用。汇票是出票人签发的委托付款人在见票时或者在指定日期无条件支付确定的金额给收款人或者持

demand or at a fixed date to the payee or the bearer. It can be classified into: banker's draft and commercial draft according to the drawer, sight draft and time draft according to the tenor; clean draft and documentary draft according to whether there are documents attached. A promissory note is an unconditional promise in writing made by the maker to the payee or the holder signed by the maker engaging to pay on demand or at a fixed or determinable future time a sum certain in money to or to the order of a specified person or the bearer. A check is an unconditional order in writing addressed by the customer (drawer) to a bank signed by that customer authorizing the bank to pay on demand a sum certain in money to or to the order of a specified person or bearer.

Term of payment in international settlement refers to the way used to settle debt and liability between individuals, enterprises, and groups in different country. It has three major of payment methods: remittance, collection, and letter of credit. Remittance especially in international trade refers to the importer remits money to the exporter on his initiative through a bank according to the terms and time stipulated in the contract. Generally, it is mostly used in payment in advance, commission payment, sample fee payment, prepayment, performance bond, and compensation and so on.

The parties in remittance generally involve in remitter, payee, remitting bank, and paying bank. There are three kinds of remittance: mail transfer (M/T), telegraphic transfer (T/T) and demand draft (D/D). M/T refers to importer send the fee of goods to the local bank, and this remitting bank issues a trust deed for payment, then sends it to paying bank by mail, and entrusts the latter to notify and pay a certain amount of money to payee. T/T is the remitting bank, at the request of the remitter, transfers funds by means of cable/telex/swift message to the paying bank, asking the latter to pay a certain sum of money to the beneficiary. D/D refers to the remitting bank, at the request of the remitter, draws a bill of exchange to the paying bank, ordering the latter to pay on demand a certain sum of money to the beneficiary who will

票人的票据。按不同的出票人可分为银行汇票与商业汇票，同时按到期日的不同，又可分为即期汇票与远期汇票，还有根据是否附有跟单，分为光票和跟单汇票。本票是一个人向另一个人签发的保证即期或定期（可以确定的将来时间），对某人或其指定人或持票人付一定金额的无条件书面承诺。支票是活期存款的存户对银行发出的一种支付通知。委托办理支票存款的银行或其他金融机构在见票时无条件支付确定金额给收款人或持票人的票据。

国际结算的支付方式是指以一定的形式与条件，实现不同国家的个人、企业、团体间为债权债务的清算所用的方式。它有三种基本方式：汇付、托收、信用证。在国际贸易中，汇付是指一国的进口商根据合同的条款及时间通过银行将款项支付给出口商。一般在预付货款、支付佣金、支付样品费、代垫费用、履约保证金及赔款等方面用得较多。

汇付的当事人一般涉及汇款人、收款人、汇出行和汇入行。最通常的汇款方式有信汇、电汇与票汇三种。信汇（M/T）是由进口人将货款交给所在地银行，由该行用信件委托出口人所在地银行把贷款付给收款人。电汇（T/T）由汇付银行应汇款人的要求通过电报、电传等方式通知付款行将资金付给受益人。票汇（D/D）指汇付行应汇款人的要求向付款银行开具汇票，要求后者在见票后将款项付给受益人，即汇票的收款人。无论哪种汇付方式，货运单据都是由出口人直接

also be payee of the draft. Whatever kinds of remittance, the document is always sent to the importer directly by the exporter, and bank does not involve in. In international business, the remittance generally involves in payment in advance, cash with order, cash on delivery, and open account trade.

Collection means the handling by banks of financial documents and/or commercial documents, in accordance with instructions received, in order to obtain payment and/or acceptance, or deliver documents against payment and/or against acceptance, or deliver documents on other terms and conditions. The parties in collection refer to principal, remitting bank, collecting bank, presenting bank, and drawee. Collection can be classified into clean collection and documentary collection. Clean collection means collection of financial document not accompanied by commercial documents. Depending on difference of conditions of payment, documentary collection can be divided into document against payment (D/P) and documents against acceptance (D/A).

D/P means: the collecting bank releases the title right and other shipping documents to the importer subject to payment. According to difference of time, it can be divided into D/P at sight and D/P after sight. D/P at sight requests importer immediately pay money to get document. D/P after sight allows that importer is given a certain period to make payment at 30, 45, or 60 days after presentation of documents, but he is not allowed to get hold of the documents until he pays. D/A calls for delivery of documents against acceptance of the draft drawn by the exporter. D/A is always after sight. Payment by collection is not always safe, especially D/A.

Letter of credit is a written undertaking by the issuing bank (the agent for the importer) to the beneficiary (the exporter), under which the bank undertakes to pay the beneficiary a sum certain in money within a designated time period and against any stipulated terms and documents. In international business, irrevocable letter of credit is most popular form of L/C. It cannot be amended

自行寄给进口人，银行并不接手。在国际贸易中，汇付方式通常运用于预付货款、随订单付现、交货付现和记账交易这些业务中。

托收是指银行根据所收到的指示，对金融票据或商业票据的处理，以便取得贷款或承兑，或付款交单，或承兑交单，或按其他条件交付单据。托收业务通常要涉及委托人、汇出行、托收银行、提示银行、付款人。托收分光票托收和跟单托收。光票托收是指出口人（出票人）开具汇票，不附随任何货运单据托收。跟单托收根据交单条件不同分为付款交单（D/P）和承兑交单（D/A）。

付款交单是指代收行在收到进口方货款后，将汇票及所附的货运单据交付给进口方。按时间不同，分为即期付款交单和远期付款交单。即期付款交单要求进口商立即付款获得单据，而在远期付款交单情况下，允许进口商在见单后一段时间，如30天、45天或60天付款，只有当他付款后，他方能获得单据。承兑交单要求买方凭书面承兑出口商开来的汇票获得各类票据，承兑交单总是远期付款。托收付款并非永远可靠，尤其是承兑交单。

信用证是指出开证行（进口商的代理）出具给受益人（出口商）的书面保证，确保在指定的时间，凭规定的单据和条款向受益人付款。在国际贸易中，不可撤销信用证的使用最为广泛。未经信用证有关当事人的一致同意，

or cancelled without prior mutual consent of all parties to the credit. Such a letter of credit guarantees payment by the bank to the seller as long as the terms and conditions of the credit have been met. From different angles, L/C can be divided into clean L/C and documentary L/C, revocable L/C and irrevocable L/C, and confirmed L/C and unconfirmed L/C. The parties in L/C include opener, issuing bank, advising bank, beneficiary, negotiating bank, and paying bank.

The main content of L/C includes

(1) Illustration of L/C itself, such as L/C's kinds, nature, value, time of validity, location and so on;

(2) Request for the goods. The name of goods, specification, quantity, packing, price and so on;

(3) Request for transport. The due date of shipping, shipment place and destination place, terms of shipping, allowing or prohibiting transhipment or partial shipment and so on;

(4) Request for documents, including three kinds of documents as follows:

①Goods documents (commercial invoice as a center, including packing list, quantity list, certificate of origin, inspection certificate and so on)

②Transport documents (bill of lading, which is an evidence of an agent of authority of goods)

③Insurance documents

Except above three documents, other documents may be required, such as sample certificate and copy of shipping advice;

(5) Special clauses, making different stipulations according to the change of political and trade conditions in importing countries and the needs of a specific transaction;

(6) The obligation sentences made by the issuing bank on guaranteeing to make payment provided the documents.

From the 2 to 5 condition, they all need to be showed

开证行不得撤销信用证或修改信用证的内容。只要受益人提供的单证符合信用证规定，开证行必须履行付款义务。信用证根据不同的角度分为：光票信用证和跟单信用证；可撤销信用证和不可撤销信用证；保兑信用证和不保兑信用证。信用证一般的当事人有开证申请人、开证银行、通知银行、受益人、议付银行和付款银行。

信用证的主要内容：

（1）对信用证本身的说明，如信用证的种类、性质、金额及其有效期和地点等；

（2）对货物的要求，如货物的名称、品种规格、数量、包装、价格等；

（3）对运输的要求，如装运的期限、起运地和目的地、运输方式、可否分批装运和可否中途转运等；

（4）对单据的要求，这主要分三类：

①货物单据（以商票为中心，包括装箱单、数量单、产地证、商检证明书等）

②运输单据（提单，这是代理货物所有权的证据）

③保险单据

除上述三种单据外，也可能需要其他单证证明，如寄样证明、装运通知副本等；

（5）特殊要求。根据进口国政治经济、贸易情况的变化或每一笔具体业务的需要，可以做出不同规定；

（6）开证行对受益人及汇票持有人保证付款的责任。

第（2）～（5）各项要求，都

in document provided by beneficiary (exporter), and make sure be same as conditions of L/C.

Payment by L/C usually goes through the following procedure:

(1) The importer applies to his local bank to open L/C in favor of the exporter;

(2) The importer's bank issues an L/C and sends it to its branches or correspondent banks in exporter's place;

(3) The exporter's bank checks the L/C of issuing bank received, and forwards the L/C to the exporter;

(4) The exporter effects shipment according to the L/C and prepares all shipping documents and the draft. He presents them to his local bank within the validity period for negotiation. The negotiating bank verifies the draft and documents, and makes payment to the exporter;

(5) The advising bank sends the draft and documents to the issuing bank to ask for payment;

(6) The issuing bank gets draft and documents, then sends them to importer;

(7) The issuing bank is called as the paying bank now, which sends money to advising bank;

(8) After the advising bank receives money, he sends it to the exporter.

要在受益人（出口人）所提供的单据中表示出来，并做到与信用证条款完全一致。

信用证一般经过以下支付程序：

(1) 进口商要求其当地银行开立以出口商为受益人的信用证；

(2) 进口商银行开立信用证，并将其寄给出口商国家的往来银行或其分行；

(3) 出口商银行审查完开证行的信用证后将其递交给出口商；

(4) 出口商根据信用证进行装运并准备汇票及所有的装运单据，然后把汇票和装运单据在有效时间内递交通知行要求议付，议付行验证汇票及单证，付款给出口方；

(5) 通知行把汇票及装运单据寄给开证行要求支付；

(6) 开证行收到汇票及装运单据后把它们递交给进口商；

(7) 开证行（此时被称为付款行）把货款汇给通知行；

(8) 通知行收到货款后交给出口商。

6.2 信例
Sample Letters

Letter 1 Establishment of Letter of Credit

Dear Sirs,

Re: Your Order No. 123 for Dresses

With reference to our faxes dated the 5th of February and 10th of March, requesting you to establish the L/C covering the above mentioned order, we regret having received no news from you up till now.

> We wish to remind you that it was agreed, when placing the order, that you would establish the required L/C upon receipt of our confirmation. Needless to say, we are placed in a very embarrassing situation now that one month has elapsed and nothing whatsoever has been heard from you. As goods have been ready for shipment for quite some time, it behoves you to take immediate action, particularly since we cannot think of any valid reason for further delay of opening the credit.
>
> We look forward to receiving your favorable response at an early date.
>
> Yours faithfully,

Notes

1. establish 开立
   开立信用证，最普通的说法是 open an L/C，正式说法是：establish an L/C，从银行角度说是 issue an L/C。
2. L/C 信用证
   confirmed, irrevocable L/C 保兑的、不可撤销的信用证　　transferable L/C 可转让的信用证
   documentary L/C 跟单信用证　　clean letter of credit 光票信用证
   sight credit 即期信用证　　time/ usance credit 远期信用证
   anticipatory L/C 预支信用证　　packing credit 打包贷款
   deferred payment credit 延期付款信用证
3. With reference to our faxes dated the 5th of February and 10th of March, requesting you to establish the L/C covering the above mentioned order, we regret having received no news from you up till now. 参阅我方2月5日和3月10日的传真，要求贵方开立有关标题订单的信用证。非常遗憾，直到目前我方仍没有收到任何信息。
4. needless to say 不用说
5. embarrassing situation 尴尬的境地
6. whatsoever = whatever 任何
7. behove（主语用 it）对（某人）来说应该（做）
8. As goods have been ready for shipment for quite some time, it behoves you to take immediate action, particularly since we cannot think of any valid reason for further delay of opening the credit. 由于货物早已备妥待装，所以贵方应立即采取措施。我方尤其难以想象贵方还能有何正当理由推迟开立信用证。

Letter 2　Amendment of Letter of Credit

> Dear Sirs,
>
> We acknowledge your L/C No. 234 covering your order for 2 000 dozens of dresses. On examination, we have found some discrepancies from our S/C. Please make the following amendments without the least possible delay:

> 1. Allow partial shipment and transhipment and delete the clause "by direct steamer".
> 2. Increase the amount of your L/C by $ 200.
> 3. There is no word "about" before the quantity and amount in the L/C, although the word is clearly used before them in our S/C.
> 4. Your L/C stipulates the proportion of goods in an assortment of Type A, B, C is 20%, 40%, 40% respectively. But the assortment contracted for is Types A 30%, B 30%, and C 40%.
>
> We hope that in future you will establish your L/C exactly according to the terms and conditions of the relevant sales confirmation. By so doing you will not only save much trouble, but also help us facilitate shipment of your products.
>
> We are waiting your bank's credit amendment.
>
> Sincerely,

Notes

1. on examination 当检查时
2. discrepancy 差异，不符，与 difference 同义，但前者多用于书面语
3. S/C Sales confirmation 的缩写，销售确认书
4. On examination of the L/C, we have found some discrepancies from our S/C. 经检查，发现贵方信用证有些地方与销售确认书不符。
5. Allow partial shipment and transhipment and delete the clause "by direct steamer". 允许部分装运和转船，删去"由直达船装运"的条款。
6. the terms and conditions 条件（商业上表示贸易条件和合同条款的习惯总称。）
7. We hope that in future you will establish your L/C exactly according to the terms and conditions of the relevant sales confirmation. 我们希望将来贵方能完全按照相关销售确认书的条款开立信用证。
8. By so doing you will not only save much trouble, but also help us facilitate shipment of your products. 这样，不仅可以省去许多麻烦，而且有助于我们及时装运贵方所需货物。

Letter 3　Extension of L/C

> Dear Sirs,
>
> We thank you for your L/C for the captioned goods. We are regretful that owing to some delay on the part of our supplier at the point of origin, we are not able to get the goods ready before the end of this month. As a result, we sent you an e-mail yesterday.
>
> It is expected that the consignment will be ready for shipment in the early part of April and we are arranging to ship it on S. S. "PEACH" from "Lian Yungang" on or about 10th April.

This being the case, we have to ask you to extend the date of shipment to 25th April, under advice to us by fax.

Faithfully,

Notes

1. owning 未付的，欠着的
   large sum still owing 尚未偿付的大笔款项
   owning to 由于
   Owning to our joint efforts the transaction has been eventually concluded. 由于我们共同努力，这笔交易终于达成了。
2. It is expected that the consignment will be ready for shipment in the early part of April and we are arranging to ship it on S. S. "PEACH" from " Lian Yungang" on or about 10th April. 期望货物能在 4 月初装运，我们正在安排驶往贵港的货轮"桃子"号，计划在 4 月 10 日左右从连云港起航。
3. This being the case, we have to ask you to extend the date of shipment to 25th April, under advice to us by fax. 既然如此，我方只好请贵方将装运日期延至 4 月 25 日，并用传真通知我方。

Letter 4　Payment by D/A

Dear Sirs,

We have received with many thanks your letter of 13th April, which give us a competitive and reasonable quotation.

We are pleased to accept your quotation and do business with you. However, after long years of satisfactory cooperation, we are surprised that you still demand D/P. So we wish to draw your attention to the term of payment, and we fell that we are entitled to easier and more convenient terms. Most of our suppliers have been drawing on us by their documentary draft at 30 days sight on D/A basis. We should be grateful if you could make out draft for payment 30 days after sight, and the documents will be handed to us on acceptance.

We hope to work with you for a longer time and look forward to hearing from you.

Faithfully,

Notes

Most of our suppliers have been drawing on us by their documentary draft at 30 days sight on D/A basis. We should be grateful if you could make out draft for payment 30 days after sight, and the documents will be handed to us on acceptance. 多数供应商都是按照 30 天承兑交单向我方开出跟单汇票，如果贵方愿意接受见票后 30 天付款，承兑交单，我方将不胜感激。

Letter 5　Refusing Payment by D/A

Dear Sirs,

Subject: Your proposal for making payment by D/A

We were glad to learn from your letter of May 15 that you are interested in Smart Choice. We also noticed that you wish to make payment by D/A.

We have considered your proposal but regret to say that we cannot accept it, as we do not have sufficient credit information to offer you D/A terms at present. However in order to help you push the sales of our new product, we are prepared to accept payment by D/P at sight. This is the best thing we can do.

We have already concluded business with several buyers from Europe and North America. We are pleased to inform you that Smart Choice is getting popular on the market. We have even received some repeat orders. We hope this will encourage you to place an order with us.

We are looking forward to receiving your order soon.

Yours faithfully,

Notes

We do not have sufficient credit information to offer you D/A terms at present. 目前我方没有足够的信用信息向你方提供 D/A 付款条件。

Tips

1. SWIFT 信用证简介

SWIFT 又称"环球银行金融电信协会"，是国际银行同业间的国际合作组织，成立于 1973 年，目前全球大多数国家的大多数银行使用 SWIFT 系统。SWIFT 的使用，使银行的结算提供了安全、可靠、快捷、标准化、自动化的通信业务，从而大大提高了银行的结算速度。由于 SWIFT 的格式具有标准化，目前信用证的格式主要用 SWIFT 电文。

根据国际商会所制定的电信信用证格式设计，利用 SWIFT 网络系统设计的特殊格式，通过 SWIFT 网络系统传递的信用证的信息，即通过 SWIFT 开立或通知的信用证称为 SWIFT 信用证，也称为"环球电信信用证"。凡采用 SWIFT 信用证，必须遵守 SWIFT 使用手册的规定，使用 SWIFT 手册规定的代号（tag）。目前开立 SWIFT 信用证的格式代号为 MT 700 和 MT 701。

2. 收到客户发来的汇款凭证，是否可以邮寄或电放提单

最好不要。保险起见，还是等货款到账后再安排。因为银行的凭证未必是真实的，客户可以造假，或故意安排一笔款项。在一些细节故意写错一些信息，比如 SWIFT 号，或者公司名跟地址对应不上等。银行收到电汇申请后，审核发现问题，就会退回款项。所以跨国交易要特别注意收款安全，如果款项没有到账，仅仅凭借对方的一份银行凭证，是不可以提供提单的。

3. 几种常用支付方式的比较

预付款（advance payment）：采用预付款的方式即在合同签订或订货的时候，进口商就按约定的方式，一般是通过银行，向出口商支付全部货款。预付款对于出口企业来说是一种极为安全的做法。出口企业可以在第一时间收到款项，盘活资金。但是对于进口企业来说就要承担较大的风险。因为它们在支付货款之后能否收到与合同相符的货物就不得而知了。这很大一部分取决于出口企业的商业信用。因此这种付款方式的使用范围较窄，大多用于那些小额交易或订造货品。

跟单信用证（documentary credit）：开证行凭跟单汇票或单纯凭单据付款的信用证。它是进口商要求银行（开证行）签发的文件，证明银行承诺在出口商的商品符合跟单信用证具体规定的情况下，向出口商支付指定金额。这里所包含的单据主要是指代表货物或证明货物已交运的运输单据，如提单、铁路运单、航空运单等。通常还包括发票、保险单等商业单据。

跟单托收（documentary collections）：出口商如要在收款之前或获得付款的承诺前保留对货物的控制权，可安排跟单托收。其基本做法是出口商先行发货，然后备妥包括运输单据（通常是海运提单）在内的货运单据并开出汇票，把全套跟单汇票交出口地银行（托收行），委托其通过进口地的分行或代理行（代收行）向进口方收取货款。

相比信用证，付款交单（D/P）、承兑交单（D/A）等付款方式实际采用的较少。主要是由于这两种付款方式属于商业信用，即出口商能否收到货款，完全取决于进口商的信用。进口商能否按时、按质、按量收到货物也取决于出口商的信用。对于信用好的进口商，一般不会出现不付货款的现象。但是遇到信用差的进口商，常常发生拖欠或拒付货款的现象。因此，这两种付款方式多用于信誉较好的进出口商。

记账（open account）：记账又称专户记账。出口商将货物装运出口后，即将货运单据交付给进口商，货款则借记进口商账户，然后按约定的期限，定期进行结算。结算时既可规定由进口商将账款通过银行汇款给出口商，也可规定由出口商开具汇票向进口商收款。

实质上记账是一种赊销交易。出口商要在交货若干时日后才能收回货款，所承担的风险较大，一般也难于向银行取得资金融通。所以这种方式多半应用于出口商与其分支机构或有特殊关系的客户之间的贸易。

6.3 有用的短语和句子

Useful Expressions

1. Common used phrases about terms of payment 支付条款常用词组

   financial document 金融票据
   certificate of creditor's right 债权凭证
   sight draft 即期汇票
   banker's draft 银行汇票
   documentary draft 跟单汇票
   promissory note 本票

   negotiable instrument 可转让票据
   bill of exchange 汇票
   time draft 远期汇票
   commercial draft 商业汇票
   commercial document 商业单据
   remitting bank 汇出行

paying bank 汇入行	mail transfer 信汇
trust deed（信汇）委托书	telegraphic transfer 电汇
demand draft 票汇	banker's demand draft 银行即期汇票
remitting bank 托收银行	collecting bank 代收银行
presenting bank 提示银行	drawee 付款人
issuing bank 开证银行	advising bank 通知银行
beneficiary 受益人	negotiating bank 议付银行
paying bank 付款银行	Irrevocable Letter of Credit 不可撤销的信用证
Confirmed Letter of Credit 保兑信用证	Transferable Letter of Credit 可转让信用证
Sight Letter of Credit 即期信用证	Usance（Term, Time）Letter of Credit 远期信用证
Anticipatory Letter of Credit 预支信用证	Revolving Letter of Credit 循环信用证
Documentary Letter of Credit 跟单信用证	Clean Credit 光票信用证

2. We will open the L/C upon receipt of your reply.
   待收到贵方答复后立即开立信用证。

3. In spite of our respected requests, still we have not received your letter of credit up to now. Please open the credit immediately, otherwise, we cannot effect shipment in January.
   尽管再三催请开证，信用证仍未收到，请立即开证，否则不能在 1 月交货。

4. Your L/C No. 1234 calls for shipment in two equal monthly lots while S/C No. 2345 stipulates shipment in a single lot to be made not later than 1st July. Please amend accordingly.
   第 1234 号信用证规定两批装运，每月一次，每次数量相等，而 2345 号合同规定 7 月 1 日前一次装运，请对信用证做相应修改。

5. Because of the recent fire in the factory, all the stocks were destroyed. In this case, we cannot make shipment as arranged before. Please extend the date of shipment and the expiry date of L/C No. 1234 to 23rd March and 12th April respectively.
   由于最近工厂发生的火灾烧毁了全部库存，已不能按照原安排交货。请将 1234 号信用证交货期和有效期分别展延至 3 月 23 日和 4 月 12 日。

6. Shipment will be effected subject to an advanced payment amounting 30% to be remitted in the seller's favour by T/T, and the remaining part on collection basis, documents will be released against payment at sight.
   装运货物系以即期信用证规定的电汇方式向卖方提交预付金 30% 为前提，其余部分采用托收，凭即期付款交单。

7. We have received your letter of credit No. 215 issued by the Bank of China. After reading it carefully, we found that transhipment is not allowed, which is just on contrary to our S/C.
   兹收到贵方由中国银行开具的第 215 号信用证。仔细审阅后，我们发现该信用证不允许转船装运，而这恰恰与我们的销售确认书不符。

8. The shipment covered by your Credit No. 12 has been ready for quite some time, but the amendment advice has not yet arrived, and an extension of 15 days is required.
   第 12 号信用证下的货物早已备好，但尚未收到信用证修改通知书，因此要求延期信用证 15 天。

9. You are kindly appreciated to see to it that punctual delivery is made within the validity of the L/C.
   恳请务必在信用证有效期内按时装运。

10. Much to our regret, we haven't received your letter of credit against our Sales Confirmation No. 0426, although it should have reached us by the end of May, as stipulated.
很遗憾,尚未收到第 0426 号销售确认书的有关信用证,按规定它本应在 5 月底到达我方。

11. The documentary bill of exchange has been upon you at 60 days under L/C No. 123 and has been delivered to the Royal Bank of this city. Documents:
(1) Full set of Clean "On Board" Bill of Lading with insurance cover.
(2) Commercial Invoice in triplicate.
(3) Inspection certificate issued by Logic Inspection House.
我们已按第 123 号信用证规定向贵方开出 60 天见票付款的跟单汇票,并已提交本市皇家银行。
单据为:
(1) 连同保险单在内的全套清洁,"已装船"提单。
(2) 商业发票一式三份。
(3) 检验证书(由洛吉检验所签发)。

12. Our Bankers in Tokyo, Ohiro Bank, will accept your draft on them on our behalf.
我方东京大平银行将代表我方承兑你们开给他们的汇票。

13. We grant your request for payment by L/C with draft at 60 days sight.
我们同意接受见票后 60 天付款的远期信用证付款的要求。

14. We enclose a bank draft for \$ 200, being the amount less 2% discount.
我们附寄银行汇票一张,金额计 200 美元,已扣除 2% 折扣。

15. The requesting party shall bear the bank charges for amendment to or extension of Letter of Credit as and when such situations arise.
如果发生需要修改或扩充信用证的情况,提出的一方必须承担有关银行的费用。

16. We would like you to instruct your bank to authorize their correspondent bank to confirm the L/C when advising us the same.
我们希望你能告知贵方银行授权其代理行确认通知我们相同内容的信用证。

17. We shall open through a bank an irrevocable Sight Letter of Credit to reach you 10 days before the month of shipment, stipulating that 50% of the invoice value available against clean draft at sight while the remaining 50% on Document against Payment at sight on collection basis.
我们应通过银行开立不可撤销的即期信用证,装运月份前 10 天内到达你处,按发票金额的 50%,以清洁的即期汇票支付,其余 50% 以托收方式下即期付款交单。

18. Since there is no direct steamer sailing for your port, we would request you to amend your L/C to allow transhipment.
因为没有驶往你港的直达轮,我方要求贵方修改信用证,允许转船。

19. Bank of China, Shanghai hereby undertakes to honor all reimbursement claims presented to us under this letter of credit on or before the expiry date stipulate herein/above.
中国银行上海分行确认并承诺在上述所规定的有效期或之前兑付本信用证项下提交我行的索偿。

20. Payment to beneficiaries under reserve or against indemnity by debiting our account is not accep-

table.

不允许不经过开证行,通过保留追索权或保函的方式付款给受益人。

21. Signed commercial invoice issued in 2/3 original, 1 copy certifying issuance in strict conformity with proforma invoice regarding the unit price and if available trade mark of the manufacture.

    签署的商业发票两正一副,证明本发票的出具在单价上和产品的商标(如有)与形式发票完全一致。

22. Commercial invoice in four fold showing detailed description of goods.

    商业发票一式四份,具有对商品的详细描述。

23. Signed commercial invoice in 3 copies duly certifying that the goods shipped are as per confirmation letter mentioned in field 45A above.

    签署的商业发票一式三份,证实所装运货物与上述栏位45A所提及的确认函相符。

24. Documents dated prior L/C opening are not acceptable.

    如果单证日期早于信用证开立日期,将不予接受。

25. Weight and measurement list in two fold bearing the code of each shipped article.

    写有每次装运货物编码的重量单和尺码单一式两份。

26. Without prejudice to the generality of foregoing, we shall have no such liability regarding the fitness for purpose, quality or merchantability of this software, whether statutory or otherwise.

    在不违反前述一般性规定的情况下,我方不会就本软件的用途、质量或产品性能的合适性问题承担其法律责任,无论此法律责任是法定的还是非法定的。

27. Any fees associated with discrepancy notification, payment refusal and rejection and/ or payment will be deducted from the proceeds.

    与不符点通知、拒付或其他支付引起的有关费用将从款项中扣除。

28. Additional instruction to paying/accepting bank/negotiating bank:Royal bank of Canada confirms the aforementioned letter of credit and thereby undertakes to honor all drafts drawn as indicated therein.

    对付款行/承兑行/议付行的附加指示:加拿大皇家银行保兑上述信用证,并承诺对依信用证所示的所有汇票付款。

29. Certificate of origin issued by chamber of commerce in the original must be certified by chamber of commerce and legalized by Saudi consulate/embassy in China stating the country of origin, name and full address of the manufacturer/producer and shipper, confirming that the goods relevant to this L/C are of Chinese origin.

    由商会出具的产地证的正本必须由商会证实,并由沙特阿拉伯驻中国的大使馆/领事馆认证。产地证必须说明原产国、制造商/生产商和托运人的名称和地址,同时确认与本信用证有关的货物为中国产。

30. The transferring bank must endorse the amount of such transfer on this letter of credit.

    转让行必须对本信用证的转让数额进行背书。

31. Upon receipt of the documents which conform to the terms and conditions of the credit, we shall remit the proceeds to the negotiating bank according to their instruction.

    在收到和本证条款/条件相符的单证的情况下,我行将根据对方指示向议付行汇款。

练习
Exercises

Ⅰ. Comprehension Questions
1. What are the definition and function of international business payment?
2. What are the definition and kinds of bills of exchange, promissory notes and checks?
3. What are the definition, parties and kinds of remittance and collection?
4. Does D/P after 30 days sight have more risks than D/A? Why?
5. What are the difference between T/T, M/T and D/D?

Ⅱ. Translating the Following Terms and Expressions
1. financial transhipment
2. draw a draft/bill on sb.
3. documents to be released to the drawee
4. in duplicate
5. marine insurance
6. 支付条件
7. 商业信用
8. 清偿债款

Ⅲ. Fill in the Blanks
1. We send you hospital equipment and supplies _____ US $ 1 234. You agreed to make payment _____ 30 days or by March 4. Now, 60 days later, and _____ three reminders, a telephone call, you still have made _____ effort to _____ your account or even give us a valid reason why you have not done so.

   I had every faith- especially after our telephone conversation that you would abide by the _____ terms offered you. We did, after all, _____ you with materials and equipment you needed and which, so far as I know, were entirely satisfactory. Do not you think you have _____ to reciprocate?

   The idea of using other _____ of collecting the money _____ us has not even occurred to me until now because I know what this can mean to one's credit _____. I know you value yours just as we do ours.

2. Payment should be made _____ sight draft.
3. Payment by L/C is our method of _____ trade in chemicals.
4. Mr. Yin could agree _____ D/P terms.
5. 90% of the credit amount must be paid _____ the presentation of documents.
6. You do not say whether you wish the transaction to be _____ cash or _____ credit.
7. We shall be glad if you agree to ship the goods to us as before _____ Cash against Documents basis.
8. In view of the small amount of this transaction, we prepared to accept payment by D/P at _____ for the value of the goods shipped.
9. We regret to say that the payment terms stipulated in your order are not _____ to us.
10. To amend the L/C would involve a delay _____ two weeks in shipment.
11. We extend to you this accommodation in _____ of our friendly relations.

Ⅳ. Translating the Following Sentences
1. We have received your covering L/C, but we find it contains the following discrepancies.
2. The L/C must be confirmed by the bank which may be acceptable to us.
3. You should be at least ship half of this order within one month upon receipt of the L/C.

4. Much to our regret that owing to the oversight on part of us, L/C was wrongly established.
5. The amendment to L/C No. 121 has not been received. Please amend it immediately in order to effect shipment at earliest convenience and cable reply.
6. 为了节省大量开立信用证的费用，我方将在所订购的货物已备齐待运、舱位已定下时，电汇全部金额。
7. 很遗憾地通知贵方，我们的贸易惯例不接受承兑交单的付款条件。
8. 贵方须在本合同签订后的 7 天内将合同金额 30% 的定金电汇给我方，其余金额以托收方式，即期付款交单支付。
9. 我方的付款要求是凭附带全套已装船单证的即期汇票开立的信用证，在装货港所在地银行议付。
10. 贵方须在 2010 年 4 月 20 日前开出信用证，否则我方保留撤销合同的权利，不另行通知。

Ⅴ. Translate the Following Paragraph into English

我们仍然保留将本单据给申请人的权利（如果开证申请人放弃不符条件，愿意接受不符单据的话），只要我们在放单前没有收到交单人书面的相反指示，那么，这就不构成我们的失职（没有考虑交单人的风险和持单听候指示），并且在此情况下的放单，我们将对交单人不负任何责任。

Ⅵ. Translate the Following Letter into Chinese

Dear Sirs,

Re: Your new product, Mobile HDD

Thank you for your letter of May 8 concerning your new product, Mobile HDD. We are interested in your product and wish to discuss further about it.

We noticed that you require payment by letter of credit. However we would like to propose payment by D/A for this first order. We hope to place substantial orders once the demand for this product has been ascertained.

We believe our proposal is a reasonable way to test the market and hope you will be willing to cooperate with us.

Yours faithfully,

Ⅶ. Write a letter in English asking for amendments to the following letter of credit by checking it with the given contract terms.

E. C. D. Bank Ltd.

Date: October 11, 2002

Irrevocable Documentary Credit No. 5676

To: Beijing Machinery Imp. / Exp. corp.

Gentlemen,

We hereby authorize you to draw on E. C. D. Bank for account of ABC Company to the extent of Can $ 2 750.00 (Say Canadian Dollars Two thousand And Seventy-five Only) available by draft at sight accompanied by the following documents:

1. Signed Commercial Invoice in duplicate.
2. Full set of clean on board ocean bills of lading made out to order and blank endorsed showing "freight paid" covering: five knitting machines at Can $ 550.00 per set CIFC 3% Montreal.
3. One original insurance Policy/Certificate Covering All Risks and War Risk for 130% of the invoice value.

Shipments from China Port to Montreal by direct steamer.

Shipments is to be effected not later than December 31, 2002.

This credit is valid at your end until January 15, 2002.

合同主要条款：

卖方：北京机械进出口公司

买方：ABC 公司

商品名称：针织机

数量：5 台

单价：CIF 蒙特利尔每台 550 加元含 2% 佣金

总值：2 750 加元

装运期：2002 年 12 月由中国港口运往蒙特利尔，允许转船

保险：由卖方按发票金额 110% 投保一切险和战争险

支付：不可撤销即期信用证支付，议付有效期为最后装运期后 15 天在中国到期

附录 6A　信用证
Appendix 6A　Letter of Credit

LETTER OF CREDIT—SAMPLE FORM
（PLACE ON BANK'S LETTERHEAD STATIONERY）

Date ＿＿＿＿＿＿＿＿＿＿＿＿

Montgomery County, Maryland

Department of Permitting Services

255 Rockville Pike, 2nd Floor

Rockville, Maryland 20850-4166

Re: Irrevocable Letter of Credit No. ＿＿＿＿＿＿＿＿

＿＿＿＿＿＿（Permittee）＿＿＿＿＿＿　　Expiration Date: (2 years)

＿＿＿＿＿＿（Address）＿＿＿＿＿＿

Gentlemen:

　　We hereby authorize Montgomery County, Maryland, to draw on (Bank Name and Address) ＿＿＿＿＿＿ for the account of ＿＿＿＿ (Permittee Name) ＿＿＿＿ up to an aggregate amount of $ ＿＿＿＿＿＿ available by your draft at sight.

　　Each draft drawn under this Letter of Credit must state, Drawn under ＿＿＿＿ (Bank Name) ＿＿＿＿＿＿ Letter of Credit No. ＿＿＿＿＿＿ dated ＿＿＿＿＿＿ in connection with ＿＿＿＿ (Subdivision Name) ＿＿＿＿ Subdivision, as more fully described in the application and Permit No. ＿＿＿＿＿＿ .

　　Each draft must also be accompanied by your certification that: **(CHECK BOX THAT APPLIES)**

　　□ (Name of Permittee) ＿＿＿＿ failed to complete the work authorized under Permit No. ＿＿＿＿ in ＿＿＿＿ (Subdivision Name) ＿＿＿＿ Subdivision in accordance with Section 8-27 of the Montgomery County Code, 1994, as amended, and failed to safely demolish the building or structure or clear the site described in the permit. [**FOR DEMOLITION PERMIT**] or

☐ (Name of Permittee) _____ failed to complete the work authorized under Permit No. _____ in _____ (Subdivision Name) _____ Subdivision in accordance with Chapter 49 of the Montgomery County Road Construction Code and the regulations adopted pursuant thereto. [FOR DRIVEWAY PERMIT OR GRADING AND PAVING PERMIT] or

☐ (Name of Permittee) _____ failed to complete the work authorized under Permit No. _____ in _____ (Subdivision Name) _____ Subdivision in accordance with Chapter 19 of the Montgomery County Code, 1994, as amended; or prior to issuing a completion certificate for the work authorized under the above project, and the County received notice, as provided below, that this Letter of Credit would not be renewed and the County received no replacement security from the permittee. [FOR SEDIMENT CONTROL PERMIT]

It is a condition of this Letter of Credit that it shall be automatically extended without amendment on a year-by-year basis from the expiration date unless sixty (60) days prior to such expiration date you are notified by certified letter that we elect not to consider this Letter of Credit renewed for any such additional period.

This Letter of Credit shall be governed by the Uniform Commercial Code as enacted by the Sate of Maryland and is subject to the Uniform Customs and Practice for Documentary Credits @ (1993 Revision or the most recent revision), International Camber of Commerce Publication No. 500. In case of conflict between the Maryland Uniform Commercial Code and the Uniform Customs and Practice for Documentary Credits, the Maryland Uniform Commercial Code shall control. This Letter of Credit complies with section 5-101 et seq. of the Commercial Law Article of the Annotated Code of Maryland and any litigation related thereto shall be conducted in the Courts of the State of Maryland.

We hereby agree that all drafts under this Letter of Credit, in whole or in part, and in compliance with the terms and conditions of this credit, will be duly honored if drawn and presented for payment on or before the initial expiration date or any automatic extended date as set forth above.

(Name of Financial Institution)

By: (Authorized signature of bank officer) (SEAL)
  (Printed Name and Title)
Letter of Credit Form. HS. doc. 08/03

附录6B 开立不可撤销信用证申请书

Appendix 6B Irrevocable Letter of Credit Application Form

Irrevocable Letter of Credit (L/C)
Application Form
(Import Documentary Credit Application Form)

To: Allied Irish Banks, p. l. c. ("AIB Bank") whose registered office is at Bank centre, Ballsbridge, Dublin 4 and whose business address for these purposes is Trade Finance Services, AIB International Centre, IFSC, Dublin 1.

We request you to issue an irrevocable documentary credit on the following terms.
Please complete all sections.

> This Irrevocable Documentary Credit Application Form (the "Application") and the documentary credit (the "credit") issued hereunder incorporate and are subject to and governed by the Trade Finance Terms and Conditions (the "Trade Terms") save for where any of the terms of the Trade Terms may be inconsistent with or conflict with the terms of this Application. In such case, this Application shall prevail to the extent of such inconsistency or conflict only, but all other terms and conditions of the Trade Terms shall remain unaffected. If you have not received a copy of the Trade Terms or require a further copy, copies are available on the websites, www.aibcm.com or www.aibtradefinance.com, or on request from your branch. These are our standard Trade Terms upon which we intend to rely. For your own benefit and protection, you should read the Trade Terms carefully. If you do not understand any point, please ask for further information.

GENERAL

              day month year country of beneficiary unless stated

1. Date and place of expiry of L/C in ____ ____ ____ in _____
   (Latest date for presentation of documents)
2. Currency and Value CCY _____ Figures _____ Tolerance (if any)% _____
3. Payment Terms Available with AIB Bank, unless otherwise stated. By payment/acceptance/negotiation at
   (specify sight/30 days sight/60 days from shipment date etc.) _____
4. Transferable Credit ☐ Tick box if credit is to be transferable
5. Confirmation of Credit ☐ Requested ☐ Not Requested

PARTIES

6. Applicant/Importer _____
   (Full name and address) _____
7. Beneficiary/Exporter _____
   (Full name and address) _____
8. Beneficiary's Bankers (If known)
   Name _____
   Address _____

SHIPPING

9. Partial Shipments ☐ Allowed ☐ Not allowed
10. Transhipment Allowed (unless otherwise stated) _____
11. Shipment details Shipment from
             _____
             For transportation to
             _____
12. Latest Date of Shipment day month year
    (optional)   ____ ____ ____

13. Period for presentation of _____ days from date of issuance of transport doc (21 days unless otherwise stated)
    documents to Bank   (Latest date of Shipment plus number of days for presentation should be the chosen Expiry Date)
14. Shipment terms   Ex works ____   F. O. B. ____   CFR ____   C&I ____   C. I. F. ____
    C. I. P. ____
    ____ Other, please specify _____

GOODS/SERVICES
15. Brief goods description _____
    (avoid excessive detail) _____

DOCUMENTS
16. Documents required   _____ Signed invoices in _____ (triplicate unless otherwise stated)
    _____ Insurance policy/certificate covering all risks for 110% of invoice value
    _____ Certificate of _____ origin issued by chamber of commerce
    _____ GSP certificate of _____ origin form A to be marked "issued retrospectively" if dated after date of shipment
    _____ Packing list
    _____ Other, please specify _____

    TRANSPORT DOCUMENT (please specify one document only relative to mode of transport)
    _____ Full set of clean on board marine bills of lading (Sea transport only)
    _____ Full set of combined transport bills of lading (Sea and land transport)
    _____ Air way bill (original No. 3) (Air transport)
    _____ CMR (international consignment note) (Road transport)
    _____ Other transport document, please specify (e.g. Certificate of Shipment)

17. Additional conditions _____
    (if any)   _____
18. Bank Charges   AIB Bank Charges: ☐ Applicant   FX Bank Charges: ☐ Applicant
                                     ☐ Beneficiary   ☐ Beneficiary
    AIB Bank charges for the applicant and FX Bank charges for the Beneficiary unless otherwise stated

Insurance Declaration
We declare that we have arranged for all risks insurance on this transaction (not applicable if exporter has arranged to effect insurance and a policy/certificate has been requested in 16 above).

We hereby authorize you to debit our account in respect of charges, and also at payments date (s) with the amount of each drawing as follows (complete A or B):

A. Utilize spot rate to meet drawings due for payment _____ OR Utilise Forward Contract Ref _____ Number F/C Rate _____ and Debit the following EUR account with AIB Bank in respect of drawings and charges _____

B. Debit currency account held with AIB Bank in respect of drawings _____ and debit charges to currency account _____ (please tick) or debit charges to the following EUR account with AIB Bank _____

Agreement and Acknowledgement

In consideration of your issuing at our request the above Credit, we acknowledge and agree that the credit shall be governed by and subject to the Trade Terms in addition to the terms (which include an indemnity) set out on the reverse of this Application Form.

Signed for and on behalf of the applicant:　　FOR BRANCH USE ONLY

_____　　Sanctioned:　　　　　　　　　　Branch Band
　　　(Authorised signatory)　　　　_____　　Signing
_____　　Manager's Signature　　Number
　　　(Authorised signatory)　　　　Branch address　　_____
Dated　　　　　Telephone number
_____　　_____　　TO BE USED ONLY IF WITHIN BRANCH　　Sorting code:
　　　　　　　　　　　　　　　DISCRETION OTHERWISE MUST BE　　_____
　　　　　　　　　　　　　　　ACCOMPANIED BY SANCTION FROM
Contact name　_____　　RELATIVE LENDING AREA

In consideration of AIB Bank opening and issuing the credit specified overleaf, the applicant named in this Application Form agrees and undertakes to

(1) reimburse AIB Bank for all amounts paid or incurred by AIB Bank in connection with the credit in accordance with clause 8 of the Trade Terms and

(2) Indemnify and keep AIB Bank indemnified from and against all liabilities, losses, damages, costs, expenses, claims and demands which AIB Bank may incur or sustain in connection with the credit.

AIB Bank is to have a lien on all goods, documents and policies and proceeds thereof for any obligations or liabilities present or future incurred by AIB Bank under or arising out of the credit. AIB Bank is to be bound only to see that the drafts and document purport to comply with the terms and conditions of the credit and is not to be liable for any loss or damage however caused in connection therewith (including, without limitation, loss or damage from delay or error in transmission or forwarding of the above or any future instruction or documents) not caused by the gross negligence or wilful default of AIB Bank's own officers or servants.

AIB Bank is authorised to debit the account of the applicant with sums paid under the credit, also with commission charges and any other charge which may be incurred in respect thereof. AIB Bank is authorised to be reimbursed for any loss incurred by AIB Bank due to variations or adjustments arising from the making of payments under the credit in a foreign currency by debiting such amounts from the applicant's account or accounts with any of AIB Bank's branches. If the applicant does not hold any account with AIB Bank, the applicant authorises AIB Bank to open a new account in its name at any of AIB Bank's branches and for AIB Bank to debit any such loss incurred from this account. The applicant agrees that AIB Bank shall be entitled to refuse payment of any cheque, bill note or order drawn or accepted by the applicant or upon which the applicant may otherwise be liable, if such payments would result in the credit balance of the applicant's account being less than the amounts from time to time owing or due to AIB Bank by the applicant.

In the event of a receiver and/or liquidator being appointed to the applicant or if AIB Bank determines that a material adverse change has occurred to the applicant's business assets or future prospects, AIB Bank shall be entitled to immediately debit from any of the applicant's accounts, the maximum total amount of AIB Bank's actual and contingent liability under the credit (notwithstanding that no actual payment has been made by AIB Bank) and AIB Bank shall refund to the applicant any excess promptly after the contingent liability has ceased to exist.

Unless specifically requested otherwise above, AIB Bank is not obliged to include any documents which it may have attached to this application, as an integral part of the credit neither is AIB Bank bound to examine documents presented under the credit against such attachments. The applicant agrees that AIB Bank is authorised to pay sums under the credit on first presentation of documents purported to comply with the terms and conditions of the credit and is not required to investigate the validity of any such demand for payment.

The applicant agrees that its liability hereunder shall also apply to any increase or decrease in the amount to be paid under the credit or any extension or renewal of the credit, whether pursuant to the same terms or otherwise and whether arising by agreement with AIB Bank or by operation of law or otherwise.

The credit is subject to the I. C. C. Paris. Uniform Customs and Practice for Documentary Credits in force on the date of issue.

Data Protection Notice

The information you have provided above will be held by AIB Group on a computer database or on your written application form to administer your Credit.

Details of any payment in relation to this Credit, including the identity of both the Applicant and Beneficiary may be disclosed to overseas authorities (including the United States of America) in connection with combating terrorism and other serious crime. Further information is available on request or from www. aibcm. com and www. aib. ie.

附录6C 汇票
Appendix 6C Bill of Exchange

BILL OF EXCHANGE

No. _____ （汇票编号）   Date：_____ （出票日期）

For：_____ （汇票金额）

At _____ （付款期限） sight of this second of exchange (first of the same tenor and date unpaid) pay to the order of _____ （受款人） the sum of _____

Drawn under _____ （出票条款）

L/C No. _____   Dated _____

To. _____ （付款人）

            _____ （出票人签章）

Chapter 7
第 7 章

包装与标志
Packings and Marks

Learning Objectives

Enable students to be familiar with the categories of packing and marks; to know the essential terms and conditions regarding packing and marks and have a good command of sentence structure and letter writing about packing.

使学生熟悉包装和标志的种类；了解包装的基本条款；掌握有关包装、标志的基本句型和信函写作。

7.1 背景知识
Background Information

Packing is considered as one of the very important parts in international transactions. Not only does it help to promote sales, reduce warehousing cost, freight and damages, it also reflects the achievement of a country's science, technology, culture and art, add value to the products. Good packing may create people's desire to possess them and enable the goods to reach users in perfect condition.

Packing is usually classified into two categories:

(1) Inner packing /small packing: packing for sales;

(2) Outer packing /large packing: packing for transportation.

Inner packing aids marketing, advertising, display, presentation, protection, handling and self-service retailing, while outer packing is designed to protect the goods from damaging and theft and facilitating transport, loading

包装被认为是国际贸易最重要的组成部分之一。包装不仅有助于促销，减少储存成本、运费和损失，而且也可以反映出一国的科技、文化、艺术水准，增加产品的价值。好的包装还可以唤起人们拥有商品的欲望，并使商品完好无损地到达客户手中。

通常包装可以分为两种：

（1）内包装/小包装：销售包装；

（2）外包装/大包装：运输包装。

内包装有助于营销、广告、陈列、演示、保护、操作和自助零售，而外包装主要用于运输过程中保护商品免于受损、偷窃，

and unloading while being carried from one place to another. Usually packing varies with the nature of the contents. The most commonly used packing containers are cartons, cases, crates, drums, barrels, bales, tins, carboys and so on.

A third kind of packing, neutral packing is also often used in international trade. Neutral packing means that there is neither a name of the origin, nor a name and address of the factory, nor a trade mark, a brand, or even any words on the (outer or inner) packing of the commodity. The purpose of using neutral packing by exporters is to break down the tariff and non-tariff barriers of some countries or regions, or meet the special demands of the transaction. It may also help the manufacturers in exporting countries to increase the competitiveness of their products, expand the exports and earn the foreign exchange in the importing countries.

Associated with packing is the marking of goods. Shipping marks are analogous to identification cards of people. Exporters, importers and carriers rely on them to distinguish one shipment from another. They are also the essential means of identifying and linking cargo and documents together. The marking information on the package should be identical with that on the documents.

Marks mainly include shipping marks, indicative marks and warning marks.

Shipping marks are marks of simple designs (such as triangle, diamond, rectangle, oval, star, pentagon, hexagon), some letters, numbers and simple words on packages, often stenciled, which serve as identification of the consignment to which they belong. It is one of the most important elements which are agreed on by the exporter and the importer in a sales contract. The shipping marks consist of:

(1) Consignor's or consignee's code name;
(2) Number of the contract or L/C;
(3) Port of destination;
(4) Numbers of the packed goods.

Shipping marks may also include article No, quantity, net weight, gross weight, and measurements like the following:

便于运输、装卸。通常要根据所运输商品的属性选择不同的包装方式。最常用的包装材料是硬纸箱、箱子、板条箱、桶、包、罐、大玻璃瓶等。

第三种包装即中性包装，也常用于国际贸易中。中性包装是一种既不标明生产国、厂商的地名和名称，也不标明商标和牌子的包装，甚至在商品内外包装上一个字都没有。出口商采用中性包装的目的是打破某些进口国家和地区的关税或非关税壁垒，或适应交易的特殊需要。它还能帮助生产商提高产品的竞争能力，对进口国扩大出口并赚取外汇。

与包装有关的是标志。标志类似于人的身份证，进出口商和承运人依靠它来区别货物，它们也是区别和联系货物与单证关系的手段。包装上的标志信息应与单证上的一致。

标志一般包括运输标志、指示性标志和警示性标志。

运输标志是用模板印制在包装上的标志，由一些简单的几何图形（如三角形、菱形、长方形、椭圆形、星形、五边形、六边形等）和一些字母、数字以及简单的文字组成，用来辨识货物。它是进出口商在销售合同里必须达成一致的几个重要的事项之一。运输标志由以下几个方面构成：

（1）收货人和发货人的代号；
（2）合同或信用证号码；
（3）目的港；
（4）装运号。

运输标志还可以包括商品号、数量、净重、毛重以及尺寸等，如：

- ITEM NO. 234
- QTY. 4 SETS
- N. W. 300KG.
- MEA. 100CM×50CM×60CM

- 234 号商品
- 数量：4 套
- 净重：300 千克
- 尺寸：100 厘米×50 厘米×60 厘米

For example (See Figure 7-1):

Indicative marks are eye-catching figures and concise instructions concerning manners of proper handling, storing, loading and unloading of packed goods like "USE NO HOOKS, THIS SIDE UP, HANDLE WITH CARE", etc. Indicative marks are often printed in black color.

Warning marks are usually made up of simple geometrical diagrams, word descriptions and particular pictures. It is also called dangerous cargo mark or shipping mark for dangerous commodities, which is brushed clearly on the shipping packing of the inflammable, explosive, poisonous, corrosive or radioactive goods, so as to give warning to the workers, such as "explosives, poison, hazardous article", etc.

Letters on packing are mainly concerned with materials or containers that are used for packing, shipping mark, packing charges, packing list and so on. So it should be concise and clear. In such letters, the seller can describe in details to the buyer his customary packing of the goods and also indicated clearly that he may accept any required packing at the expense of the buyer. The buyer can inform the seller of any formerly unexpected requirements or fears about the packing. Any changes regarding packing stipulated in the contract should be mutually discussed and determined before shipment.

例如（见图 7-1）：

指示性标志是一些醒目简洁的提示，以保证货物在搬运、储存和装卸过程中操作适当，如"切勿用钩""此端向上""小心轻放"等，一般用黑色标注。

警告性标志由文字和特定的图案组成，又称危险货物包装标志，是指凡在运输包装内装有爆炸品、易燃物品、有毒物品、腐蚀物品、氧化剂和放射性物质等危险货物时，都必须在运输包装上标明用于各种危险品的标志，以示警告，使装卸人员按货物特性采取相应的防护措施，以保护货物和人身的安全，如"爆炸品""有毒品""有害品"等。

包装一类的信函内容主要涉及包装材料或器具、唛头、包装费用、装箱单等，因此应简洁明了。这类信函在写作时，卖方可以给买方详细解释货物的惯常包装，也可以指出，它可以在买方承担费用的前提下，接受任何包装方式。买方也可告知卖方额外的要求或者对包装的担忧。任何合同规定的有关包装的变化都应在装运前由双方协商决定。

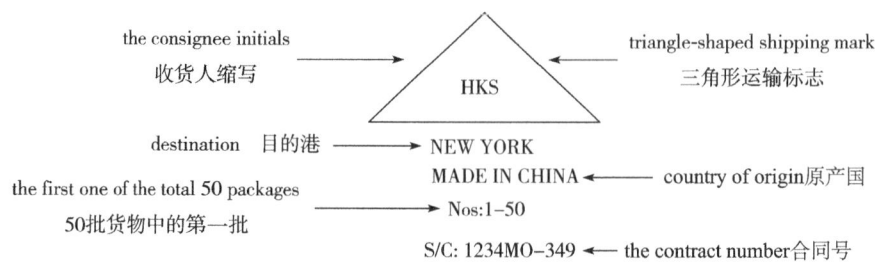

图 7-1

7.2 信例
Sample Letters

Letter 1 Packing Requirement

August 20, 2010

Dear Sirs,

Battery-driven Toy Cars

Referring to our recent exchange of fax, we would like to confirm our order for 4 thousand of your high-quality Battery-driven Toy Cars. As to the packing of our ordered goods, we suggest they should be wrapped in polythene wrappers and packed in cardboard boxes padded with foam plastic, ten toy cars each, 50 boxes to a wooded case lined with oil-cloth. We believe such packing will reduce any possible damage in transit to a minimum.

We trust that you will give careful consideration to our proposal.

Yours faithfully,
B&G Department Store
George kelin
General manager

Notes

1. battery-driven 电动的
2. ... wrapped in polythene wrappers and packed in cardboard boxes padded with foam plastic, ten toy cars each, 50 boxes to a wooded case lined with oil-cloth. 用塑料纸包裹，装在纸板箱里，垫以塑料泡沫，每箱放10个玩具车，50箱放一个木箱里，内衬油纸衬里。
   polythene wrapper 聚乙烯袋
   padded with foam plastic 垫以塑料泡沫。此处过去分词短语做定语修饰前面的 cardboard boxes。
   a wooded case lined with oil-cloth 油纸衬里的木箱。lined with oil-cloth 为过去分词做定语修饰前面的 a wooded case。
   部分常见的包装表示法：
   （1）in... 用某种容器包装
       Peanuts are packed in double gunny bags. 花生用双层麻袋包装。
   （2）in... of... each 用某种容器包装，每件若干
       Gents' shirts are packed in wooden cases of 20 dozens each. 男士衬衫用木箱装，每箱20打。
   （3）in... each containing 用某种容器装，每件内装若干
       Our raincoats are packed in wooden cases, each containing 10 dozens. 雨衣用木箱装，每箱装10打。
   （4）to 若干件装于一个容器
       Folding chairs are packed 3 pieces to a carton. 三把折叠椅装入一个纸板箱。

(5) each... in... and... to 每单位装入某容器，若干单位装入另一种较大容器
Each pair of nylon socks is packed in a plastic bag and 24 pairs to a box. 每双尼龙袜装一个塑料袋，24双装一盒。

(6) ...to... and... to 若干单位装入某种容器，若干此种容器装入另一种较大容器
Ball-point pens are packed 20 pieces to a box and 100 boxes to a wooded case. 圆珠笔20支装一盒，100盒装一个木箱。

(7) in... of... each... to... 用某物包装，每件装……若干件装于一个大件中
In boxes of a dozen each, 100 boxes to a wooden case. 用盒装，每打装一盒，100盒装一个木箱。

3. ...reduce any possible damage in transit to a minimum. 将运输过程中可能的损失减少到最低。
4. We trust that you will give careful consideration to our proposal. 敬请贵方认真考虑我们的建议。

Letter 2　Packing Suggestion

August 25, 2010

Dear Sirs,

Packing of Battery-driven Toy Cars

We thank you for your letter of August 20, confirming your Order for 4 000 high-quality Battery-driven Toy Cars together with your proposal of the packing of the captioned goods.

As regards the packing, we would use wooden cases for the outer packing if you think better. We always have our clients' interest in mind. But, our improved packing with cartons for toy cars has been widely accepted by our regular clients. Up to now, there has not been a single complaint from any of them since our adoption of this packing. Our cartons are lined with polythene sheet, reinforced by overall strapping with plastic straps to protect the contents from moisture or any possible damage from jolting and collision in transit. Therefore it is suitable for long distance ocean transportation.

Furthermore, by using cartons, the packing cost, and cargo weight can be reduced and freightage can be saved accordingly. If you insist on wooden cases for outer packing, we would strictly follow your instruction. Only that the extra charges should be borne by you.

We state the above for your reference. If we do not hear from you to the contrary before Sep. 5, we shall pack the captioned goods in cartons as we have recommended.

Yours faithfully,
High-Ace Toy Factory

Notes

1. confirm 确认
2. captioned goods 标题项下的货物
3. have our clients' interest in mind 把客户的利益放在心上
4. Our cartons are lined with polythene sheet, reinforced by overall strapping with plastic straps to

protect the contents from moisture or any possible damage from jolting and collision in transit. 我们的纸箱用聚乙烯布衬里，并用塑料包装带捆好，使内装货物在运输途中不因潮湿或颠簸、碰撞而受损。此处 reinforced by overall strapping with plastic straps to protect the contents from moisture or any possible damage from jolting and collision in transit 为过去分词短语做状语，表示伴随。

be lined with 内衬以……

5. freightage 运费
6. the extra charges should be borne by you 额外的费用应由贵方承担
7. for your reference 仅供参考
8. We shall pack the captioned goods in cartons as we have recommended. 我们将用我们推荐的纸箱包装贵方标题项下的货物。

Letter 3　Packing Requirement by the Clients

Smith & Jones Co.
25 High Street, Tottenham, London

November 23, 2010

China National Import & Export Corp.
Beijing Branch
Beijing
China

Dear Sirs,

Re: Our Order No. 226

　　Further to our telephone conversation on 22 regarding the packing of the above order for Smart Choice, we would like to propose the following:

　　1. Our clients would like to have the products packed in window packing for inner packing so that the products can be seen directly. They believe it will help to promote sales.

　　2. They prefer wooden cases to cartons for outer packing. They fear that cartons are not strong enough for ocean transportation. They might be easily damaged through rough handling. They are more susceptible to pilferage and damage by moisture.

　　3. Please indicate HANDLE WITH CARE and mark our initials CUM in diamond, under which the port of destination and our Order No. should be stenciled on the outer packing.

　　Please let us know if you can do as requested.

Yours faithfully,
Smith & Jones Co.

Notes

1. prefer wooden cases to cartons 想用木箱而不愿用纸箱
2. rough handling 粗暴搬运
3. susceptible to 易受影响的，可能或可以的
4. pilferage 偷窃
5. mark our initials CUM in diamond 将我公司首字母 CUM 标在菱形内。后面的 under which the port of destination and our Order No. should be stenciled on the outer packing 是以介词 under + which 引出的非限制性定语从句，修饰前面的 diamond。
6. stenciled 用模板印刷

Letter 4　Improper Packing

Dear Sir or Madam,

　　We regret to inform you that of the 160 cartons of machine parts delivered to us last week, two were found broken and some of the contents were badly damaged clearly through importance packing.

　　In view of our long-standing business relations, we would not lodge a claim against you for the loss this time. But we feel it necessary to stress the importance of seaworthy packing for our future dealings.

　　Usually valves and all delicate machine parts should be wrapped in soft material packed in cardboard boxes. These in turn are to be packed in wooden cases in such a manner that movement inside the cases is impossible. Besides, rope and metal handle should be fixed to the cases to facilitate consignment.

　　We look forward to your comments on the above.

Yours faithfully,

Notes

1. We regret to inform you that... 很遗憾告知贵方……
2. in view of 考虑到，鉴于
3. lodge a claim 提起诉讼，提出索赔
4. seaworthy packing 适合海上运输的包装
5. valve 阀门
6. wrapped in soft material packed in cardboard boxes 用软材料裹好装在纸板箱里
7. Besides, rope and metal handle should be fixed to the cases to facilitate consignment. 而且，箱子的外层还应扣上绳子，并配上金属把手，以便于装运。
8. consignment 货物

Tips

1. 买卖合同中的包装条款

包装条款一般包括包装材料、包装方式、包装规格、包装标志和包装费用等内容。

包装材料和包装方式应按合同中订立的内容进行包装，若合同中没有规定，卖方应按同种商品惯常的方式进行包装。按照国际贸易习惯和某些国家的法律规定，包装条款是合同的主要条款之一，是货物说明的组成部分。如果货物的包装与合同规定或行业习惯有重大不符，则属于违约，买方有权索赔损失，甚至拒收货物。因此，买卖双方必须在合同中明确规定包装条款。

2. 定牌包装和无牌包装

定牌包装（packing of nominated brand）是指卖方按买方要求在其出售的商品或包装上标明买方指定的商标或牌名。定牌包装使用的情况：①对某些国外大量的长期的稳定订货，为了扩大销售，可以接受买方指定的商标，不加注生产国别的标志，即定牌中性包装。②接受国外买方指定的商标或牌名，但在商标或牌名下标明"中国制造"。③接受国外买方指定的商标或牌名，同时在商标或牌名下注明由买方所在国家工厂制造，即定牌生产地。

无牌包装（packing without brand）是指按照买方的要求在出口商品或包装上免除任何标志或牌名的做法。它主要用于一些尚待进一步加工的半制成品，如供印染用的棉坯布，或供加工成批服装用的呢绒、布匹和绸缎等。其目的主要是避免浪费，降低成本。

除非另有约定，采用无牌时，在我国的出口商品和包装上均须标明"中国制造"字样。

7.3 有用的短语和句子
Useful Expressions

1. Types of Packing

cartons 纸箱	wooden cases 木箱	iron drum 铁桶
wooden casks 木桶	plastic casks 塑料桶	paper bags 纸袋
gunny bags 麻袋	plastic bags 塑料袋	container 集装箱
pallet 托盘	box 盒子	crate 板条箱
bale 包	can/tin 罐/听	carboy 玻璃瓶
bundle 捆	sale/marketing packing 销售包装	neutral packing 中性包装
nude cargo 裸装货		

Bale Matted Iron-band-strapped Outside.
外裹蒲包，加捆铁皮。
Block Covered with Poly Bag.
块装外加塑料袋。
Bound with Iron Bands Externally.
外绕铁皮。
Bound with Two Bands of Metal Wires Outside.

外绕铁丝两道。
Canvas Bag Filled with Water.
帆布袋内充水。
Cargo in Skids.
货物下加垫条包装。
Double Cloth Bag with Outer Bag Starched.
双层布袋外层上浆。
Non Returnable Container.
一次性包装。
Packed in Gunny Bales. Packing Sound.
布包包装,包装完好。
Packed in P. P. Woven bags Packing Sound.
塑料纺织袋装,包装完好。
Packed in Wooden Case, Packing Intact.
木箱装,箱装完整。
Packed in Cartons, Packing Sound.
纸箱装,箱装完好。
Packed in Gunny Bales, Packing Sound.
麻袋装,包装完好。
Packed on Pallets, Packing Sound.
托盘装,包装良好。
Packed in woven bales, Packing Sound.
编织包包装,包装完好。
Press Packed Bale without Wrapper.
机器榨包不带包皮。
Press Packed in Iron Hopped Bale.
机器榨包以铁皮捆扎。
Rolled on Tubes, Packing Sound.
卷筒装,包装良好。

2. Some Common Markings and Phrases
   NOT TO BE LAID FLAT 切勿平放
   USE NO HOOKS 切勿用钩
   NO TURNING OVER 切勿倒置
   OPEN HERE 此处打开
   THIS SIDE UP 此端向上
   INFLAMMABLE 易燃品
   NO DUMPING 切勿投掷
   DO NOT CRUSH 切勿挤压
   PERISHABLE GOODS 易腐物品
   FRAGILE 易碎品
   GUARD AGAINST DAMP 防潮

KEEP IN DARK PLACE 暗处存放
KEEP DRY 保持干燥
HAZARDOUS ARTICLE 危险品
KEEP AWAY FROM HEAT 请勿近热

3. in cardboard cartons, containing 30 dozens each.
   以硬纸箱包装，每箱 30 打。
4. in gunny bags, 50kg net to each.
   用麻袋包装，每袋净重 50 千克。
5. in tin-lined waterproof wooden cases, each piece wrapped in oil-cloth, 20 pieces packed in one case.
   用马口铁衬里的防水木箱包装，每件用油布裹好，20 件为一箱。
6. Packing in the same way as shipped for the previous order.
   按照上次货物装船的同一包装方法处理。
7. The shirt is packed in a polythene bag and then in a cardboard box, 10 dozens to a carton, with a gross weight of 20kg.
   衬衫用塑料袋包装，然后用纸板箱装，10 打装一个纸箱，毛重 20 千克。
8. The bed sheet under the captioned contract should be packed in plastic bags, 5 dozens to one carton, 20 cartons on a pallet, and 10 pallets in FCL container.
   该合同项下的床单必须装在塑料袋内，5 打装一个纸箱，20 纸箱装一货盘，10 货盘装一整集装箱。
9. ... strapped vertically and horizontally with metal bands and cut vent holes in the case to minimize condensation.
   用铁条横向和纵向予以加固，并在箱子上切一个通风孔以降低箱内的空气密度。
10. Cases must be nailed tightly, battened and secured by overall metal strapping.
    箱子需要用钉子钉牢，并用金属条捆扎。
11. As usual, packing for silk blouses, pink, blue and white equally assorted, size assortment is S2, M6 and L4 per dozens to a carton.
    按惯例，丝绸女衫的包装为粉色、蓝色、白色均衡搭配，每打尺码为小 2、中 6、大 4，12 打装一箱。
12. Cases should be numbered from 1 to 20, the word "FRAGILE" stenciled clearly in normal size on all four sides of the container.
    箱子外部按顺序从 1~20 编号，"易碎品"几个字按常规大小醒目地写在集装箱的四面。
13. Would you please give particular care to the fireproof lining, as our insurer insists on this.
    请特别注意使用防火内衬，因为我们的保险公司要求这样做。
14. The goods are tube marked with our initials in a diamond.
    请在货物上刷上菱形，内刷我公司名称缩写字母。
15. In iron drums of 30kg net each.
    以铁桶包装，每桶净重 30 千克。
16. 500MT net packed in 2 500 drums of 200kg net each.
    净重 500 吨，装 2 500 桶，每桶净装 200 千克。
17. Packed in 100 cartons of 2 pieces each.

装 100 箱，每箱 2 件。

18. The eggs are packed in cartons with beehives, lined with shake proof corrugated paper board, each carton contains 300 eggs.
鸡蛋用带蜂房孔的纸箱包装，内衬防震瓦楞纸板，每箱 300 个。

19. The outer packing in bags or in wooden cases is at buyer's option.
外包装用包或木箱，由买方选择。

20. We usually pack each piece of men's shirt in a plastic bag, half dozen to a box and 10 dozens to a wooden case.
我们通常将每一件男式衬衫装入一个塑料袋内，半打装一盒，10 打装一木箱。

21. Manually signed packing list in duplicate detailing the complete inner packing specification and contents of each package.
手签装箱单一式两份，详注每件货物内部包装的规格和内容。

22. Signed packing list in triplicate showing gross, net weight, net/net weight, measurement, color, size and quantity breakdown for each packing, if applicable.
签名的装箱单一式三份，如果适用，请标明每个包装的毛重、净重、净净重、尺码、颜色、尺寸和重量。

23. Packed in wooden case, for specification 6.0mm × 430mm, except one case packed with 3 reels. All were packed with 8 reels respectively; for specification 6.5mm × 300mm, every case was packed with 6 reels. The inner reels were wrapped with a poly-membrane and each reel was wrapped with a poly-membrane again.
木箱包装，6.0mm × 430mm 规格中，除 1 箱装 3 卷外，其余为 8 卷装，6.5mm × 300mm 规格为 6 卷装，箱内用塑料薄膜包裹，每卷再用塑料薄膜包裹。

24. Straightly stand on wooden pallet and wrapped with fibre borad, plastic membrane & kraft paper, board bound with iron belts externally and then mounted in the container with iron belt.
木托架包装，用纤维板、塑料薄膜及瓦楞纸皮包裹，外用铁带捆扎，再用铁带固定于集装箱内。

25. Shipped with container No. ×××with intact appearance, clear number and sound sealing. The goods were packed in cartons and packing sound.
集装箱装运，箱号×××，集装箱外观完整，箱号清晰，封识完好。货物纸箱包装，包装完好。

26. Packed in wooden case with 5 reels inside and every reel was wrapped with poly-membrane and neutral paper. The cases were bound with iron belts externally.
木箱包装，内装 5 卷，每卷用塑料薄膜及中性纸包裹，箱外铁带捆扎。

27. Packed in wooden case, the... was (were) mounted with bolts on the bottom of the case. Packing intact.
木箱装……以螺栓固定于箱底，箱装完整。

28. Packed in plastic woven flexible container, lined with plastic film bags, shipped in container, 20 bags for each.
塑料编织袋装，内衬塑料薄膜袋，集装箱装运，每箱 20 袋。

29. Packed in 2 ply cartons, lined with kraft paper and bound with four plastic belts externally packing sound.

双层纸箱装，外扎四道塑料腰带，内裹牛皮纸，包装完好。

30. Rolled on tube and packed with carton. bounded with three woven belts externally. Packing sound.

筒装，纸箱装，箱外三道编织带捆扎，包装完好。

练习
Exercises

Ⅰ. Comprehension Questions
  1. Comment briefly on the importance of packing in international trade?
  2. What is the difference between inner packing and outer packing?
  3. What are the differences among shipping marks, indicative marks and warning marks?
  4. What do the shipping marks consist of?

Ⅱ. Translate the Following Terms and Expressions into English or Chinese
  1. sales packing   2. breakage proof
  3. FCL   4. compression packing
  5. flexible container   6. brands designated by the buyer
  7. 适合海上运输的包装   8. 习惯包装
  9. 花色搭配单   10. 防水纸
  11. 指示性标志   12. 裸装货

Ⅲ. Fill in the Missing Word with the Words Given Below
  strapped, fulfill, seaworthy, covered with, directive, number, concerning, transportation, acknowledge, outer, mark, packing, with

Dear Sirs,

Re: No. 203

We have received your letter of July 23 _____ the _____ details. We are pleased to _____ them as follows:

The machine under the No. 203 order should be packed in a case of about 10 cubic meters _____ waterproof cloth and _____ vertically and horizontally, _____ metal bands and cut vent holes in the case to minimize condensation.

The packing described above is _____ export packing and fits for long distance ocean _____.

On the _____ packing please _____ the place of origin, the port of destination and the order _____. In addition, _____ marks like KEEP DRY, KEEP AWAY FROM PRESSURE, etc. should also be indicated.

We stated the above for your information, and _____ your order accordingly if we do not hear from you to the contrary before the end of this month.

Yours faithfully,

Ⅳ. Translate the Following Sentences
  1. Each tea set is to be wrapped in a plastic-film bag, fixed with hard fermented plastic padding, and put in a carton. Outside, it is to be strengthened by nylon straps.
  2. Our packing term is: in bales, each containing 30 bundles, wrapped in waterproof covering and two layers of Hessian, and firmly secured with four steel straps. Each bundle of 5 pounds should

be wrapped in craft paper and lined with one layer of polythene film.

3. The dimensions of the cartons are 15cm × 30cm × 50cm with the volume of about 0.023 cubic meter. The net weight is 21kg, the gross weight, 22kg, the tare weight, 1kg. For the shipping marks outside the carton, in addition to the gross, net and tare weight, the wording MADE IN CHINA should be stenciled on the package.

4. Each carton is lined with a polythene sheet and secured by overall metal strapping, thus preventing the contents from dampness and possible damage through rough handling.

5. 毛巾用塑料袋包装,三个不同颜色的毛巾装在一个纸板盒里,一打纸板盒装在一个纸箱里,外箍铁箍。

6. 该批货物的运输标记为一个三角形,内刷我公司名称缩写字母。

7. 三层牛皮纸袋内加一层塑料袋装,每包25公斤。

8. 每100打装一箱,刷唛头 TM,从第一号开始循序编号。

9. 除了毛重、净重和皮重外,"中国制造"字样也要在包装上加上钢印。

10. 纸箱在运输和储存时不能和木箱在一起,这样破损率比与木箱在一起要低。

Ⅴ. Translate the Following Letter into English

敬启者:

感谢贵方5月10日的来信询问我方关于花瓶的包装,现告知如下:

花瓶每个先套一塑料袋,再装入一较厚的精美的纸盒内,10盒装一垫有泡沫塑料的纸板箱中。纸箱应足够坚固,以经得起粗暴搬运和长途运输。此外,请在一个圆形内写上我方名称缩写 ASD,下面标明数量和目的港。另"易碎品""此端向上"等印刷在外包装上。

请严格按照我方要求包装,以免运输途中受损。务请尽快装运,以赶上销售旺季。

此致

Ⅵ. Translate the Following Letter into Chinese

Dear Sirs,

In reply to your fax message of May 26, we regret having forgotten to mention the inner packing requirements of Bee Brand Brown Sugar we ordered at the Guangzhou Spring Fair this year. Now we have discussed the matter with our customers. They request as follows:

As brown sugar is moisture absorbent especially in hot rainy seasons, it should be packed in kraft paper bags containing 20 small paper bags of 1 kilogram net each, two kraft paper bags to a carton lined with water-proof paper.

We hope the above requirements will be acceptable to you and look forward to your early reply.

Yours sincerely,

附录7A 装箱单
Appendix 7A Packing List

Issuer TIANJIN GARMENTS i/e INC. No.1 YOUYI ROAD, HEXI DISTRICT TIANJIN, CHINA	装箱单 PACKING LIST	
To FM TRADING SWEDEN AB KORSGATAN 13SE-41116 GOTHENBURG SWEDEN	Invoice: No.: G2010S/A2218	Date: Nov. 07, 2010
Marks and number FM TRADING CARTON NUMBER ARTICLE NAME: LAUNDRBAG NUMBER OF PCS IN THE CARTON ORDER NUMBER MADE IN CHINA	Number and kind of packages 87CTNS +7 900PCS LAUNDRBAG CTN NO.　COLOR　　　SIZE　　　　ORDER　　QTY　　TOTAL PCS 1~50　　　OFFWHITE　　72×110CM　50276　　89　　 4 450PCS 51　　　　OFFWHITE　　72×110CM　50276　　64　　 64PCS 52~57　　GREEN　　　　72×110CM　50276　　89　　 534PCS 58　　　　GREEN　　　　72×110CM　50276　　32　　 32PCS 59~64　　PURPLE　　　72×110CM　50276　　89　　 534PCS 65　　　　PURPLE　　　72×110CM　50276　　88　　 88PCS 66~85　　BROWN　　　 78×118CM　4567　　　102　　2 040PCS 86　　　　BROWN　　　 78×118CM　4567　　　90　　 90PCS 87　　　　BLUE/WHITE　72×110CM　50276　　68　　 68PCS 　　　　　　　　　　　　　　　　　　　　　　　　　7 900PCS 天津服装进出口股份有限公司 TIANJIN GARMENTS IMPORT & EXPORT INCORPORATION GROSS WEIGHT: 2 309.00KGS NET WEIGHT: 2 222.00KGS MEASURMENT: 6.35CBM	

Chapter 8

第 8 章

保　　险
Insurance

Learning Objectives

Enable the students to know the importance of insurance in international trade; to master the main insurance categories, and to be able to write letters on insurance.

使学生了解保险在外贸业务中的重要性；掌握国际贸易中主要险别的种类以及办理保险这类信函的写法。

8.1　背景知识
Background Information

Insurance is an important part in international trade. In international trade, goods from the sellers to the buyers are generally over a long- distance shipment. Ships may leak, sink or collide. Because of that, consignments may be lost or be damaged in transit. Furthermore, it has to go through the procedures of loading, unloading and storing. During this process, the goods may encounter various kinds of dangers and sometimes suffer losses. In order to protect the goods from possible losses in case of such perils, the buyers or the sellers usually apply to an insurance company for cargo transportation insurance.

International transportation insurance mainly covers Marine Cargo Transportation Insurance, On Land Cargo Transportation Insurance, Air Cargo Transportation Insurance and Mail Cargo Transportation Insurance, of which Marine Cargo Transportation Insurance is the oldest,

保险是国际贸易程序中非常重要的一个环节。在国际贸易中，每笔交易的货物，从卖方交至买方手中一般都要经过长途运输，运输途中，船只或许会渗漏、沉没或碰撞，遭受损失或灭失，而且要经过多次装卸及储运过程。在此过程中，货物可能遇到各种危险甚至灭失。为了使货物免受这些事故带来的损失，在货物运输前，买方或卖方通常向保险公司投保货物运输保险。

国际贸易运输保险的种类主要包括海上货物运输保险、陆上货物运输保险、航空货物运输保险和邮包运输保险，其中以海上货物运输保险历史最久，其他几

others are all based on it.

According to China Insurance Clauses (CIC), which is made by the People Insurance company of China (PICC), Marine Cargo Transportation Insurance has two categories: the principal risks and additional risks. The principal risks in Marine Cargo Transportation Insurance are: Free from Particular Average (FPA), with Particular Average (W P A.), All Risks.

According to *PICC's Ocean Marine Cargo Clauses* revised in January 1, 1981, F. P. A. insurance covers:

(1) Total or Constructive Total Loss of whole consignment hereby insured caused in the course of transit by natural calamities—heavy weather, lightning, tsunami, earthquake and flood. In case a constructive total loss is claimed for, the Insured shall abandon to the Company the damaged goods and all his rights and title pertaining thereto. The goods on each lighter to or from the seagoing vessel shall be deemed a separate risk. Constructive Total Loss refers to the loss where an actual total loss appears to be unavailable or the cost to be incurred in recovering or reconditioning the goods together with the forwarding costs to the destination named in the policy would exceed their value on arrival.

(2) Total or Partial Loss caused by accidents—the carrying conveyance being grounded stranded, sunk or in collision with floating ice or other objects as fire or explosion.

(3) Partial Loss of the insured goods is attributable to heavy weather, lightning and/or tsunami, where the conveyance has been grounded, stranded, sunk or burnt, irrespective of whether the event or events took place before or after such accident.

(4) Partial or Total Loss consequent on falling of entire package or packages into sea during loading, transshipment or discharge.

(5) Reasonable cost incurred by the insured in salvaging the goods or averting or minimizing a loss recoverable

类运输保险都是在海上货物运输保险的基础上起来的。

中国人民保险公司（PICC）制定的《中国保险条款》（CIC），将海上货物运输保险险别分为基本险和附加险两类。海上货物运输保险的基本险别分为平安险（FPA）、水渍险（WPA）和一切险三种。

根据1981年1月1日修订的《中国人民保险公司海洋运输货物保险条款》的规定，平安险负责赔偿：

（1）被保险货物在途中由于恶劣气候、雷电、海啸、地震、洪水等自然灾害造成整批货物的全部损失或推定全损。当被保险人要求赔付推定全损时，须将受损货物及其权利委付给保险公司。被保险货物用驳船运往或远离海轮的，每一驳船所装的货物可视为一个整体。推定全损是指被保险货物的实际全损已经不可避免，或者恢复、修复受损货物以及运送货物到原定目的地的费用超过该货物的价值。

（2）由于遭受搁浅、触礁、沉没、互撞、与流冰或其他物体碰撞以及失火、爆炸意外事故造成货物的全部或部分损失。

（3）在运输工具已经发生搁浅、触礁、沉没、焚毁以及事故的情况下，货物在此前后又在海上遭受恶劣气候、雷电、海啸等自然灾害所造成的部分损失。

（4）在装运、转运或卸货时，由于整数件货物落海造成的全部或部分损失。

（5）被保险人对遭受承保责任内危险的货物采取抢救、防止

under the policy, provided that cost shall not exceed the sum insured of the consignment so save.

(6) Losses attributing to discharge of the insured goods at a port of distress following a sea peril as well as special charges arising from loading, warehousing and forwarding of the goods at an intermediate port of call or refuge.

(7) Sacrifice and Contribution to General Average and Salvage Charges.

(8) Such proportion of losses sustained by the ship owners as is to be reimbursed by the Cargo Owner under the Contract of Affreightment "Both to Blame Collision" clause.

W. P. A. covers wider than F. P. A. Aside from the risks covered under F. P. A. conditions as above, this insurance also covers partial losses of the insured goods caused by heavy weather, lightening, tsunami, earthquake, and/or flood and so on.

The cover of All Risks is the most comprehensive of three principal insurances. Aside from the risks covered under F. P. A. and W. P. A. conditions as above, this insurance also covers all risks of loss of or damage to insured goods whether partial or total, arising from external causes in the course of transit. It should be noted that "All Risks" does not, as its name suggests, really cover all risks. The "All Risks" clause excludes coverage against damage caused by war, strikes, riots, etc. These perils can be covered by a separate clause. And it covers only physical loss or damage from external causes.

The Additional Risks in the China Insurance Clauses (CIC) include "General Additional Risks" and "Special Additional Risks".

General Additional Risk usually includes the following 11 risks:

(1) Theft, Pilferage and Non-delivery Risk, T. P. N. D. ;

或减少货损的措施而支付的合理费用，但以不超过该批被救货物的保险金额为限。

(6) 运输工具遭遇海难后，在避难港由于卸货所引起的损失，以及在中途港、避难港由于卸货、存仓以及运送货物所产生的特别费用。

(7) 共同海损的牺牲、分摊和救助费用。

(8) 运输契约订有"船舶互撞责任"条款，根据该条款规定应由供货方偿还船方的损失。

水渍险负责赔偿的范围比平安险广。除了上述平安险的各项责任以外，水渍险还负责被保险货物在运输途中由于恶劣气候、雷电、海啸、地震、洪水等造成的部分损失。

在三种基本险中，一切险承保的范围最为广泛。除了包括上述平安险和水渍险的各项责任以外，该保险还负责保险货物在运输途中由于外来因素所致的全部或部分损失。还要注意的是，一切险并不是像其名称所说的那样，承保所有的风险。一切险条款排除对由于战争、罢工、动乱等造成的损失的赔偿。这些风险可由单独的条款来负责赔偿。并且，一切险只负责赔偿由于外来原因造成的物理性灭失或损坏。

《中国保险条款》中的附加险有一般附加险和特殊附加险之分。

一般附加险有下列 11 种险别：

(1) 偷窃、提货不着险；

(2) Fresh Water and Rain Damage Risk, F. W. R. D. ;
(3) Leakage Risk;
(4) Shortage Risk;
(5) Intermixture and Contamination Risk;
(6) Clash and Breakage Risk;
(7) Taint of Odour Risk;
(8) Sweat and Heating Risk;
(9) Hook Damage Risk;
(10) Breakage of Packing Risk;
(11) Rust Risk.

Special Additional Risk includes the following 8 risks:
(1) War Risk;
(2) Strikes Risk;
(3) Import Duty Risk;
(4) Aflatoxin Risk;
(5) On Deck Risk;
(6) Rejection Risk;
(7) Failure to Deliver Risk;
(8) Fire Risk Extension Clause For Storage of Cargo at Destination Hong Kong (Including Kowloon) or Macao, F. R. E. C..

According to the stipulations in On Land Cargo Transportation Insurance Clause of the PICC, the principal risks include Overland Transportation Risks and Overland Transportation All Risks.

Air Cargo Transportation Insurance includes Air Transportation Risks and Air Transportation All Risks.

As per the stipulations in Mail Cargo Transportation Insurance, there are Mail Cargo Transportation Risks and Mail Cargo Transportation All Risks.

Institute Cargo Clauses (ICC) that is made by London Insurance Institute, is one of the most widely used clauses in the world. It mainly covers the followings:

(1) ICC (A);
(2) ICC (B);
(3) ICC (C);
(4) Institute War Clauses Cargo Clause;
(5) Institute Strike clauses Cargo Clause;

(2) 淡水雨淋险;
(3) 渗漏险;
(4) 短量险;
(5) 混杂、沾污险;
(6) 碰损、破碎险;
(7) 串味险;
(8) 受潮受热险;
(9) 钩损险;
(10) 包装破裂险;
(11) 锈损险。

特殊附加险有下列8种类别:
(1) 战争险;
(2) 罢工险;
(3) 进口关税险;
(4) 黄曲霉素险;
(5) 舱面险;
(6) 拒收险;
(7) 交货不到险;
(8) 出口货物到香港(包括九龙在内)或澳门存仓火险责任扩展条款等,简称FREC。

根据中国人民保险公司制定的《陆上运输货物保险条款》的规定,陆上货物运输保险的基本险别有陆运险和陆运一切险两种。

航空货物运输保险的基本险别有航空运输险和航空运输一切险。

根据邮包运输保险条款的规定,有邮包险和邮包一切险两种基本险。

英国伦敦保险协会制定的《协会货物条款》(ICC)是对世界各国保险业影响最大,应用最为广泛的保险条款。主要内容有:
(1) 协会货物(A)险条款;
(2) 协会货物(B)险条款;
(3) 协会货物(C)险条款;
(4) 协会货物战争险条款;
(5) 协会货物罢工险条款;

(6) Malicious Damage Clause.

In the above six risks, (A) risk, (B) risk, (C) risk are principal risks, others belong to the Additional Risks.

Insurance clause is one of the most important parts in the International Contract. Generally, it mainly includes: two participants, insurance coverage, the insurance amount, premium and the insurance policy. The two participants include the insurer and the insured. The insurer refers to the insurance company or underwriter. The insured refers to the buyer or the seller. The insured pays the premium to the insurer, and then the insured gets a policy which is one of the important documents. The insurance amount is calculated as the total value of the goods based on CIF plus 10%, i.e. 110% of the total invoice value. If the insured requires more than 110% of the total value, the importer has to bear the additional premium. In our country, the main insurance documents are insurance policy, insurance certificate, open policy and so on.

Insurance policy is a document issued by the insurer, setting out the exact terms and conditions of an insurance transaction—the name of the insured, the name of commodity insured, the amount insured, the name of the carrying vessel, the precise risks covered, the validity and any exceptions there may be. It is also a written contract of insurance between the insurance company and the insured.

Insurance Certificate is a simplified insurance policy. It has the necessary items of an insurance policy, but it doesn't set out the rights and duties of the insurer and the insured, which is still subject to the detailed insurance clauses of a formal insurance policy. An insurance certificate has the same effect as an insurance policy.

For all the CIF export contracts, the seller shall, before the shipment, effect insurance with the insurance company in time. Details such as name of commodities, insurance amount, shipping line, sailing date and insurance coverage should be listed when effecting the insurance.

（6）恶意损害险条款。

上述六种险别中（A）险、（B）险、（C）险属于基本险，其他属于附加险。

保险条款是国际货物买卖合同的重要组成部分之一。一般来说，保险条款所涉及的内容有双方当事人、投保险别、保险金额、保险费、保险单证等。保险当事人是保险人与被保险人。保险人指保险公司，被保险人为买方或者卖方。被保险人需要向保险人支付保险费以获得保单。保险金额按货物CIF价格加成10%来计算，也就是总发票金额的110%。如果被保险人需要获得高于总金额的110%，进口方需要自己另外支付保险费。我国常用的保险单证主要有保险单、保险凭证、预约保单等。

保险单是保险人签发的一种单证，它严格地规定了一笔保险业务的条款和条件——被保险人的名字、保险货物名称、保险金额、载货船只名称、承保险别、保险期限和可能产生的免责事项。它也是保险人和被保险人之间订立的书面契约。

保险凭证是一种简化的保险单，它具有保险单上的必要项目，但它并不列出保险人和被保险人的权利和义务，它们应以正式保险单详细的保险条款为准。保险凭证与保险单具有同样的效力。

凡按CIF价格成交的出口合同，卖方在装船前，须及时向保险公司办理投保手续。在投保时，投保人应将货物名称、保险金额、运输路线、开航日期及投保险别等详细列明。

For all the FOB or CFR contracts, the buyer shall effect insurance with the insurance company. Under FOB and CFR, Open Policy is signed with the PICC for goods imported in China. The formalities of insurance effecting for each lot of imports shall be deemed as being completed upon the time when the insurance company has received the notice indicating the name, the No. of B/L, the date of sailing, the name and quantity of the commodities, port of shipment and port of destination, etc.

Letters concerning insurance should include the following information:
(1) The goods or consignment to be covered;
(2) The coverage of the insurance and the insurance amount;
(3) The premium rate;
(4) The way of premium payment;
(5) The validity of the insurance;
(6) Insurance company;
(7) Express expectations for an early reply or cooperation.

Insurance letters often include three parts.

1. Acknowledge receipt of the letter concerning insurance matters.

For example:
(1) Thank you for your letter of March 8. With regard to your inquiry on insurance, we are pleased to provide you with the following details.
(2) In reply to your letter of March 10 asking us to cover the consignment of 100 cases of high-quality electric toys from Shanghai to London.

2. Express your willingness to cover insurance on the goods, state clearly the usual terms of insurance, including insurance amount, insurance premium, insurance clause, types of insurance, the way of premium payment, insurance company, etc.

For example:
(1) We cover the goods against all risks for USD 1 000 with the People's Insurance Company of China.

凡按 FOB 或 CFR 价格成交的合同，买方应该向保险公司办理投保手续。在我国按 FOB 及 CFR 条件进口货物的保险是同中国人民保险公司签订预约保险合同。每批进口货物在收到国外装运通知后，将船名、提单号、开船日期、商品名称及数量、装运港和目的港等通知保险公司即为办妥保险手续。

保险信函在写作过程中一般包括以下内容：
（1）被保险的货物；
（2）保险险别及保险金额；
（3）保险费率；
（4）保险费的支付方式；
（5）保险期限；
（6）保险公司；
（7）表达早日收到对方回复或合作的期望。

保险类信函通常主要包括三个部分。

1. 确认收到关于咨询保险事宜的信函。

举例：
（1）感谢你3月8日的来信，咨询关于保险事宜，现向你提供以下详情。
（2）兹回复贵方3月10日的来信，要求我们对从上海运往伦敦的100箱电动玩具进行投保。

2. 表达对于货物投保的意愿，清楚地说明一般保险条件，包括保险金额、保险费率、保险条款、保险类型、保险费的支付方式、保险公司等。

举例：
（1）我们向中国人民保险公司办理投保一切险，保险金额为

(2) We usually effect insurance on 100 cases of electric toys against All Risks and War risks for the full invoice value plus 10% as per CIC.

3. Hope for an early reply, and give assurance of your close cooperation.

For example:

(1) We hope you are able to send us the quotation of your rate for insurance at early date.

(2) If our rate is acceptable, please let us know immediately so that our insurance policy can reach you in time.

1 000 美元。

(2) 对于这 100 箱电动玩具,我们通常按照投保发票金额的 100% 加 10% 投保一切险和战争险,保险条款参考伦敦协会货物保险条款。

3. 希望早日收到回复,并且表达愿意与对方密切合作的意愿。

举例:

(1) 希望贵方早日给我们关于保险费率的报价。

(2) 如果保险费率合适的话,请立刻告知我们,以便我们能够及时向您寄交保险单。

8.2 信例
Sample Letters

Letter 1 Ask to Cover the Insurance

Dear Sir,

      Our Order No. 103 covering 1 000 pieces Electronic Toys

We wish to refer you to our Order No. 103 for 1 000 pieces of the captioned goods, from which you will see that this order was placed on FOB basis.

As we now desire to have the consignment insured at your end, we would be so much grateful if you will kindly arrange to insure the goods on our behalf against All Risks at invoice value plus 10%, and We shall of course refund the premium to you upon receipt of your debit note.

We hope the above will be acceptable to you.

                     Yours faithfully,

Dear Sir,

      Your Order No. 103 covering 1 000 pieces Electronic Toys

Thank you for your letter of September 20, requesting us to effect insurance on 1 000 pieces Electronic Toys for your account.

We are pleased to inform you that we have covered the above goods with the People's Insurance Company of China against All Risks. The policy is being prepared accordingly and will be sent to you on or about September 28 together with our debit note for the premium.

We believe that everything is clear now, your early reply will be highly appreciated.

                     Yours faithfully,

Notes

1. refer to 参阅

   We refer to your Offer No. 123 for 3 000 drums of petroleum. 参阅你方关于 3 000 桶石油的 123 号报盘。

2. the captioned goods 标题项下的货物

3. FOB. FREE ON BOARD （…named port of shipment） 装运港船上交货（……指定装运港），贸易术语中的一种

4. consignment 货物；寄售

   a new consignment of goods 新到的一批货物

   a consignment sale 寄售

   consignment business 寄售业务；委托买卖

5. arrange 安排；排列；协商

6. insure 投保，保险

   Please insure the goods against breakage. 请将此货物投保破碎险。

   insurance 保险

   有关保险常用词组有：

       insurance company 保险公司

       insurance agent 保险代理人

       insurance amount 保险金额

       insurance premium 保险费

       insurance certificate 保险凭证

       insurance policy 保险单

       insurance coverage 保险范围

       floating policy 流动保单

       insurance declaration 保险声明书或者保险通知单

       air transportation insurance 航运运输保险

       ocean marine cargo insurance 海洋运输货物保险

       overland transportation insurance 陆上运输保险

       parcel post insurance 邮包保险

   在表示"投保""办理保险"时，常与 insurance 搭配的动词或动词词组有：

       to arrange insurance

       to cover insurance

       to effect insurance

       to provide insurance

       to take out insurance

   与 insurance 有关的介词搭配有：

       表示所保的货物，后接 on，如 insurance on the 100 tons of wool；

       表示所保的险别，后接 against，如 insurance against all risks；

       表示保额，后接 for，如 insurance for 110% of the invoice value；

表示保险费或保险费率，后接 at，如 insurance at a slightly higher premium, insurance at the rate of 5%；

表示向保险公司投保，后接 with，如 insurance with the People's Insurance Company of China.

We have covered insurance on the 100 tons of wool for 110% of the invoice value against all risks with the People's Insurance Company of China. 对于这 100 吨羊毛，我们已按发票金额的 110% 向中国人民保险公司投保了一切险。

7. on one's behalf 代表某人或某方
8. invoice value 发票价值
9. premium 费率
10. People's Insurance Company of China 中国人民保险公司
11. debit note 索款通知书

Letter 2　Additional Risk of Breakage

Dear Sirs,

Additional Risk of Breakage

Referring to your L/C No. 123 covering Glazed Wall Tiles, which we have just received.

For the above goods, we are sorry to inform you that we do not cover Breakage. You have to, therefore, delete the word "Breakage" from the insurance clause in the credit.

Furthermore, we would like to point out that for such articles as window glass, porcelains, etc., even if additional Risk of Breakage has been insured, the cover is subject to a franchise of 5%. That is to say, if the breakage is surveyed to be less than 5%, no claims for damage will be entertained.

We believe that everything is clear now, and hope you can amend the credit as soon as possible.

Yours faithfully,

Notes

1. For the above goods, we are sorry to inform you that we do not cover Breakage. 我们很抱歉告知贵方，对于上述货物，我们不投保破碎险。

   that we do not cover Breakage 宾语从句，作 inform 的宾语

2. delete 删除

   The clause "All expenses are for the beneficiaries' account" should be deleted from the L/C. "一切费用由受益人负担"的条款应从信用证中删除。

3. franchise 免赔额

   The goods are sold with a franchise of 3%. 此类商品按免赔率 3% 出售。

Letter 3　Insurance Claim

Dear Sirs,

The goods shipped per M. V. "Yellow River" arrived here on March 10, one side of case No. 9 was found to have split. We therefore had the cases opened and the contents examined by a local insurance surveyor in the presence of the shipping company's agent. On examination, we have found that 50 cases of the 120 electric toys were badly damaged.

Therefore, We enclosed our surveyor's report and shipping agent's statement for you to approach the insurer for our claim, we should be grateful if you would take the matter up for us with the insurers.

We sincerely hope there will be no difficulty in connecting with the insurer and thank you in advance for your trouble on our behalf.

Yours faithfully,

Notes

1. insurance surveyor 保险调查员；保险公证人
2. surveyor's report 检验报告
3. shipping agent 货运代理人
4. take the matter up 处理问题

   As you hold the insurance policy, we should be grateful if you would take the matter up for us with the insurers.

   由于你公司持有保险单，希望你公司就此事与保险公司接洽。

Tips

1. "劳合社"简介

   劳合社（Lloyd's）始创于17世纪末。它最初是伦敦的一个小咖啡馆，后逐渐发展为世界上最重要的海上保险组织和重要的通信机构。劳合社和伦敦其他的海上保险公司形成了世界上最大的海上保险市场，即"伦敦市场"。劳合社本身并不经营具体保险业务，只是为其会员提供办理保险业务的场所。2000年，劳合社在北京开设了在中国的第一家代表处。

2. 《中国保险条款》（China Insurance Clauses，CIC）与《协会货物条款》（Institute Cargo Clause，ICC）

   （1）CIC沿用了传统的分类形式，即以平安险、水渍险和一切险表示基本险，附加险另文说明。风险承保范围从小到大，逐一列明，除外责任单独表示。ICC则以"（A）、（B）、（C）"等系统命名方式将保险责任明显区分为基本险和附加险。风险承保范围由大到小，承保风险采用排外式和列举式两种方法表示：ICC的（A）险以承保所有风险减除外责任的方法表示，其他两险（B）、（C）逐一列明，在列明的基础上，再去除除外责任。

（2）CIC 只有三种基本险可以单独承保（尽管近年来我国实践中也已开展战争险和罢工险业务，但是在条文形式上仍是如此），而 ICC 的战争险和罢工险由于自成体系，根据条款规定，在征得保险公司同意后，也可以单独承保。

（3）CIC 仅原则性地规定了"船舶互撞"条款的赔偿责任，而 ICC 各险均特别指明保险人在赔付时有对被保险人此种索赔进行抗辩的权利，这样可以避免保险人因单方面理算不清或"过失"而承担不应有的赔偿责任，反映出保险方在赔付时不仅要严格查明应由保险方承担的被保险方的最小损失，还要通过"双方有责碰撞"条款向索赔方抗辩的机会，将扩展赔偿的责任紧缩到最小限度。

（4）ICC 将被保险人无法控制的延迟或绕道等情况与运输契约在目的地之前终止的情况区别对待：在前一种情况下，被保险人无须发出通知。保险责任自动继续有效；在后一种情况下，只有在被保险人及时将情况通知保险人并在必要时加缴保险费的情况下，保险责任才可以继续有效。CIC 对这两种情况没有区分对待，而是均需要被保险人及时通知保险人并在必要时加缴保险费，保险责任才继续有效。显然 CIC 的规定对被保险人不利。

8.3　有用的短语和句子

Useful Expressions

1. We know that according to your usual practice, you insure the goods only at invoice value plus 10%, therefore, the extra premium will be for our account.
   我们得知，按照你们的一般惯例，你们只按发票金额另加 10% 投保，因此额外保险费由我方负担。

2. For these goods, the rate being charged by us against All Risks is 1% subject to our Ocean Marine Clauses.
   根据我方目前海运货物保险条款，承保上述货物一切险的现行费率为 1%。

3. Since Breakage is a special risk, an extra premium will have to be charged.
   破碎险是一种特殊险别，需要额外收费。

4. Since the cause of the damage is within the coverage, we would recommend you to apply to the insurance company concerned for compensation.
   由于损害的原因属于保险单的承保范围之内，我们建议贵方向有关的保险公司要求赔偿。

5. In the absence of definite instructions from our clients, we generally cover shipments against W. P. A. and War Risks. If you wish to add any extraneous risks, please let us know in advance.
   在我们没有收到客户明确通知的情况下，我们一般投保水渍险和战争险。如果贵方想投保附加险，请事先告诉我们。

6. If the consignment is insured, each case of claim on damaged goods involves three parties—i. e. the insured, the carrier and the insurer.
   如果一批货物投保，那么，有关被损坏货物的索赔程序涉及三个方面：被保险人、承运人和保险人。

7. So far as we know, there are risks of pilferage or damage to the goods during transshipment in London, so please arrange insurance against the above risks.
   据我方所知,在伦敦转船期间有货物被盗或损坏的风险,请投保上述险别。

8. Should you require the insurance to be covered as per Institute Cargo Clauses, we would be glad to comply; but if there is any difference in premium between the two, it will be charged for your account.
   假如你们需要按照协会货物保险条款投保,我们也乐于照办;但如果两者保费有所不同,则其差额由贵方负担。

9. We are also in a position to insure the goods against any additional risks if you so desire.
   如愿意,我们也能对货物投保任何附加险。

10. Our insurance company is a state-operated enterprise enjoying high prestige in settling claims promptly and equitably and has agents in all main ports and regions of the world.
    我们的保险公司是国有企业,享有理赔迅速、处理公平的声誉,并在全世界各主要港口和地区都有代理。

11. We can arrange insurance on your behalf.
    我们可以为贵方办保险。

12. We have covered the goods against All Risks and war risks.
    我们已为货物投保了一切险和战争险。

13. Since the premium varies with the extent of insurance, extra premium is for the buyer's account, should additional risks be covered.
    因为保险费随保险范围的不同而不同,如果买方要求投保附加险,额外的保险费则应该由买方负担。

14. Insurance is to be effected by the sellers for 110% of the invoice value against All Risks and War Risks as per the relevant *Ocean Marine Cargo Clause of People's Insurance Company of China* dated January 1, 1981.
    由卖方根据中国人民保险公司1981年1月1日颁布的《中国人民保险公司海洋运输货物保险条款》按发票金额的110%投保一切险和战争险。

15. Please see to it that the above-mentioned goods should be shipped before the 15th May and the goods should be covered for 150% of invoice. We know that according to value against All Risks, your usual practice, you insure the goods only for 10%, so the extra premium will be for our account.
    请注意上述货物必须确保于5月15日前装船。保险须按发票价格的150%投保一切险。我们知道按照贵方惯例贵方只按发票价格加成10%投保,因此额外保险费由我方负担。

16. Should stranding and sinking of the carrying vessel take place, then how would the insurance company handle this situation?
    万一运输船搁浅沉没,保险公司将如何处理?

17. If the insured shall make any claim knowing the same to be false or fraudulent as regards amount or otherwise, this policy shall become void and all claim there under shall be forfeited.
    若被保险人故意虚报保额或其他项目,则该保险单无效,并丧失索赔权。

18. We shall refund to you the premium upon receiving your debit note or you may draw on us at sight for the amount required.

我们收到贵方借项清单后返还保险费，或者贵方按所付金额向我方开出即期汇票。

19. For the coverage of All Risks, the insurance company shall be liable for total or partial loss on land or sea of the insured goods within the period covered by the insurance.

    投保一切险后，保险公司负责陆上和海洋上运输过程中被保险货物的全部损失或部分损失。

20. We adopt the warehouse to warehouse clause which is commonly used in international insurance.

    在国际货物运输保险中，我们采用仓至仓条款。

21. Premium will be added to invoice amount together with freight charges.

    保险费与运费将会加到发票金额中。

22. Since the premium varies with the extent of insurance, extra premium is for buyer's account, should additional risks be covered.

    保险不同，其费率也不同，如果投保附加险别，买方应该支付额外的保险费率。

23. We usually effect insurance against All Risks and War Risk for full invoice value plus 10% for the goods sold on CIF basis.

    对于按 CIF 出售的货物，我们通常按发票金额的 110% 投保一切险和战争险。

24. We are sorry to tell you that in Case No. 5, which was invoiced as containing 10 typewriters, five of them were found to be badly damaged upon arrival. Enclosed is an inspection certificate and the sipping agent's statement for your reference.

    我们很遗憾地通知你方，发票所列第 5 箱，内装 10 台打印机，在货物到达时，发现有 5 台严重受损。现随信附寄商检报告和船运代理人的报告书供你方参考。

25. Should the consignment experience any damage, you may, within 30 days after its arrival at the port of destination, approach the insurance agents at your end and file your claim with them, which is to be supported by a surveyor report.

    如果货物发生损坏，你方可在货物到达目的港后 30 天内凭公正行的检验报告与当地的保险代理人联系，并向他们提出索赔事宜。

26. We adopt the "warehouse to warehouse clause", which is commonly used in international insurance.

    我们采用"仓至仓条款"，仓至仓条款通常应用于国际保险业务中。

练习

Exercises

Ⅰ. Comprehension Questions

1. What is the definition of insurance?
2. What does International trade transportation insurance mainly cover?
3. What are the principal risks in Marine Cargo Transportation Insurance?
4. What does the Additional Risks in the China Insurance Clauses (CIC) include?
5. What does the Insurance clause include?

Ⅱ. Translate the Following Terms and Expressions

1. air transportation insurance
2. ocean marine cargo insurance
3. parcel post insurance
4. Leakage Risk

5. Hook Damage Risk
6. War Risk
7. Taint of Odour Risk
8. Fresh and/or Rain Water Damage Risks
9. 中国人民保险公司
10. 免赔额
11. 平安险
12. 水渍险
13. 一切险
14. 保险代理人
15. 保险金额
16. 保险费
17. 保险凭证
18. 保险单
19. 保险范围
20. 流动保单

Ⅲ. Read the Following Letters and Fill in the Blanks with Appropriate Words

We refer _____ our Purchase Confirmation No. 100 _____ 500 pieces of Lucky Blanket. We are notifying that we have opened _____ Citibank a confirmed irrevocable letter of credit No. 200, totaling USD 3 500, the L/C shall _____ in force till 30th, June.

Please _____ to it that above mentioned articles would be shipped before the end of June and the goods should be covered insurance _____ 130% of the invoice value _____ All Risks. We know that according to your usual practice, you insure the goods only _____ invoice value plus 10%. Therefore the extra premium will be _____ .

Please _____ insurance as our requirements and we await your advice of shipment.

Ⅳ. Translate the Following Sentences
1. Should any damage occur to the goods, you may file your claim with the insurance company, who will take up the matter without delay.
2. Our insurance company is a state-operated enterprise, enjoying high reputation in settling claims promptly and equitably and has agents in all main ports and regions of the world.
3. Your customer's request for insurance coverage up to the inland city is acceptable on condition that such extra premium is for his account. And generally we cover insurance WPA and War Risk in the absence of definite instructions from our clients. If you want to cover All Risks, we can provide such coverage at a slightly higher premium.
4. 为了使货物免受这些事故带来的损失，在货物运输之前，买方或者卖方通常向保险公司申请货物运输保险。
5. 此类货物按免赔率5%出售。
6. 如果贵方要求我方投保偷窃、提货不着险，我们也会照办，只要支付附加保险费即可。
7. 我们的保险公司在公平、迅速理赔方面享有很高的声誉，并且在世界各主要港口和地区都有自己的代理。
8. 破碎险的保险费率是5%，如果你方愿意投保破碎险，我们可以代为办理。
9. 如果货物发生损坏，你方可在货物到达目的港后30天内凭公正行的检验报告与当地的保险代理人联系，并向他们提出索赔事宜。
10. 我们采用"仓至仓条款"，仓至仓条款通常应用于国际保险业务中。

Ⅴ. Translate the Following Paragraph into English

信用证应规定所需保险的类别以及应投保的附加险别。不应使用诸如"通常险别"或"惯常险别"一类含义不明确的词语。如遇使用这类词语，银行将按照所提供的保险单据予以接受，而不负任何险别漏保之责。

Ⅵ. Write a Letter to Your Insurer to Include the Following Points
1. Begin the letter appropriately.

2. Say that goods sent on M. V. "Yellow River" from Bombay to London arrived on time but were damaged on arrival.
3. Your agent inspected the damage and noticed that the goods in containers No. 3 and No. 4 were damaged despite being packed in accordance with your instructions. The goods were also inspected by a third party and photographs of the damaged unites were taken and a detailed report written.
4. You enclose the report and photographs. Say you want to make a claim for the price of replacing the damaged goods.
5. Say that the matter is urgent as you have customers who are waiting for the products that have been damaged and need to replace them as soon as possible also by air freight.
6. Say you look forward to their prompt reply and further instructions.
7. End the letter in a suitable way.

附录 8A 保险单
Appendix 8A Insurance Policy

中国人民保险公司

The People's Insurance Company of China

运输保险单

Application for Transportation Insurance

被保险人：上海机械进出口公司

Insured's Name：Shanghai Machinery Imp. & Exp. Corp.

兹有下列物品拟向中国人民保险公司投保：

Insurance is required on the following commodities：

标记 Marks & Nos.	包装及数量 Packing & quantity	保险货物项目 Description of goods	保险金额 Amount insured
As per Invoice No.	CARTON	COLOUR TV SET	USD 8 000.00

装载运输工具
Per conveyance：S.S. PEACE

开航日期 Date of Commencement As per B/L 自 From Shanghai	提单号码 B/L NO. 至 to Singapore
请将要保的险别标明 Please indicate the Conditions and/or Special Coverage	Covering All Risks and War risk as per Ocean Marine Cargo Clauses and War Risks Clauses

备注
Remarks

投保人（签名盖章）：
Name/Seal of Proposer：Shanghai Machinery Imp. & Exp. Corp.
电话：
Telephone No：83115212
地址：
Address：700 ZHONGSHAN ROAD SHANGHAI CHINA
日期：
Date：March 24, 2010

本公司自用		
FOR OFFICE USE ONLY		
费率 Rate 0.1%	保费 Premium USD 8	经办人 By zbc

Chapter 9

第 9 章

商品检验

Commodity Inspection

Learning Objectives

Enable the students to know the writing skills of letters on Commodity Inspection; to master the useful terms and expressions, and pay attention to the problems caused during the Commodity Inspection.

使学生掌握商品检验商务信函的撰写、商品检验信函中常用的词汇和短语、商品检验中需要注意的问题。

9.1 背景知识
Background Information

Commodity Inspection is one of the important parts in foreign trade. In the process of performance of the contract, a series of activities such as delivery, payment, claims and so on are based on Commodity Inspection. So it plays an important role in foreign trade.

All import and export commodities must undergo inspection procedures. Inspections involve in quality, weight, quantity and packing of the commodities, and are carried out in accordance with the stipulations of terms and conditions laid down in foreign trade contracts. So any commodities should be applied for the inspection with the State General Administration for Quality Supervision and Inspection and Quarantine (AQSIQ), and will be released only after gaining inspection certificate issued by the Administration for Quality Supervision and Inspection and Quarantine. Normally the inspection certificates issued by AQSIQ are to be taken as final basis and have binding force to both parties. So

商品检验是国际贸易中非常重要的一个环节。在履行贸易合同的过程中，货物的交付、支付、索赔等一系列活动都是以商品检验为基础的，因此，商品检验在一国的对外贸易活动中具有重要地位。

一切进出口商品必须进行商品检验。商品检验涉及商品的质量、重量、数量及包装，并且根据国家规定及外贸合同所定的条款进行。所以，任何商品必须向国家进出口商品检验检疫局（AQSIQ）报检，且只有取得有关质量监督与检验检疫局签发的检验证书，海关才会放行。一般来说，AQSIQ签发的商品检验证书将会被视为最终的依据，并对双方具有约束力。因此，商品检验证书

inspection certificates are legal basis not only for delivery and payment but also for claims and settlement of claims.

Generally speaking, Commodity Inspection is conducted by special inspection department. In our country, it is charged by General Administration of Quality Supervision, Inspection and Quarantine of the People's Republic of China (AQSIQ). The certificates of inspection issued by the inspection department include Inspection Certificate of Quality, Inspection Certificate of Weight or Quantity, Inspection Certificate of Packing, Sanitary Inspection Certificate, Inspection Certificate of Damaged Cargo, Inspection Certificate on Tank/Hold, etc.

Commodity inspection can be divided into first inspection and re-inspection. The first inspection should be conducted by authorized inspection institution before shipment. The buyers have the right to re-inspect the quality and weight of goods after the goods arrived at the port of destination. After reinspected by the China Exit and Entry Inspection and Quarantine Bureau within certain days after discharging of the goods at the port/place of destination, if the quality, quantity or weight of the goods are found not in conformity with those stipulated in this contract, the buyer shall return the goods to or lodge claim against the sellers for compensation of losses upon the strength of Inspection Certificate issued by the said Bureau, with the exception of those claims for which the insurers or the carriers are liable. All expenses (including inspection fees) and losses arising from the return of the goods or claims will be charged by the sellers. In such case, the buyers may, if so requested, send a sample of the goods in question to the sellers, provided that the sampling is feasible.

不仅是交货与支付的法律依据，而且也是索赔与理赔的法律依据。

一般而言，商品的检验工作都由专业的检验机构负责。在我们国家，它是由中华人民共和国质量监督检验检疫总局办理的。由该检验机构出具的检验证书主要包括品质检验证书、重量或数量检验证书、包装检验证书、卫生检验证书、残损检验证书、船舱检验证书等。

商品检验可分为首次检验与复检。在货物装船前，可由权威的检验机构对货物进行检验。当货物到达目的地之后，买方有权对货物的质量、重量等进行复检。货到目的港（地）卸货后××天内经中国出入境检验检疫局复检，如发现质量或数量/重量与合同规定的不一致，除属保险公司或承运人负责外，买方可凭中国出入境检验检疫局出具的检验证书，向卖方提出退货或索赔。所有的退货或索赔引起的费用（包括检验费）及损失，一般均由卖方负责。在此情况下，如抽样是可行的，买方可应卖方要求，将有关货物的样品寄交卖方。

9.2 信例
Sample Letters

Letter 1　Information about the Commodity Inspection

Dear Sirs,
　　We have just received your letter of September 15 inquiring information about the Commodity Inspection.

> As a usual practice, all commodities that are exported are subject to inspection by an independent surveyor organization in that country, which issues a survey report after inspection.
>
> In order to benefit both the buyer and the seller, the buyer is entitled to re-inspect the goods upon arrival even though inspection has been made of the goods before shipment. That is, the buyer shall have the right to apply to the Administration for Quality Supervision and Inspection to carry out the inspection at the port of destination within the contracted limit. The re-inspection certificates shall be final and serve as the basis for making a claim if any discrepancy should be found not in conformity with the contract.
>
> We sincerely hope the above information will be helpful to you.
> Yours faithfully,

Notes

1. commodity inspection 商品检验
   re-inspection 复检
2. as a usual practice 按照惯例
3. survey report 检验报告
4. The buyer is entitled to re-inspect the goods upon arrival even though inspection has been made of the goods before shipment. 即使货物在装船前进行过检验，买方仍有权对商品进行复检。
   entitle 使有资格；使有权
   be entitled to 有……资格；有权
5. discrepancy 差异，不符合（之处）；不一致（之处）
6. The re-inspection certificates shall be final and serve as the basis for making a claim if any discrepancy should be found not in conformity with the contract. 复检证明书应作为最后依据。如复检时发现与合同不符，该证明书可作为索赔的基础。
   conformity 依照；遵从；符合一致
   in conformity with 和……相适应，和……一致；遵照

Letter 2　Inferior Quality

> Dear Sirs,
>
> <u>Our Order No. 123 for 200 case Muslins</u>
>
> With reference to the arrival of the captioned goods shipped per S.S. "Peace", we regret that on inspection we found that the goods do not conform to the samples, the quality is much inferior and the materials used are quite unsuited to the needs of our customers.
>
> We have sent you a sample of this article under separate mail so you can compare it with your original sample. The inferior quality of the goods put us into great trouble, and it is hard for us to dispose of it. Please let us know what you wish us to do with it.

> We hope you will look into the matter at once and arrange for the dispatch of the goods we ordered immediately.
> Look forward to your early reply.
> Yours faithfully,

Notes

1. muslins 平纹细布
2. The quality is much inferior and the materials used are quite unsuited to the needs of our customers. 这些商品质量低劣，所用的材料非常不适合顾客的需要。
   inferior（质量等）劣等的；差的；次的
3. under separate mail 单独邮寄
4. The inferior quality of the goods put us into great trouble, and it is hard for us to dispose of it. 由于商品质量低劣，给我们带来很大的不便，我们很难处理。
   dispose 处理；处置
   be disposed for 有意，愿意；倾向于
   feel disposed for 有意，愿意；倾向于
   be disposed to do 有意，愿意；倾向于
   feel disposed to do 有意，愿意；倾向于
   dispose sb. for sth. 使某人倾向于做某事
   dispose sb. to do sth. 使某人倾向于做某事

Letter 3　Goods not Up to Standard

> Dear Sirs,
>
> <u>Our Order No. 234 for Wool Carpet</u>
>
> We are enclosing a copy of the Inspection Certificate No. 203 issued by the Shanghai Entry-Exit Inspection and Quarantine. The certificate proved that the above goods we received on October 5 are not up to our standard and they are quite unsalable in our market.
>
> As this lot of goods is of no use at all to us, we require you refund the invoice amount and inspection fee of the goods amounting to US$ ...
>
> We trust you will promptly settle this matter. As soon as the settlement is accomplished, we will send the goods back to you. All expenses will be for your account.
>
> Yours faithfully,

Notes

1. Shanghai Entry-Exit Inspection and Quarantine 上海进出入境检验检疫局
2. The certificate proved that the above goods we received on October 5 are not up to our standard and they are quite unsalable in our market. 检验单证明我们10月5日收到的上述商品不符合我们的标准，因而很难在当地市场销售。

standard 标准，水准，规范

3. amount to 共计；意味着；发展成

   The bill amounts to ＄500. 这张账单共计 500 美元。

   His words amounted to a threat. 他的话实际上是威胁。

   If he goes on like this, he'll never amount to anything. 如果他一味这样下去，他将一事无成。

4. We trust you will promptly settle this matter. 希望贵方能及时理赔。

5. As soon as the settlement is accomplished, we will send the goods back to you. 一旦贵方理赔，我方将把货物退还贵方。

   accomplish 完成

   refund 归还，偿还

   refund the goods to the seller 把货物归还卖方

   refundable 可归还的，可偿还的

Letter 4　Shortweight

Dear Sirs,

　　When the M. V. "Prince" arrived at Qingdao on schedule, we checked the goods against your invoice, we discovered a considerable shortage in number.

　　On careful examining the ship's draft by the local Commodity Inspection Corporation and after due deductions made, a short weight of 50 tons was determined and certificated as against the invoice weight of... tons after deducting 1% allowance and moisture. In such circumstances, we have to lodge a claim on your company for the short weight as follow:

FOB value of the short delivered goods	US ＄ 800.00
Freight	US ＄ 100.00
Insurance premium	US ＄ 7.89
Inspection fees	US ＄ 110.00
Total	US ＄ 1 017.89

　　Enclosed we send you our Inspection Certificate No. 123 and a copy of the Surveyor's Report on weight by draft.

　　We look forward to your early reply.

　　　　　　　　　　　　　　　　　　　　　　　　　　　　Sincerely yours,
　　　　　　　　　　　　　　　　　　　　　　　　　　　　　　(Signature)

Encs (2): Inspection Certificate, Surveyor's Report

Notes

1. on schedule 如期，按计划

   Party A will provide the premises and attached facilities (see the appendix for detail) on schedule to Party B for using. 甲方须按时将房屋及附属设施（详见附件）交付乙方使用。

2. considerable 相当大（或多）的

   比较级：more considerable；最高级：the most considerable

3. Commodity Inspection Corporation 商品检验公司
4. In such circumstances 在这种情况下
5. surveyor's report 调查员报告

> **Tips**
> **1. 检疫的由来**
> "检疫"（quarantine）即检查并免疫，源于拉丁文"quarantum"，意为"40 天"。最早在 14 世纪中叶，欧洲本土国际港口为防范黑死病、霍乱等疾病的传播，为旅客执行卫生检查的一种措施，要求外来船舶和人员隔离 40 天。这一做法为防止疫病传播起了很大的作用，此后逐渐形成了"检疫"的概念。
>
> **2. 进出口商品检验环节**
> 主要有 4 个环节：接受报验、抽样、检验和签发证书。
> （1）接受报验：报验是指对外贸易关系人向商品检验机构报请检验。报验时需要填写"报验申请单"，填明申请检验、鉴定工作项目和要求，同时提交对外所签买卖合同、成交小样及其他必要的资料。
> （2）抽样：商品检验机构接受报验之后，及时派人员赴货物堆存地点进行现场检验、鉴定。抽样时，要按照规定的方法和一定的比例，在货物的不同部位抽取一定数量的、能代表全批货物质量的样品（标本）供检验之用。
> （3）检验：商品检验机构接受报验之后，认真研究申报的检验项目，确定检验内容，仔细审核合同（信用证）对品质、规格、包装的规定，弄清检验的依据，确定检验标准、方法，然后抽样检验，有仪器分析检验、物理检验、感官检验、微生物检验等。
> （4）签发证书：在出口方面，凡列入种类表内的出口商品，经商品检验合格后签发放行单（或在"出口货物报关单"上加盖放行章，以代替放行单）。凡合同、信用证规定由商品检验部门检验出证的，或国外要求签检验证书的，根据规定签发所需封面证书；不向国外提供证书的，只发放行单。种类表以外的出口商品，应由商品检验机构检验的，经检验合格发给证书或放行单后，方可出运。在进口方面，进口商品经检验后，分别签发"检验情况通知单"或"检验证书"，供对外结算或索赔用。凡由收、用货单位自行验收的进口商品，如发现问题，供对外索赔用。对于验收合格的，收、用货单位应在索赔有效期内把验收报告送商品检验机构销案。

9.3 有用的短语和句子
Useful Expressions

1. Common Used Phrases 常规短语
   General Administration of Quality Supervision, Inspection and Quarantine of the People's Republic of China (AQSIQ) 国家质量监督检验检疫总局（简称国家质检总局）
   Inspection Certificate of Quality 品质检验证书
   Inspection Certificate of Weight or Quantity 重量或数量检验证书
   Inspection Certificate of Packing 包装检验证书
   Sanitary Inspection Certificate 卫生检验证书

Inspection Certificate of Damaged Cargo 残损检验证书
Inspection Certificate on Tank/Hold 船舱检验证书

2. You have confirmed our order, but to our surprise, we have not yet received the goods or any advice from you when we may expect delivery.
   贵方已确认我方订货，但令人诧异的是至今尚未到货，也未收到何时可以交货的信息。

3. The goods have not turned out to our satisfaction, the quality being so poor as to render them unsuitable for the requirement of this market. As the whole parcel is quite useless to us, we must ask you to refund us the invoice value and the inspection fee as per the statement of claim enclosed. We trust that our claim will have your prompt attention, and as soon as settlement is made, we shall return the goods to you at your expense.
   该货不能令我方满意，质量如此低劣，以致不合此地市场需要。由于全部货物对我方毫无用处，请贵方退偿发票金额和检验费，详见所附索赔清单。希望贵方立即处理我方索赔，一旦解决，我们就退回货物，费用由贵方负担。

4. We are still without your advice of dispatch of the cameras, while we are receiving urgent request from customers and you will understand that this delay places us in an awkward position.
   我方仍未收到贵方照相机的装运通知，但连续接到我方客户的催促，希望贵方能理解，这次延误使我方处于困境。

5. On examination, we found that some of the commodities do not correspond with the original sample.
   经检验，我方发现一些货物与原样品不符。

6. We feel sorry to inform you that the cargo we just received is not up to your usual standard. The products seem to be too roughly made and out of shape.
   抱歉通知贵方，我方刚收到的货物未达到贵方往常的标准，看得出这些产品制作草率，而且变形。

7. On comparing the goods received with the samples, we were surprised to find that the color is not the same.
   将收到的货物与样品比较，我们发现颜色不同，感到很诧异。

8. The quality of your shipment for our Order No. 123 has been found not in conformity with the agreed specification. We must therefore lodge a claim against you for the amount of RMB 30 000. The CCIB survey report is forwarded herewith and your early settlement is requested.
   我方第 123 号订单发来的货物的质量与协议的规格不符，因此必须向贵方提出索赔，金额为人民币 3 万元。随附中国商品检验检疫局的检验报告。请早日解决索赔。

9. Your shipment of our Order No. 345 has been found short-weight by 1 500 kg, for which we must file a claim amounting to ＄987 plus inspection fee.
   贵方 345 号订单下的货物，发现短重 1 500 千克，为此，我们必须提出索赔，总值为 987 美元，外加检验费。

10. Since it is agreed that we have the right to reject the goods when they are disqualified upon examination by the China Commodity Inspection Bureau at the destination port, we regret to inform you that we have to return the goods at your expense.
    既然同意一经在目的港由中国商检局检查发现质量不符，我方就有权拒绝收货。那么很抱歉，现通知贵方我方不得不将货退回，并且费用由贵方负担。

11. The wrong pieces may be returned per next available steamer for our account, but it is preferable

if you can sell them out at our price in your market.

错发的货物由下一班轮带回来，费用由我方负担，但最好能在贵方市场按我方价格抛售。

12. As the damage is apparently due to rough handling in transit, it is only appropriate for you to file your claim with the insurance company concerned.

    显而易见，损坏是由于粗暴装卸所致，贵方应向有关保险公司索赔。

13. We have taken delivery of our order No. 324. But much to our regret, only 5 420 cases were found against the 6 500 cases in the packing list.

    我们已经提取了第 324 号订单的货物。但很遗憾地指出，只有 5 420 箱，而装箱单上注明是 6 500 箱。

14. The goods delivered are not up to the standard of samples. The pattern is uneven in places and the coloring various.

    所交货物未达到样品的质量标准，多是由于花样不匀，颜色各异所致。

15. We regret to point out that a shortage in weight of 210 lbs was noticed when the goods arrived.

    我方遗憾地指出，货物到达时短重 210 磅[①]。

16. We sent you a detailed inspection certificate of September 7 subsequence to your claim on you for the loss.

    在向贵方提出索赔之后，我方已于 9 月 7 日寄给你一份详细的检验证书。

17. The goods will be inspected by China Commodity Inspection Bureau and their findings shall be taken as final.

    货物将由中国商检局检验，其检验结果作为最后的依据。

18. We have had the case and contents examined by the insurance surveyor, but as you will see from the enclosed copy of his report, he maintains that the damage was due to insecure packing and not to any unduly rough handling of the case.

    我们已请保险公司检验人员检验了木箱和箱内货物。从随附的检验报告副本中，贵方将注意到，他认为损坏是由于包装不牢固，并非搬运不当所致。

19. This is the maximum concession we can make. Should you not agree to accept our proposal, we would like to submit the case to arbitration.

    这是我们所能做的最大让步。如贵方不接受我们的建议，我们要将此事交予仲裁机构。

20. Your claim and the survey report are now having our careful consideration. We apologize to you for this unfortunate matter and assure you that your claim will be treated with promptness.

    我们正在认真地考虑贵方的索赔和检验报告。对这一不幸事件向贵方表示歉意，并向贵方保证，我们定会及时处理贵方索赔。

21. The materials do not match the samples you sent us. The quality of them is so poor, so we think there must be a mistake in making up the order.

    材料质地与样品相差甚远，部分质量极为低劣。我们怀疑很可能是在执行订单过程中出现了差错。

22. We are really sorry for your complaint that your goods have been mixed up with others. We have made a thorough examination but the only reason we could find was the confusion of labels. Please accept our apologies for the trouble we made to you.

[①] 1 磅≈0.454 千克。

对贵方货物中混入其他物品的投诉，我方深表歉意。我方已做了彻底的调查，但可以找到的唯一原因是标签被弄混了。给贵方带来不便，请接受我方的道歉。

23. The goods were in perfect condition on leaving our warehouse and the damage had been caused in transit.

    该货从公司仓库运出时完好无损，所出现的损伤显然是在运输途中造成的。

24. Please dispatch at once a replacement of this item exactly ordered by us.

    完全按照我们所订的货物立即补发一批。

练习

Exercises

Ⅰ. Comprehension Questions
  1. What role does Commodity Inspection play in Foreign Trade?
  2. What certificate the recognized surveyors issue may be taken as the basis for negotiating payment?
  3. What should the first inspection be conducted?

Ⅱ. Translate the Following Terms
  1. Inspection Certificate on Tank/Hold   2. re-inspection
  3. Commodity Inspection   4. survey report
  5. 品质检验证书   6. 重量或数量检验证书
  7. 包装检验证书   8. 卫生检验证书
  9. 残损检验证书   10. 检验费

Ⅲ. Fill in the Blanks with Appropriate Words
  1. Our customers complain that the goods are inferior _____ quality _____ our samples.
  2. We are now lodging a claim _____ you _____ the short weight of fertilizer _____ our Order No. 123.
  3. As soon as the report is _____ our hands, we shall give the matter our best attention _____ a view to settling it at an early date.
  4. We must ask you to _____ the matter and arrange for the dispatch of replacement at once.
  5. A survey report is enclosed _____ and your early settlement is requested.
  6. There is a _____ between the contents of Case No. 68 and those described in the packing.

Ⅳ. Translate the Following Sentences
  1. A survey report is enclosed for your reference and your early settlement is requested.
  2. The goods in question are not to our satisfaction because the quality is unsuitable for this market.
  3. We trust you will consider this matter seriously, and try to prevent a recurrence of this delay.
  4. Inspection shall be conducted by the China Import and Export Commodity Inspection Bureau which enjoys international reputation for impartiality.
  5. 我们感觉贵方检验局签发的质量检验单不完全可信。
  6. 我们发现装运货物的品质与协议的规格不符。
  7. 经过检查，尽管箱子表面没有任何痕迹，但是很多货物都严重损坏了。
  8. 我们已经彻底查询，但所得到的唯一解释是标签被弄混了。
  9. 我们将在卸货完毕后检查此货。

10. 对于所遭受的损失，我们不得不要求贵方承担责任。

Ⅴ. Translate the Following into English

　　敬启者：

　　关于第234号订单项下的500吨大豆，我方已于昨天收到上述货物。但是，第20号货箱短缺15包。因箱子完好，没有损坏的迹象，我们推测一定是短装了，而且来自广州商品检验局的检验报告显示，短装了50吨。根据广州商品检验局的报告，我们向贵方提出索赔220美元。

　　随函附寄广州商品检验局的商检报告，并盼早日处理。

Ⅵ. Multiple Choices

1. The goods under Contract No. 123 left here _____ .
   A. in a good condition　　　　　　　B. in good conditions
   C. in good condition　　　　　　　　D. in the good condition
2. As the goods are ready for shipment, we _____ your L/C to be opened immediately.
   A. hope　　　　B. anticipate　　　　C. await　　　　D. expect
3. It is important that your client _____ the relevant L/C not later than April 15.
   A. must open　　B. has to open　　　C. open　　　　D. opens
4. The buyer suggested that the packing of this article _____ improved.
   A. be　　　　　B. was to be　　　　C. would be　　　D. had to be
5. _____ your needs, please write to us with your specific enquiries.
   A. Should these new products suit　　B. Had these new products suited
   C. If these new products would suit　　D. If these new products were to suit
6. Please inform us _____ the tendency of your market.
   A. for　　　　　B. in　　　　　　　C. of　　　　　　D. with
7. Will you please let us know details o any lines of goods which you think are _____ for your market?
   A. interesting　B. suitable　　　　C. proper　　　　D. desirable

附录9A　检验证明书

Appendix 9A　Inspection Certificate

江苏进出入境检验检疫局
JIANGSU Entry-Exit INSPECTION AND QUARANTINE BUREAU

地址：南京市中华路99号
Address：99, Zhong Hua Road, Nanjing
电话：025-52345020
Tel.

检验证书
INSPECTION AND QUARANTINE CERTIFICATE
No. 123

日期
Date：March 24, 2010
发货人：南京机械设备进出口公司
Consignor：Nanjing Machinery Import & Export Corporation

受货人：新加坡海外公司
Consignee：OVERASEAS COMPANY, SINGAPORE
品名：羊毛衫
Commodity：CASHMERE SWEATERS
标记及号码
Mark & No.：SINGAPORE NO. 1-4860
报检数量/重量
Quantity/Weight Declared：60 doz.
检验结果
RESULTS OF INSPECTION：
10 doz. cashmere sweaters, small
20 doz. cashmere sweaters, medium
30 doz. cashmere sweaters, large

我们已尽所知和最大能力实施上述检验，不能因我们签发本证书而免除卖方或其他方面根据合同和法律所应承担的产品数量和其他责任。

All inspections are carried out conscientiously to the best of our knowledge and ability. This certificate does not in any respect absolve the seller and other related parties from his contractual and legal obligations especially when product quantity is concerned.

主任检验员
Chief Inspection：ZB

附录9B 出口货物报关单
Appendix 9B Goods Declaration for Exportation

中华人民共和国海关出口货物报关单			
预录入编号：			海关编号：3201010101
出口口岸 SHANGHAI	备案号		出口日期 2011-March-5
经营单位 GOLDEN SEA TRADING CORPORATION	运输方式 Ocean Marine		运输工具名称 Lucky V307
发货单位 GOLDEN SEA TRADING CORPORATION	贸易方式 General trade		征免性质
许可证号	运抵国 DENMARK		指运港 COPENHAGEN
批准文号	成交方式 CIF	运费 US $ 39 350.00	保费 US $ 813.78
合同协议号 JH-FLSSC01	件数 1 200	包装种类 CARTONS	毛重（公斤） 39 600KG

(续)

集装箱号 COSU32345100-COUSU32345100	随附单据 (Commercial Invoice and packing list)		
Shipping mark	FLS 9711 COPENHAGEN 1-1200		

项号	商品编号	商品名称	规格编号	数量及单位	最终目的国(地区)	单价	总价
1	8712001	Bicycle 2ITEMS OF "FOREVER" BRAND BICYCLES	 YE803 26' YE803 24'	 600 UNITS 600 UNITS	 DENMARK	 US $ 66.00 US $ 71.00	 US $ 39 600 US $ 42 600 US $ 82 200

税费征收情况			
录入员　　录入单位	兹声明以上申报无讹并承担法律责任	海关审单批注及放行日期 审单	
报关员 赵德明 单位地址 8TH FLOOR JINDU BUILDING 27 WUXING ROAD SHANGHAI, CHINA	申报单位（签章） 填制日期 2011-March-3	征税	
		查验	

Chapter 10
第 10 章

装 运
Shipment

学习目标
Learning Objectives

Enable the students to know about modes of transportation in international trade; to be acquainted with terms of shipments; master shipping instructions, shipping advice and shipping documents; and enable to skillfully write business letters about shipment

使学生了解国际贸易的运输方式；熟悉装运条款；掌握装船指示、装运通知和装运单证；并能熟练撰写有关装运的商务信函。

10.1 背景知识
Background Information

Shipment is an indispensable part of international trade because the seller can't fulfill his obligation to deliver if the goods are not dispatched. There are three parties involved in most movements of goods: the consignor who sends the goods; the carrier who carries them and the consignee who receives them at the destination. Shipment covers rather wide ranges of work. The sales contract generally will include the following terms of shipment:

(1) Modes of transport;
(2) Time of shipment;
(3) Port of loading and unloading;
(4) Shipping advice;
(5) Partial shipment and transhipment;
(6) Shipping documents, etc.

In international trade, it is very important for the exporter to choose a correct method of delivery or transport. Modes of transport include ocean transport, railway

装运是国际贸易不可分割的组成部分，因为如果货物不能及时装运，卖方就无法履行其义务。货物运输涉及三方：发货人，发送货物；承运人，承运货物；收货人，在目的地收取货物。装运包含许多工作，一般收货合同中会列明下列装运条款：

(1) 运输方式；
(2) 装运时间；
(3) 装运和卸货港；
(4) 装运通知；
(5) 分批装运和转船；
(6) 装运单据等。

国际贸易中，出口商选择正确的运输方式很重要。运输方式包括海洋运输、铁路运输、航空

transport, air transport, container transport, international multimodal transport, postal transport, high way or inland, waterway transport, etc. The choice will be made according to the nature of products, the distance to be shipped, available means of transportation, time limit as well as freight cost. However, the most basic and common method of shipment is to use ocean cargo vessels. About two thirds of the world trade total volume are now shipped by sea.

According to its mode of transport, ocean transport can be divided into two types: Liner Shipment and Chartering Shipping /Tramp Shipping. A Liner is a vessel that sails according to regular sailing route, regular ports of call, regular sailing schedule and has fixed freight. A Tramp is a freight-carrying vessel that follows no firmed schedule, has no set route or times, and sails off to where the goods are available and the pickings are the best. These rates are not fixed but are determined by market. Tramp ships are always chartered. The shipper charters the ship from the ship owner by signing a charter party for the carriage of the goods.

When goods are shipped by road, rail or air, the contract of carriage takes the form of Consignment Notes or Air Way Bill. In sea transport, chartering of ships or booking shipping space is involved, and the contract between the ship owner and the shipper may take the form of either a Charter Party or a Bill of Lading.

Time of Shipment refers to the time for loading the goods on board the vessel at the port of shipment in accordance with the terms and conditions of the contract. The date indicated by the carrier in the bill of lading is the date of delivery. Usually the time of shipment should not be too long or too short after the contract is made. The latest date of shipment is often stipulated in the L/C. It is better to allow for a period of time rather than an exact date like the followings:
- Shipment during January/February;
- Shipment on or before March 7, 2011;
- Shipment within 30 days after receipt of the covering L/C.

Port of Loading refers to the port of shipment, while

运输、集装箱运输、国际多式联运、邮包运输、公路或内陆、水路运输等，具体要取决于产品的特性、运输距离、可利用的交通工具、期限以及运费等。但是，最基本的同时也是最常用的运输方法是海洋运输。目前大约世界贸易总量的2/3通过海上运输。

根据运输方式的不同，海洋运输可以分成两类：班轮运输和租船运输/不定期船运输。班轮运输是指船舶按照固定的线路、固定的停靠港、航行日期表和固定的运费航行。不定期船没有固定的船期表，也没有固定的航线，哪里有货就向哪里开航，哪里装船最好就去哪里接货。其费率不固定，但通常由市场决定。不定期船都是租船，发货人与船东签订租船合同，租货船装运货物。

若货物以公路、铁路或航空方式装运，则运输合同以托运单或航空货运单的方式存在。海洋运输中，则涉及租船或订舱位，船主与发货人之间的合同采取租船契约或提单的方式。

装运期指的是根据合同规定，将货物装到装运港船上的时间，承运人在提单中列明的时间就是装运期。通常装运期不应该在合同签订之后太长或太短，最晚的装运期往往在信用证中有所规定，较妥当的方法不是一个确切的时间，而是规定一个时间段，比如：
- 在1月或2月装运；
- 在2011年3月7日或之前装运；
- 在收到相关信用证之后的30天内装运。

装运港指的是发货的港口，

the port of unloading means port of destination. Several factors such as loading and unloading facilities, the location of goods, the importer, the draft of the ship, the conditions of the port, etc. should be considered as choosing the port of shipment and destination. Usually it is the seller who designates the port of loading for the convenience of shipping the goods, while the port of destination is designated by the buyer. Shipping advice needs to be sent after shipment. The exporter usually sends by fax a notice to the buyers immediately after the goods are loaded on board the ship, advising them of the shipment, especially under FOB or CFR terms. Such a notice, as the Shipping Advice, may include the following: Contract and/or L/C number, name of commodity, number of package, total quantity shipped, name of vessel and its sailing date and sometimes even the total value of the goods.

Partial Shipment means shipping the commodity under one contract by more than one shipment. In the case, a large amount of export goods is involved in one transaction and are shipped in several lots by several carriers onto different means of conveyance. When there are no or few ships sailing direct to the port of destination at the time or the amount of cargo for a certain port of destination is so small that no ships would like to call at the port, transhipment is necessary. Of course, Partial Shipment and Transhipment should be allowed by the buyer in advance.

Shipping documents usually include the Bill of Lading, Commercial Invoice, Insurance Policy, Packing List, Certificate of Inspection and Certificate of Origin, etc. The kind and number of which shall be explicitly indicated in the contract or the letter of credit.

Before shipment, the buyers generally send their shipping requirement to the sellers, and inform them in writing of the packing and marking, mode of transportation, etc. So letters regarding shipment are usually written for the following purposes: to urge an early shipment, to amend shipping terms, to give shipping advice, to dispatch shipping documents and so on. Taking the advantage of this occasion to advise the buyer of the shipment, the seller may also review the course of the transaction and express the desire for further development of business.

而卸载港则是指目的港。在选择装运港和目的港码头时，某些因素如装卸设备、货物所在位置、进口商、吃水量、港口条件等应当被考虑进去。通常，卖方指定装运港，以便装运货物，而买方则指定目的港。货物装运后就要发出装运通知。出口商在货物装船后会立刻通过传真通知进口商货物已经装运，尤其是在FOB或CFR条件下更是这样。这类通知也叫装运通知，主要包括下面几项：合同或信用证编号、品名、包装号、装运数量、船名、起航日期以及货物的总价值等。

分批装运指的是同一合同项下多于一次的装运。这种情况往往涉及大宗出口，由几个承运人分若干次由不同的运输工具装运。如果有时到达目的港的船只没有或稀少，或者到达某个目的港的货物量较少，船只不愿停泊时，就有必要采取转船的方式。当然，分批装运或者转船都要事先得到买方的许可。

装运单据通常包括提单、商业发票、保险单、装箱单、检验证书、原产地证明书等。具体种类和数量在合同或信用证中都明确写明。

装运前，买方要向卖方发出装运要求，告知对方包装方式、唛头以及运输方式。因此这类信函的写作目的主要是：催促对方早日装运；修改装运条款；发出装运通知；发送装运单据等。卖方有时也会利用通知买方货物装运的机会，回顾本次交易的过程，表达今后继续交易的愿望。

10.2 信例
Sample Letters

Letter 1　Shipping Instructions

Dear Sirs,

　　We are pleased to advise you that the whisky you ordered was dispatched by M/S "Sunlight" today, which is due to arrive at Sydney on May 5. In spite of every care in packing, it sometimes may happen that a few barrels are broken in transit. Should there be any breakages of other causes for compliant, please do not hesitate to let us know.

　　Further details, concerning the consignment including packing and shipping marks, are contained in our invoice No. 218 enclosed in triplicate. In order to cover this shipment we have drawn you a draft under L/C and negotiated it through the Bank of China, Hong Kong with relative shipping documents.

　　We trust that the goods will reach you in good condition and give you complete satisfaction.

Yours faithfully,

Notes

1. shipping instruction 装船指示
   装运前买方将装运要求以书面方式通知卖方，说明装船方式、包装要求等称为装船指示。
2. due to 预计
3. Should there be any breakages of other causes for compliant, please do not hesitate to let us know. 如果有任何破损的投诉，请立刻告知我们。（这里 Should there be any breakages of other causes for compliant, 为省掉 if 的虚拟语气的倒装形式。）
   complaint 抱怨，申诉，控告
   We can't but file a complaint against you about the poor packing. 我方不得不就包装不良向你方申诉。
   complaint 的动词形式为 complain
   The buyers complained of the delay in shipment. 买方抱怨装船延迟。
   do not hesitate to do sth. 不要犹豫做某事，类似的表达方法还有：feel free to do sth.
   If you are interested in our products, please do not hesitate to send us your inquires. 如果贵方对我方产品感兴趣，请尽快向我方询盘。
4. in triplicate 一式三份
   其他表示"一式×份"的短语还有：in duplicate（一式两份）；in quadruplicate（一式四份）；in quintuplicate（一式五份）；in sextuplicate（一式六份）；in septuplicates（一式七份）；in octuplicate（一式八份）；in nonuplicate（一式九份）；in decuplicate（一式十份）
5. draw sb. a draft 向某人开具汇票
6. negotiated it through the Bank of China, Hong Kong 通过中国银行香港分行议付

Letter 2　Transhipment

Gentlemen:

As requested in your letter of March 5, we are pleased to provide the following information for your reference:

1. There are about 2 to 3 sailings weekly from Shanghai to Hong Kong.

2. Arrangements have been made with the ABC line, which has one sailing approximately on the 10th of every month from Hong Kong to West African ports, such as Lagos, Accra, etc. Shipping space is to be booked through their Shanghai Agents, who communicate with the Line by e-mail.

After receipt of the Line's reply accepting the booking, their Shanghai Agents will issue a Through Bill of Lading. Therefore, with the exception of unusual condition which may happen accidentally, the goods will be transshipped from Hong Kong without delay.

3. In general the freight for transshipment from Hong Kong is higher than that from the U.K. or Continental port, but ABC Line agrees to the same freight, the detailed rates of which are shown on the 2 appendices to this letter.

If you want to have the goods transhipped at Hong Kong, your L/C must reach us well before the shipment month so as to enable us to book space with the Line's Agents.

We assure you of our best attention at all times.

Yours sincerely,

Notes

1. sailing 船，行驶
2. shipping space 舱位
3. Arrangements have been made with the ABC line, which has one sailing approximately on the 10th of every month from Hong Kong to West African ports, such as Lagos, Accra, etc. 已安排好 ABC 班轮，该班轮每月 10 日左右有船从香港驶往西非的拉各斯、阿克拉等港口。这里 which has one sailing approximately on the 10th of every month from... 为非限制性定语从句，修饰前面的 ABC line。
4. who communicate with the Line by e-mail 为非限制性定语从句修饰前面的 Shanghai agent。
5. Through Bill of Lading 联运提单
   提单（Bill of Lading, B/L）是指在对外贸易中，运输部门承运货物时签发给发货人的一种凭证。收货人凭提单向货运目的地的运输部门提货，提单须经承运人或船方签字后始能生效，是海运货物向海关报关的有效单证之一。根据不同的方法提单可分为以下几种类型。
   （1）已装船提单（Shipped B/L, or On Board B/L）和备运提单（Received for Shipment B/L）
   已装船提单是指货物装船后由承运人或其授权代理人签发给托运人的提单。备运提单又称待装提单、收货待运提单或简称待运提单。它是承运人在收到托运人交来的货物但还没有装船时，应托运人的要求而签发的提单。签发这种提单时，说明承运人确认货物已交由承运人保管并存在其所控制的仓库或场地，但还未装船。所以，这种提单未载明所装船名和装船时间，在跟单信用证支付方式下，银行一般都不肯接受这种提单。但当货物装船，承运人在这种提单上加注装运船名和装船日期并签字盖章后，待运提单即成为已装船提单。

(2) 清洁提单（Clean B/L）和不洁提单（Unclean B/L or Foul B/L）

在装船时，货物外表状况良好，承运人在签发提单时，未在提单上加注任何有关货物残损、包装不良、件数、重量和体积，或其他妨碍结汇的批注的提单称为清洁提单。在货物装船时，承运人若发现货物包装不牢、破残、渗漏、玷污、标志不清等现象时，将在收货单上对此加以批注，并将此批注转移到提单上，这种提单称为不清洁提单。

(3) 记名提单（Straight B/L）、指示提单（Order B/L）和不记名提单（Bearer B/L, or Open B/L, or Blank B/L）

记名提单又称收货人抬头提单，是指提单上的收货人栏中已具体填写收货人名称的提单。在提单正面"收货人"一栏内填上"凭指示"（To order）或"凭某人指示"（Order of...）字样的提单叫指示提单。指示提单是一种可转让提单。不记名提单是指提单上收货人一栏内没有指明任何收货人，而注明"提单持有人"（Bearer）字样或将这一栏空白，不填写任何名称的提单。

(4) 直达提单（Direct B/L）、转船提单（Transhipment B/L）、联运提单（Through B/L）和多式联运提单（Multimodal Transport B/L or Intermodal Transport B/L）

直达提单，又称直运提单，是指货物从装货港装船后，中途不经转船，直接运至目的港卸船交与收货人的提单。转船提单是指货物从起运港装载的船舶不直接驶往目的港，需要在中途港口换装其他船舶转运至目的港卸货，承运人签发这种提单称为转船提单。联运提单是指须经两种或两种以上运输方式（海—陆、海—河、海—空、海—海等）联运的货物，由第一承运人（第一程船运输的承运人）收取全程运费后，在起运地签发到目的港的全程运输提单。联运提单虽然包括全程运输，但签发提单的各程承运人只对自己运输的一段航程中所发生的货损负责，这种提单与转船提单性质相同。多式提单主要用于集装箱运输，是指一批货物需要经过两种以上不同运输方式，其中一种是海上运输方式，由一个承运人负责全程运输，负责将货物从接收地运至目的地交付收货人，并收取全程运费所签发的提单。提单内的项目不仅包括起运港和目的港，而且列明一程、二程等运输路线，以及收货地和交货地。

6. with the exception of ＝except 除……之外

Other terms and conditions are same as usual, with the exception of insurance which will cover, All Risks and War Risk for 110% of the total invoice value. 除保险按发票总额的110%投保一切险和战争险外，其他条款与以往一样。

7. We assure you of our best attention at all times. 我们保证会随时关注事情的进展情况。

Letter 3　Requesting Early Shipment

Dear Sirs,
　　We refer to our Purchase Contract No. 98. under the terms of the contract, delivery is scheduled for May 2010. We would like to bring delivery forward to March/April 2010.

We realize that the change of delivery date will probably inconvenience you and we offer our sincere apologies. We know that you will understand that we would not ask for earlier delivery if we did not have compelling reasons for doing so.

In view of our long-standing, cordial commercial relationship, we would be very grateful if you would comply with our request.

We look forward to your early reply.

Yours sincerely,

Notes

1. refer to 参阅
2. in view of 考虑到
3. long-standing, cordial commercial relationship 长期友好的商业关系
4. comply with 照办,同意

Letter 4 Shipping Advice

Dear Sirs,

Further to your Order No. 320, we are pleased to inform you that the bicycles have now been dispatched as requested.

Packing: 4 cases

Marking & Numbering: FA in triangle with case number one to four. Particulars of weight and measurement are given on the enclosed sheet.

Shipment: M/S Evergreen which sailed from Guangzhou on March 12, scheduled to arrive at New York on April 2.

Clean, shipped on board B/Ls in complete set, together with Commercial Invoice and Insurance Policy have been negotiated through the Bank of China with the sight draft under your L/C No. 234.

We shall be pleased to hear that the goods have arrived safely and in good order.

Yours faithfully,

Notes

1. shipping advice 装运通知
   指卖方对买方所发的告知货物已经或将于某个日期发出的通知。其内容包括订单号码、货品、装运数量、船名、装运日期、预定到达日、装运港、目的港等。
2. FA in triangle with case number one to four. 三角形内注上 FA 字样,并标上 1~4 箱。
3. Particulars of weight and measurement are given on the enclosed sheet. 重量和尺寸的详单在附单上。
4. M/S Evergreen which sailed from Guangzhou on March 12, scheduled to arrive at New York on April 2. "长青"轮 3 月 12 日从广州起航,预计 4 月 2 日到达纽约。

M/S Evergreen "长青"轮

M/S：merchant vessel 商船，与此相似的还有 S.S：steamship 船运，MV：motor vessel 内燃机船

5. scheduled to 预计
6. clean, shipped on board B/Ls in complete set 全套清洁已装船提单
7. commercial invoice 商业发票

商业发票是出口方向进口方开列的发货价目清单，是买卖双方记账的依据，也是进出口报关交税的总说明。商业发票是一笔业务的全面反映，内容包括商品的名称、规格、价格、数量、金额、包装等，同时也是进口商办理进口报关不可缺少的文件。

8. sight draft 即期汇票

Tips

1. 班轮提单的优势

承运人能够在航海运输之前或之后立即联系托运人，告知估计开船日（estimated time of departure，ETD）和估计到港日（estimated time of arrival，ETA）。这样，进口商也可以获知货物已经发出并将于确定日抵达。

2. 装运条款（terms of shipment）

装运条款又称"海洋运输条款"，是贸易合同的一个重要组成部分，主要指装运条件和相互责任。在洽商交易时，买卖双方必须就交货时间、装运地和目的地、能否分批装运和转船、转运等问题商妥，并在合同中具体订明。合同的装运条款应包括装运时间、装运港、目的港、是否允许转船与分批装运、装运通知，以及滞期、速遣条款等内容。对外磋商交易和签订合同时，要争取把合同中的装运条款订得合理、明确，以利于进出口业务的顺利开展。

10.3 有用的短语和句子

Useful Expressions

1. We are pleased to inform you that we have booked shipping space for your Order No. 147 on S/S Shanghai 1, ETA 20th August.
   很高兴通知贵方，我们已经为贵方订单 147 号货订好了"上海 1 号"的舱位，估计到达时间是 8 月 20 日。
2. Please amend the covering letter of credit to allow partial shipment, under advice to us.
   请修改有关信用证允许分装，同时通知我方。
3. As the only direct steamer which calls at our port once a month has just departed, goods can only be shipped next month.
   由于每月停靠我港一次的直达轮船刚离开，货物只能在下月装运。
4. Air waybill, giving full particulars, will be sent to you as soon as the consignment is ready for dispatch.
   航空货运单注明了详情，一旦货物备妥待运即寄予贵方。
5. Shipments during March and April 2010 in two monthly lots.

2010 年 3 月、4 月装运，每月各装一批。

6. Shipments shall be effected at intervals of every other month.
   每隔一个月装运一批。
7. Ship half of the order in May and the balance one month later.
   5 月装一半，其余的次月装运。
8. We shall be much obliged if you could effect shipment of these milk powder in two equal lots by direct steamer as soon as you receive our L/C.
   如果一收到我方信用证就能用直轮分两等批装运这些奶粉，我方将不胜感激。
9. Please ensure that all the cases are marked clearly with our initials in a triangle, under which comes the destination with the contract number below.
   请确保在所有的箱子上都将我公司的首字母标注在三角形内，下面写上目的地，其下是合同号。
10. We are pleased to inform you that the consignment under your order No. 112 has now been shipped per S. S. "Luck" which is to leave here on Aug. 1 and due to arrive at your port on Aug. 10.
    我们很高兴告知贵方，贵方 112 号订单的货物已经由"幸运"号轮装运，此轮定于 2009 年 8 月 1 日起航，预计 8 月 10 日到达贵方港口。
11. As direct steamers to your port are few and far between, we have to ship via Hong Kong.
    由于到达贵方港口的船稀少，我们不得不经由香港转船。
12. We are now enclosing one set of the shipping documents covering L/C No. 005, which comprise the following:
    (1) Commercial invoice in quintuplicate.
    (2) One original clean on board ocean bill of lading, made out to order, blank endorsed and notify applicant and marked freight prepaid.
    (3) One original certificate of origin.
    现附上 005 号信用证项下的一套装运单据如下：
    (1) 商业发票一式五份；
    (2) 一份正本清洁已装船提单，空白抬头，空白背书，以申请人为被通知人，注明运费已付；
    (3) 原产地证明书正本一份。
13. Attached to this letter is a copy of B/L together with copies of invoice and weight memo.
    随函附上一份提单及发票和重量单的复印件。
14. Would please obtain for us a ship with a cargo capacity of about 4 000 tons.
    请为我们找一条承载量为 4 000 吨位的船。
15. The goods are ready for shipment for a long time. Please inform us of the name, the voyage number and the ETA of the vessel to enable us to effect shipment in time.
    货已备妥待运，请告知船名、航次及预计抵达时间，以便我方及时安排装运。
16. Usually there are three parties involved in most transportation of goods, the consignor, the carrier and the consignee.
    通常情况下，大多数货物运输涉及三方当事人：发货人、承运人和收货人。
17. Owing to the congestion of orders coming in at the moment, we are afraid that a certain portion

of the goods may have to be shipped in the early part of June. In that case, we beg that you will overlook this unavoidable delay.

由于现在订单拥挤，有一部分货也许要到 6 月上旬才能装船，在此情况下，请原谅装船延迟不可避免。

18. Transhipment to be allowed at Singapore subject to presentation of through B/L on Rotterdam.

    允许在新加坡转船，但需要提交到鹿特丹的联运提单。

19. 3 000MT plus or minus 5%, at beneficiary's option, January, February, March shipment equally divided. Each shipment shall be regarded as a separate and independent contract.

    3 000 吨，5% 增减，由受益人选择，1、2、3 月等量装运。每次装运视为一份分开的、独立的合同。

20. Shipments at intervals of about 60 days.

    每间隔约 60 天装运。

练习

Exercises

Ⅰ. Comprehension Questions

1. What do terms of shipment include in the contract?
2. Please explain the meaning of liner shipment and charting/tramp shipping?
3. What is time of shipment and what has to be paid attention to in stipulating time of shipment?
4. What are the main kinds of B/L in international trade?

Ⅱ. Translate the Following Terms and Expressions

1. shipping advice
2. clean, on board B/L
3. transshipment and partial shipment allowed
4. ready for delivery
5. commercial invoice
6. shipping space
7. port of loading
8. mode of transportation
9. 起运价格
10. 分批或分期装运
11. 凭样交货
12. 过境货

Ⅲ. Choose the Best Answer

1. We expect _____ shipment next month.
   a. cffccting
   b. to effect
   c. effect
   d. for effecting

2. Sometimes, transshipment and partial shipment are _____ by the buyer.
   a. permission
   b. permitting
   c. prohibited
   d. prohibiting

3. We are glad to inform you that the goods you ordered last month have been shipped by M/S "Pacific" _____ leave Shanghai port on April 12.
   a. owing to
   b. due to
   c. as to
   d. thanks to

4. If shipment involves transport by more than two modes, a (an) _____ will be issued.
   a. direct B/L
   b. ocean through B/L

c. multi-modal B/L d. shipped B/L

5. Time of shipment refers to the time for loading the goods on board the vessel at the port of _____ .
   a. unloading b. loading
   c. destination d. transhipment

6. If the latest date of shipment is May 20, 2010, the goods should be shipped _____ .
   a. before May 20 b. between May 15 to 25
   c. on May 20 d. on or before May 20

7. If the goods are damaged before they reach the ship, the ship owners will issue an _____ B/L.
   a. clean b. unclean
   c. non-negotiable d. order

8. A commercial invoice is always made out by the _____ as soon as the goods are shipped.
   a. importer b. insurance company
   c. exporter d. ship owner

9. The B/L, the insurance policy and the commercial invoice are called _____ .
   a. shipping advice b. shipping instruction
   c. shipping marks d. shipping documents

10. Shipment is to be made during May to July _____ .
    a. in three equally lots b. in three lots each time
    c. in three equal lots d. in equal three lots

Ⅳ. Translate the Following Sentences

1. When the seller gives the notice that goods have been shipped on board the ship, he should include details of the transaction:
   Contract No./order No. and L/C No.
   The name of the goods /Article No.
   Quantity of the order
   The name of the vessel
   ETD and ETA
   Shipping document enclosed

2. Please see to it that you effect shipment on time and advise us of the name of the vessel, the time of departure and the approximate time of arrival so as to enable us to arrange for unloading and selling.

3. As the only direct steamer which calls at our port once a month has just departed, goods can only be shipped next month.

4. We take this opportunity to inform you that we have loaded the above goods on board S/S... which sails for your port tomorrow. Enclosed please find one set of the shipping documents covering this consignment.

5. 由于这些货物非常容易在运输过程中损坏，我们建议用集装箱船装运，以避免装卸过程中可能的毁坏。

6. 很高兴告知贵方，100 台电视已由"东风"号装运，该轮预计 3 月 25 日起航，预计 4 月 10 日到达。

Ⅴ. Translate the Following Letter into English

×××先生，

贵方 2010 年 12 月 15 日来函收悉。今歉告，尽管我方做出极大努力，但仍未预订到直达马赛的舱位。我方船公司告知，中国港口与马赛之间尚无定期船只，因而我方很难将此 1 000 吨白糖直运马赛。

鉴于我们所面临的困难，请允许在中国香港转船。若贵方能同意我方的要求，当不胜感激。

谨启

Ⅵ. Translate the Following Letter into Chinese

Complain about Late Delivery

Dear Sirs,

We regret to have to complain about late delivery of the filing cabinets ordered on 2nd July. We did not receive them until this morning though you had guaranteed delivery within a week. It was on this understanding that we placed the order.

Unfortunately, there have been similar delays on several previous occasions and their increasing frequency in recent months compels us to say that business between us cannot be continued under conditions such as these.

We have felt it necessary to make our feelings known since we cannot give reliable delivery date to our customers unless we can count on undertakings given by our suppliers. We hope you will understand how we are placed and that from now on we can rely upon punctual completion of our orders.

Yours faithfully,

附录 10A 提货单样本
Appendix 10A Bill of Lading

Shipper: JIANGSU INTERNATIONAL AIRLINE SERVICE CO., LTD. 12/F XIAONANHU BLDG NO. 23 TAIBEI FIRST ROAD NANJING CHINA	Booking Ref.: No. Sh345098 PIL, PACIFIC INTERNA TIONAL LINES LTD. (incorporated in Singapore) COMBINED TRANSPORT BILL OF LADING
Consignee TO ORDER	Received in apparent good order and condition except as otherwise noted the total number of containers or other packages or unit enumerated below for transportation from the place of receipt to the place of delivery subject to the terms hereof. One of the signed Bills of Lading must be surrendered dully endorsed in exchange for the Goods or delivery order. On Presentation of this document (dully endorsed) to the Carrier by or on behalf of the Holder, the rights and liabilities arising in accordance with the terms hereof shall (without prejudice to any rule of common law or statute rendering them binding on the Merchant) become binding in all respects between the Carrier and the Holder as though the contract evidenced hereby had been made between them. SEE TERMS ON ORIGINAL B/L
Notify Party: RAINBOW SPORTSWEAR MANUFATURING LTD. 15625 STONY PLAIN RD. NW EDMONTON. ADT3T 4Z6	

Vessel and Voyage Number: HANJING V. 100	Port of Landing: SHANGHAI	Port of Discharge: VANCOUVER
Place of Receipt: SHANGHAI	Place of Delivery: EDMONTON	Number of Original Bs/L: THREE

PARTICULARS AS DECLARED BY SHIPPER-CARRIER NOT RESPONSIBLE				
Container Nos. / Seal Nos. Marks and /Numbers	No. of Container/ Packages	Description of Goods	Gross Weight (Kilos)	Measurement (cu-metres)
RAINBOW L/C 1541322 EDMONTON MADE IN CHINA C/NO. 1-260	260CTNS CONTAINER NO. CU23577	COVERALLS AND DENIM SHIRTS	6 680KG	25.35CBM

Freight &Charges FREIGHT PREPAID	Number of Containers/Packages (in words) SAY TWO HUBDRED AND SIXTY CARTONS IN ONE TEU ONLY
	Shipped on Board Date: SEP. 10, 2010
	Place and Date of Issue: SHANGHAI, CHINA SEP. 10, 2010
	In witness Whereof this number of Original Bills of Lading stated above all of the tenor and date one of which being accomplished the other to stand void. (STAMP AND SIGNATURE OF CARRIER OR AGENT)

附录 10B 商业发票样本
Appendix 10B Commercial Invoice

湖北省五矿国际贸易股份有限公司
HUBEI PROVINCIAL MINMETALS INTERNATIONAL
TRADING CORPORATION LIMITED
8 Jianghan North Road, Wuhan, China

COMMERCIAL INVOICE

Fax: (02782811135)

To LAI SAN AND CO., LTD. 121 LOUIS PASTEUR STREET PORT LOUIS MAURITIUS	Invoice No.	TJ0604B	Date	JAN. 16, 2010
	L/C No	ILS06/00060		
	Issued by	MAURITIUS COMMERCIAL BANK LTD.		
	Contract No.	MAURO51229		

Marks &Nos.	Descriptions	Unit Price	Amount
N/M	CAST IRON MANHOLE COVERS AND FRAMES TO BS 497/79 BLACK BITUMEN COATED "HB" BRAND AS PER S/C NO MAURO51229 DD 29/12/20XX SPECIFICATION (SINGLE SEAL, LIGHT DUTY) (1) 450MM×600MM 23KG, 700SETS (2) 450MM×450MM 15KG, 200SETS (3) 375MM×375MM 12KG, 100SETS (4) 300MM×300MM 7KG, 100SETS (5) 225MM×225MM 5KG, 100SETS TOTAL: 1200SETS PACKED IN 21 PACKAGES GROSS WEIGHT 21 210KG NET WEIGHT 21 000KG MEASUREMENT: 19.00 CBM FOR VALUE OF GOODS: USD 8 391.00 FREIGHT CHARGES: USD 2 324.00 INSURANCE PREMIUM: USD 35.00 WE HEREBY CERTIFY THAT THE PARTICULARS GIVEN IN THE INVOICE ARE TRUE AND CORRECT AND THAT NO DIFFERENT INVOICE IN RESPECT OF THE GOODS HAS BEEN OR WILL BE ISSUED.	CIF PORT LOUIS USD/SET 11.5 7.50 6.00 3.50 2.50	 USD 8 050.00 USD 1 500.00 USD 600.00 USD 350.00 USD 250.00 USD 10 750.00

HUBEI PROVINCIAL MINMETALS INTERNATIONAL
TRADING CORPORATION LIMITED
(STAMP AND SIGNATURE)

Chapter 11
第 11 章

投诉、索赔和理赔
Complaint, Claim and Settlement

Learning Objectives

Enable the students to know about various kinds of complaints made by the buyers and the sellers; master the steps of settlement of claims; enable to skillfully write letters of complaint, claim and settlement.

使学生了解进出口方投诉的类型;掌握理赔的基本步骤;熟练撰写有关投诉、索赔以及理赔信函。

11.1 背景知识
Background Information

In international trade, once a contract is signed between the exporter and the importer, both parties are under the obligation to carry out the contract. Sometimes no matter how perfect the organization maybe, complaints or claims still arise. Any party's breach of the contract entitles the other party to secure himself against the losses sustained. In practice, it is not infrequent that the exporter or the importer neglects or fails to perform any of his obligations, which gives rise to breach of contract and various trade disputes. Further more, it leads to claim, arbitration, or litigation.

Generally, there are two kinds of complaints made by the buyer:

(1) The justified or genuine complaints that due to the following reasons: refusal of making delivery, shipment overdue, goods wrongly delivered, goods arrived damaged or late, shortage, inferior quality, improper

在国际贸易中,一旦进出口方签订了合约,双方都有义务执行合同。但有时,不管组织得多么完善,总会引起投诉和索赔。任何违反合同的一方都赋予另一方权利来确保自己的货物免受损失。实践中,经常会发生进口商和出口商忽略或不能履行义务的情况,由此会产生违反合同等各种各样的贸易纠纷,进而还会导致索赔、仲裁甚至诉讼。

通常,买方投诉的原因有两种:

(1) 正当的或真正的投诉。这类投诉通常是由下列原因引起的:拒绝交货、装运不及时、发错货、收到的货物受损或来迟、

packing, etc.

(2) The second type of complaints is unjustified complaint, which arises when there is a change of market or when the buyer realizes he has made a bad bargain. At this moment, the buyer finds fault with the goods as an excuse to escape from their contract obligations. In this case, they either do not need the goods any more or have found something cheaper from other sources. So it is important for the seller to distinguish the different kinds of complaints and find the right way to settle them.

Of course, the seller may have causes to file complaints or claims against the importers too. An importer may breach a contract where, under an L/C, he fails to open the relevant L/C according to the stipulated period; where he wrongly refuses to accept the goods; or where, under FOB, he fails to dispatch the vessel according to the stipulations of the contract.

The stipulation of terms and conditions of contract is too unclear to unify the understanding and explanation between two parties that arises disputes or comply with the contract. Breach of a contract occurs when any party of a contract does not follow the stipulations of the contract. The sales contract shall have a legal binding force upon the contracting parties. Any party who has violated the contract shall be legally held responsibilities for the breach, and the injured party is entitled to remedies according to the stipulations of the contract or the relevant laws.

Settlements of claims actually are two sides of a same problem. Settlement of claims refers to the action conducted by the party in breach that he entertains and settles the other party's claim. The first step in the settlement of claims is to find out what the problem is and what the liabilities are and carefully asses the amount of damage or loss due to breach of contract together with the other party. The second step is to work out a mutually acceptable scheme for compensation. Generally, the party in breach may settle the claims by replacing the cargo, giving a discount or cash compensation.

A letter of complaint or claim, whether made by the

短缺、质量低下、包装不良等。

（2）非正当投诉。这类投诉通常是由于市场发生了变化或者买方认为它买的价格不合适。买方此时会挑货物的毛病，以此为借口逃避合同义务。在这种情况下，它们要么不再需要该货物，要么又找到了更便宜的货源。因此正确区分不同形式的投诉并找到良好的解决方法对于卖方而言非常重要。

当然，卖方也可能有理由向进口方提出投诉或索赔。买方违约的情况有：在信用证支付条件下，不按期开证或不开证；无理拒收货物；在FOB条件下，不按合同规定派船等。

有时因合同条款规定不明确，会致使双方理解或解释不统一而引起纠纷，或双方均有违约行为。违约是买卖双方中的任何一方违反合同规定义务的行为。买卖合同对缔约方均具有法律约束力。任何一方违约都应该承担违约的法律责任，而受害方则有权根据合同或有关法律规定得到补救。

理赔实际上是同一个问题的两个方面。理赔指的是违约的一方处理另一方索赔所采取的行为。理赔的第一步是发现问题和责任所在，并正确评价由于违约方和其他一方造成的损坏或损失的金额。第二步是计算出双方都能够接受的补偿计划。通常，违约方可以通过替换货物、打折或现金补偿来理赔。

不管投诉或索赔是由进口方

importer or by the exporter, should be written specifically and tactfully so as to get a satisfactory settlement. The general structure of a letter of complaints is as follows:

(1) Setting the scene;
(2) Explaining the complaint;
(3) Recommending action;
(4) Making your position clear.

In the first part, we give full details such as: dates of delivery and/or order, quantity ordered, account number and invoice number, etc. This part is usually a short paragraph describing what has gone before, so that your complaint has a background, and can be understood in context. This requires simple narrative language to describe the circumstances behind the complaint.

In the second part of complaint letter, details are given such as damaged or defective goods, late delivery, incorrect bills, poor quality, delivery mistakes and so on. It is a good idea to enclose a copy of any documentation you have, such as a sales receipt, an order form, delivery note or an invoice. In this part you should also refer to the inconvenience that you have had to suffer, and if appropriate, mention the cost to your company of this inconvenience. Be sure to avoid using over-emotional or offensive language.

The last part of the complaint letter is usually very short. It should state clearly what exactly you want the company to do. You should request rather than demand. Your tone should be polite but firm.

Replies to complaints are also called adjustment letters. This is because their job is to adjust a difficult situation to benefit both the writer and the reader. Most replies to complaints contain the following four parts:

(1) Acknowledging the complaint;
(2) Describing the action you have taken since receiving it;
(3) Stating briefly your decision;
(4) Offering compensation if appropriate.

还是出口方提出的，这类信函都应写得明确且富于策略性，以便得到满意的结果。通常投诉信的结构如下：

(1) 说明当时的情景；
(2) 解释投诉的原因；
(3) 提出建议；
(4) 表明自己的立场。

信的第一部分应写明有关装运期、订单号、订购的数量、账号、发票号之类的情况。通常这部分是很短的一小段，用以描述之前发生的事情，以便你的投诉有一个背景，能够容易被人理解。这要求用描述性的语言描述投诉背后的情况。

信的第二部分描述货物受损、迟到、票据错误、质量低劣、错误发货等情形。最好的办法是随函附上一份单证，比如销售票据、订单、发货单或发票，同时说明因此给你带来的不便。合适的话，还可以提及这种不便给公司带来的成本损失，但要注意切勿用一些过激或攻击性的语言。

投诉信的最后一部分通常都很短。这一段应明确说明你希望对方做什么，是请求对方而不是要求对方，语气应当礼貌而坚决。

对投诉的回复函通常又叫理赔函，这是因为此类信函的主要任务就是解决困难从而使买卖双方都受益。多数对投诉信的回复包括以下四个方面的内容：

(1) 确认对方的投诉；
(2) 叙述自接到投诉以来所采取的行动；
(3) 简要说明你的决定；
(4) 合适的话提出补偿。

In such letter, remember to keep the tone positive by avoiding negative words such as damage, defective, poor quality, etc. A sincere apology for the inconvenience caused can be contained here, even if you have later to point out the complaint was not really justified at all. If the complaint is justified, you should explain briefly why the mistake took place, and assure the mistake will not occur again. If you accept responsibility and agree to adjustment, you should simply confirm arrangements for compensation. Even if you deny responsibility, it is also a good idea to offer a compromise so as to keep the customer happy.

在这类信函中，切记用肯定的语句而不是负面的词汇如损坏、缺损、质量低劣等。即使你在后面指出投诉是不对的，在这里也要给对方带来的不便表示真诚的歉意。如果投诉是正当的，应解释为什么会发生此类错误并确保不会再犯。如果你承担责任并同意理赔，应确认理赔安排，即使不愿负责，最好做出承诺以便使顾客满意。

11.2 信例
Sample Letters

Letter 1　Complaint

AMAZA GARMENT CO.
45 Wythe Ave, Brooklyn, NY11211

September 15, 2010
Mr. Victor Pon
General Manager
Xiamen Textile Manufacturing Limited
34 Zhangshan Road
Xiamen

Dear Pon,
Order No. XE23003

　　The order mentioned above was delivered to us on September 4, 2010. It is with great regret we have to complain about the packing of Bale 4 and the quality of the material in Bale 2.

　　Bale 4 does not appear to have packed in waterproof material and has become very sodden on arrival. As a result, the 500 meters of your material AC303 it contained has been very badly stained and show signs of rotting.

　　The material in Bale 2 750 metres of AC223, is not up to the standard of the similar material we ordered from you on May 4, 2010. It appears to be too loosely woven and pulls out of shape very easily. Under separate cover by air parcel post we have sent you a cutting of this material and also one from the material we obtained from you on your previous visit to us. You will be able to compare the two for yourselves. We have always been able to rely on the high quality of your materials and packing in the past. We are, however, disappointed on this occasion as we have received orders which need these materials for production. We will, therefore, appreciate it if you can let us know without delay what action you can take to help us to get over present difficulty.

 I look forward to your prompt reply.

Yours faithfully,
Leona
Managing Director

Notes

1. It is with great regret we have to complain about the packing of Bale 4 and the quality of the material in Bale 2. 很遗憾不得不投诉有关第 4 包的包装和第 2 包的质量问题。
2. waterproof material 防水材料
3. sodden 湿透的，湿漉漉的
4. ... badly stained and show signs of rotting 被严重染色，并有腐烂的迹象
5. The material in Bale 2 750 meters of AC223, is not up to the standard of the similar material we ordered from you on May 4, 2010. AC223 材料中有 2 750 米不符合我们在 2010 年 5 月 4 日订购的类似材料的包装要求。这里 we ordered from you on May 4, 2010 是定语从句修饰 similar material。
6. It appears to be too loosely woven and pulls out of shape very easily. 看上去编织松散，容易变形。
7. under separate cover by air 另封航邮
8. We have sent you a cutting of this material and also one from the material we obtained from you on your previous visit to us. You will be able to compute the two for yourselves. 现邮寄你方此材料的剪样以及上次贵方拜访我们时带来的材料剪样，你们自己可以进行一下比较。
9. We are, however, disappointed on this occasion as we have received orders which need these materials for production. 尽管对这次事件我们感到很失望，但我们已经收到许多订单要用这些材料生产。
10. We will, therefore, appreciate it if you can let us know without delay what action you can take to help us to get over present difficulty. 如果贵方能尽快告诉我们贵方将采取何种措施来帮助我们渡过难关，我们将不胜感激。

Letter 2 Response to the Complaint

Xiamen Textile Manufacturing Limited
34 Zhangshan Road
Xiamen
September 22, 2010
Ms Leona
Amaza Garment Co.
45 Wythe Ave, Brooklyn, NY11211
Dear Ms Leona,
 Thank you for your letter of September 15 in which you complain about the packing for Bale

4 and the quality of the material contained in Bale 2. We are sincerely sorry this has happened and trust we can help you overcome your difficulties.

With regard to Bale 4, we regret we are at a complete loss to understand how this came to be packed without any waterproofing material inside the Hessian covering. Our packers have a very good reputation and normally every possible precaution is taken to ensure our export packing is well up to standard. In response to your complaint, we are sending John Smith, our representative, to inspect the bale, and subject to their report, we will replace the part that can't be used. We trust, however, that most of this material can be saved. We will be most grateful if you will assist him to inspect the bale.

As far as the contents of Bale 2 are concerned, we are sorry to say this is not AC223 at all, but AC224, an inferior material that is not for export. Our packing Department is always extremely busy, and unfortunately 750 metres of AC224 were accidentally packed in your Bale 2. We greatly regret this has happened and we are at present arranging to ship the replacement to you. We sincerely hope this bale will arrive in time to meet your production deadline.

We would like to say again how very sorry we are that you have been put to so much trouble in this matter. We hope it will not affect our future business dealings. We will, of course, do all we can to ensure the mistakes made on this occasion are not repeated. In order to offer you some slight additional compensation for the inconvenience caused, we will be pleased to offer you an additional 5% discount on the next order you place with us.

We assure you of our best services at all times.
Yours sincerely,
Victor Pon
General Manager

Notes

1. We are sincerely sorry this has happened. 对此事件的发生表示诚挚的歉意。
2. with regard to 关于
3. at a complete loss 非常茫然，不知所措
4. hessian 棕色粗麻布；打包麻布
5. ... every possible precaution is taken to ensure our export packing is well up to standard. 采取一切可能的预防措施，以确保我们的出口包装符合标准。
6. as far as the contents of Bale 2 are concerned 关于第2包的商品
7. We greatly regret this has happened and we are at present arranging to ship the replacement to you. 发生此事我们深感遗憾，现在我们正安排装运以替换该批货物。
8. We sincerely hope this bale will arrive in time to meet your production deadline. 我们诚挚希望该包货物能够及时到达你方以满足你方生产要求。
9. In order to offer you some slight additional compensation for the inconvenience caused, we will be pleased to offer you an additional 5% discount on the next order you place with us. 作为给您造成不便的额外补偿，我们将乐于在贵方下次订单中提供5%的额外折扣。
10. We assure you of our best services at all times. 我们保证随时提供优良服务。

Letter 3 Claim

Dear Sirs,

Re: Claim on Curtain Materials

The captioned goods you shipped per S. S. "Dongfeng" on May 2 arrived here yesterday. On examination, we have found that many of the curtain materials are severely damaged. Considering this damage was due to the rough handling by the steamship company, we claimed on them for recovery of the loss, but an investigation made by the surveyor has revealed the fact that the damage is attributable to improper packing. For further particulars, we refer you to the surveyor's report enclosed.

We are therefore, compelled to claim on you to compensate us for the loss, $ 23 600, which we have sustained by the damage to the goods.

We trust that you will be kind enough to accept this claim and deduct the sum claimed from the amount of your next invoice to us.

Sincerely,

Notes

1. claim 索赔，赔偿要求
   lodge a claim against sb. for an amount for a reason on sth. 对于某物因为某种原因而向某人索赔一笔金额
   可用于此句型的动词还有 file, raise, register, lay, put in 等。
   表示向某人索赔，一般用介词 against, with 或 on。
   a claim against the underwriters 向保险公司索赔
   表示索赔的原因，一般用介词 for 或 on。
   a claim for/on damaged goods 由于货物损坏而索赔
   表示索赔的金额一般用介词 for。
   a claim for US $ 20 000 索赔 2 万美元
   to accept a claim 接受索赔；to entertain a claim 考虑并接受索赔
   to reject a claim 拒绝索赔；to withdraw a claim 撤回索赔
   to settle a claim 解决索赔、理赔
   例如：to lodge/file /enter/register/make/raise/put in a claim against/with sb. on a certain shipment for a certain reason for amount of money... 对于某批货物由于某种原因向某人提出金额为……的索赔。
2. rough handling 粗暴搬运、野蛮装卸
3. be attributable to 归因于
4. For further particulars, we refer you to the surveyor's report enclosed. 具体情况请参阅随附鉴定报告。这里 refer to 意思是"参阅、参考"。
5. compel to do sth. 被迫做某事
6. ... deduct the sum claimed from the amount of you next invoice to us. 从下次我方的发票金额中扣除该笔索赔费用。

Letter 4　Settlement

Dear Sirs,

　　We have received your letter of 15th May, informing us that the curtain materials we shipped to you arrived damaged on account of imperfectness of our packing.

　　Upon receipt of your letter, we have given this matter our immediate attention. We have studied your surveyor's report very carefully.

　　We are convinced that the present damage was due to extraordinary circumstances under which they were transported to you. We are therefore not responsible for the damage; but as we do not think that it would be fair to have you bear the loss alone, we suggest that the loss be divided between both of us, to which we hope you will agree.

Sincerely,

Notes

1. on account of 因为, 由于
2. We are convinced that the present damage was due to extraordinary circumstances under which they were transported to you. 我们认为现有损失是由于运输途中遭遇的特殊情况所导致的。这里 under which they were transported to you 是介词+which 引出的定语从句修饰前面的 extraordinary circumstances。
3. ...to have you bear the loss alone 贵方独自承担损失

Tips

1. 如何回复客户的索赔

（1）直接接受

I'm sorry for the defectives. We will afford all the claim charge.

对于产品的品质问题我非常抱歉。我方会承担所有赔款。

（2）委婉拒绝

To be honest, it is not our mistake to cause the claim. Please check the following issue: ...

坦白说，不是我们的问题造成索赔。具体原因如下：……

（3）暂时拖延

Sorry to hear that the claim issue happened. We'll do the internal investigation, and give you reply soon.

很抱歉听到索赔的事情发生。我们会做内部调查，并尽快给您答复。

2. 订单延期，是不是需要第一时间跟客户说"sorry"

答案是"不"！在英文交流中，"sorry"这个词是不能随便用的。因为，在欧美文化中，对就是对，错就是错，都是直来直去的。如果这件事是你的责任，大方道歉，并提出补救方案，未尝不是一种诚恳的做法。但如果不是你的原因造成的，就应该据理力争，把情况说明白。你可以帮客户想办法，帮客户补救，但是这句"sorry"是不能讲的。

很多人喜欢在邮件里用"sorry"表示客气，回复晚了说"sorry"，客户嫌价格高了也说"sorry"，总之，只要客户有一点不开心马上就说"sorry"，这是不合适的。这样会使你显得卑躬屈膝，失去合作双方对彼此的尊重，把自己置于一个弱势的不利地位。

订单延期了，这很正常，先要调查和了解清楚原因，为什么延期，如何处理和解决，是谁的问题造成的延期，将来如何避免和改进，这些才是应该去做和去跟客户说明的。如果真的是己方错了，说抱歉完全应该。如果是对方的错，可以指出，并提出补救方案和建议，这反而更能得到对方的尊重和感激。

3. 收到投诉，如何在第一时间应对

一般做法是第一时间给出正面回应，但是不要纠结于谁对谁错，而是先争取一定时间进行思考和讨论，等公司内部达成一致的处理意见或几套处理方案后，再跟客户讨论和商量。这样既有时间进行内部紧急磋商，也可以避免在客户气头上火上浇油，先冷处理一下，对双方都有好处。可以这样回复客户的投诉邮件：

Dear ×××,

    We got your claim massage. I'll do the investigation and get you back ASAP.

    Best regards,

    ×××

11.3 有用的短语和句子
Useful Expressions

1. All disputes in connection with this contract or the execution thereof shall be settled amicably by negotiation.
   凡涉及本合同的争执或在执行本合同中所发生的一切争执应通过友好协商的方式解决。
2. The color deviation is so big that we cannot help lodging a claim against you.
   色差如此之大以至于我们不得不向贵方提出索赔。
3. Owing to your delay in shipment, we have no choice but to make apology to our customers and trouble them for L/C extension.
   由于贵方装运延迟，我们不得不向客户致歉并麻烦他们展证。
4. We immediately looked into the matter and found that the wrong goods were shipped to you through an error on the part of our packers.
   我们迅速介入此事，发现这批货物发运错误是由于我方装箱人员的错误导致的。
5. After inspection we found that the goods were short-delivered by 20 tons.
   检验后发现，货物短交20吨。
6. Since you have refused to negotiate an adequate offer of compensation, we will seek other suppliers and halt all business dealings with your company.
   因贵方拒绝就补偿事宜磋商，我们将寻找新的供应商并终止与贵方所有的业务往来。
7. We have no record of your claim for compensation and ask you to resubmit a copy of the original.
   我方没有贵方的索赔记录，请您将索赔信函原件的副本递交给我们。
8. The total shortage amounts to 1 250kg.

短重总共达 1 250 公斤。
9. The buyer submits a claim for USD 3 000 on account of breakage.
买方对货物的破损要求赔偿 3 000 美元。
10. Since the dispute cannot be settled through negotiation, we agree to settle it by arbitration.
由于争议无法通过谈判解决,我们同意通过仲裁解决。
11. We are sorry to inform you that your claim against us for short weight is unsuited to the international insurance claim standards.
歉告,贵方提出的短重索赔与国际保险索赔标准不相适应。
12. We hope that you will not take this case as a breach of the contract and refrain from making any claims against us as the loss can be negligible.
我们希望贵方不要将此事视为违约,也不要提出索赔,因为这些损失是可以忽略不计的。
13. The shortage you raised might have occurred in the course of transit, and that is a matter over which we can exercise no control.
贵方提出的短重可能是在运输途中发生的,其中的情况我们是无法控制的。
14. We should be grateful if you would give us a complete refund for the defective goods delivered.
对于已交付的这批有瑕疵的货物,如贵方能全数退还货款,我方将不胜感激。
15. We appreciate your offer to keep the goods wrongly delivered, and we are ready to allow 10% off the invoice price if you would like to accept.
我们感谢贵方保留错发的货物,如果贵方愿意接受这批货物,我们愿按照发票价给予 10% 的折扣。
16. We may compromise, but in no case should the compensation exceed $800. Otherwise, this case will be submitted to arbitration.
我们可以让步,但赔偿金额不能超过 800 美元,否则将提交仲裁解决。
17. The seller said the quantity of the shipment was correct. On the contrary, the surveyor testifies that the goods are short-delivered by 50 tons.
卖方说装运的数量准确,但正相反,检验人员证实货物短交 50 吨。
18. Claim can be defined as a demand made upon a person or persons for payment on account of a loss sustained through its negligence.
索赔是指由于一方的疏忽而造成了损失,另一方向其提出赔款的赔偿要求。
19. We take all our customers' comments seriously. We shall arrange for a replacement consignment to be sent to you immediately and would be grateful if you could return the faulty products to us. We shall reimburse freight charges.
我们非常重视顾客的评价,并会即刻安排替换那批货物,如果贵方能够把残次货物退还我方,我们将补偿运费。
20. We have investigated the case carefully, but found no error on our part. We packed the goods according to the contract. They were in good condition as shown by the certificate of packing inspection. The clean B/L further proved that. We suggest you file a claim with the insurance company. We shall try our best to assist you in your claim.
我们已就这件事做了仔细的调查,发现错误不在我方。我方是按照合同规定进行包装的,而且包装检验显示包装良好,清洁提单可进一步证明。建议贵方向保险公司提出索赔,对此我方会尽力帮助。

练习
Exercises

Ⅰ. Comprehension Questions
1. How does the exporter distinguish different kinds of complaints made by the importer?
2. May the seller file the complaints or claims against the buyer? Why?
3. What may happen if any party fails to fulfill his contractual obligations?
4. How to settle the claims?
5. What should we do when writing the letter of complaints or claims?

Ⅱ. Translate the Following Terms and Expressions
1. 合同违约
2. 仲裁条款
3. 提出索赔
4. 索赔短重
5. 拒赔
6. 品质不良
7. arbitration award
8. resort to litigation
9. short delivery
10. settle a claim

Ⅲ. Supply the Missing Words in the Blanks
Dear Sirs,

We have just received the Survey R_____ from Shanghai Commodity Inspection B_____ evidencing that the captioned goods unloaded here yesterday was short weight 1 200kg. A thorough e_____ showed that the short weight was d_____ to the improper packing, for which the suppliers should be definitely r_____. On the b_____ of the SCIB's Survey Report, we hereby l_____ a claim a_____ you f_____ Stg. 270.00 in all. We are e_____ the Survey Report No. 567 and look f_____ to settlement at an e_____ date.

Yours faithfully,

Ⅳ. Translate the Following Sentences
1. We hope that you will not take this case as a breach of the contract and refrain from making any claims against us as the loss can be negligible.
2. We have investigated the case carefully, but found no error on our part. We packed the goods according to the contract. They were in good condition as shown by the certificate of packing inspection. The clean B/L further proved that. We suggest you file a claim with the insurance company. We shall try our best to assist you in your claim.
3. We take all our customers' comments seriously. We shall arrange for a replacement consignment to be sent to you immediately and would be grateful if you could return the faulty products to us. We shall reimburse freight charges.
4. Claim on short-weight is caused by packing damage or short-loading. While claim on delayed shipment is that seller fail to make the delivery according to time schedule. Claim on quality originates from inferior quality of goods or quality changes.
5. Any complaint about the quality of the products should be lodged within 15 days after their arrival.
6. 请尽快告知我方是否可以在7月底交货，如果不能，我们将取消订单，因为我们无法再等下去了。
7. 完好无损的包装证明货物是在装运前损坏的。
8. 对你们遭受的不便我们深表歉意，保证尽心高效地办理你们今后的订单。

9. 考虑到我们之间长期的业务关系，我们准备接受25吨短装的索赔。
10. 很遗憾从你方9月15日来函得知，发往你方的第100号订单下10箱货物中有3箱受损严重。由于该货物均进行了精心包装，我们只能认为箱子是被粗暴搬运的。

Ⅴ. Translate the Following Letter into English

×××先生：

现随函寄去无锡商检局签发的第20号检验报告，该报告证明所购货物的质量与以前送来的样品相差甚远。由于这些货物对我方毫无用处，因此我方要求贵方归还这批货物的发票金额和商检费用，共计5 000美元。

Ⅵ. Translate the Following Letter into Chinese

A Claim for Short-weight and Inferior Quality

Dear Sirs,

We have received the goods of our Order No. P2001, which you shipped by S. S. "Morning Star". From the Survey Report issued by the Commodity Inspection Bureau here you will see that there is a shortage of 868 kilos. As the packing remains intact, it is beyond doubt that the shortage occurred prior to shipment. Meanwhile the goods are much inferior to the samples you submitted to us before. Under the circumstances, we have to lodge claims with you as follows.

Claim Number	Claim for	Amount
GM-30	Short weight	USD 1 120.85
GM-40	Quality	USD 1 028.60
	Plus survey charges	USD 60
	Total Amount	USD 2 209.45

Enclosed please find one copy each of Survey Reports No. 3018 and No. 3028 together with our Statement of Claims. We hope you will give the matter your most favorable consideration and settle the claims as soon as possible.

Yours sincerely,

Chapter 12
第 12 章

促　　销
Promotion

Learning Objectives

Enable the students to know the concept of promotion, the way to make promotion; and master the main points of writing these letters.

使学生了解促销的含义、促销的手段及特点,掌握促销这类信函的写作要领。

12.1　背景知识
Background Information

Promotion is one way for marketers to convey information of their enterprise and products to the consumers, persuade them to buy the products so as to expand the sales. It is actually a form of communication, the marketers (information providers or senders) send information that can stimulate consumption to one or more target (namely the information receiver, such as the audience, readers, consumers or end-users) to affect their attitude and behavior. The ordinary promotion methods are advertising, personnel selling, network marketing, business promotion and public relations. A firm may not use all of these promotional techniques to sell a product. However many firms will rely on two or three of them because one technique cannot usually do the job.

Advertising is a world wide major mode of communicating with customers. As a part of promotional strategy, it

促销就是营销者向消费者传递有关本企业及产品的各种信息,说服或吸引消费者购买其产品,以达到扩大销售量的目的。促销实质上是一种沟通活动,即营销者(信息提供者或发送者)发出作为刺激消费的各种信息,把信息传递到一个或更多的目标对象(信息接收者,如观众、读者、消费者或用户等),以影响其态度和行为。常用的促销手段有广告、人员推销、网络营销、营业推广和公共关系。一个企业不一定运用所有促销手段来销售一种产品,但许多企业会依靠其中的两种或三种,因为仅依靠一种往往不能奏效。

广告是世界范围内与顾客交流的主要方式。它们作为促销战

is important not only in foreign market, but also in export markets where customers are unfamiliar with firms and their products.

To some extent, the letter of promotion is a form of advertising, aiming at selling particular kinds of goods or services to specific types of customers. It is usually written by companies to their potential buyers, former customers and existing customers. It generally includes four basic characters: to draw attention; to arouse interest; to create desire of buying and to induce action of buying. When writing, we should follow the following rules:

(1) Arousing the buyer's interest is very important. Remember trying to start your letter with an attractive opening sentence to catch the reader's interest;

(2) Introducing the unique features, advantages and purposes of the products, such as whether products are fashionable, romantic, convenient or healthy;

(3) Emphasize what benefits customers can receive from the goods or services;

(4) Keep the letter short, concise and attractive, persuade your customers to act as what you want them to do.

12.2 信例
Sample Letters

Letter 1　Sales Letters

Dear Sirs,
　　We are one of the leading exporters of Textiles in this city and are pleased to send you with this letter a copy of our catalogue for Chinese Cotton Pieces Goods. Our products are finely woven, hard wearing, creaseless materials with most attractive designs. We are confident that a trial order will convince you that the goods we are offering you are excellent value for money.
　　In order to popularize these products, all the catalogue prices are subject to a special discount of 10% during this month only.

> Please note that we have given you our most favorable price and highly appreciate your early reply.
>
> Yours faithfully,

Notes

1. leading exporter 主要出口商
2. Our products are finely woven, hard wearing, creaseless materials with most attractive designs. 此产品质地精良、外观漂亮、耐穿且不打皱,因而非常畅销。
3. trial order 试订单

   excellent value for money 物有所值

   We are confident that a trial order will convince you that the goods we are offering you are excellent value for money. 我们相信贵方对这些货物的试订单将会让你确信我们提供的商品物有所值。
4. In order to popularize these products, all the catalogue prices are subject to a special discount of 10% during this month only. 为了促销这些商品,在本月内对所有目录价格给予10%的折扣。

   popularize 普及;推广

   discount 折扣

   at a discount 折价,减价发行;低于面值的价格

   with some discount 打折扣;以保留的态度

Letter 2　Advertisement

> Xuzhou Construction Machinery Group (XCMG) has always been the leading construction machinery manufacturer and provider in China since its establishment in March 1989. Now it ranks 1st in China construction machinery industry and 10th in the world construction machinery. XCMG is well known in China for its most competitive and high-quality construction machinery including construction lifting equipment, road machinery, road and maintenance machinery, compaction equipment, loaders, bulldozers and graders, excavators, concrete pump machinery etc. Most of XCMG products are market leaders both domestically and internationally in terms of market share.
>
> XCMG now has its own sales network all over the world and has always been faithful in carrying out its contract. Reasonable in price, superior in quality, good after-sale services, timely in delivery, the Corporation serves clients wholeheartedly.
>
> The corporation wishes to join hands with business people from home and abroad for economic development.
>
> Address: Industrial Zone 1
>
> 　　　　　Xuzhou Economic Development Zone
>
> 　　　　　Jiangsu, China

Notes

1. Xuzhou Construction Machinery Group (XCMG) 徐州工程机械集团
2. construction lifting equipment 工程起重机械
3. road machinery 路面机械
4. road and maintenance machinery 筑路及养护机械
5. compaction equipment 压实机械
6. loaders 装货设备
7. bulldozers and graders 推土挖掘机械
8. excavators 开凿机械
9. concrete pump machinery 混凝土泵机械
10. excellent value for money 物有所值
11. after-sale services 售后服务
12. The corporation wishes to join hands with business people from home and abroad for economic development. 公司竭诚希望海内外人士共同携手，为公司发展做贡献。

Letter 3 Introduce Company to New Clients

Dear Sir,

  We understand from your information posted on Alibaba.com that you are in the market for Electric Appliances. We would like to take this opportunity to introduce our company and products, with the hope that we may work together in the future.

  We are a joint venture specializing in the manufacture and export of all kinds of household appliances. Our company has a long history with over 80 kinds of the corporation-manufactured goods won prizes at international and domestic contests. Our products have been sold well in more than 150 countries and regions. Recently we have received enquiries from Japan, Germany, Australia and South Africa. The large number of repeat orders we regularly receive from distributors is a clear evidence of the widespread popularity of our products.

  We have enclosed our catalogue, which introduces our company in details and covers the main products we supply at present. You may also visit our online company introduction at http://www.alibaba.com includes our latest product line.

  We are awaiting your early reply.

Yours faithfully,

Notes

1. Our company has a long history with over 80 kinds of the corporation-manufactured goods won prizes at international and domestic contests. 本公司的产品历史悠久，享誉中外，80多种产品在国内及国际评比中屡获殊荣。
2. The large number of repeat orders we regularly receive from distributors is a clear evidence of the widespread popularity of our products. 从分销商处收到的大量重复订单表明，我们的产品深

受消费者欢迎。
distributor 分销商

3. We have enclosed our catalogue, which introduces our company in details and covers the main products we supply at present. 随函附寄了我们的目录，上面详细介绍了我们的公司及目前可供的主要产品。
in details 详细地

Letter 4　Promotion Letter of Woman Handbag

Dear Sirs/ Madams,

　　We are pleased to get to know that you are presently in the market for Woman Handbag, and as a specialized manufacturer and exporter for this product in China, we sincerely hope to establish business relations with your esteemed corporation.

　　Our handbag is known for its durability and artistic appearance and we are confident that a trial order would convince you of more purchase. Furthermore, we believe that the goods are highly worthy of the price we are offering.

　　Herewith please find our competitive offer as follows:

Net weight: 821g

Type NO.: AWOOK235

Outer material: fair leather

Inner material: dyed fancy cloth

Logo: fair hardware

Dimensions: 14cm × 32cm × 27cm

Shoulder straps: 24cm (flexible)

　　Considering our longstanding business relationship, all the catalogue prices are subject to a special discount of 10% with less profit during this month only.

　　We are offering you the goods of the highest quality on unusually generous terms and would welcome your earliest orders.

Yours faithfully,

Notes

1. esteemed 受人尊敬的
   esteem 的过去式和过去分词
2. We believe that the goods are highly worthy of the price we are offering.
   我们相信我们所提供的产品肯定会被认为是物有所值。
3. competitive offer 有竞争力的报价
4. a special discount of 10%　10% 的特别折扣
   special price 特价

> **Tips 怎样写促销信**
>
> 促销信分为两种：一种是直接推销产品的信，另一种是答复对方咨询产品的信。
>
> 和其他促销方式比起来，促销信成本低廉，还可以传递更多、更详细的产品信息。下面是写促销信应遵循的一些基本原则。
>
> （1）Emphasize the benefits rather than the features of the product or service.
>
> （2）Use active voice in picturing the reader enjoying the use or performance of the product or service.
>
> （3）Focus on one of the main appeals.
>
> （4）Subordinate the price, unless it is an obvious bargain, by mentioning it after most of the benefits have been listed.
>
> （5）Use a promotion piece (eg. An enclosed brochure) to illustrate the details of the product or service.
>
> （6）Specify the action by providing the ways of obtaining the products.

12.3 有用的短语和句子

Useful Expressions

1. In order to popularize these products, all the catalogue prices are subject to a special discount of 10% during this month only.

   为了促销这些产品，在本月内对所有目录价格给以10%的折扣。

2. We request you to make a careful comparison of these goods, both in respect to quality and prices, with those you are now buying elsewhere.

   在质量与价格方面，贵方可以把我们的这些产品与从别处购买的产品进行详细比较。

3. We would be glad to have the opportunity of supplying any of these goods which would be most suited to your needs.

   很高兴能有机会向您提供其中的任一产品，来满足贵方的需求。

4. With a history dating back to..., ... has grown to become one of the 100 largest industrial companies in the United States, with 2010 sales in excess of ＄5 billion.

   ……的历史可追溯到……年，现已发展成美国最大的100家工业公司之一，2010年的销售额超过了50亿美元。

5. As far as construction lifting equipments are concerned, we have sent only one set of literature to you as we would first like to find out whether you are interested and then whether the export licensing position is favorable.

   就机械起重设备而言，我们只寄给你们一套说明书，因为我们首先想了解你们是否有兴趣、出口许可证情况是否有利。

6. The corporation has made many export achievements and has been appraised as advanced local company by the provincial government for ten years running.

   该公司出口业绩显著，连续十年被省政府评为先进的地方外贸公司。

7. With the right of import and export authorized in 1989, the corporation has been expanding its

import and export trade greatly. Friends from all parts of the world are welcome to make a choice.

自1989年公司拥有自营进出口权以来，公司的进出口业务取得了很大的发展，欢迎世界各国朋友前来选购。

8. You will be interested to hear about our latest ... which we have just introduced to the market. The product is a multi-purpose type with the highest technical development and very economical.

   贵公司一定有兴趣了解我公司刚刚上市的最新型……（产品）的消息，该产品采用了最高技术，具有多项功能，并极具经济效益。

9. We see from our sales figures that you placed a considerable number of orders with us last year for our.... As we are selling off this popular range of ... in preparation for the introduction of new models, we are willing to make you an offer at prices 15% below the listed prices. But the quantity is limited, please make up your decision as soon as possible.

   根据销售数量得知，去年贵公司向我方订购了相当数量的……由于我方欲将此本年度中广受欢迎的……清出，以便推出新型产品。故我方愿意向贵方按低于价目表15%的价格报价，但数量有限，欲购从速。

10. With the increase of the general retail costs which become conspicuous this spring, the next consignment will be much dearer, so we recommend you to take prompt advantage of this offer which is firm for a week only.

    由于今春以来，一般零售成本显著上涨，因此下一次的出货价格势必更加昂贵。故建议贵方从速把握时机，该报价有效期仅为一周。

11. We have been requested by the above mentioned company to approach you and your main branches for introducing their manufacturing program, which is briefly outlined in the heading.

    上述公司要求我们与你们及你们的主要分公司联系，介绍其生产计划，该计划已在标题中简要列出。

12. Regarding Plastic Welding Equipment, it may well be that manufacturers here will not be able to compete against Japan.

    关于塑料焊接设备，很可能该厂竞争不过日本。

13. Headquartered in Chicago, Illinois, FMC Corporation is a major producer of technically advanced machinery and chemicals for industry and agriculture.

    FMC公司总部设于伊利诺伊州芝加哥市，是一家技术先进的生产机械和工农业化工原料的大厂家。

14. We believe FMC to be one of the leaders of the packing industry both in the U. S. and abroad.

    我们相信FMC在美国和在国外都是包装工业界的主要厂家之一。

15. Our corporation is established for the purpose of carrying on import and export as well as other activities in connection with foreign trade.

    本公司是以经营进出口业务以及对外贸易有关的活动为宗旨而建立的。

16. We are active in commercial intercourse with the trade and financial circles of various countries and districts.

    本公司致力于各国和各地区的贸易和金融界的商业往来。

17. To give you a general idea of our exports, we are sending you under separate cover a catalogue together with a range of pamphlets for your reference.

    为使贵方对我方出口产品有全面的了解，我方另函寄去一本目录册及一套小册子以供参考。

18. We hope you will do your utmost to promote trade as well as friendship.
    我们希望贵方尽最大努力,既促进业务,又增进友谊。
19. As you know, it is our foreign trade policy to trade with merchants from all over the world on the basis of equality and mutual benefit.
    如你所知,我们的外贸政策是在平等互利的基础上与各国人民做生意。
20. To encourage you to place orders with us, we would allow for a 3% special discount for any order received at the end of September.
    为了鼓励贵方向我方下订单,特对9月底之前的订单给予3%的优惠折扣。
21. In order to popularize these products, all the catalogue prices are subjected to a special discount of 20% during this month only.
    为了推广这些产品,产品目录上所有价格在本月都享有20%的特殊折扣。
22. We are offering you goods of the highest quality on unusually generous terms and would welcome your earlier orders.
    我们将在特殊的优惠条件下为您提供优质的产品,欢迎您早日订购。
23. You will see that prices this season are slightly higher, but you will find that this is offset by marked improvements in almost every line.
    贵方将看到本季价格轻微上涨,但这一上涨几乎可以被产品的每一项显著改进所抵消。
24. We believe it will surely find a good/ready market in your country.
    我们相信该产品在贵国市场一定会很畅销。
25. We are an exclusive exporter of parts and components of various types of motorcycles in this district and would take the liberty to send a quotation sheet covering our current range of this line for your reference. We hope you will find it interesting.
    我们是本地区各种摩托车零部件的独家出口商,愿借此机会寄去现有的这类产品的报价供您参考,希望您对此有兴趣。
26. With a view to supporting your sales, we have specially prepared some samples of our new comodities and are sending them to you, under separate cover, for your consideration.
    为了支持你们的销售,我们特别准备了一些新产品的样本,另外寄给贵方供参考。
27. We take pleasure in enclosing the latest designs of our products, which are superior in quality and moderate in price and are sure to find a good market at your end.
    我们很高兴随函寄给贵方我们产品的最新设计样式,这些新设计质量高、价格适中,肯定会在贵地市场畅销。
28. Owing to its superior quality and reasonable price, our poplin has met with a warm reception and quick sale in most European countries. We think it is to your advantage to buy this item for sale in your market.
    我们的府绸品质优良、价格公道,深受大多数欧洲国家欢迎,销售很快。我们认为订购我们的府绸在贵方市场销售是很有利的。
29. Since the required articles are not available, we would like to recommend the under-mentioned products which can be supplied from stock for prompt shipment. This recommendation is made in the interest of both parties.
    由于所需的品种目前无货供应,我们想推荐下列库存产品,可以即装。这一推荐照顾到了双方的利益。

30. We trust that you will take advantage of this opportunity to offer your customer with first-class products.

我们确信您会把握此机会，向贵公司客户提供一流的产品。

练习
Exercises

Ⅰ. Comprehension Questions
1. What is the definition of promotion?
2. What are the general methods of promotion?
3. What are the features of promotion?

Ⅱ. Translate the Following Terms and Expressions
1. leading importer
2. excellent value for money
3. after-sale services
4. personnel selling
5. 网络营销
6. 营业推广
7. 公共关系

Ⅲ. Translate the Following Sentences
1. In order to support your sales, we are glad to enclose some sales literatures for your reference.
2. If you find our products of interest, please let us have your specific inquiry.
3. If you are interested in any of our items, please let us know immediately.
4. We shall be glad to have your comments on its sales possibilities.
5. 在质量与价格方面，贵方可将我们的产品与您从别处购买的产品进行仔细比较。
6. 很高兴能有机会向您提供您所需要的产品。
7. 我们向贵方保证，我们提供的试订单的货物都会像你亲自挑选的一样。
8. 这是这类商品中最畅销的品种，如果贵方感兴趣，请通知我方。
9. 此类商品由上海公司经营，请与他们直接联系。
10. 我们有幸自荐，盼望能有机会与你们合作，扩大业务。

Ⅳ. Read the Following Letters and Fill in the Blanks with Appropriate Words

Product packaging is an important aspect of overseas promotion. Most American companies know that packaging must be _____ to attract buyers' attention, _____ the product, and provide a reason to buy.

Some of American packaging needs to be redesigned for foreign _____. Certain photographs, signs, colors, and symbols may be considered _____ overseas. Another important _____ by the Americans in designing packages _____ foreign shipment and sale is protection _____ breakage and spoilage _____ in shipment. Overseas sales agents can often make valuable suggestions _____ package design. Adapting or redesigning packaging can be expensive, and this cost are generally considered when they _____ foreign markets.

Ⅴ. Translate the Following into English

什么是营销？营销一词的含义是什么？许多人都认为营销就是推销和广告。可是，事实上，营销是为了引发令人满意的服务和商品交换而进行的一系列活动。营销活动可以始于弄清楚人们想要得到的产品是什么，也可以始于激发起一种新的需要然后再去满足这种需要。营销活动包括营销调研、零售、推销人员管理、广告和运输。

VI. Fill in the Gaps in This Letter with One of the Words From the Box

| a. position | b. experience | c. referees | d. CV | e. convenient | f. interview |
| g. information | h. hear | i. forward | j. advertisement | k. responsible | |

Dear Sir,

  I am writing in answer to your ___(1)___ in The Times of April 19, 2014 for the ___(2)___ of Export Manger.

  I have had eight years ___(3)___ in the export departments of two large organization, starting as a trainee and gaining promotion to my present position as Assistant Sales Manager in charge of exports. During the last three years I have been ___(4)___ for finding and expanding new markets in the Far East and I believe this experience would enable me to undertake full responsibility for your Export Department.

  I enclose a ___(5)___, together with the address of two ___(6)___: my present manager Mr. John Wills and Mr. James Booth, who supervised my training at the Far East Trading Company.

  I will be pleased to give you any further ___(7)___ you may require and come to an ___(8)___ at any ___(9)___ time. I should mention, however, that I will be out of the country from 1-9 May. I hope this will not cause any inconvenience to you.

  I look ___(10)___ to ___(11)___ from you soon.

Yours faithfully,

Chapter 13
第 13 章

代　　　理
Agency

Learning Objectives

Enable the students to know about the basic knowledge of agency; to understand its function and categories; to master the writing skills of this kind of letter, such as asking for agency, appointing agency, signing an agency agreement.

使学生了解代理的作用、代理的分类，掌握寻找代理、请求代理、指定代理及拟定代理协议的写作要领。

13.1　背景知识
Background Information

Agency is one of the usual practices in the international trade. Except negotiating directly to come into business, the exporters and the importers can also choose a reliable firm as their agent. One important reason why the exporters look for foreign agents is that they are familiar with local market and the end-users. What's more, the exporters can also take advantage of the agent to help them explore, strengthen and extend world market.

An agent acts on behalf of the other. The party for whom an agent acts is the principal. Agents ordinarily have authority to bind their principals. Agents may enter into contracts on behalf of their principals. And, principals are liable for the tortious acts committed by agents within the scope of their agency.

Once an agency relationship exists, the law imposes

代理是国际贸易中采用的贸易方式之一。在国际贸易中，除了由买卖双方直接逐笔洽谈业务并达成交易外，可根据业务需要选择可靠的客户建立代理关系。委托国外客户代理商的一个重要原因，在于代理商熟悉当地的市场和实际买户的情况，出口商可以利用代理在当地市场上的有利条件帮助其开拓、巩固和扩大出口市场。

代理人以他人名义行事，而被代理人又称委托人。代理人通常有权约束委托人并代表委托人签订合同。委托人对代理人在代理范围内的侵权行为负责。

一旦代理关系成立，代理双

certain duties and obligations of that relationship on both parties. The principal has certain responsibilities to the agent. And, the agent, in turn, owes certain duties to the principal.

Agents are characterized as fiduciaries. A fiduciary holds a position of trust and has the highest enforcement in the law. As fiduciaries, they owe to their principals the duties of obedience, care, loyalty, and responsibility. An agent who breaches any of these duties is liable for damages to the principal and forfeits any compensation.

The principal owes certain duties to the agent, which includes the duty to comply with the contract and reimburse the expenses and losses resulting from the agency.

Terms of agency are sometimes set out through correspondence between the parties, while dealings are on a large scale, a formal agreement drafted by one of the parties after negotiation is desirable. All or some of the following may cover some or all of following contents:

(1) The nature and duration of the agency;
(2) The territory to be covered;
(3) The duties of the agent and principal;
(4) Details of commission and expenses to be allowed;
(5) The law of the country by which the agreement is governed;
(6) The sending of reports, accounts and payments;
(7) The arrangements of arbitration in the event of disputes.

The establishment of agency relations, the rights and duties of the two parties are based on the agency agreement. Under this agreement, the one who appoints an agent to work for him/her is called the principal, the person or the firm authorized by the principal to promote sales is called the agent. The agent always represents the principal to sign contracts or engage into other commercial business. The principal will pay the agents in the form of commission on the value of the sales level.

A principal-agency relationship may terminate in many ways. It may terminate under the terms of the agency

方便承担了法律责任和义务。委托人对代理人承担一定责任，代理人对委托人也负有相应的义务。

代理人具有受托人的特点，受托人受人之托，这种形式具有最高的法律效力。作为受托人，他们对授托人服从、审慎、忠心并负有责任。若有违约，代理人需要对因此给委托人造成的损失负责并且赔偿。

委托人对代理人也负有义务，包括遵守合约并向代理人偿付由代理引起的费用和损失。

有时候双方通过信函来确定代理条件，但是，在业务量较大时，较理想的做法是由一方与另一方磋商后草拟一份正式协议。代理协议可包括以下全部或部分内容：

(1) 代理的性质以及期限；
(2) 代理的地区；
(3) 代理人及委托人的职责；
(4) 佣金及费用明细情况；

(5) 协议可适用的法律；

(6) 报表的寄送、账户及付款；
(7) 发生争执时的仲裁安排。

代理关系的建立，双方的权利及义务，是根据双方签订的代理协议来确立的。在这种关系下，被称为委托人的一方，授权给被称为代理人的另一方，由后者代表前者与第三方订立合同或进行其他商业行为。委托人对代理方按其经营金额，以佣金的形式支付酬金。

代理关系可以通过各种方式终止，这种终止可能是代理合同规定

contract. For example, "this agency shall terminate in two years", which specifies the validity. If there is no specific provision for termination in the contract, the parties may always terminate the agency relationship by mutual consent.

Sometimes, a change in circumstances may terminate principal-agency relationship suddenly, which include death of the principal agent, impossibility of performance, and destruction of the subject matter of the agency.

The agency relationship may also terminate on the unilateral action of either party. Either party may terminate the relationship, even if he or she does not have the right. Simply stated, the law does not force a party to continue to carry out the service against his or her will. Unilateral termination, however, may constitute a breach of contract, in which case the non-breaching party may have an action for damages.

There are usually three types of agency:

(1) Sole/Exclusive agent: A sole/exclusive agency enjoys the sole/exclusive rights to promote sales of certain commodities for the principal in a certain area;

(2) Ordinary agent: An agent does not have the sole/exclusive rights of selling commodities in a certain area, but the entrusted by the principal to promote sales of commodities on the basis of commission;

(3) General agent: With more extensive rights than sole/exclusive agent entitled by the principal, they will act as a representative of the principal in a certain area not only in promoting sales of commodities, signing contracts but also executing other non-commercial business, for which the principal will be responsible in law.

If you are a company who are seeking for agent to expand your business, the following elements should be included:

(1) Express your wishes to appoint an agent;

(2) State the reason why you choose this company to represent for you;

(3) Favorable terms that you can provide for the agency.

的。比如说,条款中指明"代理关系两年后终止",这就规定了终止期限。即使合同中没有明确规定终止期限,合同双方总可以在互相同意的基础上结束代理关系。

有时,一些突发情况可能终止代理关系,这些情况包括委托人或代理人的死亡、代理行为不能执行、代理的主体事件消亡。

代理关系也会因单方面的行动而终止。任何一方都能够终止代理关系,即使他没有这种权利。简单来说,法律并不强迫合同一方违背自己的意愿继续履约。但是,单方面终止合约可能造成违约,非违约人可能会采取行动要求赔偿损失。

代理的形式主要有三种:

(1) 独家代理:委托人授予代理人在某一特定区域和时期内享有独家代理销售某项指定商品的专营权;

(2) 一般代理:代理人在特定区域内不享有销售代理商品的专营权利,只是接受委托人的委托代为销售商品,收取佣金;

(3) 总代理:总代理人具有由委托人授予的较为广泛的权限,可以代表委托人在推销商品、签订合同之外,从事其他业务活动和办理一些非商业性的事务,而由委托人承担法律责任。

公司指定代理发展业务的信函,应该包括以下内容:

(1) 表达想要指定代理的意愿;

(2) 说明选择该公司作为代理的理由;

(3) 为代理商提供的优惠条件。

When you are ready to act as an agent for a foreign firm, you will write to ask for sole agent. The letter includes followings:

(1) Express your wishes to represent as their sole agent;

(2) State your abilities serving as an agent;

(3) What terms you can accept.

Through friendly negotiations between both parties, they will conclude an agency agreement. In practice, complete agreements will consist of the following matters:

(1) The nature and duration of the agency;
(2) The covered territory of agency;
(3) The duties of agent and principal;
(4) The method of mail sale.

当要申请作为某一公司的代理商时，可以写一封要求作为独家代理的信函。内容如下：

(1) 表达要成为代理商的意愿；

(2) 说明作为代理商所具有的能力；

(3) 可以接受的代理条件。

通过友好协商，双方将会达成代理协议。在实践中，完整的代理协议应包括以下方面：

(1) 代理的性质及有效期；
(2) 代理地区；
(3) 代理人和委托人的责任；
(4) 寄售的方式。

13.2 信例
Sample Letters

Letter 1 Asking to be Sole Agent

Dear Sirs,

We learn from B/C Corporation that you are looking for a reliable firm with good connections in Machinery Equipment trade to represent you in North America.

We are experienced dealers in marketing Machinery Equipment, having been in the business for more than twenty years and enjoying good business relations with all the leading wholesalers and retailers in this line. Furthermore, we have spacious and well-equipped showrooms and experienced staff of sales representatives who could push your business effectively.

If you have interest in our proposal, please inform us of your requirement and on what terms you would be willing to conclude an agency agreement.

For our credit standing and integrity in the trade, please refer to B/C Corporation.

Your immediate reply would be highly appreciated.

Yours faithfully,

Notes

1. We learn from B/C Corporation that you are looking for a reliable firm with good connections in Machinery Equipment trade to represent you in North America. 我公司从 B/C 公司获悉，贵方正在寻找一家在机械设备贸易方面具有广泛联系的商号作为在北美地区的代理。

   represent 代表，象征，表示；作为……的代表

The Foreign Minister represented the country at the conference. 外交部长代表该国出席大会。
2. spacious 广阔的，宽敞的
3. We have spacious and well-equipped showrooms and experienced staff of sales representatives who could push your business effectively. 我公司拥有宽敞且设备良好的展室，并拥有经验丰富的工作人员，他们一定能有效地促进贵方的业务。
   well-equipped 设备良好的
4. inform 告诉，通知
   be informed of 听说；接到……的通知
5. If you have interest in our proposal, please inform us of your requirement and on what terms you would be willing to conclude an agency agreement. 期望贵方对我公司的建议感兴趣，并希望能了解贵方愿以何种条件达成代理协议。
6. agency 代理；代理处，代理商，代理机构
   agency agreement 代理协议
   agency commission 代理佣金
   sole agency = exclusive agency 独家代理
   For our credit standing and integrity in the trade, please refer to B/C Corporation. 关于我公司的资金状况及商业信誉，请向 B/C 公司查询。

Letter 2　Appointing Agent

> Dear Sirs,
> 　　We appreciate your proposal to act as our sole agent for the sale of our Machinery Equipment in North America.
> 　　After a careful consultation with B/C Corporation, we should like to go further into the matter. But before we make our final decision, we should be glad to know on what terms you would be willing to represent us, also the terms on which business is generally conducted in your country. As your manager Mr. Wang will visit Beijing in two weeks, we think it would be better to discuss this with him rather than communicating through a lengthy correspondence. May we therefore ask you to let us know when we may expect Mr. Wang to call?
> 　　We look forward to your early reply.
>
> 　　　　　　　　　　　　　　　　　　　　　　　　　　　　　　　　Yours faithfully,

Notes

1. We appreciate your proposal to act as our sole agent for the sale of our Machinery Equipment in North America. 贵方提出担任在北美地区销售我方机械设备产品的代理，对此我们表示感谢。
   act 充当，担任
2. agent 代理商
   sole agent = exclusive agent 独家代理人

commission agent 佣金代理人
general agent 总代理人
advertising agent 广告代理人
shipping agent 运输代理人
insurance agent 保险代理人

agent 与 agency 不同，前者为代理人（外经贸业务中，一般即简称代理），后者为代理权或机构。所以我们说 agency agreement 而不能说 agent agreement，即有关代理权的协议。因此，我们只能说 We appoint you as our agent；而不能说 We appoint you as our agency。

3. consultation 咨询，磋商

Letter 3 Seeking for Agent

Dear Sirs,

Further to our discussion with Mr. Wang when he called on us on the 23rd, we have decided to entrust you with the sole agency for our Machinery Equipment in the territory of North America.

The appointment will be for a trial period of twelve months in the first instance. We shall pay you a commission of 5% on the net value of all sales against orders received through you.

If you find these terms and conditions acceptable, we will arrange for a formal agreement to be drawn up and, when this is signed, prepare a circular for distribution to our customers in North America, announcing your appointment as our agent.

Yours faithfully,

Notes

1. In view of our experience and extensive business connections, we hope you will entrust us with the sole agency for the territory. 鉴于我方丰富的经验和广泛的联系，希望贵方能委任我方为该地区的独家代理商。

    entrust 委托，托付

    entrust sb. with sth. 委托某人做某事

    entrust sth. to sb. 将某事委托给某人

2. The appointment will be for a trial period of twelve months in the first instance. We shall pay you a commission of 5% on the net value of all sales against orders received through you. 委托期限先定为12个月的尝试期，我方将根据从贵方获得的订单按所有销售额的净值支付贵方5%的佣金。

    in the first instance 起初，首先

    commission 佣金

3. drawn up 草拟，拟定

    circular 通函

    If you find these terms and conditions acceptable, we will arrange for a formal agreement to be drawn up and, when this is signed, prepare a circular for distribution to our customers in North America, announcing your appointment as our agent. 如果贵方确认上述条件,我方将拟定正式协议。协议一经签署,我们将立即向我方北美地区的客户发出通函,宣布委托贵方为我方代理。

Letter 4　Confirmation of Agency Terms

Dear Sirs,

With reference to your letter of October 2, we are pleased to confirm our readiness to act as your Agents for the sale of your Machinery Equipment in North America. Before you send us your formal Agency Agreement, we would like to restate the main points as follows:

1. We act as your sole agents for a trial period of twelve months, commencing on 1st December;

2. We shall receive a commission of 5% on our sales of your products;

3. During the validity of the agency agreement, we shall not handle any other foreign products of the same line and competitive types.

4. Payments for the sales will be made by an irrevocable letter of credit against our invoices.

5. We undertake to forward you detailed reports in writing on current market conditions as well as consumer's comments on price, quality, packing and the sales prospective in the duration of this agreement.

We believe the agreement will be mutually beneficial and open up way to further cooperation.

Yours faithfully,

Notes

1. With reference to your letter of October 2, we are pleased to confirm our readiness to act as your agents for the sale of your Machinery Equipment in North America. 兹参阅贵方10月2日的来函,我们很高兴能够作为贵方在北美地区销售机械设备的独家代理商。
   with reference to 兹参阅

2. Before you send us your formal agency agreement, we would like to restate the main points as follows. 在给我们发正式协议之前,我们重申以下几点内容。
   restate 重申

3. During the validity of the agency agreement, we shall not handle any other foreign products of the same line and competitive types. 在协议有效期内,我们不会为其他公司销售类似商品及具有竞争性的商品。
   during the validity of... 介词短语,作时间状语,在……有效期内
   agreement 协议
   sole agency agreement 独家代理协议
   exclusive sales agreement 包销协议,独家经销协议

consignment agreement 寄售协议书

4. We undertake to forward you detailed reports in writing on current market conditions as well as consumer's comments on price, quality, packing and the sales prospective in the duration of this agreement. 我们会向贵方呈交一份有关当地市场情况和客户关于商品价格、质量、包装及销售前景评价的书面报告供贵方参考。

forward 提交

detailed reports 详细报告

Letter 5 Ask a Firm or Individual to Represent Us

Dear Sirs,

　　We are writing to you on the recommendation of the Consular section of your Embassy in Beijing, who informed us that you are an experienced agent for domestic appliances in your country.

　　We are well-known manufactures of over 15 years' standing in producing domestic appliances. Now there is a steady increase in demand for our products overseas, we are seeking a really active agent that can handle a considerable amount of business. Being aware of your long experience in this line and have extensive networks in your market, we feel that your firm is the right one to do this and we have pleasure in offering you a sole agency.

　　We sincerely hope that you are interested in representing us, and contact us to discuss the matter further. Should you not be able to accept it, perhaps you could recommend some other reliable firms whom we might approach.

　　We look forward to hearing from you.

　　　　　　　　　　　　　　　　　　　　　　　　　　　　　　　Yours faithfully,

Notes

1. domestic appliances 家用电器

   A microwave oven and a dishwasher are domestic appliances. 微波炉和洗碗机是家用电器。

2. a considerable amount of 相当数量的

3. Should you not be able to accept it, perhaps you could recommend some other reliable firms whom we might approach. 如果您不接受，也许您能推荐一些可靠的声誉卓越的公司，我们可以同它们联系。

   此句式为非真实条件从句。非真实条件从句用来描述说话人想象的、非真实的情景，这些情景通常是不可能发生的，与客观实际相反的，或发生可能性极小，只表示说话者的一种主观愿望、假想和建议等。非真实条件从句表示对现在、过去、将来的事实进行虚拟时，主句和 if 从句中的谓语动词形式如下：

表示虚拟的时间	If 从句谓语形式	主句谓语形式
现在	did or were	Would (should, might, could) + do
过去	had done or had	Would (should, might, could) + have done (been)
将来	were to (should) + do	would (should, might, could) + do

这就是虚拟语气的三种基本形式。
(1) 与现在的事实相反：If they were here, they would help you.
(2) 与过去的事实相反：If she had worked harder, she would have succeeded.
(3) 与将来的事实相反，表示对将来的假想：If you succeeded, everything would be all right.

> **Tips 外贸代理协议**
>
> 　　外贸代理协议指出口企业与国外代理商就贸易交往中双方的共同目标、权利、义务和业务关系、法律关系等进行磋商而达成的书面协议。出口企业与外商进行商品交易、经济合作，在协商一致的基础上，最后都需要签订协议书或合同。
>
> 　　外贸代理协议的格式与其他商务协议书相同，一般由标题、正文和签署构成。要求条款清楚、项目齐全、法律关系及责任规定明晰。除此之外，外贸代理协议还应着重注意以下两点。
>
> 　　代理的权限及义务。代理商的权限，或限于为委托人寻找买主、中介交易，或代委托人缔约以及规定是否授予独家代理商和约定商品的专营权。
>
> 　　代理佣金。由于代理双方是委托关系，代理方不拥有货物的所有权，不承担风险，因而由委托人向代理方支付佣金。在代理协议中，除明确规定佣金率外，还规定佣金的计算基础和支付方法。佣金的计算基础可按发票总值，也可按 FOB 值，一般按发票总值计算。支付方式可以逐步结算，逐笔支付，也可以定期结算，累计总付。

13.3　有用的短语和句子
Useful Expressions

1. However, after serious consideration, we do not think conditions are ripe to entrust you with the agency at the present stage as the sales volume mentioned in your letter is too small for us to grant you the agency.
   然而，郑重考虑后，我们认为现阶段委任贵方代理的条件尚不成熟，因贵方的来信中所提及的销售量太小，我们不能给你代理权。
2. Referring to the question of sole agency, we are not yet prepared to take the matter into consideration for the time being. We feel it would be better to consider it after you have done more business with us.
   关于独家代理一事，目前我们还不打算考虑。我们认为在贵方与我方做了大量交易后，再考虑此事为宜。
3. We should be glad to know on what terms you would be willing to represent us, also the terms on which business is generally conducted in your country.
   我们想知道在什么条件下贵方愿做我们的代理，以及什么条件下可以在贵国展开贸易。
4. We appreciate your proposal to act as our sole agent for..., but we are sorry that it has been taken over by someone else.
   非常感激贵方欲做我方独家代理的要求，但很抱歉已由其他人接任。

5. We suggest a trial period of one year. If everything turns out satisfactory, we can renew the agreement on its expiry.
   我们建议试行期一年。如果双方都满意,可在协议期满时续签。
6. During the validity of the agency agreement, we shall not handle any other foreign products of the same line and competitive types.
   在协议有效期内,我们将不经营其他国外相同的有竞争性的商品。
7. We undertake to forward you detailed reports in writing on current market conditions as well as consumer's comments on price, quality, packing and the sales prospective in the duration of this agreement.
   在协议有效期内,我们有义务向贵方提供目前市场情况的详细报告以及消费者对商品价格、质量、包装及销售前景等方面的意见。
8. Neither party will be liable to the other for any default here under if such default is caused by an event beyond such party's control, including without limitation acts or failure to act of the other party, strikes or labor disputes, component shortages, unavailability of transportation, governmental requirements and any Force Majeure Event.
   本协议中任何一方不对另一方承担超出其操控能力的事件引发的本协议项下的过错,包括但不限于另一方作为或不作为、罢工、劳动纠纷、零件短缺、未有交通工具、政府命令和任何不可抗力事件。
9. The styles and colors are very much to the taste of our market.
   式样和颜色很适合我们的市场。
10. For your reference, we would propose a sole agency agreement for a duration of three years with annual turn over of 50 000, 60 000 and 70 000 pieces for the first, second and third year respectively.
    供你参考,我们建议订立独家代理协议,期限三年,第一年、第二年和第三年的每年销售量分别为 5 万只、6 万只和 7 万只。
11. Referring to the question of sole agency, we are not yet prepared to take the matter into consideration for the time being. We shall revert to this subject as soon as the business between us has developed to our mutual satisfaction.
    关于独家代理问题,目前我们还不准备考虑。但当彼此业务发展至双方都感到满意时,我们可以再谈此事。
12. In spite of this, please do not misinterpret our above remark which in no way implics dissatisfaction.
    虽然这样,请不要误解我们上面所说,我们的话绝没有暗示不满意。
13. In view of increasing demand for our products at your end and the business you have brought to us, we have, at your request, decided to appoint you to be our agent in your country.
    由于贵方市场对我们产品的需求量越来越大,并且给我们带来了很多业务,我们决定委托贵方作为在贵国的代理。
14. We appreciate the confidence you show in us by offering us a sole agency here for your products.
    很感激贵方对我们的信赖,委托我方作为该产品的独家代理。
15. We would suggest that we leave aside the problem of agency until circumstances necessitate doing so.
    我们建议必要的时候再讨论代理问题。

16. After three years of mutual cooperation in this business, we should like to act as your agent in our city in order to most effectively market your products.

    经过 3 年在该贸易领域的相互合作,为了能更有效地推广贵方产品,我们愿意成为贵方在我们城市的代理。

17. We should be glad if you would consider our application to act agent for the sale of your plastic slippers.

    如果你们能够考虑我方作为塑料拖鞋的代理申请,我们将会很高兴。

18. Your proposal to be our sole agent is under serious consideration. In reply, we would like to know your detailed plan for handling our products, your sales channels, prospective sales turnover and your commercial and financial references so that we can decide on your proposal.

    我们正在认真考虑贵方提出的独家代理申请。在做出决定之前,我们希望了解贵方有关代理我方产品的具体计划、销售渠道、预计的销售额以及商界和金融界证明人的名单。

19. Thank you for your proposal of acting as our agent. In view of your past efforts in pushing the sale of our products, we have decided to accept your proposal and appoint you as sole agent.

    感谢贵方作为我方代理的建议,鉴于你们过去努力推销我方产品,现决定接受贵方建议,委派贵方为独家代理。

20. After careful consideration, we have decided to entrust you with the sole agency for Textiles in the territory of China.

    经过仔细考虑,决定委托贵方为我们纺织品在中国地区的独家代理。

21. We think that it would be premature to commit ourselves at this stage when the record of transaction shows only a moderate volume of business.

    我们认为现在做出承诺不免为时过早,因为交易的记录表明目前的交易额尚不太可观。

练习

Exercises

Ⅰ. Comprehension Questions
   1. What role does agency play in Foreign Trade?
   2. What does an agency agreement include?
   3. What is a sole agency?
   4. What is a general agent?

Ⅱ. Translate the Following Terms
   1. shipping agent   2. insurance agent
   3. consignment agreement   4. exclusive sales agreement
   5. 代理协议   6. 代理佣金
   7. 独家代理   8. 佣金代理人
   9. 总代理人   10. 广告代理人

Ⅲ. Read the Following Letters and Fill in the Blanks with Appropriate Words
   1. Transactions _____ Governmental Bodies: Transaction _____ between governmental bodies of Party A and Party B are not restricted the terms and conditions of this agreement, _____ shall they be considered as the target fulfilled by party B _____ this agreement.

2. Party B shall undertake to supply Party A once every three months with a market report in writing on _____ market conditions as well as customers' comments _____ quality, packing, and price, etc. of the bicycles under this agreement. If there is any particular change of local import regulations, Party B shall notify Party A at once.

3. _____ of a breach of any of the provisions of this agreement by one party, the other party shall have the right to _____ this agreement forthwith by giving notice in writing to its opposite party.

Ⅳ. Translate the Following Sentences

1. We are also interested in handing a sole agency for you, which we think would be to our mutual advantage.
2. With the sole agency in your hand, you could easily control the market.
3. We wish to sell our hand tools in your country, and should like to be put in touch with a company or individual who would be willing to represent us.
4. In view of the steady increase in the demand for our beauty preparations, we have decided to appoint an agent to handle our export trade with your country.
5. We have noticed that in canvassing for orders, you have more than once exceeded the limit of your district. We wish that it wouldn't happen again as it is against the stipulations in our agreement.
6. 本协议有效期为一年，除非另行书面通知，期满后自动延长相同的期限。
7. 作为我们的独家代理，未经我们事先同意，不得为其他商家销售类似产品。
8. 对你们想担任独家代理的请求，我们正在认真考虑。同时，我们很想了解你方推销我们产品的计划。
9. 由于这种类型的设备对我们地区来说完全是新产品，因此销售起来非常困难，所以我方希望你方考虑增加我们的佣金。
10. 感谢你们对皮鞋的询价，但由于该商品在贵地已由 ABC 公司独家代理，目前不能直接报盘，请同他们联系订货。

Ⅴ. Translate the Following into English

本协议一经双方签署立即生效，有效期为 2 年。自 2009 年 1 月 1 日到 2010 年 12 月 31 日。在期满前一个月如果双方未用书面提出异议，本协议将自动延长一年。如果一方未按本协议条款执行，另一方有权终止本协议。

Ⅵ. Fill in the Gaps in This Letter with One of the Words From the Box

a. freigh	b. rates	c. factory	d. terms	e. documentation
f. commisssion	g. principals	h. recommendation	i. offer	j. delcredere
k. brochure				

Dear Sirs,

We are writing to you on the ___(1)___ of the Berlin Chamber of Commerce who inform us that your company is looking for an agent to be responsible for purchasing high precision machine tools from Germany.

We have long experience in this line and have an extensive network of contacts with the major manufacturers of machine tools in Germany and believe we have a good opportunity to forge a successful business relationship.

I would first of all like to give you a brief summary of our ___(2)___ of business.

We generally place orders for our ___(3)___ with our suppliers and our customers settle direct with the manufacturers. We also arrange all costs, insurance and ___(4)___ facilities for our clients, sending the goods from the ___(5)___ to the destination in the clients country.

Because of our long experience in this area and our extensive contacts, we can offer you the most competitive ___(6)___ for shipment, and in addition will handle all the ___(7)___, including the customs formalities.

We usually operate on a 5% ___(8)___ on CIF values, but if credit risk is involved, can offer ___(9)___ facilities for an additional 2.5% commission.

We hope you will be interested in our ___(10)___ and can guarantee a fast and efficient service at competitive prices. Please contact us if you require more detailed information or would like to discuss the matter further. Please find enclosed our ___(11)___ with full details of our company and services.

We look forward to hearing from you further in due course.

Yours faithfully,

附录 13A 代理协议
Appendix 13A Agency Agreement

Through friendly negotiations, this Sole Agency Agreement is entered into between China National Machinery Equipment Import and Export Corporation, Jiangsu, China (hereinafter called Party A) and B/D Corporation, USA (hereinafter called Party B) on the following terms and conditions:

(1) Party A entrust Party B with the sole agency for the sale of Machinery Equipment in the territory of North America.

(2) Price: Party B is under obligation to push sales energetically at the price quoted by Party A. Each transaction is subject to Party's final confirmation.

(3) Quantity: During the above-mentioned period, Party B shall endeavor to push sales of not less than 5 000 sets of Machinery Equipment. Party B shall order at least 3 000 sets in the first six months from the date of signing this agreement. Should Party B fail to fulfill the above-mentioned quantity (namely 3 000 sets) in this duration, Party A shall have the right to sell the goods under this agreement to other customers in North America. In case Party B places orders for less than 1 000 sets in three months from the date on which the agreement is signed, Party A shall have the right to terminate this agreement by giving notice in writing to Party B.

(4) Payment: Payment is to be made by confirmed, irrevocable letter of credit, without recourse, available by sight draft upon presentation of shipping documents. The letter of credit for each order shall reach Party A 30 days before (prior to) the date of shipment. Should Party B fail to establish the Letter of Credit in time, which Party A may sustain shall be borne by Party B.

(5) Commission: Party A agrees to pay Party B a commission of 5% on FOB value of orders. No commission shall be paid until after Party A receives the full payment for the order concerned.

(6) Advertising & Publicity: In order to expand the sales of the products in the duration of this agreement, Party A shall take every effective measure to advertise the products. Party A shall also provide Party B, free of charge, with the advertising materials, if available.

(7) Arbitration: All disputes arising from the execution of, or in connection with, this Agree-

ment shall be settled amicably through friendly negotiations. In case no settlement could be reached, the case shall be referred to the Foreign Trade Arbitration Commission of the China Council for the Promotion of International Trade. The decision made by this Commission shall be regarded as final and is binding on both parties.

(8) Market Report: Party B shall undertake once every three months to supply Party A detailed reports on current market conditions and on consumers' comments. Party B shall also forward to Party A samples pf similar commodity offered by other suppliers, together with their prices, sales position and advertising material.

(9) Validity of Agreement: This Agreement, when duly signed by the parties, shall remain in valid for a period of twelve months commencing from 1st December to the next 30th November. If no written objection is raised by either Party one month before its expiration, this Agreement shall be automatically extended for another one year.

(10) Other Terms & Conditions:

a. Party A shall not handle any of the contracted commodities to other buyers in the above-mentioned territory. Direct enquired, if any, will be referred to Party B. However, should any other buyers insist on dealing direct with Party A, Party A shall have the right to do so, but have to reserve for Party B a 2% commission on the transaction.

b. For any transactions concluded between Government bodied of Party A's country and those of Party B's are not restricted by the terms and conditions of this Agreement, nor shall the amount of such transactions be counted as part of without being bound by this Agreement.

c. In the event of a breach of any of the provisions of this Agreement by one of the parties, the other is entitled to cancel this Agreement by giving notice in writing to the defaulting party.

This Agreement is made out in Chinese and English, both versions being equally valid. Each party shall keep one original of this Agreement.

  Party A (Supplier)   Party B (Agent)

Chapter 14
第 14 章

国际商务合同
International Business Contracts

Learning Objectives

Enable the students to know about the varieties of contract; to be acquainted with the format of business English contract, the writing requirements, language features; to be able to skillfully translate related contracts, and master the main points regarding business contracts translation.

使学生了解商务英文合同的种类；熟悉商务合同的格式及写作要求、语言特色；能较熟练地翻译相关合同；掌握合同翻译的注意事项。

14.1 国际商务合同简介
A Brief Introduction to International Business Contract

A contract is an agreement between two or more persons, concerning something to be done, whereby both parties are bound to each other, or one is bound to the other. It is an agreement which sets forth binding obligations of the relevant parties. Should any conflicts between the two sides arise later, reference is generally made to the contract in an effort to resolve the misunderstandings.

A contract may be formal or informal, oral or written, which is plain to understand. Some contracts are required to be in writing in order to be enforced. In international trade, contract varies in both names and forms, which mainly include: Agreement, Sales Note, Sales Agreement, Sales Contract, Sales Confirmation/Confirmation of Sales/ Acknowledgement of Sales, Confirmation of Order, Purchase Agreement Contract, Purchase Note, Order Sheet/ Purchase Order, Purchase Confirmation/ Confirma-

合同是两个或两个以上的法人之间为实现某一经济目的而确定相互的权利和义务所达成的关系。它是对有关当事人规定了约束性责任的一种协定。一旦日后双方发生纠纷，则要根据合同来解决争端。

合同可以是正式的，也可以是非正式的，书面的或口头的，应明了易懂。有些合同要求必须是书面的以便执行。国际贸易中，进出口贸易书面合同的名称和形式均无特定的限制。合同主要有协议书、售货单、销售协议、销售合同、销售确认书、订货确认书、购货合同、购货单、订单、

tion of Purchase, Trade Agreement, Bilateral Trade Agreement, Multilateral Trade Agreement, Import Contract, Export Contract, Consignment Contract, Agency Agreement, Agency Contract and Compensation Trade Contract. But the names that often appear are contract, confirmation, agreement and memorandum.

In international trade, a contract can be drawn up either by the seller or the buyer. Respectively, it is called a sales contract/ confirmation or a purchase contract/ confirmation. Whatever they are named, they are equally binding on the parties. The sales or purchase contract is more formal than the sales or purchase confirmation. The former usually consists of commodities, specifications, quantity, packing, marking, price, shipment, port of shipment and port of destination, and payment as well as those clauses concerning insurance, commodity inspection, claims, arbitration and force majeure, etc; while the later only includes several main items. What's more, the former is appropriate to transactions of large amount and huge quantity because of its detailed clause which can prevent the occurrence of disputes. If the amount is not large or the business is done by means of agency arrangement or exclusive sale agreement, the sales or the purchase confirmation is often used.

Generally, a formal written contract includes the following parts:

1. Title
2. Preamble
(1) Date of signing;
(2) Signing parties;
(3) Place of signing;
(4) Recitals or WHEREAS clause.
3. Body
(1) Definition clause: To give specific explanation to the key words repeatedly appearing in a contract or agreement, which have special meanings or easily cause misunderstanding and controversy.
(2) Specific conditions: Such as the name and the specification of the commodity, quantity, unit price and total value, package, the time of shipment, the port of

购货确认书、贸易协议、双边贸易协议、多边贸易协议、进口合同、出口合同、寄售合同、代理协议、代理合同、补偿贸易合同等，但是经常出现的有合同、确认书、协议书和备忘录。

国际贸易中，合同和确认书可以由任何一方起草，分别称为售货合同/确认书，或购货合同/确认书。不管叫什么，它们对双方都有约束力。售货或购货合同往往比售货或购货确认书正规。前者通常包含商品名称、规格、数量、包装、唛头、价格、装运、装运港、目的港、付款方式以及有关保险、商检、索赔和不可抗力等条款；后者只包括几项主要条款。另外，售货或购货合同对价值和数量较大的交易较为合适，因为合同制订了详细的条款以避免产生争议。如果数量不大或交易是通过代理或独家销售协议来进行的，则经常使用售货或购货确认书。

通常正规的书面合同包括下面几个部分：

1. 合同名称
2. 前文
(1) 订约日期；
(2) 订约当事人；
(3) 订约地点；
(4) 订约缘由。
3. 正文
(1) 定义条款：用于解释合同或协议中重复出现的关键词，这些词有特殊的含义或容易引起误解和争议。
(2) 具体条款：如商品名称及型号、数量、单价、总价值、包装、装运期、装运港、目的地、

shipment, the port of destination, terms of payment, insurance, inspection, claim and arbitration, etc.

(3) General conditions: Including duration, termination, force majeure, assignment, arbitration, governing law, jurisdiction, notice, "Entire agreement" clause, amendment and others.

4. Witness clause
(1) Concluding sentence;
(2) Signature;
(3) Seal.

付款条件、保险、检验、索赔、仲裁等。

(3) 一般条款：包括合同有效期、合同的终止、不可抗力、合同的让与、仲裁、适用的法律、诉讼管辖、通知手续、完整条款、合同的修改以及其他。

4. 立证结尾条款
(1) 结尾语；
(2) 订约人签名；
(3) 盖印。

14.2　国际商务合同的语言特色
Language Features in International Business Contracts

International business contracts are the combination of business English, trade laws and international economics and trade practice. After long term practice it has formed its own language features.

国际商务合同是商务英语、贸易法、国际经贸实务三者融合的产物，通过长期的实践形成了自己独特的语言特色。

14.2.1　使用正式、法律用语
Using Formal, Legal Words and Phrases

Written form as well as formal and legal words and phrases is often used in some important contracts so as to show the accuracy, normality and solemnity of contracts.

重要的合同习惯采用书面的形式和正式、法律用语以显示合同的正规性、准确性和庄严性。

For example

(1) At the request of Party B, Party A agrees to send technicians to assist Party B to install the equipment. 应乙方要求，甲方同意派遣技术人员帮助乙方安装设备。
这里 assist 较 help 正式。

(2) This contract shall be governed by and construed in accordance with the laws of China. 本合同受中国法律管辖，并按中国法律解释。
这里 construe 较 explain、interpret 正式。

(3) In case one party desires to sell or assign all or part of his investment subscribed, the other party shall have the preemptive right. 如一方想出售或转让其所投资的全部或一部分，另一方应有优先购买权。
这里 assign 和 preemptive 都是法律用语。

(4) The term "Effective Date" means the date on which this agreement is duly executed by the parties hereto. "生效期"是指双方合同签字的日子。
这里，法律用词 execute 较 sign 正式。

14.2.2　成对使用同义词
Using Synonyms

Synonyms which have a little difference in their meaning are often used in the contracts so as to avoid possible misunderstanding.

合同中成双成对地使用含义只有细微差别的同义词以避免产生歧义。

For example

(1) Each party to this Agreement shall perform and fulfill any of the obligations under this Agreement. 本协议的各方均履行协议规定的义务。

这是同义词的成对使用。perform 和 fulfill 均为"履行",但前者强调的是主观的努力,后者强调的是客观的结果。

(2) Change in the Work shall mean any modification, amendment or, addition to, alteration in or deletion from the Work. 工程施工的变化是指对该项工程的更改、修正,或增减变动。

14.2.3　用"shall"强化合同的功能
Using "shall" to Intensify the Function of the Contract

"Shall" is often used to express specific regulations and legal enforcement instead of "must" or "have to". It can be also used in various of tenses and persons with a tone of strong command, which fully reflected the binding and authority of legal documents.

要表述合同中各项具体的规定和表示法律上可以强制执行,常用 shall 而不是 must 或 have to。shall 可以用于各种时态和人称,带有浓厚的命令语气,充分体现法律文件的约束力和权威性。

For example

(1) This contract shall become effective upon and from the date on which it is signed. 本合同签字生效。

(2) The employer shall make a prepayment of 20% of the contract value to the Contractor within 10 days after signing the Contract. 雇主应于签约后的十天内向承包人支付相当于承包合同价值 20% 的预付款。

14.2.4　使用古体词
Using Archaic Words

Some archaic words are still used in contract today. As some words are mentioned in the same contract more than one times, it is more concise and accurate to use the archaic words so as to avoid repetition and redundancy. The most common used ones are the compound adverbs such as hereafter, whereby, therein and so on. The word "here" stands for "this", "there" for "that", "where" for "what/which".

迄今合同中仍使用一些古体词,由于在同一合同中要多次提及某些单词,使用这些古体词可避免用词重复和冗长,从而使合同语句简练、准确。最常见的是复合副词如 hereafter、whereby、therein 等,这里"here"代表"this","there"代表"that","where"代表"what/which"等。

For example

(1) This agreement is made and entered into by and between AA Corporation (hereinafter called supplier) and BB Company (hereinafter called Distributor) whereby Supplier agrees to grant to Distributor the exclusive right to sell the Products in the Territory on the terms and conditions stipulated as follows. 本协议由 AA 公司（以下简称供货人）与 BB 公司（以下简称经销商）签订。凭此协议供货人同意授予经销商按下列条款在指定地区销售指定产品的独家权利。

在这里，古体词 hereinafter = later in this agreement, whereby = by which。

(2) 常用的此类副词有：

hereafter ＝ after this time, following this
hereby ＝ by this means or by reason of this
herein ＝ in this
hereof ＝ of this
hereinafter ＝ later in this contract
hereunder ＝ under this
hereafter ＝ afterwards
hereinbefore ＝ in a preceding part of this contract
thereafter ＝ after that
thereby ＝ by that means
therefore ＝ for that
therein ＝ in that
thereinafter ＝ in that part of a contract
thereof ＝ of that
thereto ＝ to that
thereunder ＝ under that part of a contract
thereupon ＝ as a result of that
whereby ＝ by which
whereof ＝ of which

14.2.5 多用现在时态，少用将来时态
Using Present Tense More, Simple Future Tense Less

Though many clauses in the contract is for future using, present tense is still be used instead of simple future tense.

尽管合同的许多条款是规定签约后的事项，但习惯上使用现在时而不是将来时。

For example

Licensee may terminate this contract 90 days after a written notice thereof is sent to Licensor upon the happening of the following events:

a. Licensor becomes involvement or a liquidator of Licensor is appointed;

b. The patent described in Article 2 is not issued within 30 days from signing this contract.

当有下列事件之一发生，被许可人在提前 90 天向许可人发送书面通知后，可以终止本合同：

a. 许可人无力偿付债务，或许可人的破产清算已被指定；
b. 第二条规定的专利在签约后 30 天内尚未发布。

14.2.6　多用主动语态，少用被动语态
Using Active Voice More and Passive Voice Less

As active voice is more direct, natural and definite, it is often used in the contract.

由于主动语态更直接、自然和明确，所以合同中主动语态用得较多。

For example

(1) Party B is hereby appointed by Party A as its exclusive sales agent in France. 乙方被甲方委托为在法国的独家销售代理。

(2) Party A hereby appoints Party B as its exclusive sales agent in France. 甲方委托乙方作为在法国的独家销售代理。

这两句的意思虽然相同，但主动语态比被动语态更为自然、有力。

14.2.7　使用专门术语
Using Special Phrases

Some special phrases are used to express contract idioms. They are as follows:

常用以下专门术语来表达合同惯用语：

whereas 鉴于
in witness whereof 作为协议事项的证据
now, therefore 兹特
in consideration of 以……为约/对价、报酬
now these presents witness 兹特立约为据
in witness whereof/thereof/in testimony whereof 特此立据，以此立据，以此为证
in the presence of ……见证人
for and on behalf of ……代表某人
per pro. = per procurator 代表，代理
unless otherwise 除非有……者外
in respect of / in respect thereof 涉及，至于，关于……
subject to 在……条件下，在规定的范围内，须经，服从于

14.2.8　使用定义条款
Using Defining Words

For a very important contract, definitions are given at the very beginning of the contract to avoid misunderstanding later.

重要的合同往往一开始就使用定义条款，以免日后产生分歧。

For example

Licensed Patents, as used herein, shall mean all patents and patent applications. 此处所用"许可专利权"一词，系指一切专利权和专利申请权。

14.2.9 利用附录和表格来描述某些细节
Using Appendix, Schedule to Give the Details of the Contract

Appendix and schedule are the integral part of the contract and are equally binding on both parties.

附录和表格是合同不可分割的组成部分,对双方具有同等的约束力。

14.3 合同样例
Sample Contract

SALES CONTRACT

Ref. No. HR20110319
Date: Mar. 19, 2011

The Buyers: Beijing Hengxin Import Trading Co., Ltd.
Address: Room 309, Liye Mansion,
Fengtai District, Beijing, China.
Tel: 86-10-34567233
Fax: 86-10-34567234
The Sellers: NETZSCH Geraete bau Gmbh
Address: Wittels bacher str. 45, C-90 200 Selb/Bavaria Germany
Tel: 49-93-88761235
Fax: 49-93-88761240

This contract is made by and between the Buyers and Sellers, whereby the Buyers agree to buy and the Sellers agree to sell the following mentioned commodity according to the terms and conditions stipulated below:

Commodity and Specification	Quantity	Unit Price (EUR)	Total Amount (EUR)
Laser Flash Apparent for measuring thermal conductivity, Model LFA 457, Micro Flash TM, manufactured by NETZSCH Geraete bau Gmbh, with technical specifications as described in Annex No. 01 which is an integral part of this contract. (Assembly and Installation charge of equipment included.)	1Set	114 000.00	114 000.00
Say one hundred and fourteen thousand Euros only			

1. Country of Origin and Manufacturers: NETZSCH Geraete bau Gmbh, Germany.
2. Payment: By L/C at 60 days before shipment, the Buyers shall establish with Bank an

Irrevocable 100% L/C in favor of the Sellers. 90% against presentation of the shipping documents, and 10% against acceptance certificate issued by the end user. If the end user is responsible for the fact that the acceptance certificate cannot be issued within 100 days after delivery, the remaining 10% will be negotiated without acceptance certificate from 101st day after delivery.

The Seller's Bank: Hypo-Vereins Bank AG, P. O. Box1338, D-95012 Hof/Saale, Germany.

Beneficiary: NETZSCH Geraete bau Gmbh.

3. Port of shipment: German Main Ports (Airport).

4. Port of Destination: Beijing Airport.

Shipping address: Room 309, Liye Mansion, Fengtai District, Beijing, China.

5. Time of shipment: Four months after the contract effects. The cost for freight will be paid by the Sellers.

6. Transport Method: By Air.

7. Shipping Advice: Immediately after the goods being completely loaded, the sellers shall cable to notify the buyers of the contract number, name of commodity, quantity, gross weight, and invoice value, name of the flight and the date of flight.

8. Documents: The sellers shall present the following documents to the paying bank for negotiation, collection or to the Buyers in case of payment by T/T.

(1) Air Way Bill.

(2) Insurance Policy or Certificate, covering All Risks and War Risk, All Risks includes TPND, Breakage and Leakage irrespective of percentage and indicating "In the event of loss or damage, request for survey upon arrival of the cargo at the port of destination be made to The Entry-exit Inspection and Quarantine Bureau of the People's Republic of China of that port".

(3) Signed Commercial Invoice issued by the seller, in 03 original and 04 copies, including Contract number and Shipping Marks.

(4) Detailed Packing List issued by the seller, in 03 original and 04 copies with indication of both gross and net weight, measurement and quantity of each item packed.

(5) Certificate of Origin to Beijing Hengxin Import & Export Trading Co., Ltd., issued by the Germany Chamber of Commerce: 01 original and 04 copies.

(6) Certificate of Quantity and Quality to Beijing Hengxin Import & Export Trading Co., Ltd., issued by the manufacturer, in 02 original and 04 copies.

(7) Certificate of Warranty to Beijing Hengxin Import & Export Trading Co., Ltd., issued by the manufacturer, in 02 original and 04 copies.

(8) Certificate of Inspection to Beijing Hengxin Import & Export Trading Co., Ltd., issued by issued by the manufacturer, in 02 original and 04 copies.

(9) Beneficiary's Certificate stating that one set of non-negotiable documents has been sent to the applicant by DHL within 07days after AWB date.

(10) Within 10days after shipment being effected, the sellers shall prepare one set of the above mentioned documents and the airmail to the buyers.

9. Technical Documents.

Two complete sets of the following technical documents written in English shall be packed and dispatched together with each consignment:

(1) Wiring instructions, diagrams of electrical connections and /or pneumatic and/or hydraulic and transhipment manual.

(2) transhipment Manual for the assembly, operation and maintenance, etc.

The Seller shall send the Technical documents (1) to the Buyer by airmail one month ahead of time of delivery of the goods.

10. Packing: To be packed in strong cartons, suitable for long distance parcel post/air freight transportation and change of climates, well protected against moisture and shocks etc.

Shipping Marks:

HENGXIN CORP
S/C HX20110319
BEIJING
C/NO. 1-UP

On the surface of each package, the package number, measurements, gross weight, net weight, the lifting positions, such caution as "THIS SIDE UP" "HANDLE WITH CARE" "KEEP DRY" etc. shall be stenciled legibly in fadeless paint.

11. Guarantee of Quality: The Sellers shall guarantee that the goods are made of best materials, with first class workmanship, brand new, unused and correspond in all respects with the quality, specifications and performance as stipulated in this contract. The Sellers shall also guarantee that the goods when correctly mounted and properly operated and maintained, will give satisfactory performance for a period of 12 months starting from the date of signing of the acceptance certificate.

12. Insurance: to be effected by the Sellers for full invoice value plus 10% against All Risks, War Risk and Strikes as per the relative insurance clauses of PICC dated January 1, 1981. Claims payable at Beijing and irrespective of percentage.

13. Force Majeure: The Sellers shall not be held responsibility for any delay in delivery or on delivery of the goods due to Force Majeure. The Sellers shall advise the Buyers immediately of the occurrence above, and if requested, the Sellers shall send by airmail to the Buyers a certificate to the accident as evidence thereof. Under such circumstance the Sellers, however are still under the obligation to take all necessary measures to hasten the delivery of the goods. In case the accident lasts for more than 10 weeks, the Buyers shall have the right to cancel the Contract.

14. Confidential Terms: The contents in this Contract, especially the pricing issue, should be confidential among the sellers, the buyers, and the end user. Neither party should disclose the information to a fourth party. Or the party with loss has the right to claim compensation from the party who discloses the information.

15. Penalty: The sellers shall indemnify the buyer for 0.2% of the total contract value for each full day of delivery delay, but the total amount of penalty shall not exceed 20% of the total contract value. If the delay in delivery exceeds 30 days, or any unconformity with the No. 1 and No. 12, the buyer has the right to cancel the contract.

16. Arbitration: Any disputes arising from the execution of, or in connection with this contract should be settled through negotiation. In case no settlement can be reached, the case shall then be submitted to The Foreign Trade Arbitration Commission of China Council for the Promotion of International Trade, Beijing for settlement by arbitration in accordance with the Commission's Provisional Rules of Procedure. The award rendered by the Commission shall be final, and binding on both parties.

17. Enclosure: This Contract has one attachment, which is non-separable part of the Contract.

Attachment: Technical Contract.

IN WITNESS THEREOF, this contract is made in both Chinese and English with equal authentication, and signed by both parties on March 19, 2011 in two original copies each party holds one copy; In the event of any discrepancy between the two versions, the Chinese version shall prevail.

The Buyers: The Sellers:

Notes

1. sales contract 售货合同
   售货合同是卖方转移标的物的所有权给买方,买方支付价款的合同。这种合同的内容通常包括合同的名称、编号、订约的日期、地点、检验、索赔、不可抗力、仲裁条款等。
2. Laser Flash Apparent for measuring thermal conductivity 激光导热性能测试仪
3. If the end user is responsible for the fact that the acceptance certificate cannot be issued within 100 days after delivery, the remaining 10% will be negotiated without acceptance certificate from 101st day after delivery.
   如果因为最终用户的原因致使货物在装运后100天内无法提交已经签署的验货报告,则这10%的款项在装运后的第101天无验收报告即可支付。
4. The Sellers shall present the following documents to the paying bank for negotiation, collection or to the Buyers in case of payment by T/T. 卖方应将下列单据交付银行议付、托收,如果为汇付,则应寄给卖方。
5. irrespective of percentage 不计免赔
6. In the event of loss or damage, request for survey upon arrival of the cargo at the port of destination be made to The Entry-exit Inspection and Quarantine Bureau of the People's Republic of China of that port. 万一发生损坏或灭失,当提请货物目的地的中国出入境检验检疫局在目的地对货物实施检验。
7. certificate of warranty 质量保证书
8. ... one set of non-negotiable documents has been sent to the Applicant by DHL within 07days after AWB date. 一套不可议付的单据在提单日期后的7天之内已经通过敦豪快递公司寄给申请人。

9. Wiring instructions, diagrams of electrical connections and /or pneumatic and/or hydraulic and transhipment manual. 布线说明，电气及/或气动及/或液压接线图。
10. long distance parcel post/air freight 长途邮政运输/空运
11. ... will give satisfactory performance for a period of 12 months starting from the date of signing of the acceptance certificate. 自货物验收合格之日起的 12 个月内运转良好。
12. The sellers shall indemnify the buyer for 0.2% of the total Contract value for each full day of delivery delay. 如果发生延迟交货的情况，卖方将担保按每延迟一天向买方支付本合同金额 0.2% 的罚金。
13. The Foreign Trade Arbitration Commission of China Council for the Promotion of International Trade, Beijing 北京中国国际贸易促进委员会对外贸易仲裁委员会
14. in accordance with the Commission's Provisional Rules of Procedure 根据仲裁委员会的仲裁程序暂行规定
15. The award rendered by the Commission shall be final. 仲裁的裁决是最终裁决。
16. ... which is non-separable part of the Contract. 此附件为本合同不可分割的组成部分。
17. In the event of any discrepancy between the two versions, the Chinese version shall prevail. 如果文字解释有异议，应以中文为准。

Tips 1. 协议（agreement）与合同（contract）

协议往往着眼于宏观，重在对原则性问题做出规定，涉及的标的比较广泛，内容和条款则不是很具体，书写格式也较为灵活多样；协议的重要性不等，可以指普通的非正式协议，也可指国与国之间的正式协定。

合同多致力于微观，重在把具体问题做出明确详细的规定，往往是一个标的签订一个合同，书写格式也多基本相似，有的甚至可以格式化；合同多是见诸文字并且受法律保障的正式契约。

在实际经贸业务中，双方对某一项目往往是就先达成的原则性问题订立一个协议，然后据以签订一个或多个合同，以全面确定具体执行的细节，并说明合同是根据协议签订的，或者协议是合同的组成部分。

2. 出口合同的履行

可分为四大部分：货（备货）、证（催证、审证、改证）、船（租船订舱、托运）、款（制单结汇）。

货。根据外贸订单的要求备货，包括产品的质量、数量、包装等。

证。订单签订后，催客户开立信用证。信用证开出后，审查信用证中是否有不合理条款，如有，及时跟客户联系要求对方改证。

船。货物备齐，信用证审核无误的情况下，租船订舱，安排发货。注意发货期要在信用证规定的发货期内。

款。货物发出后，按照信用证要求准备交单单据：发票、装箱单、提单、保单、产地证和其他客户要求的文件。在信用证规定的交单日期内交单办理收汇。

14.4　有用的短语和句子
Useful Expressions

1. The Buyers agree to buy and the Sellers agree to sell the following goods on terms and conditions as set forth below.
   双方同意按下列条款由卖方售出下列商品。
2. The award of the arbitration shall be final and binding upon both parties.
   仲裁决议是终局，对双方都有约束力。
3. This agreement, when duly signed by the both parties concerned, shall remain if force for 12 months from October1, 2009 to September 30, 2010, and it shall be extended for another 12 months upon expiration unless notice in written is given to the contrary.
   本协议经有关双方如期签署生效后，有效期为一年，从2009年10月1日至2010年9月30日。除非做出相反通知，本协议期满后将延长12个月。
4. Subject to terms of this Agreement, the Buyer and Seller agree to be bound by the terms to the following marketing agreement.
   在本协议的条件下，买方和卖方同意接受下列销售协议中各项条款的约束。
5. Unless otherwise specified in the Contract, the supplied goods shall be packed by standard measures.
   除非在合同中有明确规定外，所供应的货物要用标准方法包装。
6. IN WITNESS THEREOF, the guarantor has caused this Guarantee to be duly executed by its authorized representative on this 1st day of March 2011.
   有鉴于此，担保人授权其代表于2011年3月1日对本保函签字。
7. The parties mutually agree that said Agreement shall be and is hereby cancelled.
   缔约双方彼此同意，特此取消该协议。
8. Party B shall be held responsible for the delay in shipment and Party A may lodge claims against Party B for the losses arising therefrom.
   乙方对迟装负责，且甲方有权就由此产生的损失向乙方提出索赔。
9. Royalty shall be paid if any patented invention of A is embodied therein.
   如果其中包含甲方的已有专利权的创造发明，则应支付专利权使用费。
10. Additions thereto or deductions therefrom may be made under this Article.
    由此增加或由此减少（条款）可按本条规定进行。
11. This agreement shall begin on the date hereof and shall continue for 5 years thereafter.
    此协议由协议书之日开始，并在该日之后连续五年有效。
12. The following documents shall be deemed to form and be read and construed as an integral part of this contract.
    下列文件应被认为、读作、解释为本合同的组成部分。
13. NOW THESE PRESENTS WITNESS that it is hereby agreed between the parties hereto as follows.
    兹特立约为据，并由订约双方协议如下。
14. IN THE PRESENCE OF THE PARTIES hereto have hereunder set their respective heads and seals.
    作为协议事项的证据，订约双方各自签名盖章如下。

15. Should the articles stipulated in this contract be in conflict with the following supplementary condition, the supplementary conditions should be taken as valid and binding.
   本合同其他条款如与本附加条款有冲突,当以本附加条款为准。
16. Beneficiaries' certificate certifies that one set of N/N shipping documents has been sent to buyer immediately after shipment has been made.
   受益人证书证明一套不可转让运输单证在装运后已立即寄送买方。
17. Unless otherwise stipulated all documents should be issued in English language.
   除非另有规定,所有单证都需要使用英语。
18. Without prejudice to the provisions of this letter of credit, all matters relating to the procedure of enforcement shall be regulated by the law of the state where enforcement takes place.
   在不违反本信用证规定的条件下,与执行程序有关的所有事项均应遵守执行国际法律的规定。
19. This is to certify that the goods stated in this certificate had not been subjected to any processing during their stay /transshipment in Hong Kong.
   谨此证明,本证所述商品在香港停留/转运期间没有经过任何加工。
20. The sellers shall not be held responsible for late delivery or non-delivery of the goods owing to the generally recognized force majeure causes.
   卖方对由于普遍认可的"不可抗力事件"的发生所造成的货物迟交或不交将不负任何责任。

练习
Exercises

Ⅰ. Comprehension Questions
1. What is the definition for contract?
2. What is the difference between a sales contract and a sales confirmation?
3. What does the setting up of a contract generally contain?
4. What are the language features in the Contracts?

Ⅱ. Translate the Following Terms and Expressions into English or Chinese
1. governing law
2. recitals or WHEREAS clause
3. bidding contract
4. licensing agreement
5. 双边贸易协定
6. 补偿贸易合同
7. 书面合同
8. 合同正文
9. 不可抗力
10. 合同有效期

Ⅲ. Choose the Best Answer
1. This Sales Contract is made by and between the Sellers and the Buyers _____ the Sellers agree to sell and the Buyers agree to buy the under-mentioned goods.
   a. whereby   b. that   c. which   d. what
2. The findings of theirs shall be considered final and binding _____ both parties.
   a. by   b. against   c. covering   d. as per
3. The contract stipulates that shipment is to be made within one month _____ receipt of the L/C.

a. after   b. during   c. before   d. for

4. If any terms and conditions to this Contract are breached and the breach is not corrected by any party within 15 days after a written notice thereof is given by the other party, then the non-breaching party shall have the option to _____ this Contract by giving written notice thereof to the breaching party.
   a. implement   b. eliminate   c. contaminate   d. terminate

5. _____ the seller fail to make delivery on time as stipulated in the contract the seller should pay a penalty which _____ be deducted by the paying bank from the payment under negotiation.
   a. Shall, shall   b. Shall, should   c. Should, should   d. Should, shall

6. It is mutually agreed that Party B shall undertake to sell not less than... of the said commodity in the _____ of this Agreement.
   a. durante   b. during   c. duration   d. duty

7. Party A agrees to reserve for Party B a commission of 1% on the _____ of FOB value of the business thus concluded.
   a. form   b. base   c. basis   d. way

8. For any business transacted between governments of both parties, party A may handle such direct dealings as authorized by party A's government without _____ himself to this Agreement.
   a. binding   b. bonding   c. bounding   d. bouncing

9. If the obligations in the contract can not be fulfilled, _____ of the contract may occur.
   a. void   b. comply   c. breach   d. against

10. _____ the employer is desirous that manpower can be rendered available for the construction of the building.
    a. hereby   b. thereupon   c. witness   d. whereas

Ⅳ. Translate the Following Sentences

1. All disputes rising from the execution of or in connection with this confirmation shall be settled amicably through friendly negotiation.
2. The present contract is drawn in duplicate in Chinese and English, both two texts being equally authentic. In case of any divergence of interpretation, the Chinese text shall prevail.
3. Any complaint which either party does not wish to refer to a Conciliation Committee may then be submitted by the first party to arbitration as hereinafter provided.
4. ×× company, USA (hereinafter called Party A) and ×× company, PRC (hereinafter called Party B) through friendly negotiation reached the following agreement on the basis of equality and mutual benefit.
5. We regret to tell that we have to cancel this contract as a result of your default and reserve the right to file a claim for the loss sustained.
6. 由于不可抗力的原因，卖方不应承担货物迟到或无法装运的责任。
7. 违约的一方有义务采取一切必要的措施减轻发生的损失。
8. 如果一方不执行合同，另一方有权撤销该合同。
9. 合同是一份具有法律效力的协议，并对双方或更多方具有约束力。
10. 合同已于今日生效，我们不能反悔了。

Ⅴ. Fill in the Contract Form in English with the Particulars Below

2011年2月19日江苏食品进出口公司与加拿大温哥华食品公司在南京签订第10/109号

合同，内容如下：

　　商品：一级核桃仁

　　单价：每吨 CIF 温哥华价 250 美元

　　数量：30 吨

　　包装：用麻袋包装，每袋重 100 千克

　　装运：分三次装运，每月运 10 吨，从 2011 年 4 月起，由中国港装运，目的港为温哥华

　　付款方式：以卖方为受益人的不可撤销信用证，信用证须于装运前 30 天开到卖方，在中国议付有效至装运后的第 15 天。

　　保险：根据 1981 年 1 月 1 日的伦敦协会货物保险条款按发票总值的 110% 投保一切险和战争险。

Contract No. 10/109

Date:

Sellers:

Buyers:

This contract is made by and between the Buyers and the Sellers, whereby the Buyers agree to buy and the Sellers agree to sell the under-mentioned commodity on the terms and conditions stipulated below:

Commodity:

Specifications:

Quantity:

Unit Price:

Total Value:

Packing:

Insurance:

Time of Shipment:

Port of Shipment:

Port of Destination:

Terms of Payment:

Force Majeure: The Sellers shall not be held liable for failure of delay in delivery of the entire lot or a portion of the Commodity under this contract in consequence of any force majeure incidents.

Ⅵ. Fill in the Contract Form in English with the Particulars Given in the Following Letters

　　Sellers: Beijing Light Industrial Products Imp. & Exp. Corp.

　　Buyers: Boston Trading Co., Ltd.

　　Letter 1: Please quote your lowest price for 1 000 dozens Fountain Pens Model LC001 CFR Boston.

　　Letter 2: As requested, we are making you a firm offer as follows:

　　　　　　1 000 dozens Fountain Pens, Model LC001. Packed in boxes of one dozens each, and 20 boxes to a carton, at US $ 20 per dozens CFR Boston for shipment during March/April 2002. Payment is to be made by confirmed, irrevocable L/C payable by draft at sight.

　　Letter 3: While we thank you for the above offer, we regret to say that your price is too high to be acceptable. There is no possibility of this deal unless you reduce your price by 5%.

　　Letter 4: In view of our long business relations, we accept your counter offer. Please send us your order by return.

Letter 5: We are pleased to confirm having ordered 1 000 dozens Fountain Pens on the terms and conditions stated in our counter offer. Please send us the relevant S/C.

Letter 6: Enclosed is our S/C No. 5454 signed in Beijing on 18th January, 2002.

CONTRACT No.

Sellers:

Buyers:

This contract is made by and between the Buyers and the Sellers, whereby the Buyers agree to buy and the Sellers agree to sell the under-mentioned commodity on the terms and conditions stipulated below:

Commodity:

Specifications:

Quantity:

Unit Price:

Total Value:

Packing:

Shipping Mark:

Insurance:

Time of Shipment:

Port of Shipment:

Port of Destination:

Terms of Payment:

Done and signed in _____ on this _____ day of _____

附录 14A 贸易单证实例 1
Appendix 14A Trade Documents 1

案例名称：户外健身器材出口/英国　　业务时间：2015-03-01

案例概述：

　　商品名称：户外运动器材

　　贸易方式：一般贸易

　　成交方式：FOB XINGANG

　　结汇方式：T/T

　　运输方式：水路运输

　　启运港：XINGANG

　　抵运港：SOUTHAMPTON, UK

该案例涉及主要贸易单证：形式发票、采购合同、商业发票（报关）、装箱单（报关）、报关合同、出口货物报关单、商业发票（结汇）、装箱单（结汇）。

1. 形式发票

Beijing Okstar Sporting Goods Co., Ltd.
北京奥康达体育用品有限公司
Add: No. 16, Beisan Street, Yanqi Economic Development Area, Huairou District, Beijing
Tel: +86 010-61669488   E-mail: sales@okstarfitness.com

PROFORMA INVOICE

SOLD TO: Sunshine Gym
Unit A3 Halesfield 11
Telford, Shropshire, TF7 4PH
P: +44 (0) 1952 580520 F: +44 (0) 1952 580520
Email: info@sunshinegym.co.uk

P/I NO.: OS1503015UK
DATE: 1-Mar-15

SHIPPED: BY SEA   FROM: XinGang Port, TianJin   TO: SOUTHAMPTON   W/T Freight Collect

No.	ITEM NO.	PICTURE	DESCRIPTION & SIZE	QUANTITY	UNIT-PRICE FOB XINGANG	AMOUNT
1	OB-M01D		Air Walker (Double) Dimension: 1 820 × 475 × 1 440 (mm) (72″ × 19″ × 57″) Color: Blue RAL5002, Yellow RAL1018 Material: Non-galvanized steel Post Diameter: 3.5 inch	60 pcs	$328.00	$19 680.00
2	OB-Z05		Waist Twister Dimension: 1 600 × 1 310 (mm) (63″ × 52″) Post Diameter: 4.5 inch Material: Non-galvanized steel	20 pcs	$308.00	$6 160.00
TOTAL:			1 × 40HQ			$25 840.00
TOTAL:						

**SAY U.S. DOLLARS: TWENTY FIVE THOUSAND EIGHT HUNDRED AND FORTY ONLY.
REMARK: 10% MORE OR LESS IN TOTAL QUANTITY OR VALUE ACCEPTABLE.
5 years warranty for main parts; 1 year warranty for spare parts, such as top hat, screw bolt, screw nut.
Package: Bubble wrap + knitting strap wrapping
PAYMENT: 30% Deposit; 70% T/T after shipment
SHIPMENT: within 25 days after receipt of payment
ADDITIONAL:
INSURANCE: TO BE EFFECTED BY THE BUYERS
保险:
CLAIMS: IN CASE THE QUALITY AND/OR QUANTITY/WEIGHT ARE FOUND BY THE BUYERS TO BE NOT IN CONFORMITY
赔偿: WITH THE CONTRACT AFTER ARRIVAL OF THE GOODS AT THE PORT OF DESTINATION, THE BUYERS MAY LODGE CLAIM WITH THE SELLERS SUPPORTED BY SURVEY REPORT ISSUED BY AN INSPECTION ORGANISATION AGREED UPON BY BOTH PARTIES, WITH THE EXCEPTION, HOWEVER, OF THOSE CLAIMS, FOR WHICH THE INSURANCE COMPANY AND/OR THE SHIPPING COMPANY ARE TO BE HELD RESPONSIBLE. CLAIM FOR QUALITY DISCREPANCCY SHOULD BE FILED BY THE BUYERS WITHIN 30 DAYS AFTER ARRIVAL OF THE GOODS AT THE PORT OF DESTINATION WHILE FOR QUANTITY/WEIGHT DISCREPANCY CLAIM SHOULD BE FILED BY THE BUYERS WITHIN 15 DAYS AFTER ARRIVAL OF THE GOODS AT THE PORT OF DESTINATION THE SELLERS SHALL WITHIN 30 DAYS AFTER RECEIPT OF THE NOTIFICATION OF THE CLAIM, SEND REPLY TO THE BUYERS.
ARBITRATION: ANY DISPUTE ARISING FROM THE EXECUTION OF/OR IN CONNECTION WITH THIS CONTRACT SHOULD
仲裁: BE SETTLED THROUGH NEGOTIATION. IN CASE OF SETTLEMENT CAN BE REACHED, THE CASE SHALL THEN BE SUBMITTED TO THE FOREIGN TRADE ARBITRATION COMMISSION OF THE CHINA COUNCIL FOR THE PROMOTION OF INTERNATIONAL TRADE, BEIJING, FOR SETTLEMENT BY ARBITRATION IN ACCORDANCE WITH COMMISSION'S POVISIONAL RULES OF PRODUCE THE AWARD REDERED BY THE COMMISSION SHALL BE FINAL AND BINDING ON BOTH PARTIES.

2. 采购合同

下单通知

采购方：（甲方）	北京奥康达体育用品有限公司 Attn：Judy	合同编号：	OSN130102
售卖方：（乙方）	永宁健身器材设备厂 Attn：靳新	签订日期：	2015-03-06
		签约地点：	北京（BEIJING）

经双方商定，按以下条款由采购方出售，通知方安排购进下列货物。条款如下：

一、产品名称、规格、数量、金额

产品货号	产品生产要求	数量	单价	金额
YN283452	太空漫步机（双人） 外观尺寸：1 820×475×1 440（mm） 颜色：Blue RAL5002，Yellow RAL1018 材质：主架采用50mm×50mm×3mm及以上优质钢管，塑钢盖帽 扶手采用φ32mm×3mm及以上优质钢管；连接件选用防盗防松不锈钢螺丝 表面静电粉末喷涂处理 毛重/净重：kg/87kg	60件		
YN283331	三位扭腰器 外观尺寸：1 600×1 310（mm） 颜色：Blue RAL5002，Yellow RAL1018 材质：主立柱采用φ114mm×3mm及以上优质钢管，塑钢盖帽 摆腿采用30mm×60mm×3mm及以上优质钢管 连接件选用防盗防松不锈钢螺丝；表面静电粉末喷涂处理 毛重/净重：kg/41kg	20件		
数量合计：	1×40HQ	80件		
金额总计：	人民币元整			RMB

二、交货时间和地点：2015-03-10 工厂交货

三、其他

1. 品质：售卖方保证按本订单所出售的货物品质良好，符合采购方的品质及规格要求。无论在出货前的检验过程中还是在出货后产品在国外市场流通中发现品质问题，工厂都必须负责。该产品不得使用对人体有害的材料，在正常情况下不得造成人身伤害，否则，由工厂负责。
2. 包装。
3. 唛头。
4. 交货：工厂（特别指定除外）。
5. 付款：出货后采购方凭售卖方所开的增值税发票及缴款书，安排30个工作日内一次性付清货款。
6. 约定事项：
   1）工厂需要严格按照合同要求的品质准时交货，如因工厂延期交货或不履行合同而导致最终客人所产生的一切经济损失由工厂承担。
   2）工厂应严格执行本单中产品描述的所有要求，任何与本单中所列尺寸、材质、规格、颜色不符之处，应及时通知对方解决，并需要取得书面确认。否则由此引起的一切损失由工厂承担。
   3）工厂在接到装柜通知书时，应准时装柜，工厂必须负责检查货柜没有破漏、浸水、变形、生锈及被化学物污染等现象，装柜时要在柜底加上防潮的纸箱（纸板）或PE布等。工厂装货后应于4个小时以内，第一时间将有关实际装货数量、车牌号及货柜号码传真通知甲方。如因未传真准确资料而引起的一切争议及责任由卖方承担。出货前每个产品需要按客人要求提供船头板。

3. 商业发票（报关）

Beijing Okstar Sporting Goods Co., Ltd.
北京奥康达体育用品有限公司
Add: No.16, Beisan Street, Yanqi Economic Development Area, Huairou District, Beijing

INVOICE

TO: Sunshine Gym
    Unit A3 Halesfield 11
    Telford, Shropshire, TF7 4PH

Invoice No. OS1503015UK
S/C No.
Date: 2015-04-05

From   XINGANG, CHINA   To   SOUTHAMPTON, UK   Via
L/C No.   Issued by:

Marks & Nos.	Quantities & Descriptions	Amount
N/M	OUTDOOR FITNESS EQUIPMENT 80 pcs $ 323.00 户外运动用品 1. 品名：太空漫步机；2. 用途：健身；3. 种类：户外健身器材；4. 品牌：无牌；5. 型号：OB-M01D	FOB XINGANG $ 25 840.00

4. 装箱单（报关）

Beijing Okstar Sporting Goods Co., Ltd.
北京奥康达体育用品有限公司
Add: No.16, Beisan Street, Yanqi Economic Development Area, Huairou District, Beijing

PACKINGLIST

TO: Sunshine Gym
    Unit A3 Halesfield 11
    Telford, Shropshire, TF7 4PH

Invoice No. OS1503015UK
S/C No.
Date: 2015-04-05

From   XINGANG, CHINA   To   SOUTHAMPTON, UK   Via
L/C No.   Issued by:

Marks & Nos.	Descriptions	Qty (pc)	G.W. (kg)	N.W. (kg)	Meas. (cbm)
N/M	OUTDOOR FITNESS EQUIPMENT 户外运动器材 1. 品名：太空漫步机；2. 用途：健身；3. 种类：户外健身器材；4. 品牌：无牌；5. 型号：OB-M01D	80	6 540	6 040	

5. 报关合同

Beijing Okstar Sporting Goods Co., Ltd.
北京奥康达体育用品有限公司
Add: No.16, Beisan Street, Yanqi Economic Development Area, Huairou District, Beijing

<u>SALES CONTRACT</u>
销售合同

S/C NO:
销售合同号: OS1503015UK
DATE: MAY 10, 2015
签约日期:
SIGN AT: BEIJING
签约地点:

THE SELLERS: Beijing Okstar Sporting Goods Co., Ltd.　　THE BUYERS: Sunshine Gym
卖方:　　　　　　　　　　　　　　　　　　　　　　　　　买方:

COMMODITY 商品名称	QUANTITY 数量	UNIT PRICE & TERMS 单价及价格条款	AMOUNT 金额
OUTDOOR FITNESS EQUIPMENT 户外运动器材 1. 品名: 太空漫步机; 2. 用途: 健身; 3. 种类: 户外健身器材; 4. 品牌: 无牌; 5. 型号: OB-M01D	80 PCS	FOB XINGANG	
		TOTAL AMOUNT 金额合计:	USD

TOTAL: SAY U.S.　　　　DOLLARS:
PAYMENT: D/P
付款条款:
SHIPMENT: Xingang, CHINA　　　　　　　　　　DESTINATION: SOUTHAMPTON, UK
装运港:　　　　　　　　　　　　　　　　　　　目的港:
SHIPMENT DATE: MAY 15, 2015
装运日期:
SHIPMENT DATE: TO BE EFFECTED BY THE BUYERS
保险:
CLAIMS: IN CASE THE QUALITY AND/OR QUANTITY/WEIGHT ARE FOUND BY THE BUYERS TO BE NOT IN CONFORMITY
赔偿: WITH THE CONTRACT AFTER ARRIVAL OF THE GOODS AT THE PORT OF DESTINATION, THE BUYERS MAY LODGE CLAIM WITH THE SELLERS SUPPORTED BY SURVEY REPORT ISSUED BY AN INSPECTION ORGANISATION AGREED UPON BY BOTH PARTIES, WITH THE EXCEPTION, HOWEVER, OF THOSE CLAIMS, FOR WHICH THE INSURANCE COMPANY AND/OR THE SHIPPING COMPANY ARE TO BE HELD RESPONSIBLE. CLAIM FOR QUALITY DISCREPANCCY SHOULD BE FILED BY THE BUYERS WITHIN 30 DAYS AFTER ARRIVAL OF THE GOODS AT THE PORT OF DESTINATION WHILE FOR QUANTITY/WEIGHT DISCREPANCY CLAIM SHOULD BE FILED BY THE BUYERS WITHIN 15 DAYS AFTER ARRIVAL OF THE GOODS AT THE PORT OF DESTINATION. THE SELLERS SHALL WITHIN 30 DAYS AFTER RECEIPT OF THE NOTIFICATION OF THE CLAIM, SEND REPLY TO THE BUYERS.
ARBITRATION: ANY DISPUTE ARISING FROM THE EXECUTION OF/OR IN CONNECTION WITH THIS CONTRACT SHOULD
仲裁: BE SETTLED THROUGH NEGOTIATION. IN CASE OF SETTLEMENT CAN BE REACHED, THE CASE SHALL THEN BE SUBMITTED TO THE FOREIGN TRADE ARBITRATION COMMISSION OF THE CHINA COUNCIL FOR THE PROMOTION OF INTERNATIONAL TRADE, BEIJING, FOR SETTLEMENT BY ARBITRATION IN ACCORDANCE WITH COMMISSION'S POVISIONAL RULES OF PRODUCE THE AWARD REDERED BY THE COMMISSION SHALL BE FINAL AND BINDING ON BOTH PARTIES.
THE BUYERS: Sunshine Gym　　　　　　　　　　THE SELLERS: Beijing Okstar Sporting Goods Co., Ltd.
买方:　　　　　　　　　　　　　　　　　　　　卖方:

6. 出口货物报关单

中华人民共和国海关出口货物报关单

预录入编号：　　　　　　　　　　　　　　　　　　　　　　　　　　　海关编号：

出口口岸 新港海关 0202		备案号		出口日期 20150518	申报日期 20150518
经营单位 北京奥康达体育用品有限公司		运输方式 水路运输	运输工具名称	提运单号	
发货单位 北京奥康达体育用品有限公司		贸易方式 一般贸易（0110）		征免性质 一般征税（101）	结汇方式 电汇
许可证号		运抵国（地区） 英国		指运港 南安普顿	境内货源地 北京其他
批准文号		成交方式 FOB	运费	保费	杂费
合同协议号 OS1503015UK		件数	包装种类	毛重（公斤） 6 540	净重（公斤） 6 040
集装箱号		随附单据			生产厂家
标记唛码及备注 N/M					

项号	商品编号	商品名称、规格型号	数量及单位	最终目的国（地区）	单价	总价	币制	征免
1	9506919000	户外运动器材 太空漫步机/健身/户外健身器材/无牌/OB-M01D	6 040 公斤 80 件	英国	323.00	25 840.000 0	美元（502）	照章征税

税费征收情况

录入员　　　录入单位	兹声明以上申报无讹并承担法律责任	海关审单批注及放行日期（签章）	
		审单	审价
报关员			
	申报单位（签章）	征税	统计
单位地址			
邮编　　　电话　　　填制日期		查验	放行

7. 商业发票（结汇）

Beijing Okstar Sporting Goods Co., Ltd.
北京奥康达体育用品有限公司
Add: No. 16, Beisan Street, Yanqi Economic Development Area, Huairou District, Beijing

INVOICE

TO: Sunshine Gym　　　　　　　　　　　　　　　　　　　　Invoice No. OS1503015UK
　　Unit A3 Halesfield 11　　　　　　　　　　　　　　　　　S/C No.
　　Telford, Shropshire, TF7 4PH　　　　　　　　　　　　　Date: 2015-04-05

From　　XINGANG, CHINA　　　To　　SOUTHAMPTON, UK　　Via
L/C No.　　　　　　　　　　　　Issued by:

Marks & Nos.	Quantities & Descriptions		Amount
N/M	OB-M01D $ 328.00 Air Walker(Double) Dimension: 1 820 × 475 × 1 440(mm)(72″×19″×57″) Color: Blue RAL5002, Yellow RAL1018 Material: Non-galvanized steel Post Diameter: 3.5 inch	60 pcs	FOB XINGANG $ 19 680.00
	OB-Z05 $ 308.00 Waist Twister Dimension: 1 600 × 1 310(mm)(63″×52″) Post Diameter: 4.5 inch Material: Non-galvanized steel	20 pcs	$ 6 160.00
	TOTAL:	80 pcs	$ 25 840.00

**SAY U.S. DOLLARS: TWENTY FIVE THOUSANDS EIGHT HUNDRED AND FORTY ONLY.

8. 装箱单（结汇）

Beijing Okstar Sporting Goods Co., Ltd.
北京奥康达体育用品有限公司

Add: No.16, Beisan Street, Yanqi Economic Development Area, Huairou District, Beijing

PACKINGLIST

TO: Sunshine Gym
    Unit A3 Halesfield 11
    Telford, Shropshire, TF7 4PH

Invoice No. OS1503015UK
S/C No.
Date: 2015-04-05

From XINGANG, CHINA   To SOUTHAMPTON, UK   Via
L/C No.   Issued by:

Marks & Nos.	Descriptions	Qty (pc)	G.W. (kg)	N.W. (kg)	Meas. (cbm)
N/M	OB-M01D Air Walker (Double) Dimension: 1 820 × 475 × 1 440 (mm) (72″×19″×57″) Color: Blue RAL5002, Yellow RAL1018 Material: Non-galvanized steel Post Diameter: 3.5 inch	60	5 520	5 220	
	OB-Z05 Waist Twister Dimension: 1 600 × 1 310 (mm) (63″×52″) Post Diameter: 4.5 inch Material: Non-galvanized steel	20	1 020	820	
	TOTAL:	80	6 540	6 040	

附录 14B 贸易单证实例 2
Appendix 14B Trade Documents 2

案例名称：医疗器械出口/美国　　　业务时间：2014-05-30
案例概述：
　　商品名称：医疗器械
　　贸易方式：一般贸易
　　成交方式：FOB
　　结汇方式：L/C
　　运输方式：海运
　　目的地：美国

该案例涉及主要贸易单证：报关发票、装箱单、出境货物报检单、汇票、商业发票、装箱单。

1. 报关发票

MEHEO GEN MEDICAL MACHINE CO., LTD.
COMMERCIAL INVOICE

Sold to Messrs: 美国医药国际有限公司　　　　　　　　　　　　No.: 24T22005
　　　　　　　71 NW 50TH STREET MIAMI, FL 33176, U.S.A.　　　Date: May 13, 2014
　　　　　　　　　　　　　　　　　　　　　　　　　　　　　Contract No.: TE14MKE098

Shipped Per:　　　　BY SEA　　　From: SHANGHAI　　　　To: TRUJILLO, HONDURAS

Marks & Nos.:
N/M

ITEM	DESCRIPTION OF GOODS	QUANTITY	UNIT PRICE	AMOUNT
1	2WAY FOLEY CATHETER	18 000.00	USD 0.70/PIECE	USD 12 600.00
2	SURGICAL BLADES	90 000.00	USD 0.03/PIECE	USD 2 700.00
3	TONGUE DEPRESSOR	2 000.00	USD 0.617/PIECE	USD 1 234.00
4	URINE COLLECTOR	21 000.00	USD 0.076/PIECE	USD 1 596.00
5	BURETTE INFUSION SET	30 080.00	USD 0.56/PIECE	USD 16 844.80
6	SHOE COVER	25 000.00	USD 0.044/PIECE	USD 1 100.00
7	SURGICAL GOWN	27 000.00	USD 0.292/PIECE	USD 7 884.00
8	ENDOTRAQUEAL TUBE	10 500.00	USD 0.45/PIECE	USD 4 725.00
9	IDENTIFICATION BAND	20 000.00	USD 0.038005/SET	USD 760.10
10	WOOL APLICATOR	1 200.00	USD 0.368/PIECE	USD 441.60
11	IV CATHETER	168 000.0	USD 0.19/PIECE	USD 31 920.00

2. 装箱单

MEHEO GEN MEDICAL MACHINE CO., LTD.
PACKING LIST

DATE: May 13, 2014
INVOICE NO.: 24T22005

Marks & Nos.:
N/M

ITEM	Name of Commodity	Quantity	Gross Weight (kg)	Net Weight (kg)
	2WAY FOLEY CATHETER	30.00 CTNS	360.00/12.00	330.00/11.00
	SURGICAL BLADES	18.00 CTNS	135.00/7.50	99.00/5.50
	TONGUE DEPRESSOR	40.00 CTNS	520.00/13.00	440.00/11.00
	URINE COLLECTOR	27.00 CTNS	309.00/11.44	282.00/10.44
	BURETTE INFUSION SET	192.00 CTNS	3 064.00/15.96	2 684.00/13.98
	SHOE COVER	25.00 CTNS	162.50/6.50	150.00/6.00
	SURGICAL GOWN	270.00 CTNS	1 815.00/6.72	1 680.00/6.22
	ENDOTRAQUEAL TUBE	105.00 CTNS	451.50/4.30	367.50/3.50
	IDENTIFICATION BAND	4.00 CTNS	56.00/14.00	52.00/13.00
	WOOL APLICATOR	10.00 CTNS	50.00/5.00	40.00/4.00
	IV CATHETER	84.00 CTNS	882.00/10.50	756.00/9.00

3. 出境货物报检单

中华人民共和国出入境检验检疫
出境货物报检单

报检单位（加盖公章）：   编号：
报检单位登记号：   联系人：朱力   电话：6711   报检日期：2014-05-13

发货人	（中文）				
	（外文）				
收货人	（中文）×××				
	（外文）To order				
货物名称（中/外文）	H.S.编码	产地	数/重量	货物总USD	包装种类及数量
2 WAY FOLEY CATHETER 导尿套/管	90183900	天津	18 000.00	12 600.00	30.00 CTNS
SURGICAL BLADES 刀片	90189090	天津	90 000.00	2 700.00	18.00 CTNS
TONGUE DEPRESSOR 压舌板	4421902190	天津	2 000.00	1 234.00	40.00 CTNS
URINE COLLECTOR 尿袋	39269090	天津	21 000.00	1 596.00	27.00 CTNS
BURETTE INFUSION SET 一次性注射器	90183100	天津	30 080.00	16 844.80	192.00 CTNS
SHOE COVER 鞋套	6307900090	天津	25 000.00	1 100.00	25.00 CTNS
SURGICAL GOWN 化纤制一次性或医用无纺织物服	6210103020	天津	27 000.00	7 884.00	270.00 CTNS
ENDOTRA QUEAL TUBE 导管、插管及类似品	90183900	天津	10 500.00	4 725.00	105.00 CTNS
IDENTIFICATION BAND 其他医疗、外科或兽医用仪器器具	90189090	天津	20 000.00	760.10	4.00 CTNS
WOOL APLICATOR 棉签	30059010	天津	1 200.00	441.60	10.00 CTNS
IV CATHETER 静脉针	90183210	天津	168 000.00	31 920.00	84.00 CTNS
总 计：			412 780.00	81 805.50	805.00 CTNS

运输工具名称号码	By Sea	贸易方式	一般贸易	货物存放地点	美康库		
合同号	TE14MKE-B003	信用证号				用途	药用
发货日期	2014-03-22	输往国家（地区）	AMERICA	许可证/审批号	×××		
启运地	Shanghai	到达口岸	TRUJILLO, Honduras	生产单位注册号	×××		
集装箱规格、数量及号码	×××						
备注							

需要单证名称（划"√"或补填）		检验检疫费	
□ 品质证书 □ 重量证书	□ 植物检疫证书 □ 熏蒸/消毒证书	总金额 （人民币元）	
□ 数量证书 □ 兽医卫生证书	□ 出境货物换证凭单 □ 通关单	计费人	
□ 健康证书 □ 卫生证书 □ 动物卫生证书		收费人	
报检人郑重声明： 1. 本人被授权报检。 2. 上列填写内容正确属实，货物无伪造或冒用他人的厂名、标志、认证标志，并承担货物质量责任。		领取证单	
		日期	
		签名	

4. 汇票

No. 24T22005

Exchange for   USD 81 805.50   Beijing, China,   May 13, 2014

LC 45 DAYS   At   ×××   Sight of this SECOND of exchange

(the FIRST of the same tenor and date being unpaid) pay to the order of

The sum of

US DOLLARS EIGHTY ONE THOUSAND EIGHT HUNDRED AND FIVE AND CENTS FIFTY

drawn under

value received and charge to account

To 美国医药国际有限公司

71NW 50TH STREET MIAMI, FL 33176, U.S.A.

Account of

(Invoice No. 24T22005)

5. 商业发票

MEHEO GEN MEDICAL MACHINE CO., LTD.
COMMERCIAL INVOICE

Sold to Messrs: 美国医药国际有限公司   No.: 24T22005
             71 NW 50TH STREET MIAMI, FL 33176, U.S.A.   Date: May 13, 2014
                                                              Contract No.: TE14MKE098
Shipped Per: BY SEA   From: SHANGHAI   To: TRUJILLO, HONDURAS

Marks & Nos.:
N/M

ITEM	DESCRIPTION OF GOODS	QUANTITY	UNIT PRICE	AMOUNT
1	2WAY FOLEY CATHETER	18 000.00	USD 0.70/PIECE	USD 12 600.00
2	SURGICAL BLADES	90 000.00	USD 0.03/PIECE	USD 2 700.00
3	TONGUE DEPRESSOR	2 000.00	USD 0.617/PIECE	USD 1 234.00
4	URINE COLLECTOR	21 000.00	USD 0.076/PIECE	USD 1 596.00
5	BURETTE INFUSION SET	30 080.00	USD 0.56/PIECE	USD 16 844.80
6	SHOE COVER	25 000.00	USD 0.044/PIECE	USD 1 100.00
7	SURGICAL GOWN	27 000.00	USD 0.292/PIECE	USD 7 884.00
8	ENDOTRAQUEAL TUBE	10 500.00	USD 0.45/PIECE	USD 4 725.00
9	IDENTIFICATION BAND	20 000.00	USD 0.038005/SET	USD 760.10
10	WOOL APLICATOR	1 200.00	USD 0.368/PIECE	USD 441.60
11	IV CATHETER	168 000.00	USD 0.19/PIECE	USD 31 920.00

6. 装箱单

MEHEO GEN MEDICAL MACHINE CO., LTD.
PACKING LIST

DATE: May 13, 2014
INVOICE NO.: 24T22005

Marks & Nos.:
N/M

ITEM	Name of Commodity	Quantity	Gross Weight (kg)	Net Weight (kg)
	2WAY FOLEY CATHETER	30.00 CTNS	360.00/12.00	330.00/11.00
	SURGICAL BLADES	18.00 CTNS	135.00/7.50	99.00/5.50
	TONGUE DEPRESSOR	40.00 CTNS	520.00/13.00	440.00/11.00
	URINE COLLECTOR	27.00 CTNS	309.00/11.44	282.00/10.44
	BURETTE INFUSION SET	192.00 CTNS	3 064.00/15.96	2 684.00/13.98
	SHOE COVER	25.00 CTNS	162.50/6.50	150.00/6.00
	SURGICAL GOWN	270.00 CTNS	1 815.00/6.72	1 680.00/6.22
	ENDOTRAQUEAL TUBE	105.00 CTNS	451.50/4.30	367.50/3.50
	IDENTIFICATION BAND	4.00 CTNS	56.00/14.00	52.00/13.00
	WOOL APLICATOR	10.00 CTNS	50.00/5.00	40.00/4.00
	IV CATHETER	84.00 CTNS	882.00/10.50	756.00/9.00

综合练习题 1
Comprehensive Exercises 1

Ⅰ. Translate the Following Terms
  1. From English into Chinese
    (1) PNTR
    (2) Irrevocable Letter of Credit
    (3) Blank Endorsement
    (4) General Average
    (5) FAQ
    (6) DES
    (7) Franchise
    (8) FPA
    (9) Bill of Exchange
    (10) Auction
  2. From Chinese into English
    (1) 世界银行
    (2) 电子商务
    (3) 托运人
    (4) 进口许可证
    (5) 国际商会

Ⅱ. Choose the Best Answer for Each of the Following Question
  1. Contracts must be renewed one week _____ their expiration.
    A. on   B. against   C. the moment of   D. before
  2. The commodities you offered are _____ line with the business scope of our clients.
    A. outside   B. out of   C. out   D. without
  3. We are arranging for an inspection tour of _____ the material was processed.
    A. place   B. the place   C. where   D. there
  4. We are reconsidering those trade terms _____ might be adverse to the interest of our principals.
    A. what   B. that   C. when   D. where
  5. Information indicates that some similar goods of Indian origin have been sold here _____ about 30% lower than yours.
    A. with a level   B. at something   C. at quotation   D. with a figure
  6. As we are _____ of these goods, please expedite shipment after receiving our L/C.
    A. in badly need   B. badly in need   C. urgent in need   D. in urgently need
  7. We give you on the attached sheet full details regarding packing and marking, which must be strictly _____.

A. observed   B. abide by   C. submitted   D. seen

8. We _____ to allow you a special discount if you increase your order to 5 000 pairs.

    A. have prepared   B. are prepare   C. are prepared   D. were prepared

9. The importance of delivery on time _____ overstressed, because failure to receive goods or services will cause serious inconvenience to the end-users.

    A. can   B. be   C. cannot be   D. could be

10. We wish to stress that shipment must be made within the prescribed time limit, as a further _____ will not be considered by our end-users.

    A. prolong   B. protract   C. extension   D. expansion

11. With computer users linked to the Internet growing _____ every year, business is trying to cash in on the worldwide network.

    A. at million   B. with a million   C. with one million   D. by millions

12. We regret having to remind you that 30% of the freight is still _____ .

    A. owned   B. owning   C. outstanding   D. understanding

13. It should be _____ if you could immediately _____ what quantity you can supply us at present.

    A. thankful, advise   B. appreciate, advise

    C. appreciated, advise   D. appreciating, inform

14. We thank you for your e-mail of November 25 _____ your purchase of 10 MT wild rice.

    A. confirm   B. confirming   C. to confirm   D. confirmed

15. Subject to satisfactory arrangements _____ terms and conditions, we should be pleased to act as your sole agent.

    A. as   B. as per   C. as if   D. as to

16. Our usual terms of payment are _____ L/C and we hope they will be satisfactory _____ you.

    A. by, for   B. by, to   C. for, to   D. for, with

17. That helps to explain _____ businesses are setting up Net sites even though profits aren't yet very big.

    A. that   B. the reason for   C. why   D. why that

18. We find that there is no stipulation of transshipment _____ in the relative L/C.

    A. allowing   B. which allows   C. which allowed   D. being allowed

19. After unpacking the case we found that the goods did not _____ with the original sample.

    A. match   B. come up   C. agree   D. measure

20. If the first shipment _____, we guarantee that we will send you many repeat orders.

    A. will prove satisfactory   B. proves satisfactory

    C. turns out a satisfaction   D. turns out to be satisfied

21. It is necessary that an arbitration clause _____ in the contract.

    A. will be included   B. must be included

    C. be included   D. has been included

22. Please see that your written confirmation _____ by the end of this month; otherwise we will be free from the obligation for his offer.

   A. reaches us   B. will reach us   C. reach us   D. reached us

Ⅲ. Translate the Following into an English Letter in a Proper Form

写信人：新路华贸易有限公司，

地址：中国上海，兴达路999号金星大厦（Golden Star Mansion）33层

收信人：James Brown & Sons，由日用品部（Daily Articles Department）办理

地址：#304-310 Jalan Street，Toronto，Canada

日期：2000年6月30日

内容：感谢你6月15日的来函和样品。

特告知，我方客户对你方样品的试用结果非常满意，但现在仍有些犹豫。

经与同类货物做仔细比较，我们发现你方报价有点高。当前的洗发精（shampoo）市场充斥着各种各样的品牌，像 Rejoice、Pond's 等优质产品很容易买到，而且这些品牌都已得到我地市场的认可。就洗发精而言，很多消费者不愿接受新产品。你方产品作为新品牌，最大的卖点将是它的护发（hair care）功能；质量上虽然已经达到客户要求，但要想在我地市场打开销路，必须还要具备价格优势，否则很难与一些老牌产品竞争。

鉴于此，我方客户建议将原报价减10%。请考虑并及时答复。

Ⅳ. Fill in the Contract Form with Information Gathered From the Following Correspondences

1. Outgoing Letter

Beijing, November 5, 1999

Dear Sirs,

　　Thank you for your enquiry of October 30 for Women's Nylon Garments. In compliance with your request, we have enclosed a price list and an illustrated brochure. Although we still have certain amount of stock we can hardly keep them for a long time because of the heavy demand. Samples will be sent on request. We are looking forward to our early reply.

Yours faithfully,

Beijing Garments Imp./Exp. Corporation

2. Incoming Letter

Dear Sirs,

　　Many thanks for your quotation of November 5 and the samples of Women's Nylon Garments. We are satisfied with the quality and pleased to enclose our Order NO. 333 for 3 sizes mentioned in your latest catalogue. We note that you can supply these items from stock and hope you will send them before December 31. Our company will reserve the right to cancel this order or reject the goods for any late arrival. For your reference, we want to effect payment by D/P 60 days. Please kindly let us have your confirmation.

　　ORDER

　　　NO. 333

　　　Beijing Garments Imp./Exp. Corp.

　　　Beijing, China

　　　Please supply the following items:

Quantity (doz)	Item	Size	Unit Price (per doz) CIF London
15	Women's Nylon Garments	Small	US $ 75.00
16	ditto	Medium	US $ 110.00
14	ditto	Large	US $ 150.00

London Trading Co., Ltd.

3. Outgoing Letter

Dear Sirs,

We've received your letter of November 13 and your Order No. 333. Much to our regret, we can hardly accept your order at the prices you bid since the prices of raw materials have increased recently. We're afraid the best we can do is as follows:

Commodity	Unit Price(per doz) CIF London	Size	Quantity(doz)
Woman's Nylon Garments	USD 80.00	Small	15
Woman's Nylon Garments	USD 120.00	Medium	16
Woman's Nylon Garments	USD 160.00	Large	14

As to payment terms, we usually require letters of credit. However, in view of our long and pleasant relations, we will accept D/P 60 days this time. But it must be clearly understood that, in so doing, we are not establishing a precedent. We hope you will accept our prices and give us a reply as soon as possible.

Yours faithfully,

4. Incoming Letter

Dear Sirs,

Your letter of November 20, 1999 has been received. As we are anxious to finalize this transaction, we have been exerting ourselves to persuade our clients to accept your prices. Eventually, they have decided to accept. We are glad to have been able to conclude the business with you and await your sales confirmation.

Yours faithfully,

5. Outgoing Letter

Dear Sirs,

We're glad that your clients have accepted our prices, which are narrowly calculated. These goods will be packed in boxes of half dozen each and 10 dozens to a carton, and shipped in December from China port to London with transshipment and partial shipments allowed. Insurance is to be covered by us against ALL Risks and War Risk for 100% of the invoice value. Enclosed is our Sales Contract No. 116 signed in Beijing on November 28, 1999 in duplicate, a copy of which please sign and return.

Yours faithfully,

  CONTRACT

  No. _____

  SELLERS:

  BUYERS:

This Contract is made by and between the Buyers and the Sellers, whereby the Buyers agree to buy and the Sellers agree to sell the under - mentioned commodity according to the terms and conditions stipulated below:

Commodity Size Quantity (doz) Price per doz CIF London Amount

Total Value:

Packing:

Shipping Mark:

Insurance:

Time of Shipment:

Port of Shipment:

Port of Destination:

Terms of Payment:

Done and signed in on this day of

V. Write a letter in English asking for amendments to the following letter of credit by checking it with the given contract terms.

Copenhagen Bank

Date: January 4, 2000

To: Bank of China, Beijing

We hereby open our Irrevocable Letter of Credit NO. 112235 in favor of China Trading Corporation for account of Copenhagen Import Company up to an amount of GBP 14 550 (Say Pounds Sterling One Thousand Four Hundred And Fifty - five Only) for 100% of the invoice value relative to the shipment of:

150 metric tons of Writing Paper Type 501 at GBP97 per MT CIF Copenhagen as per your S/C No. PO5476 from Copenhagen to China port. Drafts to be drawn at sight on our bank and accompanied by the following documents marked "×":

(×) Commercial Invoice in triplicate.

(×) Bill of Lading in triplicate made out to our order quoting L/C No. 112235, marked FREIGHT COLLECT.

⋮

(×) One original Marine Insurance Policy or Certificate for All Risks and War Risk, covering 110% of the invoice value, with claims payable in Copenhagen in the currency of draft (s) Partial shipments and transshipment are prohibited.

Shipment must be effected not later than March 31, 2000.

This L/C is valid at our counter until April 15, 2000.

附：PO5476 号合同主要条款：

卖方：中国贸易公司

买方：哥本哈根进口公司

商品名称：写字纸

规格：501 型

数量：150 吨

单价：CIF 哥本哈根每吨 97 英镑

总值：14 550 英镑

装运期：2000 年 3 月 31 日前自中国港口至哥本哈根

保险：由卖方按发票金额的 110% 投保一切险和战争险

支付：不可撤销的即期信用证，于装运前 1 个月开到卖方，并于上述装运期后 15 天内在中国议付有效

Ⅵ. Translate the Following Passages

1. From English into Chinese

   Discount means that sellers offer buyers a certain percentage of reduction on the original price. When competition in the market is fierce, discount will help to improve sellers' competitiveness. There are different kinds of discount, for example, quantity discount, seasonal discount and exceptional discount. The specific amount or percentage of discount varies in different situations. The percentage of discount can be clearly written down in a contract if the seller and the buyer have reached an agreement.

   The amount of discount is usually deducted from the buyers' payment.

2. From Chinese into English

   (1) 国际市场营销是重要的，因为世界已变成了一个全球化的场所，国际营销每日都在我们身旁发生，对我们的生活产生着深刻的影响。

   (2) 国际贸易中，只有很少一部分服务贸易。因为，就某种程度来说服务并不像商品那样可以交易。

   (3) 在执行合同的过程中，签约双方都应该遵守合同条款。任何一方如果不严格履行，就会给另一方带来麻烦，甚至使另一方遭受损失。

   (4) 国际贸易中，时间因素至关重要，所以买方通常坚持货物必须在指定截止日期前或一段时间内装运是很自然的。

   (5) 技术转让是生产某个产品、使用某个程序或提供某种服务的系统化知识的转让。其要素有"人件""软件"和"硬件"。

综合练习题 2
Comprehensive Exercises 2

Ⅰ. Multiple Choice
1. We shall highly appreciate _____ if you will send us a brochure and two sample books by air immediately.
    A. you   B. that   C. it   D. when
2. We hope that you will find many items of _____ to you.
    A. interest   B. interesting   C. interested D. being interested
3. Please note that our offer remains firm _____ ten days for your acceptance.
    A. for   B. until   C. in   D. on
4. Our sewing machines _____ fast, and there have been numerous enquiries about them.
    A. are sold   B. selling   C. are selling D. are being sold
5. We would be most thankful if you could extend this favor to us and agree _____ 50% by L/C and 50% by D/P at sight.
    A. with   B. upon   C. at   D. to
6. We have arranged with the Bank of Japan, Tokyo, to _____ a credit in your favor.
    A. draw   B. establish   C. make   D. extend
7. We thank you for your letter of 12 June, _____ you have opened the covering L/C.
    A. in which   B. from which   C. informing   D. informing us
8. Please call your attention _____ our newly developed bicycles which will surely have good sale in your market.
    A. to that   B. to the fact that   C. that   D. to
9. We are sending you by separate airmail a copy of our _____ catalog for your reference.
    A. new   B. fresh   C. latest   D. later
10. If you had opened the letter of credit to reach us in July, we _____ the goods now.
    A. could have dispatched   B. could dispatch
    C. dispatch   D. can dispatch
11. Consequently we find no _____ to compensate for the loss you claimed for.
    A. ground   B. place   C. land   D. position
12. We are making you our quotation for shoes _____ .
    A. as follow   B. as follows   C. following   D. at following
13. We are willing to renew the agreement on the same terms _____ last.
    A. like   B. as   C. to   D. with
14. We shall fulfill you order according to the remarks in our last letter _____ we hear from you to the contrary.
    A. if   B. unless   C. that   D. which
15. While placing our order, we emphasized that any delay in delivery would definitely

_____ the cost of the goods.
   A. add   B. add to   C. amount to   D. plus
16. Are the goods _____ Contract No. 1986 are now ready for shipment, please rush your L/C.
   A. against   B. of   C. under   D. for
17. Please _____ us your lowest price for 500 men's bicycles.
   A. quote   B. offer   C. make   D. enquire
18. Part of your payment has been received, but $20 000 is still _____.
   A. withstanding   B. paid   C. owned   D. outstanding
19. As a result of the _____ switches, we are now faced with the following losses.
   A. effective   B. broke   C. fault   D. defective
20. _____, we discovered that the goods were inferior in quality to the sample.
   A. After exam   B. On examination   C. When exam   D. Upon examining

II. Fill in the Blanks with the Proper Words
21. We will _____ a sight draft on you on collection basis.
22. The buyer should open a letter of credit with a bank _____ to the seller.
23. As to terms of payment, we often require a confirmed and irrevocable L/C _____ by draft at sight.
24. Your goods will be loaded _____ S. S. "Green Wood".
25. We are now _____ need of the following specialties of your corporation.
26. Our offer is _____ to your reply reaching us before May 15.
27. We file a _____ with you _____ this cargo for the short-weight.
28. The port of festination is _____ buyer's option.
29. We hope the matter can be settled _____ our mutual benefit.
30. You must be aware that any further delay _____ shipment will bring about adverse effect _____ future business.
31. We will inform our customers _____ arrival of the shipment ourselves.
32. I need to receive the replacement not later _____ Monday, April 29.
33. We are sure your help will be beneficial _____ both parties.
34. We are unable to comply _____ your request in your letter of January 31.
35. We look forward _____ receiving your early reply.
36. We are pleased to enclose a detailed quotation _____ bathroom showers.
37. Such a growing demand can only result _____ increased price.
38. We assure you _____ our full attention _____ executing the contract.
39. As you fail to make delivery _____ time, we have no choice _____ to cancel our order with you.
40. All prices must be quoted _____ US dollars.
41. I am afraid I cannot supply you _____ their information you request.

III. Translate the Following Sentences
42. Thanks to your close cooperation, we have successfully concluded a number of deals.
43. We are expecting to receive your earliest reply to this enquiry.

44. We will allow you 10% discount if you purchase 5 000 dozens or more.
45. The offer is made subject to our final confirmation.
46. Unless you make a reduction of 5%, no business is possible.
47. We are willing to make you a firm offer at this price.
48. We appreciate your counter-offer but find it too low.
49. We will surely honor the sight draft on us upon presentation.
50. We are studying your offer and hope that it will remain open till the end of the month.
51. In case of transshipment, we have to pay extra transportation charges.
52. 这是一套有关这批货的装运单据。
53. 额外的保险费将由买方承担。
54. 你们本应该在上个月就发送我们订的货物。
55. 你们能否将价格提高5%。
56. 我们将在装船前一个月开立信用证。

Ⅳ. Writing an English Letter

57. 尊敬的先生：

　　收到贵方2006年2月1日的来函，要求我方办理5 000双男皮鞋的投保事宜，保险费由贵方承担。

　　现欣然奉告，我方已向中国人民保险公司按发票金额的110%为上述货物投保了一切险。投保金额为3万美元。保险单正在准备中，将在本周连同保险费的收款单（debit note）一并寄给贵方。

　　货物将由"东风"号货轮运出，该货轮将于2月18日出发，预计3月10日左右抵达目的港。

　　此致

综合练习题 3
Comprehensive Exercises 3

I. Multiple Choice
1. For goods concluded on FOB basis, freight for shipment from Shanghai to Hong Kong is to be _____ to buyer's account.
   A. borne   B. paid   C. changed   D. charged
2. We wish to call your attention _____ the L/C covering your order No. 185 has not reached us.
   A. to the fact that   B. to that   C. to   D. that
3. We have received your enquiry of October 15 _____ you show great interest in our electric heaters.
   A. which   B. at which   C. in which   D. from which
4. You can file a claim with the insurance company in your area, who will _____ the loss incurred.
   A. compensate   B. compensate for C. compensate to you D. compensate you
5. _____ will be highly appreciated if you will send us a brochure.
   A. We   B. You   C. I   D. Which
6. Please effect shipment immediately as L/C will _____ on July 31.
   A. valid   B. firm   C. due   D. expire
7. Your order No. 123 was confirmed by our fax of September 15 subject to _____ of your credit within 15 days from the date.
   A. arrival   B. reaching   C. arrive   D. reach
8. We are now _____ your inquiry of October 12.
   A. on receipt   B. on receipt of C. in receipt   D. in receipt of
9. Our new low cost solutions may be _____ particular interest to you.
   A. in   B. of   C. with   D. for
10. Drafts drawn in compliance with the terms of credit shall be duly _____ on presentation and paid at maturity.
    A. honored   B. dishonored   C. discounted   D. declined
11. Please _____ the shipment date of your L/C to October 15 and validity to October 30.
    A. amend   B. extend   C. establish   D. expand
12. We look forward to _____ the goods in fourth quarter.
    A. the delivery of B. your delivery C. deliver   D. delivery
13. Should your price _____ reasonable, we will place an order with you _____ the item.
    A. is, for   B. is, from   C. be, for   D. be, with
14. _____, we are airmailing you our latest quotation sheet for your consideration.

  A. As request B. At request C. At requested D. As requested
15. We are sorry for the trouble the printer has caused you, but we are confident that it can be fixed _____ your complete satisfaction.
  A. to B. with C. in D. for
16. We hope the goods you ordered will arrive at the port of destination _____ .
  A. in good condition   B. in good conditions
  C. in a good condition   D. in the good condition
17. We lodge a claim _____ you _____ the short-weight.
  A. with, on B. for, for C. with, for D. for, with
18. Please insure _____ WPA _____ 110% of the invoice value.
  A. with, for B. against, at C. for, for D. against, for
19. 90 percent of the credit amount must be paid _____ the presentation of documents.
  A. at B. by C. when D. against
20. _____ you don't reduce your quotations, we shall have to buy elsewhere.
  A. Before B. If C. Unless D. When

Ⅱ. Fill in the Blanks with Proper Words
21. The goods _____ Contract No. 3617 left here yesterday.
22. As the goods are now ready _____ shipment, please rush your letter of credit.
23. The buyer is required to _____ a confirmed and irrevocable letter of credit in seller's favor.
24. As to terms of payment, we often require a confirmed and irrevocable L/C _____ by draft at sight.
25. If additional risks are to be covered, the extra premium is for buyer's _____ .
26. We will try our best to satisfy you _____ the additional 10 000 tons of coal.
27. Don't you think it is troublesome to transship the goods _____ Sydney?
28. While placing our order we emphasized that any delay in delivery would definitely add _____ the cost of the goods.
29. As for the shortage, we suggest your making it _____ in your next shipment.
30. You can see the clear difference _____ these two grades.
31. So far as we know, there are risks of pilferage or damage _____ the goods if they are transshipped.
32. Your refusal to amend the L/C is equivalent _____ cancellation of the order.
33. We have been doing quite well in our business, and we are willing to open an account _____ you.
34. The machine requested has been replaced by a new model, which can provide you _____ a more satisfactory service.
35. If the goods are _____ to our customer's expectation, we shall place further orders with you.
36. We are enclosing our pro-forma invoice in triplicate for your application _____ import license.
37. We are studying your offer and hope that it will remain valid _____ the end of the

month.
38. The products we supplied are _____ fine quality.
39. Please refer _____ our last order in which model F-65 is included.
40. Enclosed are three copies of our catalog, _____ which we hope you will find your preferences.
41. Now we are looking forward to your replying _____ our offer.
42. Thanks _____ your enquiry dated May 18, we are now sending you our latest price list _____ your reference.
43. Please quote us lowest price _____ cotton pieces goods CIF Singapore.
44. We are making you our quotation for shoes _____ follows.

Ⅲ. Translate the Following Sentence
45. We don't think we can cut our price to that extent you required. Shall I suggest that we meet each other half way?
46. Please let us know at what price per metric ton, and upon what terms of payment, you are able to deliver large quantities of best rock sugar.
47. In order to start some concrete business, we are glad to make you the following special offers subject to our final confirmation.
48. If quality and price are satisfactory, there will be prospects of good sales here.
49. The goods you intend to order are out of stock, but we recommend Art. No. 123 as an excellent substitute.
50. If you insist on your price, we will have no way but to turn to other sources for supply.
51. The draft was discounted in Shanghai.
52. We shall appreciate it very much if you can accept Documents against Payment terms.
53. Please make sure the terms in the L/C are exactly the same as those in our contract so that there is no need for amendment, which is costly and time consuming.
54. Our offer is based on reasonable profit margin.
55. 这些货花了我们 100 万美元。
56. 该订单以我们获得进口许可证为条件。
57. 我们已经在"海河"号货船上订了货仓。
58. 如果没有你们的明确指示，我们将按惯例投保水渍险和战争险。
59. 货物短交 1 540 公斤。

Ⅳ. Writing an English Letter
60. 先生：
　　我们按时收到了由"东风"号运来的货。对于你方迅速执行订单，深表谢意。
　　经检查第 3 号箱子内所装货物完全不对。我们猜想是货物错装了，箱子内的货物属于别的订单。
　　由于需要用所订货物来完成对我们客户的交货，务请更换，立即发运。随函附上第 3 号箱货物清单一份，请与我方订单核对。
　　盼复。
　　此致

综合练习题 4
Comprehensive Exercises 4

Ⅰ. Multiple Choice
1. Documentary Collection is to be made with the documents to be _____ to the draft.
    A. enclosed	B. attached	C. together	D. along with
2. We will instruct our bank to issue an L/C _____ favor of your company.
    A. on	B. for	C. with	D. in
3. We have instructed the bank to _____ the amendment you ask for.
    A. perform	B. fulfill	C. effect	D. do
4. The notice given by the shipper after the shipment of the goods is called _____.
    A. shipping notice	B. shipping instruction
    C. shipping advice	D. shipping documents
5. Your terms of payment are _____ to us.
    A. agree	B. agreed	C. agreement	D. agreeable
6. The shipment time is June or July at our _____ and the goods will be shipped in one _____.
    A. choice, shipment	B. option, lot
    C. decision, cargo	D. option, consignment
7. We thank you for your letter of May 17 and the _____ catalogue.
    A. sent	B. enclosed	C. given	D. presented
8. While _____ an enquiry, you ought to enquire into quality, specification and price etc.
    A. giving	B. offering	C. sending	D. making
9. We would _____ very much if you send us some samples immediately.
    A. thank you	B. appreciate it	C. appreciate	D. appreciate you
10. We are anxious to _____ the market for our Antimony Trioxide, which at present enjoys a limited sale in Europe.
    A. increase	B. enlarge	C. expand	D. extend

Ⅱ. Match
    A. "INCOTERMS" ( )	1. 货交承运人
    B. FOB ( )	2. 信用证
    C. FCA ( )	3. 欧洲主要口岸
    D. T/T ( )	4. 海运提单
    E. D/P ( )	5. 装运港船上交货
    F. L/C ( )	6. 电汇
    G. EMP ( )	7. 国际贸易术语解释通则
    H. FPA ( )	8. 平安险

1. B/L   (   )   9. 付款交单

Ⅲ. Business Terms Translation
1. Chamber of commerce _____   2. Quotation _____
3. Counter-offer _____   4. Customs invoice _____
5. Open account terms _____   6. Certificate of origin _____
7. Import quotas system _____   8. Bill of exchange _____
9. Promissory note _____   10. Confirmed L/C _____

Ⅳ. Sentence Translation
1. 贵国驻华大使馆商务参赞处告知，你拟从我国进口车床（lathe），故特致函你公司，希望能在该项产品方面建立业务关系。
2. 我们想请你们代为查询一下伦敦一家商行的财务和信用情况，它们是James Neils & Co.。它们的银行是香港汇丰银行。谢谢。
3. 我们是世界上最大的丝绸进口商之一。我们过去一直从日本进口，现在我们想到中国市场订购。
4. 我们很遗憾不能接受你方的还价。自从我们报价给你们后，我们已按原报价与其他许多客户成交，故如你方仍有需要，请立即订购。
5. 你公司8月10日来函收悉，内附有关第100号订单订购500台缝纫机的销售确认书第90SP-5861号一式两份。今签退一份请查收。
6. 对这次交易，我们例外同意用信用证方式付款，但对以后的交易，我们要求更有利的付款条件，也就是付款交单。
7. 今收到你公司对第×××号销售确认书开来的第×××号信用证，但发现少开500美元。请与上述销售确认书核对并希望及早修改。
8. 我们报的是CFR价格，因此，货物将由你方投保，但我们在货物装运后，将立即通知你们有关的装运情况。
9. 如果指定我们做你们在巴基斯坦的代理，我们将集中精力，努力推销你们的商品。这对我们双方都是有利的。
10. 在收到你方具体询价时，我将立即寄上报价单及样品。

Ⅴ. Fill in the Blanks With the Words/Phrases Given

amendments   special discount   in   confirm   effect
originals   conform to   for   stipulations   on

Dear Sirs,

We want to say how pleased we were to receive your order of 15th April for Ladies' and Children's Shoes.

We ___(1)___ supply of 1 000 pairs of the shoes at the prices stated in your order No. 888 and will allow a 5% ___(2)___ on you order worth $5 000 or above. Our Sales Confirmation No. BC-510 in two ___(3)___ were airmailed to you. Please sign and return one copy of them ___(4)___ our file.

It is understood that a letter of credit ___(5)___ our favour covering the said shoes should be opened immediately. We wish to point out that ___(6)___ in the relative L/C must strictly ___(7)___ the stated in our Sales Confirmation so as to avoid subsequent ___(8)___. You may rest assured that we will ___(9)___ shipment without delay ___(10)___ receipt of your letter of credit.

We appreciate your cooperation and look forward to receiving from your further orders.

Yours truly,

VI. Letter Translation

With reference to our Sales Confirmation No. 7904 dated August 8, 2000, we regret to say that your letter of credit has not yet reached us up to the time of writing. This has caused us much inconvenience as we have already made preparations for shipment according to the stipulations of the said Sales Confirmation.

You must be aware that the terms and conditions of a contract once signed should be strictly observed, failure to abide by them will mean violation of contract. If you refer to our Sales Confirmation, you will see the clause reading:

"The Buyer shall establish the covering letter of credit before August 30, 2000, failing which the Seller reserves the right to rescind the contract without further notice."

The goods you ordered have been ready for quite some time and the demand of late has been so great that we find it hard to keep them for you any longer. However, in consideration of our friendly business relations, we are prepared to wait for your L/C, which must reach us not later than October 5, 2000. If we again fail to receive your L/C in time, we shall cancel our Sales Confirmation and ask you to refund to us the storage charges we have paid on your behalf.

Your cooperation in this respect will be appreciated.

VII. Contract Filling According to the Following Information

Letters between buyer and seller:

1. At your request, we send you under cover a quotation sheet showing our lowest price for walnut meat of first grade at RMB ￥15 000 per metric ton on CIF Vancouver basis.

2. We wish to place an order for 60 MT of walnut meat of first trade at the price you quoted.

   Please pack the goods in sacks of 100 kg each and ship our order in three shipments of 20 tons each month, commencing from October 2002.

   We will open an irrevocable L/C by sight draft in your favour after receipt of your Sales Contract. We hope the goods will be insured against All Risks and War risk for 110% of the invoice value as per CIC of January 1, 1981.

3. We are pleased to inform you that we have booked your order and are sending you our Sales Contract No. 4173 signed in Shijiazhuang on 28th July 2002 in duplicate. Kindly return one copy countersigned at your earliest convenience.

Note: Sellers: Hebei Imp./Exp. Corp.

Buyers: Vancouver Foodstuffs Company

CONTRACT No. 4173

Sellers:

Buyers:

This contract is made by and between the Buyers and the Sellers, whereby the Buyers agree to buy and the Sellers agree to sell the under-mentioned commodity according to the terms and conditions stipulated below:

Commodity:

Specifications:

Quantity:

Unit Price:

Total Value:

Packing:

Shipping Mark:

Insurance:

Time of Shipment:

Port of Shipment:

Port of Destination:

Terms of Payment:

Done and signed in Shijiazhuang on this 31st day of July, 2002.

综合练习题 5
Comprehensive Exercises 5

Ⅰ. Multiple Choice
1. Your request for payment _____ Letter of Credit is unacceptable.
   A. with   B. by   C. using   D. of
2. As instructed, we will draw _____ you a sight draft for collection through the Bank of China.
   A. for   B. against   C. on   D. from
3. The bank who opens the L/C is called _____ .
   A. issuing bank   B. notifying bank   C. establishing bank   D. paying bank
4. Please send us the amendment _____ L/C immediately or we shall not be able to ship your order on time.
   A. of   B. to   C. as to   D. with
5. As the goods are _____ great demand we regret being unable to cover your requirements.
   A. in   B. on   C. of   D. having
6. Our company has 30 years' experience _____ the machinery line.
   A. on   B. in   C. about   D. of
7. We regret to report that a consignment of silk piece goods _____ Order No. 567 has not been delivered.
   A. with   B. for   C. on   D. under
8. _____ your Enquiry No. 123, we are sending you a catalog and a sample book for your reference.
   A. According   B. As per   C. As   D. About
9. We are sending you the samples _____ requested.
   A. be   B. are   C. as   D. for
10. We would like to take this _____ to establish business relations with you.
    A. opening   B. opportunity   C. step   D. advantage

Ⅱ. Translate the Following Sentence
1. 我们愿意在平等互利、互通有无的基础上与贵公司建立业务联系。
2. 我们的惯例是接受即期付款交单而不是信用证。因此，对这笔交易和以后的交易，我们希望你能接受付款交单的支付条件。
3. 在随附的单子上我们列出了关于包装的具体要求，请你方务必照办。
4. 请报 CIF 温哥华最低价，包括我方 5% 的佣金。
5. 随函寄去我们的报价，此报价有效期仅为两周。
6. Insurance on the goods shall be covered by us for 110% of the CIF value, and any extra premium for additional coverage, if required, shall be borne by the buyers.

7. We are sorry to say that the quality of your shipment for our order No. 758 has been found not in conformity with the agreed specification.
8. With wide and varied experience in this trade, we convinced that we can handle as an agent the goods you are exporting in the most effective manner.
9. We are very happy to place an order on the following goods basing on the condition that you must supply products your quotation.
10. We would ask you to cooperate with us in advancing the shipment to the end of September to enable us to catch the brisk demand in Christmas.

Ⅲ. Translate the Following Letters
1. Dear Sirs,
   We have obtained your name and address from Aristo Shoes, Milan, and we are writing to enquire whether you would be willing to establish business relations with us. We have been importers of shoes for many years. At present, We are interested in extending our, range and would appreciate your catalogues and quotations. If your prices are competitive we would expect to transact a significant volume of business. We look forward to your early reply.
   Very truly yours

2. 敬启者：
   布朗宁父子公司的指示已通过香港办事处收到，我们已开出了以你方为收益人的金额是 55 000 美元的不可撤销信用证，有效期至 11 月 30 日。你们有权就布朗宁父子公司的 2 000 吨钢向我按金额开出期限为 60 天的汇票。
   你们的汇票必须随附下列单据，这些单据将在我们承兑汇票时提交我们：提单一式三份、商业发票、保险单和原产地证。
   如你方履行信用证的条款，我方将承兑并在到期时兑付本信用证项下的汇票。另外，如有要求，我们还可以按现行利率提供贴现的便利。

Ⅳ. Fill in the Blanks with the Suitable Words
1. We should appreciate _____ if you would quote us your lowest price.
2. You may refer _____ the catalogue _____ complete details of our mobile phone.
3. The buyer will only accept a clean and shipped Bill of Lading made out _____ order.
4. Any delay _____ delivery will cause us much inconvenience.
5. Our garments should be packed _____ special water-proof cases.
6. Our quotation _____ groundnuts is valid _____ five days.
7. The S. S. "Haihe" is scheduled to sail _____ Shanghai _____ the port of destination about April 10.
8. We are sending you herewith the required invoice _____ triplicate.
9. Extra premium will be _____ your account.
10. We are glad to inform you that the goods _____ Contract NO. 6732 have arrived here _____ good condition.
11. You are not supposed to duplicate our design _____ our written approval.
12. If any of the items in the booklet are _____ interest to you, please let us have your specific enquiry.
13. The goods have been ready _____ shipment _____ a long time, but we still ha-

ven't received your L/C.

14. The insurance will be responsible _____ the claim as far as it is _____ the scope of cover.
15. _____ examination, we have found that some of the cases are severely damaged.
16. We would like to pay you a commission _____ 5%.
17. We can not make you an offer as the goods are _____ of stock.
18. Dear Sirs,

    We refer to your L/C No. 157 _____ Glazed Wall Tiles, which we have just _____.

    Please _____ for this article we do not cover Breakage. You have to, therefore, delete the word "Breakage" from the insurance _____ in the _____.

    Furthermore, we wish to point out that for such articles as window glass, porcelains, etc, even if _____ Risk of Breakage has been insured, the cover is subject _____ a franchise of 5%. In other words, if the breakage is surveyed to be less than 5%, no _____ for damage will be _____.

    We trust that the position is now clear. Please cable the _____ at once.

Ⅴ. Write a letter in English asking for amendments to the following letter of credit by checking it with the given contract terms.

Eastern Bank
    Date: April 14, 2002
    TO: Bank of China, Tianjin

We hereby open our revocable Letter of Credit No. LC5123 in favour of Tianjin Textiles Corporation for account of Vancouver Trading Company up to an aggregate amount of HK $ 16 000.00 (Say HK Dollars Sixteen Thousand Only) CIF Vancouver for 100% of the invoice value relative to the shipment of: 8 000 pieces of Art. No. 81000 printed Shirting 30×36, 72×69, 35/6×42 yards as per Contract NO. 1098 dated April 9, 2002.

Shipment from China port to Vancouver. Drafts to be drawn at sight on our bank and accompanied by the following documents, marked "×":

(×) Bill of Lading in triplicate made out to our order quoting L/C No. 5123, marked FREIGHT PAID.

(×) Signed Commercial Invoice in triplicate.

(×) One original Marine Insurance Policy or Certificate for 110% full invoice value covering All Risks and War Risk, and TPND with claims shipments are allowed.

⑤Transshipment is prohibited.

Shipment must be effected not later than July 31, 2002.

Draft (s) drawn under their credit must be negotiated in China on or before August 15, 2002.

合同主要条款：
卖方：天津纺织公司
买方：温哥华贸易公司

商品名称：81000 号印花布

规格：30×36，72×69，35/6×42 码①

数量：8 000 码

单价：CIF 温哥华每码 2 加元

总值：16 000.00 加元

装运期：2002 年 7 月 31 日前自中国港口至温哥华，从 6 月开始按月等量分两批装运，不允许转船。

付款条件：凭不可撤销即期信用证付款，于装运期前 1 个月开到卖方，并于最后装运期后 15 天内在中国议付有效。

保险：由卖方根据中国人民保险公司 1981 年 1 月 1 日中国保险条款按发票金额的 110% 投保一切险和战争险。

合同号码：1098

---

① 1 码 = 0.914 4 米。

练习答案
Key to Exercises

Chapter 1

II.
1. 信内地址
2. 参考编号
3. 半平头式
4. 事由
5. 结尾敬语
6. 附件
7. attention line
8. left margin
9. indented format
10. the semi-blocked format
11. 包裹邮件
12. 赠阅本
13. 印刷品
14. with compliments
15. sample post

III.

Manley Ventilations PLC
22 Warden Hill Street, Padiham, Burnley BRO 1 RQ, England
Tel：3021 4567 Fax：0321 6789
Website：manley@bigbiz.co.uk

September 21, 2009

Atomic Shielding International
234 Park Avenue, Cranford, NJ07015 USA
Tel：973 778-1234 Fax：973 778-4321
Dear Sirs,

Household Porcelain Articles

  We have received your letter dated September 2, 2009. We are very much interested in your household porcelain articles produced by your company.

  We shall greatly appreciate it if you will kindly forward us some samples and relative pamphlets for our inspection.

  Thank you for your attention to this matter and looking forward to your early reply.

Yours faithfully,
Manley Ventilations PLC

Ⅳ.

Manley Ventilations PLC
22 Warden Hill Street
Padiham, Burnley BRO 1 RQ
England

Atomic Shielding International
234 Park Avenue
Cranford, NJ07015
USA

Ⅴ.

Indented form:

ZHEJIANG YIWU GLASSWARE PRODUCT LIMITED CO.
19 North Zhongshan Road, Yiwu, Zhejiang, 322000, China
Telephone No. 86-0579-88957213
E-mail: ywglass@hotmail.com

May 10, 2016

Fox International Co.
   150 Fifth Avenue, New York
     NY231, USA

Dear sirs,

Re: Glassware products

    The glass sample you need was sent to you on May 8. It has been very popular in Europe and America market. Please send us order information as soon as you received the sample.

    Thank you for your attention.

Yours faithfully,
Zhejiang Yiwu Glassware Product Co., Ltd.

Block form:

ZHEJIANG YIWU GLASSWARE PRODUCT LIMITED CO.

19 North Zhongshan Road, Yiwu, Zhejiang, 322000, China
Telephone No. 86-0579-88957213
E-mail: ywglass@hotmail.com

May 10, 2016

Fox International Co.
150 Fifth Avenue, New York
NY231, USA

Dear sirs,
Re: Glassware products

The glass sample you need was sent to you on May 8. It has been very popular in Europe and America market. Please send us order information as soon as you received the sample.

Thank you for your attention.

Yours faithfully,
Zhejiang Yiwu Glassware Product Co., Ltd.

Semi-block form with indented paragraphs:

ZHEJIANG YIWU GLASSWARE PRODUCT LIMITED CO.
19 North Zhongshan Road, Yiwu, Zhejiang, 322000, China
Telephone No. 86-0579-88957213
E-mail: ywglass@hotmail.com

May 10, 2016

Fox International Co.
150 Fifth Avenue, New York
NY231, USA

Dear sirs,

Re: Glassware products

The glass sample you need was sent to you on May 8. It has been very popular in Europe and America market. Please send us order information as soon as you received the sample.

Thank you for your attention.

Yours faithfully,
Zhejiang Yiwu Glassware Product Co., Ltd.

Chapter 2

II.

1. 与……相一致
2. 与……联系
3. 业务伙伴
4. 开立账户
5. 询购,询问
6. Commercial Counselor's Office
7. financial position
8. be in the market for
9. at sb.'s convenience
10. after-sale service

III.
expand, do with, with, concerns, importing, enclosed, Having, As to, standing, to

IV.
1. 我们想知道订货 2 000 打,能给多少优惠。
2. 贵方 2 月 23 日函悉,并已转交了上海分公司。他们会直接答复你们,因为你所询问的商品是他们经营的。
3. 我们已经经营金属矿产多年,希望能有机会与贵公司合作。

4. 我们相信通过双方的努力，贸易往来定会朝着互利的方向发展。

5. 根据要求，兹另封航邮货号 1025 和 1026 样品一份，以供参考。

6. 如果贵方能与我方合作，不胜感激。

7. The attached pamphlet will give you complete information on our vacuum cleaners.

8. The Overseas Department of local Bank of China recommended that you are interested in establishing business relations with a company in China to promote your light industry products.

9. According to your request, we are sending samples of our new products now, hoping they can arrive at your place in time.

10. Please notice us the price, terms and quantities you can supply us with the following products.

V.

We write to introduce ourselves as one of the largest exporters in China of a wide range of Machinery and Equipment. We enclose a copy of our latest catalogue covering the details of all the items available at present, and hope some of these items will be of interest to you.

It will be a great pleasure to receive your inquires for any of the items against which we will send you our lowest quotations.

Should, by chance, your corporation not deal with the import of the goods mentioned above, we would be most grateful if this letter could be forwarded to the correct import company.

We are looking forward to your favorable and prompt reply.

VI.

Date：April 20

Foothill Enterprises Trade Development Co., Ltd.
Taiz Street
P. O. Box 22789
Sana'a Republic of Yemen
Dear Sirs,

Your company has been introduced to us by Commercial Counselor's Office of your embassy in Beijing as a prospective buyer of arts & crafts.

In order to introduce our products to the Middle East, we are writing to you in the hope of establishing trade relations.

The main line of our business covers the export of chinaware of superb quality, fashionable design and competitive price, which enjoys a good reputation all over the world. For your information, we are enclosing an illustrated catalogue and the latest. Samples and quotations will be airmailed to you upon receipt of your specific inquiries.

Looking forward to your early reply.

Yours faithfully,

Chapter 3

II.

1. 数量折扣
2. 损害信誉
3. 享有信誉
4. 原价

5. 先行价格
6. special discount
7. under separate cover
8. fair average quality
9. shipping papers
10. a ready market

Ⅲ.

in, for, in, for, on, by, prompt, captioned, current, conclude, assure, annual demand, a win-win, sincerely, appreciate, due to, similar, main, sets, margin, requirements

Ⅳ.

1. 易碎物品须小心装卸。
2. 从 ABC 公司处得知贵公司现能供应水果和干果。
3. 一旦收到贵方具体询盘，我们将立即给你们报最优惠的拉格斯到岸价。
4. 关于支付条件，我们需要不可撤销的凭即期汇票支付的信用证。
5. 随函附上根据贵方第 16 号询价单所开的报价单，期待贵方确认。
6. As demand for our tea has been increasing since last year, we are unable to make you the offer as requested.
7. We have quoted our most favorable prices so that we cannot be able to entertain any counter offer.
8. We are favorable to your proposal.
9. We have been suggested by one of our business partners to have your help.
10. As you know we are a state-owned company handling this kind of items for many years.
11. The price of the product has been lowered by 20% due to the strong competition.
12. Please send us your quotation for 7 inches Teddy Bear in grey color packed in board carton, every dozen per carton on a FOB basis.
13. We would like to draw your attention to the potential market.
14. As soon as we receive your competitive offer, we will place our order for 500 dozens of electronic toy cars with you.
15. You are recommended to us by our partner in Silicon Valley in reply to our inquiry for database system software.

Ⅴ.

We are interested to buy large quantities of Iron Nails of all sizes and should be obliged if you would give us a quotation per metric ton CIF Lagos, Nigeria. It would also be appreciated if samples and/or brochure could be forwarded to us. We used to purchase this article from other sources but we now prefer to buy from your corporation because we are given to understand you are able to supply larger quantities at more attractive prices. Besides, we have confidence in the quality of Chinese products.

Chapter 4

Ⅱ.

1. 做出让步
2. 装运
3. 实盘
4. 延长报盘
5. be in line with
6. raise the price by 8%
7. accept a counter-offer
8. inquiry list

Ⅲ.

from, for, for, to, on, within, from, in, to, of, of, to, of, to, at, in, from, for, offer, of

Ⅳ.

1. 尽管本公司无法满足贵方的特殊要求，但我们仍寄送另一份报价单给贵方。
2. 兹报实盘，以我方时间7月10日星期二下午5时以前收到为有效。
3. 请接受此难得再有的报盘。最近可望有大笔订单自美国方面来，届时将导致价格猛涨。
4. 我方的产品质量好、价格合理，因此相信贵方能大量订货。
5. 我们正在仔细研究贵方报盘，希望将此盘保留到月底有效。
6. This offer is firm for five days.
7. Our offer is subject to change without notice.
8. If you think this offer is acceptable, please cable us in order that we can confirm it.
9. In order to start the concrete business between us, we are glad to make you a special offer, subject to our final confirmation.
10. If you reduce by 3% the price of quotation sheet dated September 3, we are desirous of accepting your offer.

Ⅴ.

We have carefully studied your letter of 18th September. As our two firms have done business with each other for so many years, we should like to grant your request to lower the prices of our products. But there are difficulties. Our cost of raw materials has risen sharply in the past four months and to reduce prices by 20% you mention could not be done without considerably lowering our standards of quality. This is something we are not prepared to do. Instead of 20% reduction on underwear, we suggest a reduction of 15% on all lines on order for $ 5 000 or more. On order of this size we could manage to make the reduction without lowering our standards.

Ⅵ.

1.

Dear Adam,

We thank you for your letter asking for our new catalogues and shall be glad to enter into business relations with your firm.

Complying with your request, we are sending you under separate cover our latest catalogues and price list covering our exports available at present and hope that you will find many items in it which interest you.

We look forward to receiving your inquiries soon.

Sincerely,
Frank

2.

Dear Frank,

Thanks for your information. We are interested to buy large quantities of Angle Grinder and shall appreciate it if you would give us the best FOB Ningbo price. I have now listed below the models that are of interest:

AG105L, AG203S, AG880H

Please send us some samples for testing. We will pay the sample fees.

We are waiting for your reply.

Best Regards,
Adam

3.

Dear Adam,

With reference to your last inquiry, we have already forwarded you the samples and take pleasure in making the following offer:

Art No. AG105L: USD 25.30/PC FOB Ningbo;

Art No. AG203S: USD 30.50/PC FOB Ningbo;

Art No. AG880H: USD 13.00/PC FOB Ningbo.

Please feel free to contact us if you have any question.

Sincerely,
Frank

4.

Dear Frank,

We have already done a test for the samples, I have to say that the quality and function are really good.

But comparing to the price which is showed in the price list, the new price has not changed much. We hope you can give us a discount of 5% on the basis of the order, 5 000 pieces of Angle Grinder.

Best Regards,
Adam

5.

Dear Adam,

The new price has already reached to the bottom of price range. You can not buy Angle Grinder of similar quality at such a price anywhere else. However, as this is the first time to do business with you, we accept your request to give you a discount of 5%.

As we have received large numbers of orders from our clients, it is quite probable that our present stock may soon run out. We would therefore suggest that you take advantage of this attractive offer.

We look forward to receiving your first order.

Sincerely,
Frank

6.

Dear Frank,

Thank you for your letter of October 8, 2010. We do appreciate your concession and want to accept your revised price and please send us your PI.

Best Regards,
Adam

Chapter 5

Ⅱ.

1. 熟练工人
2. 竖放
3. 双边贸易
4. 双边清算
5. 海运保单
6. collecting bill
7. closing rate
8. export loan
9. amount of exports
10. written document

Ⅲ.

received, Order, confirming, accept, from, owing, from, amended, appreciated.

Ⅳ.

1. 现附上我方第4567号合同正本两份，请会签，并早日寄回一份。

2. 这笔交易的达成并不意味着结束，它仅仅是个开端，并且是我们之间长期友好业务关系的开端。

3. 请按下列颜色搭配供货，最好红、黄、绿、蓝及棕色各6打。

4. 由于我方目前已承担过多的订单，因此无法接受今年之内交货的新订单。

5. 参阅我方5月15日675号订单，由于我方至今尚未收到有关贵方交货的任何消息，故我方不得不取消该订单。

6. Please deliver the following goods according to your quotations and samples sent us on June 10.

7. The recent exceptional demand for our fax machines makes it impossible to promise delivery of any further orders before November 30.

8. We place this order on the clear understanding that the consignment is dispatched in time to reach us by May 31, and reserve the right to cancel and refuse delivery after this date.

9. As supplies of the items are becoming difficult to obtain, we have no alternative but to decline your order.

10. As you have failed to deliver within the specified time, we have to cancel our order.

Ⅴ.

Our buyers have agreed to allow partial shipments for this order, which will enable you to make shipment with the three months from April to June. If you could spread our shipments by forwarding a proportionate quantity each month instead of letting the whole lot of 100MT be congested into the same month, it would be of much assistance to our customers. It might interest you to know that the buyers concerned are among the leading importers of edible oils in this city. It is very likely that they might want to duplicate their order before the month is out.

Ⅵ.

Andy Burns,

你方2015年10月19日电邮收悉，经考虑，我方愿意接受你方报盘如下：

Article No. DR2010 USD 19.00 CIF Toronto per set
Article No. DR2202 USD 23.80 CIF Toronto per set
Article No. DR2211 USD 30.00 CIF Toronto per set
Article No. DR2401 USD 23.50 CIF Toronto per set

很乐于接受你方来函及其中的价格和条款，随函附 NE0911 订单，请查收。期待更多合作。

祝好

Chapter 6

Ⅱ.
1. 金融工具
2. 向某人开出汇票
3. 放单给受票人
4. 一式两份
5. 海运保险
6. terms of payment
7. commercial credit
8. pay off the trade debt

Ⅲ.
1. in the amount of, within, after, no, settle, credit, supply, an obligation, means, owed to, reputation
2. by 3. doing 4. on 5. upon 6. paid by, by 7. on 8. sight 9. acceptable to 10. about 11. view

Ⅳ.
1. 我们已收到有关信用证，但发现以下事项不符合要求。
2. 信用证必须由我方公司接受的银行加以保兑。
3. 在收到信用证后的一个月内，你们至少应装运这笔订货的一半。
4. 由于我们的疏忽，开立信用证有错误，很抱歉。
5. 信用证 121 号修改书未到，请立即改信，以便早日装运，电复。
6. In order to save a lot of expenses on opening the L/C, we will remit you the full amount by T/T when the goods purchased by us are ready for shipment and the freight space is booked.
7. We regret to inform you that it is our usual practice of business not to accept payment by D/A.
8. You have to pay us 30% amount for deposit by T/T in 7 days after signing the contract, and the remaining part on collection basis, documents will be released against payment at sight.
9. We require confirmed and irrevocable L/C available by draft at sight against a full set of shipping documents presented to the negotiating bank at the port of loading.
10. You shall establish the covering letter of credit before 20th April, 2010, failing which we reserve the right to rescind the contract without further notice.

Ⅴ.

we shall retain the right to accept a waived of discrepancies from the applicant and, subject to such wavier being acceptable to us, to release documents against that waiver without reference to the presenter provided that no written instructions to the contrary have been received by us from presenter before the release, instruction shall not constitute a failure on our part to hold the documents at the presenter's risk and disposal, and we will have no liability to the presenter in respect of any such release.

Ⅵ.

事由：关于你方新产品移动硬盘一事

感谢你方 5 月 8 日来函关于移动硬盘一事。我方对此产品很感兴趣，希望能进一步商议。我方已注意到贵公司希望用信用证付款，但对第一笔订单我们还是建议承兑交单，一旦该产品市场需求有保证,我们即会下大量订单。

相信我方建议是检验市场的合理方法,希望贵方愿意与我公司合作。

祝好

Ⅶ.

Dear Sirs,

Thank you for your L/C No. 5676. After checking the L/C, we have found quite a few discrepancies, and would therefore request you to make the following amendments:

1. The amount in words should read "Say Canadian Dollars Two thousand Seven Hundred And Fifty Only".

2. The commission should be 2%, not 3%.

3. "130% of invoice value" should read "110% of invoice value".

4. Delete "by direct steamer" and put in "allowing transshipment".

5. The Credit is valid until "January 15, 2003" instead of "January 15, 2002".

As the date of shipment is drawing near, please send us the L/C amendments as soon as possible so that we can effect shipment in time.

Chapter 7

Ⅱ.

1. 销售包装
2. 防破碎
3. 整箱货
4. 压缩包装
5. 集装包
6. 定牌
7. seaworthy packing
8. customary packing
9. assortment list
10. waterproof paper
11. indicative marks
12. nude cargo

Ⅲ.

concerning, packing, acknowledge, covered with, strapped, with, seaworthy, transportation, outer, mark, number, directive, fulfill

Ⅳ.

1. 每套茶具必须用透明塑料袋包好,固定在硬质泡沫塑料衬垫里,放在硬纸板箱中,外用尼龙袋加固。

2. 我们的包装条件是:捆包,每包内含30束,用防水材料和双层麻布包裹,并用4条钢带捆紧。每束重5磅,用牛皮纸包裹,衬以单层塑料薄膜。

3. 纸板箱的尺码是15cm×30cm×50cm,体积约0.023立方米,净重21公斤,毛重22公斤,皮重1公斤,箱外的唛头除印有毛重、净重及皮重外,还须印有"中国制造"的字样。

4. 每一纸板箱衬以塑料纸,全箱用铁箍加固,以防内装货物受潮及因粗暴搬运可能引起的损坏。

5. Please pack the towels in a polythene bag, 3 pieces in different colors to a cardboard box, a dozen cardboard boxes to a carton with two iron hoops outside.

6. The shipping mark of this shipment is a triangle, with the initials of our corporation stenciled inside.

7. Packed in 3-ply Kraft Paper Bags with PE Liner, 25kg/bag.

8. Every 100 dozens should be packed in a wooden case marked TM and numbered from No. 1 upward.

9. In addition to the gross, net and tare weights, the wording "Made in China" is also stenciled on the package.

10. Cartons are not likely to be mixed with wooden cases while in transport or storage, so that the rate of breakage is lower than that of wooden cases.

V.
Dear Sirs,

In reply to your letter of the 10th May inquiring about the packing of vases, we wish to state as follows:

Each vase packed in a plastic bag first, then in a thick, exquisite paper box, 10 boxes to a cardboard carton padded with foamed plastic. The cartons should be strong enough to withstand rough handling and long ocean transportation. In addition, please mark our initials BOC in a circle, under which the quantity and port of the destination should be indicated. And warning marks such as "Fragile" "This Side Up" should be stenciled on the outer packing.

Please pack the goods strictly according to our requirements to avoid damage during transit. As the selling season is approaching, please expedite shipment for us to catch it.

Yours truly,

Ⅵ.
敬启者:

兹复你方5月26日传真,很遗憾忘记提醒你们关于我们今年在春季广交会上订购的蜜蜂牌红糖的内包装要求。经与客户协商,现提出要求如下:

由于红糖在炎热多雨的季节容易受潮,所以应用牛皮纸包装,内含20个小纸袋装,每个净重1公斤,每两个牛皮纸袋放进一个纸箱,内衬防水纸。

希望贵方能够接受上述要求,期待着您的早日回复。

此致

Chapter 8

Ⅱ.
1. 航运运输保险
2. 海洋运输货物保险
3. 邮包保险
4. 渗漏险
5. 钩损险
6. 战争险
7. 串味险
8. 淡水雨淋险
9. People's Insurance Company of China
10. franchise
11. Free Particular Average
12. With Particular Average
13. All Risks
14. insurance agent
15. insurance amount
16. insurance premium
17. insurance certificate
18. insurance policy
19. insurance coverage
20. floating policy

Ⅲ.
to, for, through, remain, see, for, against, at, for our account, arrange

Ⅳ.

1. 如果货物发生损坏，你们可以向保险公司提出索赔，他们将迅速办理。

2. 我们的保险公司是一家享有理赔迅速、处理公平声誉的国有企业，并在全世界各主要港口和地区都有代理。

3. 贵方客户要求投保到内陆城市的请求可以接受，但条件是由此导致的额外保险费要由买方自行承担。在客户没有明确指示的情况下，我们一般投保水渍险和战争险。倘若你方想投保一切险，我们可以提供这种险别，但保险费率要稍高一些。

4. In order to protect the goods against possible loss in case of such perils, the buyer or seller, before the transportation of the goods, usually applies to an insurance company for insurance covering the goods in transit.

5. This class of goods is sold with a franchise of 5%.

6. If you wish to secure protection against T. P. N. D., we may do accordingly upon receipt your payment of an additional premium.

7. Our insurance company enjoys high prestige in settling claims promptly and equitably and has agents in main ports and regions all over the world.

8. The premium for Breakage is 5%. If you would like to insure against Breakage, we will effect it for your account.

9. Should the consignment experience any damage, you may, within 30 days after its arrival at the port of destination, approach the insurance agents at your end and file your claim with them, which is to be supported by a surveyor report.

10. We adopt the "warehouse to warehouse clause", which is commonly used in international insurance.

Ⅴ.

Credits should stipulate the type of insurance required and, if any, the additional risks which are to be covered. Imprecise terms such as "usual risks" or "customary risks" should not be used; if they are used, banks will accept insurance documents as presented, without responsibility for any risks not being covered.

Ⅵ.

Dear Sirs,

I write to inform you that the goods you sent on M. V. "Yellow River" from Bombay to London arrived on time but were found on arrival to be damaged.

Your agent inspected the damage and reported that the goods in containers No. 3 and No. 4 were damaged even though they had been packed according to your instructions. The goods were then inspected by a third party who took photograph of the damaged items and wrote a detailed report.

I hereby enclose the report and photograph. We would like to make a claim for the costs of replacing the damaged items. This matter is urgent as our own customers are waiting for the products that have been damaged and we need to replace them as soon as possible also by air freight.

We await your immediate attention to this matter and a prompt reply with further instructions.

Yours faithfully,

Chapter 9

Ⅱ.
1. 船舱检验证书
2. 复检
3. 商品检验
4. 检验报告
5. Inspection Certificate of Quality
6. Inspection Certificate of Weight or Quantity
7. Inspection Certificate of Packing
8. Sanitary Inspection Certificate
9. Inspection Certificate of Damaged Cargo
10. inspection fees

Ⅲ.
1. in, to
2. against, for, under
3. in, with
4. look into
5. for your reference
6. discrepancy.

Ⅳ.
1. 现随函寄去检验报告一份,供参考。并请早日解决此案。
2. 由于该货质量不适销我处市场,我方对该货不感兴趣。
3. 相信贵方对这个问题一定会给予认真考虑,并设法防止再次发生这样的延迟事故。
4. 检验由中国进出口商品检验局执行。该局检验公正,在国际上享有盛誉。
5. We feel that the quality certificates issued by your inspection bureau are not entirely trustworthy.
6. We found that the quality of the shipped goods was not conform with those specified in the agreement.
7. Upon examination, we found that many of the goods were severely damaged, though the cases themselves show no trace of damage.
8. We have looked into the matter thoroughly but the only explanation is that labels were mixed.
9. We will examine the goods after the completion of unloading.
10. We can not but hold you responsible for the losses thus sustained.

Ⅴ.
Dear Sirs,

Re: Our Order No. 234 for 500MT Soybean

We have just received the captioned goods yesterday. But Case 20 was found to be 15 packages short. As the case was in good shape and did not appear to have been tampered with, we surmise that they must have been short-shipped, and the Survey Report from Guangzhou Commodity Inspection Bureau evidencing that the unloaded goods was short weight 50 MT.

On the basis of the GCIB's Survey Report, we hereby register a claim with you for $ 220 in all.

We are enclosing the Survey Report and looking forward to the settlement at an early date.

Yours faithfully,

Ⅵ.

1. C 2. D 3. D 4. A 5. A 6. C 7. B

Chapter 10

Ⅱ.

1. 装运通知   2. 清洁已装船提单
3. 允许转船和分批装运   4. 备妥待运
5. 商业发票   6. 舱位
7. 装货港   8. 运输方式
9. shipment price   10. shipment by installments
11. shipment per sample   12. transit shipment

Ⅲ.

1. b 2. c 3. b 4. c 5. b 6. d 7. b 8. c 9. d 10. c

Ⅳ.

1. 当卖方通知货物已装船时，应说明下列交易细节：合同号/订单号/信用证号、货物名称或品名、订单数量、船名、预计开船时间和到达时间、所附装运单据等。

2. 请务必按时装运，并告知船名、起航日期及预计抵港日期，以便安排销售。

3. 由于停靠在我港的直达轮一个月只有一趟，货物只能在下个月发运。

4. 借此告知贵方上述货物已由××轮装运，该轮将于明天起航前往贵方港口。随函附有关货物的装运单据一套，请查收。

5. As these goods are apt to break if not handle with care in transportation, we suggest that the parcel should be sent by container vessel, to avoid possible damage in loading and discharge.

6. We are glad to inform you that your consignment of 100 sets of TV sets has been loaded on S.S. "East Wind", which is due to sail for NewYork on March 25 the estimated time of arrival is on April 10.

Ⅴ.

Dear Sirs,

We are in receipt of your letter of December 15, 2010. We regret very much to inform you that, despite great efforts made by us, we are still unable to book space on a direct vessel sailing for Marseille. The shipping company here told us that, for the time being, there is no regular vessel sailing between ports in China and Marseille. Therefore it is very difficult for us to ship these 1 000 metric tons of sugar to Marseille direct.

In view of the difficult situation faced by us, please allow transshipment at Hong Kong where arrangements can easily be made for transshipment. Your agreement to our requests and your understanding of our position will be highly appreciated.

Yours faithfully,

Ⅵ.

关于延迟交货的投诉

敬启者：

很遗憾，我们要投诉关于7月2日我方订购的文件柜推迟交货一事。尽管你们保证一周内交货，但直到今天早上我们都没有收到。考虑到一周内能发货，我们才下的订单。

不幸的是以往也有几次类似的耽搁，最近几个月频繁发生此类事件使我们不得不说，在此条件下我们无法继续双方的交易。

我们觉得有必要表明我们的想法，因为我们无法给客户一个确切的发货期，除非供货商能给我们明确的答复，希望你们能理解我们的处境，并且从现在起及时完成我方订单。

祝好

Chapter 11

II.

1. breach of a contract
2. arbitration clauses
3. file a claim
4. claim for short weight
5. refuse the claim
6. inferior quality
7. 仲裁裁决
8. 提起诉讼
9. 短交
10. 理赔

III.

Report, Bureau, examination, due, responsible, basis, lodge, against, for, encloseing, forward, early

IV.

1. 我们希望你不要将此事视为违约，也不要提出索赔，因为这些损失是可以忽略不计的。

2. 我们仔细进行了调查，但认为责任不在我们。我方按照合同对货物进行包装，检验证明书表明货物状况良好，清洁提单进一步证明了这一点。建议贵方向保险公司提出索赔，对此我方将尽力协助。

3. 我方会认真对待客户的意见，并立即安排给你们换货。如能将有问题的产品退给我们，我们将不胜感激，运费由我方承担。

4. 短重索赔是由包装破损或短装引起的；延期索赔是对卖方没有按时装运货物而提出的索赔。品质索赔是在货物质量低劣或是质量改变的条件下发生的。

5. 任何有关该产品质量问题的申诉应该在货物到达后的15天内提出。

6. Please inform us soon whether you can deliver the goods by the end of July. If your answer is the negative, we shall have to cancel the order as we cannot wait any longer.

7. The intact packing evidenced that the goods were damaged before shipment.

8. We apologize for your trouble and promise to execute your future orders with maximum care and efficiency.

9. In view of our friendly business relations, we are prepared to meet your claim for the 25 tons shortage weight.

10. We regret to learn from your letter of Sep. 15 that 3 cases out of the 10 shipped against your order No. 100 arrived in a badly damaged condition. As the goods were packed with the greatest care we can only presume that the cases have been roughly handled.

V.

Dear Sirs,

We enclose herewith Survey Report No. 20 issued by Wuxi Commodity Inspection Bureau certifying that the quality of the goods ordered is much inferior to that of the sample sent previously. As this consignment is entirely useless to us, you are requested, therefore, to return us the invoice value and inspection charges involved, totaling $ 5 000.

Ⅵ.

关于短重和产品质量低劣的索赔

我方已收到由"晨星"号装运的第 P2001 号订单的货物。根据本地商品检验局开具的检验报告显示，868 公斤短缺。由于包装完整，所以毫无疑问，短缺发生在装运之前。此外，该批货物要比先前你给我方的样品质量差很多。在此情况下，我们只好提出索赔如下：

索赔号	索赔原因	金额
GM-30	短重	USD 1 120.85
GM-40	质量	USD 1 028.60
加上检验费		USD 60
总计		USD 2 209.45

随函附 3018 号检验报告以及索赔说明一份，希望贵方对此事予以重视并尽快理赔。

祝好

Chapter 12

Ⅱ.

1. 主要进口商
2. 物有所值
3. 售后服务
4. 人员推销
5. network marketing
6. business promotion
7. public relations

Ⅲ.

1. 为了促进销售，我们随函附寄了样品册供你参考。
2. 如果贵方对我们的产品感兴趣，请向我们发具体询盘。
3. 如果贵方对我们其中的产品感兴趣，请立即告知我们。
4. 很高兴能得到您对我们销售产品的评价。
5. We request you to make a careful comparison of these goods, both in respect to quality and prices, with those you are now buying elsewhere.
6. We would be glad to have the opportunity of supplying any of these goods which would be most suited to your needs.
7. We can assure you that, for any trial order you may send us, the goods will be carefully selected as if you personally made the choice.
8. This is the best-selling item in this line. Please tell us in case you are interested.
9. As this item is handled by our Shanghai Office, please get in touch with them directly.
10. We have pleasure of introducing ourselves to you with the hope that we may have an opportunity of cooperation with you in your business extension.

Ⅳ.

designed, identify, tastes, inappropriate, consideration, for, against, while, regarding, evaluated

Ⅴ.

What is marketing? What does the word marketing mean? Many people think of marketing only as selling and advertising, but actually, marketing is a set of activities undertaken to stimulate satisfactory exchanges of goods and services. A marketing effort may begin with finding out what product people want, or it may begin with stimulating a new want and then satisfying it. Marketing activities include such things as marketing research, retailing, sales force management, advertising, and transportation.

Ⅵ.
(1) advertisement (2) position (3) experience (4) responsible (5) CV
(6) referees (7) information (8) interviews (9) convenient (10) forward
(11) hearing

Chapter 13

Ⅱ.
1. 运输代理人
2. 保险代理人
3. 寄售协议
4. 包销协议
5. agency agreement
6. agency commission
7. sole agency
8. commission agent
9. general agent
10. advertising agent

Ⅲ.
1. with, concluded, nor, under
2. prevailing, on
3. In case, terminate

Ⅳ.
1. 我们很高兴能够作为你的独家代理,这对我们双方都是双赢的。
2. 作为独家代理,你可以很容易控制整个市场。
3. 我们希望能够在贵国销售手工工具,并且希望能够联系某个公司或个人作为我们的代理。
4. 鉴于你们对化妆品的需求稳步上升,我们决定委托贵方在贵国经营我方的出口业务。
5. 我们注意到,在招揽订单中你方曾不止一次超越你方代理的地区范围,希望不再发生这类违反协议规定的事情。
6. The agency agreement has been drawn up for the duration for one year, automatically renewable on expiration for similar period unless written notice is given to the contrary.
7. To be our sole agent, you could not sell similar products from other manufactures without our prior approval.
8. We are taking your request of acting as our sole agent into account and at the same time we are keen to know your plan for promoting our products.
9. We hope you will consider increasing our commission to accommodate the difficulty in selling this type of equipment, which is entirely new in our district.
10. While appreciating your inquiry for leather shoes, we wish to inform you that this item is under the exclusivity of ABC Co. in your district. We regret being unable to make you an offer directly at present. You may contact them for your requirement.

Ⅴ.
This Agreement, when duly signed by the parties concerned, shall remain in force for 2 years

to be effective as from January 1, 2009 to December 31, 2010. If no written objection is raised by either party one month before its expiry, this agreement will be automatically extended for an other year. Should one of the parties fail to comply with the terms and conditions of the Agreement, the other party is entitled to terminate the Agreement.

Ⅵ.

(1) ~ (6): h-recommendation; d-terms; g-principals; c-factory; b-rates

(7) ~ (11): e-documentation; f-commission; j-delcredere; i-offer; k-brochure.

Chapter 14

Ⅱ.

1. 遵从的法律
2. 订约缘由
3. 投标合同
4. 许可证协议
5. bilateral agreement
6. compensation trade contract
7. written contract
8. body of the contract
9. force majeure
10. valid of the contract

Ⅲ.

1. a 2. c 3. a 4. d 5. d 6. c 7. c 8. a 9. c 10. d

Ⅳ.

1. 有关或执行本售货确认书的一切争议应当友好协商。

2. 本合同以中英文两种文字书写,两种文字具同等效力,但在对其解释产生异议时,以中文文本为准。

3. 如缔约方中的每一方都不愿将任何申诉提交调解委员会处理,则可由第一方按下文规定提请仲裁解决。

4. ××国××公司(以下简称甲方)与中华人民共和国××公司(以下简称乙方)在平等互利的基础上经过友好协商达成以下协议。

5. 我们很遗憾告知你方,由于你方的不作为,我们只能取消合同,同时对于我们所遭受的损失保留索赔权。

6. The seller shall not be held responsible for late delivery or non-delivery of the goods owing to generally recognized Force Majeure causes.

7. The party, who sets up a breach of the contract, shall be under a duty to take all necessary measures to mitigate the loss which has occurred.

8. In case one party fails to carry out the contract, the other party is entitled to cancel the contract.

9. A contract is an agreement that creates an obligation, that is a binding, legally enforceable agreement between two or more competent parties.

10. The contract comes into effect today, we can't go back on our word now.

Ⅴ.

Contract No. 10/109

Date: February 19, 2011

Sellers: Jiangsu foodstuffs Imp&Exp Corp.

Buyers: Vancouver Foodstuffs Company, Canada

Thus contract is made by and between the Buyers and the Sellers, whereby the Buyers agree to buy and the Sellers agree to sell the under-mentioned commodity on the terms and conditions stipulated below:

Commodity: Walnutmeat of first grade

Specifications: First grade

Quantity: 30MT

Unit Price: US $ 250 per metric ton

Total Value: US $ 7 500 (Say seven thousand and five hundred US dollars only)

Packing: Packing in sacks of 100kg each

Insurance: Insured against All Risks and War Risk for 110% of the invoice value as per CIC of January 1, 1981.

Time of Shipment: In three shipment of 10 tons each month, start from April, 2011

Port of Shipment: China port

Port of Destination: Vancouver, Canada

Terms of Payment: By irrevocable L/C to reach the Sellers 30 days before shipment and remain Valid for negotiation in China within 15 days after shipment.

Force Majeure: The Sellers shall not be held liable for failure of delay in delivery of the entire lot or a portion of the Commodity under this contract in consequence of any force majeure incidents.

Ⅵ.

CONTRACT No. 5454

Sellers: Beijing Light Industrial Products Imp. & Exp. Corp.

Buyers: Boston Trading Co., Ltd.

This contract is made by and between the Buyers and the Sellers, whereby the Buyers agree to buy and the Sellers agree to sell the under-mentioned commodity according to the terms and conditions stipulated below:

Commodity: Fountain Pens

Specifications: Model LC001

Quantity: 1 000 dozens

Unit Price: At US $ 19 per dozen CFR Boston

Total Value: US $ 19 000 (Say US Dollars Nineteen Thousand Only)

Packing: In boxes of one dozen each, and 20 boxes to a carton

Shipping Mark: At Sellers' option

Insurance: To be covered by the Buyers

Time of Shipment: During March/April 2002

Port of Shipment: China Port

Port of Destination: Boston

Terms of Payment: By confirmed, irrevocable L/C payable by draft at sight

Done and signed in Beijing on this 18th day of January, 2002.

综合练习题答案
Key to Comprehensive Exercises

Comprehensive Exercises 1

Ⅰ.
1.
(1) 永久性正常贸易关系
(2) 不可撤销信用证
(3) 空白背书
(4) 共同海损
(5) 良好平均品质/大路货
(6) 目的地船上交货
(7) 免赔额/特许经营权
(8) 平安险
(9) 汇票
(10) 拍卖

2.
(1) World Bank
(2) e-commerce/e-business
(3) shipper/consigner
(4) import license
(5) International Chamber of Commerce (ICC)

Ⅱ.
1. D 2. B 3. C 4. B 5. B 6. B 7. A 8. C 9. C 10. C
11. D 12. C 13. C 14. B 15. D 16. B 17. C 18. D 19. C 20. B
21. C 22. A

Ⅲ.
Xinluhua Trading Company Ltd.
Floor 33. Golden Star Mansion. No. 999 Xingda Road
Shanghai China
June 30, 2000
James Brown & Sons
#304-310 Jalan Street, Toronto, Canada
　　ATTN: Daily Articles Department
Dear Sirs,
　　Thank you for your letter and samples sent on June 15. We're glad to inform you that our customers are very satisfied with the test result of your samples, but they are still hesitating at the mo-

ment.

After careful comparison with similar goods, we find your quotation on the high side. The current shampoo market is swollen up with various brands, and quality brands such as Rejoice and Pond's are easily available. These brands have already gained recognition of the local market. In terms of shampoo, many consumers are reluctant to accept new products. As a new brand, the biggest selling point of your product will be its hair care function. Although its quality has already measured up to our customers' requirements, it still needs price advantage in order to open up a market here. Otherwise it can hardly compete against the established brands.

In view of this our customers request you to reduce your original price by 10%. Please consider this and give us a prompt reply.

Yours faithfully,

(Signed)

Ⅳ.

NO.

SELLERS: Beijing Garments Imp./Exp. Corp.

BUYERS: London Trading Co., Ltd.

This Contract is made by and between the Buyers and the Sellers, whereby the agree to buy and the Sellers agree to sell the under-mentioned commodity to the terms and conditions stipulated below:

Commodity	Size	Quantity (doz)	Price per doz CIF London	Amount
Women's Nylon Garments	Small	15	US $ 80.00	US $ 1 200
Women's Nylon Garments	Medium	16	US $ 120.00	US $ 1 920
Women's Nylon Garments	Large	14	US $ 160.00	US $ 2 240

Total Value: US $ 5 360.00

Packing: In boxes of half dozen each and 10 dozens to a carton

Shipping Mark: At Seller's option

Insurance: To be covered by the Sellers against All Risks and War Risk for 110% of the invoice value

Time of Shipment: In December allowing transshipment and partial shipments (During December with transshipment and partial shipments allowed)

Port of Shipment: China port

Port of Destination: London, U.K.

Terms of Payment: By D/P60 days (By D/P at 60 days after sight)

Done and signed in Beijing on November 28, 1999

Ⅴ.

China Trading Corporation

Dear Sirs,

While we thank you for your L/C No. 112235, we regret to say that we have found some discrepancies. You are therefore requested to make the following amendments:

1. The amount both in figures and in words should respectively read "GBP 14 500" (Say Pounds Sterling Fourteen Thousand Five Hundred And Fifty Only);

2. "Form Copenhagen to China port" should read "form China port to Copenhagen";

3. The Bill of Lading should be marked "Freight Prepaid" instead "Freight Collect";

4. Delete the clause "Partial shipments and transshipment prohibited";

5. "This L/C is valid at our counter" should be amended to read "This L/C is valid at your counter";

Please confirm the amendments by fax as soon as possible.

Yours sincerely,

(Signed)

Ⅵ.

1.

折扣是指卖方按照商品的原价给对方一定比率的价格减让。在市场竞争激烈的情况下，此法是加强竞争力的一种手段。折扣的名目比较繁多，有数量折扣、季节性折扣、额外折扣等。具体折扣数额或比例的多少应根据情况而定。当双方确定了折扣比率后，可在买卖合同中明确地表示出来。折扣部分的金额一般是在买方付款时从货款中扣除。

2.

（1）International marketing is important because the world has become globalized. International marking takes place all around us every day and has a major effect on our lives.

（2）There is only a small proportion of service activity in international trade. Because to some extent services are much less tradable than goods.

（3）In executing a contract, both sides should abide by the stipulations in the contract. If one part fails to fulfill all of the obligations, it will bring inconvenience or even loss to anther party.

（4）In international trade time is of the essence, so it is natural that the buyer usually insists that shipment be made before a specified deadline or within a period of time.

（5）Technology transfer is the transfer of systematic knowledge for the manufacture of a product for the application of a process, or for the rending of a service. The elements of the transfer are "human ware" "soft ware" and "hard ware".

Comprehensive Exercises 2

Ⅰ.

1~5 CAACD   6~10 BDDCB   11~15 ABBBB   16~20 CADDB

Ⅱ.

21. draw   22. acceptable   23. available   24. on   25. in   26. subject
27. claim, on   28. at   29. to   30. in, on   31. of   32. than
33. to   34. with   35. to   36. for   37. in   38. of, to
39. in, but   40. in   41. with

Ⅲ.

42. 由于你方的密切合作，我们成功达成了一批交易。

43. 我们正在等待你方早日答复这一询盘。

44. 如果你方能够订购5 000打以上，我们将给予10%的折扣。

45. 此报盘以我方确认为准。

46. 除非你方降价5%，否则不可能达成交易。

47. 我们愿意以此价格向你方报实盘。

48. 感谢你方的还盘，但我方认为你方还价过低。
49. 一经提示，我们一定会兑付你方向我开具的汇票。
50. 我们正在研究你方的报盘，希望将此报盘保留到月底有效。
51. 货物如果转运，我们得多付运费。
52. This is a set of the shipping documents covering the consignment.
53. The additional premium will be for buyer's account.
54. You should have dispatched the goods we ordered last month.
55. Is it possible for you to raise the price by 5%?
56. We will open the letter of credit one month before shipment.

Ⅳ.
Dear Sirs,

We have received your letter of February 1, 2006, requesting us to insure 5 000 pairs of men's leather shoes for your account.

We are pleased to inform you that we have insured the above shipment with the People's Insurance Company of China against All Risks for 110% of the invoice value. The insured amount is $ 30 000.

The insurance policy is being prepared accordingly and will be forwarded to you by the end of this week together with our debit note for the premium.

For your information, the goods will be shipped on S.S. "East Wind", setting sail on February 18 and due to arrive at the port of destination on or about March 10.

Yours faithfully,

Comprehensive Exercises 3

Ⅰ.
    1~5 DACBA   6~10 DADBA   11~15 BACDA   16~20 ACDDC

Ⅱ.
21. under	22. for	23. establish/open
24. payable	25. account	26. with
27. at	28. to	29. up
30. between	31. to	32. to
33. with	34. with	35. satisfactory
36. for	37. by	38. of
39. to	40. from	41. to
42. for, for	43. for	44. as

Ⅲ.
45. 我方不能降到贵方所提出的价格，我们能否各让一半？
46. 请告知高级块状砂糖每公斤的价格，以及在什么付款条件下，你方能大量供货。
47. 为了双方之间能开展具体的业务，我们很高兴向贵方报特盘，以我方最后确认生效。
48. 如果质量和价格令人满意的话，该产品会有很好的销售前景。
49. 贵方拟订购的产品已售尽，我们推荐123号货物作为理想的替代品。
50. 如你方坚持不降价，我们只好从其他地方购买。

51. 汇票已在上海贴现。

52. 如你方能接受付款交单的话，我们将感激不尽。

53. 请确保信用证条款与合同的条款一致，保证无须修改信用证。如要修改信用证，既费时又费钱。

54. 我方所报价格是基于合理的利润。

55. We spent USD one million on the goods.

56. The order is subject to our obtaining the import license.

57. We have booked shipping space on S. S. "Haihe"

58. If no your definiteinstructions, we will cover your goods against W. P. A. and War Risk according to usual practice.

59. There is a shortage of 1 540 kilograms in this shipment.

Ⅳ.
Dear Sirs,

We have received the consignment ex S. S. "Dongfeng" in time and highly appreciate your promptly executing our order.

After a check-up by our staff, it was found that the contents packed in CTN No. 3 wasn't the goods we have ordered. I guess that the shipment was for someone else and packed in CTN No. 3 by mistake.

Since the goods we ordered will be delivered to our customers, it will be appreciated if you replace it and arrange for the immediate dispatch of the replacement.

Enclosed is the contents list of CTN No. 3 with which you could compare our order.

We look forward to your early reply.

Yours sincerely,

Comprehensive Exercises 4

Ⅰ.
　　1~5　BDCCD；6~10　BBDBC

Ⅱ.
　　7, 5, 1, 6, 9, 2, 3, 8, 4

Ⅲ.
　　1. 商会　　　2. 报盘（价）　　3. 还盘　　4. 海关发票　　5. 赊账方式
　　6. 原产地证　7. 进口配额制　　8. 汇票　　9. 本票　　　　10. 保兑信用证

Ⅳ.

1. The Commercial Counsellor's Office of your Embassy in China has informed us that you intend to import lathes from China and we are writing to you in the hope that we may establish business relations with you in this line.

2. We should appreciate it if you could obtain for us all information about the financial and credit standing of James Neils & Co. in London. The reference they have given us is their bank, The Hongkong and Shanghai Banking Corporation.

3. Please be informed that we are one of the largest importers of silk in the world. We have been importing this item from Japan and now intend to extend our business to import the same from

China.

4. We regret being unable to accept your counter-offer. Since we quoted you we have concluded business with many clients at the price originally quoted. Therefore, if you are still in need of this item please place your order without delay.

5. We have received your letter of the 10th August, enclosing S/C No. 90SP-5861 in duplicate against our Order No. 100 for 500 sets of Sewing Machines. Attached hereto is a copy of the said Sales Confirmation, duly countersigned. Please find it in order.

6. For this transaction, we exceptionally agree to make payment by L/C but for future transactions, we would ask for more favourable payment terms, i.e. D/P.

7. We have received your L/C No. ××× against S/C No. ×××, but found its amount is US $ 500 short. You will find the shortage by referring to the said contract. It is hoped that you will make it up at your earliest convenience.

8. Our price is quoted on CFR basis and consequently the insurance is to be covered by yourselves. However, as soon as we ship the goods we will let you know the relative shipping position.

9. If you appoint us your agent in Pakistan we will concentrate our effort on pushing the sales of your products, this being to the benefit of both parties.

10. We will send you our quotations and samples immediately upon receipt of your specific enquiry.

Ⅴ.
(1) confirm (2) special discount (3) originals (4) for (5) in
(6) stipulations (7) conform (8) amendments (9) effect (10) on

Ⅵ.
敬启者：

关于我方2000年8月8日第7904号销售确认书，我们很遗憾地告知你方，信用证在写信时还没到。这给我们带来很大的麻烦，因为我们已按上述所说的销售确认书的规定做好了装运准备。

你必须知道，一旦合同签署，合同的条款和条件就必须遵守，不遵守就意味着违约。如果你查阅我方的销售确认书，你就可以看到这样的条款："买方应在2000年8月30日前开出有关的信用证，没能做到的话，卖方保留撤销合同而不另行通知的权利。"

你方所订的货物已备妥多时了，最近需求如此旺盛以至于我们难把货物留太久。然而，考虑到我们之间友好的业务关系，我们还是打算等你们的信用证。该证必须在2000年10月5日以前到。如我们没能及时收到你们的信用证，我们将取消销售确认书，并请你们退回我们代付的仓储费。

非常感谢你们在这一方面的合作。

Ⅶ.
Sellers: Hebei Imp./Exp. Corp.
Buyers: Vancouver Foodstuffs Company

This contract is made by and between the Buyers and the Sellers, whereby the Buyers agree to buy and the Sellers agree to sell the under-mentioned commodity according to the terms and conditions stipulated below:

Commodity: Walnut Meat

Specifications: First Grade

Quantity: 60MT

Unit Price: At RMB ￥15 000 per metric ton CIF Vancouver

Total Value: ￥900 000 (Say RMB Nine Hundred Thousand Only)

Packing: In sacks of 100 kg

Shipping Mark: At the Sellers' option

Insurance: To be covered by the Sellers against All Risks and War Risk for 110% of the invoice value as per CIC of January 1, 1981

Time of Shipment: In three shipments of 20 tons each month, commencing from October 2002

Port of Shipment: China Port

Port of Destination: Vancouver

Terms of Payment: By irrevocable L/C by draft at sight

Done and signed in Shijiazhuang on this 31st day of July, 2002.

Comprehensive Exercises 5

Ⅰ.

    1~5 BCABA; 6~10 BDBCB

Ⅱ.

    1. We are willing to enter into business relations with your firm on the basis of equality and mutual benefit, and to exchange what on has with what one needs.

    2. It has been our usual practice to do business with payment by D/P at sight instead of by L/C. we should, therefore, like you to accept D/P terms for this transaction and future ones.

    3. We give you on the attached sheet full details regarding packing and marking. These must be strictly observed.

    4. Please quote us your lowest prices. CIF Vancouver, including our 5% commission.

    5. Enclosed please find our quotations which are open for two weeks.

    6. 我们将为货物投保 CIF 价值的 110%，如果要求额外险别，则额外保费由买方负担。

    7. 很遗憾，你们运来的我方 758 号订单的货物与双方谈定的规格不符。

    8. 凭着我们在这一行业的丰富经验，我们对自己能以最有效的方式代理你方出口产品这一点非常自信。

    9. 我们很高兴向你订购下列货物，其条件是按你所报价现货供应。

    10. 请你方给予合作，将装运期提前到 9 月底，以使我们能够赶上圣诞节销售旺季。

Ⅲ.

    1. 敬启者：

自米兰 Aristo Shoes 公司得知贵公司和贵公司的地址，特此修函，祈能发展关系。多年来，本公司经营鞋类进口生意，现欲扩展业务范围。盼能惠赐商品目录和报价表。如价格公道，本公司必大额订购。烦请早日赐复。

    此致

    2. Dear Sirs,

The instructions from Browning & Sons, received through our Hong Kong office, we have opened an irrevocable letter of credit for $55 500 in your favor, valid until November 30 next. You have authority to draw on us at 60 days against this credit for the amount of your invoice upon shipment of 2 000 tons of Steels to Browning & Sons.

Your drafts must be accompanied by the following documents, which are to be delivered to us against our acceptance of the draft, Bill of Lading in triplicate, Commercial Invoice, Insurance Certificate and Certificate of Origin.

Provided you fulfill the terms of the credit we will accept and pay on maturity the draft presented to us under this credit and if required, provide discounting facilities at current rates.

Ⅳ.

1. it 2. to, in 3. in 4. in 5. in 6. on, for
7. from, to 8. in 9. on 10. under, in 11. without 12. of
13. to, for 14. for, within 15. After 16. of 17. out
18. covering, received, note, clause, credit, additional, to, claims, entertained, amendment

Ⅴ.

Dear Sirs,

We have received the above mentioned L/C against our Contract No. 1098. After checking the L/C, we have found a number of discrepancies. It is requested that you amend the L/C as follows:

(1) The L/C should be "irrevocable" instead of "revocable".

(2) "HK $" should be "CAN $".

(3) "8 000 yards" instead of "8 000 pieces".

(4) Delete "and TPND" from insurance clause.

(5) Add "in two equal monthly instalments beginning from June" before "transshipment is prohibited".

Your early fax amendments will be highly appreciated.

Yours faithfully,

参考文献
Reference

[1] 暴金玲. 外贸英语函电 [M]. 北京：对外经济贸易大学出版社，2008.
[2] 程同春. 新编国际商务英语函电 [M]. 南京：东南大学出版社，2001.
[3] 常玉田. 英语商务信函写作 [M]. 北京：对外经济贸易大学出版社，2006.
[4] 樊红霞. 英文外贸函电 [M]. 北京：外语教学与研究出版社，2007.
[5] 葛萍，周维家. 外贸英语函电 [M]. 上海：复旦大学出版社，2009.
[6] 胡鉴明. 商务英语函电 [M]. 北京：中国商务出版社，2004.
[7] 黄丽威. 外贸函电与单证 [M]. 北京：高等教育出版社，2006.
[8] 侯玉珍. 涉外函电写作 [M]. 北京：海洋出版社，1996.
[9] Karla C Shippey. 国际商务合同 [M]. 上海：上海外语教育出版社，2009.
[10] 刘慧玲. 国际商务函电 [M]. 北京：对外经济贸易大学出版社，2002.
[11] 刘超先. 外贸英语单证与函电 [M]. 上海：复旦大学出版社，2008.
[12] 凌华倍，朱佩芬. 外经贸英语函电与谈判 [M]. 北京：对外经济贸易出版社，2002.
[13] 李金林. 外贸制单 [M]. 北京：对外经济贸易大学出版社，2008.
[14] 梁金水. 外贸英语函电实战 [M]. 北京：中国海关出版社，2010.
[15] 蓝天. 外贸英语函电 [M]. 大连：东北财经大学出版社，2008.
[16] 李文彪，等. 国际商务函电学习指导 [M]. 北京：北京理工大学出版社，2009.
[17] 李雅静. 涉外经贸英语函电 [M]. 青岛：青岛海洋大学出版社，1997.
[18] 廖瑛. 实用外贸英语函电 [M]. 武汉：华中科技大学出版社，2004.
[19] 刘慧玲. 国际商务函电 [M]. 北京：对外经济贸易大学出版社，2002
[20] 刘卓林. 外经贸英语函电 [M]. 北京：科学出版社，2006.
[21] 毛丁，等. 商务英语常用信函文书 [M]. 成都：西南财经大学出版社，2003.
[22] 马宗贤. 外贸英语函电 [M]. 北京：北京科学技术出版社，1994.
[23] 欧阳护华，朱永基. 国际商务英语公文写作 [M]. 重庆：重庆大学出版社，2005.
[24] 翟步习. 商务英语信用证英语分析 [M]. 北京：对外经济贸易大学出版社，2008.
[25] 戚云芳. 新编外经贸英语函电与谈判 [M]. 杭州：浙江大学出版社，2002.
[26] 苏根林. 实用商务英语函电 [M]. 南京：东南大学出版社，2006.
[27] 束光辉. 新编商务英语函电 [M]. 北京：清华大学出版社，2007.
[28] 孙继红，瞿启平. 国际贸易单证实务 [M]. 北京：清华大学出版社，2009.
[29] 滕美荣. 外贸英语函电 [M]. 北京：首都经济贸易大学出版社，2008.
[30] 檀文茹，等. 外贸函电 [M]. 北京：中国人民大学出版社，2004.
[31] 田运银. 国际贸易单证精讲 [M]. 北京：中国海关出版社，2010.
[32] 王虹，耿伟. 外贸英语函电 [M]. 北京：清华大学出版社，2009.
[33] 王慧敏. 外贸函电 [M]. 北京：北京大学出版社，2005.
[34] 王俊. 外贸函电 [M]. 合肥：合肥工业大学出版社，2006.
[35] 吴敏，吴明忠. 国际经贸英语合同写作 [M]. 广州：暨南大学出版社，2002.
[36] 王燕. 商务英语函电 [M]. 武汉：武汉理工大学出版社，2009.
[37] 夏宏钟，等. 外贸英语 [M]. 成都：西南财经大学出版社，2008.
[38] 徐明莺，李强. 无敌商务英语信函 [M]. 大连：大连理工大学出版社，2009.

[39] 徐启华. 英语外贸函电 [M]. 沈阳：东北大学出版社，2004.
[40] 易露露，等. 国际贸易实务双语教程 [M]. 北京：清华大学出版社，2010.
[41] 尹小莹. 外贸英语函电：商务英语应用文写作 [M]. 西安：西安交通大学出版社，2008.
[42] 张干周. 国际贸易函电 [M]. 杭州：浙江大学出版社，2007.
[43] 周蔚，等. 国际商务单证实务 [M]. 杭州：浙江大学出版社，2008.
[44] 邹勇，等. 国际商贸英语实务 [M]. 成都：西南财经大学出版社，2007.
[45] 张永莉，张中强. 国际商务英语 [M]. 上海：上海财经大学出版社，2010.
[46] 石定乐，蔡蔚. 实用商务英语写作 [M]. 北京：北京理工大学出版社，2008.
[47] 杨乐梅. 商务英语函电及单证 [M]. 天津：南开大学出版社，2009.
[48] 马瑞华，等. 商务英语 [M]. 武汉：武汉理工大学出版社，2009.
[49] 刘庆秋. 商务应用文写作 [M]. 北京：对外经济贸易大学出版社，2009.
[50] 王妍，刘亚卓. 外贸函电 [M]. 北京：北京大学出版社，2013.
[51] 余敏，邹勇. 国际商贸英语实务 [M]. 成都：西南财经大学出版社，2015.
[52] 金泽虎，王桂平. 国际商务函电 [M]. 北京：北京大学出版社，2013.
[53] 吴百福，徐小薇. 进出口贸易实务教程 [M]. 上海：上海人民出版社，2011.